Hard Choices: Security, Democracy, and Regionalism in Southeast Asia

Edited by
Donald K. Emmerson

I0125384

SHORENSTEIN
APARC
STANFORD

THE WALTER H. SHORENSTEIN
ASIA-PACIFIC RESEARCH CENTER

SHORENSTEIN
APARC
STANFORD

This book is the second of a three-part series, published by the Walter H. Shorenstein Asia-Pacific Research Center, on contemporary issues of regionalism and nationalism in Asia.

Cross Currents: Regionalism and Nationalism in Northeast Asia
(edited by Gi-Wook Shin and Daniel C. Sneider, 2007)

Hard Choices: Security, Democracy, and Regionalism in Southeast Asia
(edited by Donald K. Emmerson, 2008)

Does South Asia Exist? Prospects for Regional Integration in South Asia
(edited by Rafiq Dossani, Daniel C. Sneider, and Vikram Sood, forthcoming 2009)

THE WALTER H. SHORENSTEIN ASIA-PACIFIC RESEARCH CENTER (Shorenstein APARC) is a unique Stanford University institution focused on the interdisciplinary study of contemporary Asia. Shorenstein APARC's mission is to produce and publish outstanding interdisciplinary, Asia-Pacific–focused research; to educate students, scholars, and corporate and governmental affiliates; to promote constructive interaction to influence U.S. policy toward the Asia-Pacific; and to guide Asian nations on key issues of societal transition, development, U.S.-Asia relations, and regional cooperation.

The Walter H. Shorenstein Asia-Pacific Research Center
Freeman Spogli Institute for International Studies
Stanford University
Encina Hall
Stanford, CA 94305-6055
tel. 650-723-9741
fax 650-723-6530
http://APARC.stanford.edu

Hard Choices: Security, Democracy, and Regionalism in Southeast Asia may be ordered from:
The Brookings Institution
c/o DFS, P.O. Box 50370, Baltimore, MD, USA
tel. 1-800-537-5487 or 410-516-6956
fax 410-516-6998
http://www.brookings.edu/press

First printing, 2008.
13-digit ISBN 978-1-931368-13-1

HARD CHOICES: SECURITY, DEMOCRACY, AND REGIONALISM IN SOUTHEAST ASIA

THE WALTER H. SHORENSTEIN ASIA-PACIFIC RESEARCH CENTER

CONTENTS

PREFACE

Asian regionalism is a major topic of research for the Walter H. Shorenstein Asia-Pacific Research Center (Shorenstein APARC) at Stanford University. This volume is the second of a three-part series of books on Asian regionalism that the center is publishing. The first volume, *Cross Currents: Regionalism and Nationalism in Northeast Asia* (2007), looked at the tensions between increasing regional integration and rising nationalism in Northeast Asia. Its content was based on an international conference that was held at Stanford in May 2006.

The following year, in May 2007, my colleague, Professor Donald K. Emmerson, led a conference at Shorenstein APARC that examined the interplay between security, democracy, and regionalism in Southeast Asia. This book is an edited volume of the revised conference papers, written by scholars from across Southeast Asia and outside the region.

For the final installment of our inquiry into Asian regionalism, we held a third conference, in June 2008, in cooperation with the Observer Research Foundation of India, which focused on the prospects for regionalism in South Asia. The papers from that gathering—which brought together scholars from across South Asia with experts from Russia, China and the United States—will be published in 2009.

This book and its companion volumes offer provocative, detailed perspectives by some of the finest scholars working in Asian studies today. In publishing these books, we hope to bring this important material to a wider audience, and thereby to advance understanding of Asian regionalism and its impact on nations, both within Asia and beyond.

Gi-Wook Shin
Professor, and Director
Shorenstein APARC
Stanford University

ACKNOWLEDGMENTS

It is a pleasure in a book entitled *Hard Choices* to begin with easy ones—deciding whom to thank, for making this volume possible, for writing or improving its chapters, and for intellectual stimulation, collegial patience, and good humor along the journey whose destination these pages represent.

Plans for our voyage grew from a series of conversations with Southeast Asianist colleagues beginning in April 2006. I knew that 2007 would mark the fortieth anniversary of the Association of Southeast Asian Nations (ASEAN), and that its leaders planned to celebrate the occasion by underpinning the organization with a new and innovative ASEAN Charter. It seemed a good time for a fresh look at regionalism in Southeast Asia.

What I had in mind was an analytic account of security, democracy, regionalism, and their interactions. Combining these topics in a multiauthored book struck me as usefully novel. With talent and support, the result could appeal to a diverse set of interested readers—teachers and students, scholars and officials, professionals and businesspeople, and specialists as well as the general public.

My coauthors supplied the talent. Core support came from Stanford University's Walter H. Shorenstein Asia-Pacific Research Center (Shorenstein APARC). In May 2006, the Center held a conference at Stanford on regionalism and nationalism in Northeast Asia. The resulting collection, *Cross Currents*,[1] was the first of three planned volumes on regionalism in Northeast, Southeast, and South Asia. *Hard Choices* is the second in this series. A third book, on South Asian regionalism, is scheduled for 2009.

First drafts of our chapters were discussed over two days at a workshop held at Stanford in May 2007. Many of the essays implied or raised "hard choices" for ASEAN. Should Southeast Asia's leaders recommit themselves to an "ASEAN Way" of ignoring whatever its member regimes chose to do behind their own borders—sacrificing fairness inside member states to friendliness between them? Or should the Association, on the contrary, encourage democracy and respect for human rights throughout the region—trading diplomatic amity for political reform?

How, in particular, should ASEAN deal with the enduring dictatorship in its most reviled member state, Myanmar (Burma)? Should regional leaders maintain cooperation with the junta in hopes of moderating its behavior and preserving regional unity, even at the cost of appearing to abet repression,

---

[1] Gi-Wook Shin and Daniel C. Sneider, eds., *Cross Currents: Regionalism and Nationalism in Northeast Asia* (Stanford, CA: Walter H. Shorenstein Asia-Pacific Research Center, 2007).

and thereby damaging ASEAN's international reputation? Or should ASEAN criticize, impose sanctions upon, or even expel Myanmar's predatory regime for the sake of political accountability, human rights, and the Association's own image among democrats, even at the cost of opening a destructive rift between its most and least authoritarian member states?

How could regional priorities be allocated between the security of states and the security of persons, in countries whose regimes were responsible for human insecurity? Could ASEAN's respect for member-state sovereignty and consensus be squared with its interest in responding promptly to environmental disasters, infectious diseases, and other threats that ignored state borders? Could regionalism be reorganized to lessen the tension and increase the complementarity between stability on the one hand and freedom on the other? How? Would ASEAN's new Charter help or hinder its ability to manage such dilemmas?

In Myanmar in August–September 2007, antiregime protests broke out, grew, and were repressed by the junta with force and loss of life. Soon after, in November in Singapore, the final text of the ASEAN Charter was finally and officially announced and signed. At the end of November, to take these late-breaking events into account, authors who had focused on Myanmar or the Charter gathered for a one-day workshop in Singapore to present and discuss revised versions of one another's chapters. The editing process continued well into 2008.

Editors of multiauthored books run the gamut from A to Z, where A is the Absentee and Z is the Zealot. The Absentee is content to slap covers on whatever comes in and call it a book. The Zealot edits the manuscript to reflect his or her own opinions. Most editors distribute themselves between these extremes of indifference and imposition. I tried to respect the contrasting perspectives and arguments offered herein while striving for a consistency of style that would convey them more effectively. My coauthors were as responsive to my suggestions as they were magnanimous about being edited in detail. They tolerated my "Americanisms"—for example, a preference for the active as opposed to the passive voice. I am indebted to them for the quality of their work and the generosity of their understanding.

Edited books differ as well in the extent to which a reader must absorb the earlier chapters in order to understand the later ones. Readers of this book are under no such constraint. Because each author was free to fill in the background necessary for his or her argument, each reader is free to go directly to the chapters that interest him or her most. In addition to making this benefit possible, the occasional duplication of information regarding the Charter process and the controversy over Myanmar usefully exposes readers to differing interpretations of the same events. (This modular aspect should also be of value to teachers who might like to assign only certain chapters in their courses.)

Beyond writing this book, my coauthors helped in many other ways. Termsak Chalermpalanupap graciously answered my interminable questions about ASEAN. Mely Caballero-Anthony shared her vast knowledge of "nontraditional security." Jörn Dosch provided a helpful link to parallel scholarship in Europe.[2] Kyaw Yin Hlaing met our deadlines despite being caught up in the maelstrom that his topic—Myanmar—turned out to be. David Martin Jones and Erik Kuhonta were kind enough to agree to write chapters in which they would disagree. Michael Malley helped me to remember that ASEAN as an organization and Southeast Asia as a region are hardly synonymous. Rizal Sukma was willing to change his travel schedule in order to attend the Singapore workshop. As noted below, that gathering could not have taken place without Simon Tay's help. Together, in these and other ways, my fellow authors showed me how simultaneously stimulating and collegial a research community can be.

I am grateful to Shorenstein APARC and its director, Gi-Wook Shin, for providing the core budget for our first workshop, in May 2007. That event benefited as well from supplemental funding by Stanford's Center on Development, Democracy, and the Rule of Law (CDDRL), and from travel support from the University of Leeds (for Jörn Dosch) and the ASEAN Secretariat (for Termsak Chalermpalanupap). For hosting and funding our second workshop, in November 2007, I am happy to thank the Singapore Institute of International Affairs and its chairman, Simon Tay. His willingness to schedule our meeting one day before his own Institute's ASEAN and Asia Forum 2007 enabled several of us to participate in both events. (The Forum's co-sponsors included the International Foundation for Arts and Culture [in Tokyo], the Japan External Trade Organization, and the Singapore Institute of Management.)

Southeast Asianist colleagues in many countries merit appreciation. Surin Pitsuwan graciously agreed to preface our book. Amitav Acharya was unstinting in his encouragement and his ideas. Ong Keng Yong would have joined us at Stanford had he not been in Almaty at the time. Didi Babo-Soares relayed word of events and hopes in his country, Timor-Leste, a would-be and maybe-someday member of ASEAN. Brian Job shared his thoughts on regionalisms outside Southeast Asia.

Shorenstein APARC's publications manager Victoria Tomkinson prepared the manuscript for publication. Her editorial skills, quick turnaround, and high professionalism deserve major credit for the readability, consistency, and appearance of our book. I am also grateful to Triena Ong of the Institute of Southeast Asian Studies for being so responsive, over lunch in Singapore, to the idea of copublication—and for all of her and her Institute's subsequent efforts on the book's behalf. Barbara Milligan ably copyedited *Hard Choices*; the Brookings Institution facilitated its circulation; and Shorenstein APARC's

---

[2] Revised versions of a number of the papers written for a conference on "40 Years of ASEAN: Performance, Lessons and Perspectives" (held in May 2007 in Freiburg, Germany) were scheduled for publication in December 2008 in a special issue of *The Pacific Review* to be edited by Jürgen Rüland and Anja Jetschke. See also the essays in "ASEAN at 40: Progress, Prospects and Challenges," *Contemporary Southeast Asia* 29, no. 3 (December 2007), 395–523.

director for research, Daniel Sneider, was always supportive. Throughout the process, Carolyn Emmerson's love, generosity, and tolerance kept me going.

Last but not least, for relevant information and advice, not to mention friendship, I am grateful to Muthiah Alagappa, Ali Alatas, Jennifer Amyx, Dewi Fortuna Anwar, Maureen Aung-Thwin, David Camroux, Kavi Chongkittavorn, John Ciorciari, Priscilla Clapp, Ralph Cossa, James Cotton, Catharin Dalpino, Barry Desker, Larry Diamond, Alan Dupont, Ralf Emmers, Paul Evans, Cherian George, Natasha Hamilton-Hart, Mohamed Jawhar Hassan, Richard Higgott, Paul Hutchcroft, Erik Jensen, Clara Joewono, Joseph Liow, Noel Morada, Maria Ortuoste, Thitinan Pongsudhirak, José Ramos-Horta, Michael Richardson, Christopher Roberts, Jürgen Rüland, Sheldon Simon, Hadi Soesastro, Ian Storey, Tan See Seng, Tan Siok Choo, Eric Thompson, Jusuf Wanandi, Donald Weatherbee, and Maung Zarni.

It would be nice if I could implicate all these people in collective guilt for whatever inaccuracies or infelicities have survived their assistance. That would, alas, be unfair and untrue. But if I am accountable for whatever shortcomings *Hard Choices* may retain in the wake of such ample and excellent advice, responsibility for the merits of the book belongs first and foremost to my coauthors and, in concentric circles of receding involvement, to the many others whose contributions are acknowledged here.

Donald K. Emmerson
Stanford, California
1 October 2008

Acronyms and Note on References to the ASEAN Charter

Many acronyms appear throughout this book. Some are used frequently; others appear on only a handful of occasions. To aid the reader, all the acronyms used in this book are spelled out here, in alphabetical order. In each chapter, they are likewise spelled out on the instance of their first usage. The one exception to this rule is ASEAN—the Association of Southeast Asian Nations—which appears so often that repeatedly spelling it out is unnecessary.

ABAC	ASEAN Business Advisory Council
ACAMM	ASEAN Chiefs of Army Multilateral Meeting
ACC	ASEAN Coordinating Council
ACB	ASEAN Centre for Biodiversity
ACD	Asia Cooperation Dialogue
ACDC	ASEAN Centre for Disease Control
ACE	ASEAN Centre on Energy
ACFTA	ASEAN-China Free Trade Area
ACSC	ASEAN Civil Society Conference
ADB	Asian Development Bank
ADMM	ASEAN Defense Ministers Meeting
AEC	ASEAN Economic Community
AFC	Asian financial crisis
AFTA	ASEAN Free Trade Area
AIPA	ASEAN Inter-Parliamentary Assembly, formerly AIPO
AIPMC	ASEAN Inter-Parliamentary Myanmar Caucus
AIPO	ASEAN Inter-Parliamentary Organisation, renamed AIPA
AltSEAN	Alternative ASEAN Network on Burma
AMAF	ASEAN Ministers of Agriculture and Forestry
AMM	ASEAN Ministerial Meeting
AMME	ASEAN Ministerial Meeting on the Environment
APA	ASEAN People's Assembly
APEC	Asia-Pacific Economic Cooperation
APSC	ASEAN Political and Security Community, formerly ASC
APT	ASEAN Plus Three (ASEAN plus China, Japan, and South Korea)
ARF	ASEAN Regional Forum

ASA	Association of Southeast Asia
ASC	ASEAN Security Community, renamed APSC in ASEAN Charter
ASCC	ASEAN Socio-Cultural Community
ASCPA	ASEAN Security Plan of Action
ASEAN	Association of Southeast Asian Nations
ASEAN-CCI	ASEAN Chamber of Commerce and Industry
ASEAN DG	ASEAN Director-General
ASEAN-ISIS	ASEAN Institutes of Strategic and International Studies
ASEM	Asia-Europe Meeting
ASOEN	ASEAN Senior Officials on the Environment
AU	African Union
AWGHR	ASEAN Working Group on Human Rights
BSPP	Burma Socialist Program Party
CAFTA	China-ASEAN Free Trade Area
CIBs	conventional international bodies
CPV	Communist Party of Vietnam
CRPP	Committee Representing People's Parliament, Myanmar
CSIS	Centre for International and Strategic Studies, Jakarta
CSO	civil society organization
CSU	Coordination and Support Unit, RHAP, Indonesia
DG	director-general
DIPs	detailed implementation plans
DPR	People's Representative Council, Indonesia
DSGs	deputy secretaries-general
DSM	Enhanced Dispute Settlement Mechanism
EAI	Enterprise for ASEAN Initiative
EAS	East Asia Summit
ECO	Economic Cooperation Organization, Tehran
EEZ	exclusive economic zone
EPG	Eminent Persons Group
ERIA	Economic Research Institute for ASEAN and East Asia
EU	European Union
FDI	foreign direct investment
FEALAC	Forum for East Asia and Latin America Cooperation
FTA	free trade agreement
G8	Group of Eight
GCC	Gulf Cooperation Council, Riyadh
GDP	gross domestic product
GONGO	governmental nongovernmental organization
HDI	Human Development Index
HLTF	High-Level Task Force
HTTF	Haze Technical Task Force
IAEA	International Atomic Energy Agency
IAI	Initiative for ASEAN Integration

ICISS	International Commission on Intervention and State Sovereignty
ICG	International Crisis Group
ICJ	International Court of Justice
IMF	International Monetary Fund
IOM	International Organisation for Migration
IR	international relations
ISDS	Institute for Strategic and Development Studies, Manila
ISEAS	Institute of Southeast Asian Studies, Singapore
IWEP	Institute of World Economics and Politics, Hanoi
JCM	Joint Consultative Meeting
JMM	Joint Ministerial Meeting
LPRP	Lao People's Revolutionary Party, Laos
NATO	North Atlantic Treaty Organization
NC	National Convention, Myanmar
NGO	nongovernmental organization
NF	National Front, Malaysia
NLD	National League for Democracy, Myanmar
NPT	Treaty on the Non-Proliferation of Nuclear Weapons
NTS	nontraditional security
NTU	Nanyang Technological University
NU	Nahdlatul Ulama
NUP	National Unity Party, Myanmar
NWS	nuclear-weapon state
OPEC	Organization of Petroleum Exporting Countries
ORHAP	Operational Regional Haze Action Plan
PAP	People's Action Party, Singapore
PIF	Pacific Island Forum, Suva, Fiji
PMC	ASEAN Post-Ministerial Conference
PPP	purchasing power parity
PRC	People's Republic of China
R2P	"responsibility to protect"
RHAP	Regional Haze Action Plan, Indonesia
SAARC	South Asian Association for Regional Cooperation, Kathmandu
SADC	Southern African Development Community
SALW	small arms and light weapons
SAPA	Solidarity for Asian People's Advocacy
SARS	Severe Acute Respiratory Syndrome
SCO	Shanghai Cooperation Organization, Beijing
SEAMEO	Southeast Asian Ministers of Education Organization
SEANWFZ	Treaty on the Southeast Asia Nuclear-Weapon-Free Zone
SEARCCT	Southeast Asia Regional Centre for Counter-Terrorism, Kuala Lumpur
SEATO	Southeast Asia Treaty Organization
SEOM	ASEAN Senior Economic Officials Meeting
SG	secretary-general

SLORC	State Law and Order Restoration Council, Myanmar
SOM	ASEAN Senior Officials Meeting
SPDC	State Peace and Development Council, Myanmar
TAC	Treaty of Amity and Cooperation in Southeast Asia
TCG	ASEAN-Myanmar-UN Tripartite Core Group
UMNO	United Malays National Organization, Malaysia
UN	United Nations
UNDP	United Nations Development Programme
UNEP	United Nations Environment Programme
UNSC	United Nations Security Council
USDA	Union Solidarity and Development Association, Myanmar
VAP	Vientiane Action Program
WALHI	Indonesian Forum for Environment
WTO	World Trade Organization
ZOPFAN	Zone of Peace, Freedom and Neutrality

Note on References to the ASEAN Charter

The contributors to this book regularly refer to the ASEAN Charter, which was signed by the leaders of all ten ASEAN member states in November 2007.

For ease of reference, the text of the Charter is reproduced as an appendix at the end of this book. The Charter has fifty-five articles, numbered consecutively throughout using Arabic numerals. Most of the articles are divided into Arabic-numbered paragraphs, and many of these contain alphabetically lettered clauses.

Throughout this book, sections of the Charter are identified as necessary by article, paragraph, and clause. For example, a reference to the article, paragraph, and clause stating that ASEAN and its member states shall act in keeping with the principle of noninterference would read: Charter, Art. 2.2(e). In the Charter, articles are also grouped under Roman-numbered chapters, but these merely identify the topics they subsume and are therefore not needed for reference purposes.

FOREWORD

Surin Pitsuwan
Secretary-General
Association of Southeast Asian Nations (ASEAN)

In writing this preface I feel as if I were briefly back in a previous life, the life of an academic with the luxury of time—time to read and think and write books like *Hard Choices*.

In the first seven months of my term as ASEAN Secretary-General, I have been constantly in motion, trying to meet numerous commitments in ASEAN and elsewhere. Cyclone Nargis, which devastated Myanmar's Irrawaddy Delta in early May 2008, suddenly thrust both ASEAN and me into the international spotlight. We have had to help the government of Myanmar help the cyclone survivors in a massive humanitarian operation that is unprecedented in the more than forty years of ASEAN's history to date. The Nargis operation constituted yet another challenge to ASEAN's lengthening agenda. It has also multiplied the flights I have to take, the meetings and negotiations I pursue, and the new commitments to request and to make. In addition to the region's economic plans and challenges, it is as if I have been living, on a daily basis, the topics of this book—security, democracy, and regionalism in Southeast Asia.

I am glad that the authors of *Hard Choices* pay major attention to nontraditional security (NTS). The new regionalism in Southeast Asia is not only about free trade and economic engagements with external trading partners. This new regionalism is about community-building in ASEAN. It is about narrowing the development gaps and removing pockets of poverty. It also involves mobilizing regional efforts and international support to cope with new and NTS challenges.

The nature of insecurity in Southeast Asia has undergone great changes in recent decades. New kinds of dangers have arisen that cannot be solved by governments alone. These threats have taken root in the cracks between sovereignties, the spaces between states. Major natural disasters, global warming, cross-border pollution, infectious disease, and international crime are just a few examples. Human security is at stake, not just the security of states. To overcome these challenges, we need the help of civil society—nongovernmental experts to partner with governments in studying and solving problems, whistle-blowers to expose abuses, activists and journalists to help render authorities accountable. ASEAN needs its civil society to serve as the link, the channel of communication to convey to the Association's leaders, ministers, and senior officials what is in the hearts and minds of nearly six hundred million Southeast Asians.

We in ASEAN need to reach out and inspire everyone in our ASEAN community to appreciate and adopt a double identity, both national and regional, so that someday every Southeast Asian can say: "I am a Thai (or an Indonesian, a Vietnamese, and so on), but I am also an ASEAN citizen." But first we need to show and convince our peoples that everything our Association is trying to do in creating the three pillars of our community—a Political-Security Community, an Economic Community, and a Socio-Cultural Community—is aimed chiefly at improving their own welfare and well-being.

The third of these three pillars should be especially attractive to individuals and civil society organisations because it directly concerns development, human security, and regional identity. The Socio-Cultural Community is a wide-open opportunity to contribute to Southeast Asia's identity across many sectors and topics.

I am pleased to note the attention paid to democracy in this book. Democracy, human rights, participation, accountability, justice, tolerance, and equality are just some of the big issues that we need to address in building a regional identity that is more than merely geographic. Democracy and human rights are no longer taboo topics for ASEAN. The days when domestic political controversies could not be discussed in regional settings are over.

My greatest challenge these past seven months has been organizing ASEAN's response to the death and damage done to Myanmar by Cyclone Nargis. This has been a defining moment for our Association. ASEAN could not stand idly by and watch a natural disaster turn into a man-made one. So many lives were at stake, and so was ASEAN's reputation. Our task was twofold. First, we sought to assure Myanmar's leaders that foreign donors and aid workers would respect their sovereignty and that humanitarian relief would not be politicized. Second, based on that assurance, we worked to expand and speed the flow of assistance to the 2.5 million cyclone survivors. For this purpose we even opened a coordination office in Yangon in ASEAN's name—an unprecedented move for the Association. ASEAN has risen to the occasion. We have been doing what our peoples rightfully expect of us. This is the New ASEAN—a community that puts people at the center of concern.

Many ASEAN initiatives are necessarily begun by the member governments, in top-down fashion. It was the leaders of Southeast Asia who decided that ASEAN should have a Charter. It was the foreign ministers, meeting in Singapore on 19 May 2008, who decided that ASEAN would lead a humanitarian assistance operation in Myanmar. But if we are to succeed in establishing a genuine ASEAN Community by 2015, top-down leadership alone will not suffice. ASEAN will also need grassroots support, including the participation of civil society organisations.

Security and democracy are part of the ASEAN Charter. Once the Charter is ratified, it will become part of ASEAN. As I hope our response to the tragedy of Nargis already illustrates, ASEAN is not and will not be part of the problem. Rather, it is and will be part of the solution to a range of challenges that are described and analyzed from various perspectives in this book. The book's title is appropriate. These challenges pose hard choices—hard, but not impossible to make.

My message to the readers of this book is that the New ASEAN, led by its ten member states and focused on their peoples' needs, can and will make the tough decisions necessary to achieve a secure and prosperous, open and tolerant, caring and sharing community of Southeast Asian societies in the twenty-first century.

Surin Pitsuwan
Jakarta, Indonesia
1 August 2008

[Editor's Update: On 21 October 2008, as this book was going to press, the ASEAN Secretariat announced that the ASEAN Charter had been "fully ratified by all ten ASEAN Member States."]

INTRODUCTION

CRITICAL TERMS: SECURITY, DEMOCRACY, AND REGIONALISM IN SOUTHEAST ASIA

Donald K. Emmerson
Stanford University
United States

Security, democracy, regionalism, and Southeast Asia are critical terms in many ways. There is a critical lack of knowledge about how they interact, yet the topics they denote are critically important. The concepts themselves invite critical—discerning—analysis of the kind represented in this book. As an instance of regionalism, the Association of Southeast Asian Nations (ASEAN) has been criticized for its inability to alleviate the insecurity and lack of democracy suffered by citizens of its most brutally ruled member state, Myanmar (or Burma).[1] Events in 2007–08 underscored the critical—urgent—need for reform and relief in that misgoverned country. In 2007, ASEAN's effort to reform itself by drafting and signing a new Charter to orient its actions in the twenty-first century elicited critiques from inside and outside the region. In 2008, scathing criticism was leveled at the Association for failing to criticize the Myanmar junta's malign neglect of the surviving but homeless and hungry victims of Cyclone Nargis.[2]

The egregious case of Myanmar evokes a wider range of issues, ideas, and interactions involving security, democracy, and regionalism that are fostering

---

[1] For example, in May 2008, eight globally known personalities, including former Czech president Václav Havel, South African activist cleric Desmond Tutu, and Russian reformer Grigory Yavlinsky, urged "Burma's neighbors in ASEAN" to "stop looking the other way as Burma's rulers trample on Burma's citizens." ("Referendum Farce in Burma," Forum 2000, <http://www.forum2000.cz/en/about-us/news-archive/detail/referendum-farce-in-burma-1/>.)

[2] In the words of one respected American analyst, Myanmar's junta continued "to kill its own people through brute idiocy," by obstructing relief to the cyclone's victims, and "conspicuous in its absence" was "one harsh word to Burma's rulers from ASEAN." Experts in Washington, he reported, were asking—in the light of ASEAN's silence—how the organization could expect to be taken seriously, let alone respected. (Chris Nelson, *The Nelson Report*, Washington DC, 12 May 2008.)

hard choices for Southeast Asia[3] in the twenty-first century. These matters form the subject of this book. Following this introduction, Jörn Dosch and Termsak Chalermpalanupap offer, respectively, a scholar's and a practitioner's assessment of ASEAN as it faces the challenges of ensuring security, advancing democracy, and reforming regionalism itself.

Five key issues are then taken up by as many authors. Rizal Sukma asks whether ASEAN can augment its concern for security with an agenda for democracy. Kyaw Yin Hlaing reviews the resilience of autocracy and the suppression of democracy in Myanmar, and asks what if anything ASEAN can do about its most reviled member. Mely Caballero-Anthony examines ASEAN's nontraditional security agenda—coping with nonmilitary threats that ignore national borders—and asks whether human rights and democracy could become a new regional policy frontier. Simon SC Tay chronicles regional efforts to quell one of these nontraditional threats, the damaging smoke from fires in Indonesia, and asks whether that country's democracy could be part of the problem. Michael S. Malley explores the nexus between domestic political competition and nuclear energy security in light of plans to open nuclear plants in the region, and asks what ASEAN has done to forestall this future security risk.

Hard Choices ends with two views on whether, and under what conditions, regionalism should include a right to intervene in a country's domestic affairs. David Martin Jones argues for the value of decency over democracy and against the idea that ASEAN should promote liberal pluralism in Southeast Asia. Erik Kuhonta, with Myanmar in mind, argues against unconditional sovereignty and for regional intervention proportional to the severity of harm inflicted by a repressive government upon its own people.[4]

Critical Terms

My own purpose in this introductory chapter is to ask and discuss, in this order, these questions: What do security, democracy, and regionalism mean? How

---

[3] In the later twentieth century, political observers conventionally defined "Southeast Asia" as a set of ten countries: Brunei, Cambodia, Indonesia, Laos, Malaysia, Myanmar (or Burma), the Philippines, Singapore, Thailand, and Vietnam. In 2002, the tiny ex-Indonesian province of East Timor gained full independence as Timor-Leste. Opinions differ as to whether Timor-Leste should be counted as Southeast Asia's eleventh state. It is explicitly included, in passing, in the chapters by Mely Caballero-Anthony and Termsak Chalermpalanupap. In the other chapters, with one exception, Timor-Leste is not mentioned and the question therefore does not arise. The exception is this chapter, where I discuss the issue but remain agnostic about whether Timor-Leste is or is not a "Southeast Asian" state.

[4] Some basic information is repeated in these nine chapters—that ASEAN was born in 1967, for example, and held its fortieth-birthday summit in 2007. The duplication has been retained to allow the essays to be read and understood in any order, depending on one's interest and regardless of prior knowledge.

are they related to a theme that is, for lack of space, underrepresented in this book, namely, the economy? What is the relevance of these topics for Southeast Asia? Why focus on this particular part of the world? What is the "ASEAN Way"? Is it on the way out? Does the ASEAN Charter augur reform, or will it reinforce the status quo? What about Myanmar? How did ASEAN respond to the repression of mass protest in 2007 and the mismanagement of natural disaster in 2008, and with what implications for the (in)ability of regionalism to promote security and democracy in Southeast Asia? After summarizing and interpreting my conclusions, I will close with some "unfinal thoughts" on the topics I have raised. By posing and exploring critical terms and hard choices in this first chapter, I hope to sketch a helpful context in which to read the findings and views of my co-authors: their assessments of ASEAN, their analyses of issues, and their arguments over intervention.

I now turn to the terms themselves. What do security, democracy, and regionalism mean—and what do they mean for this book?

Security

Like the other critical terms, security has many facets. These vary depending on the entity whose security is threatened, the nature and gravity of the threat, the source of the threat, and the authority responsible for identifying and describing the entity, the threat, and the source.[5] Such an authority could be, for example, a government, an association, an activist, or a scholar. In this book, my co-authors and I all perform this identifying role.

Consider merely the choice of an entity in danger. This could be our physical planet and all humankind, particular regions and populations, specific states and societies within a given region, or areas and peoples either within a country or spanning the borders of countries. Or one could descend still farther down the ladder of abstraction and consider the security of ever smaller physical spaces or social groups, including—finally—the security of individual human beings, or "human security" as it is referred to in this book.

Nor is this an exhaustive list. One could consider as well the security or sustainability of a tradition, a language, a religion, an organization, a theory, or a practice—including the organization, theory, and practice of this book's other conceptual pillars: democracy and regionalism. I will shortly note the ecological,

---

[5] On the scope of security, see my "Goldilocks's Problem: Rethinking Security and Sovereignty in Asia," in *The Many Faces of Asian Security: Beyond 2000*, edited by Sheldon W. Simon (Lanham, MD: Rowman & Littlefield, 2001), 89–111; and Muthiah Alagappa's discussion of "security with adjectives" in "Introduction," 11–13, and "Conceptualizing Security: Hierarchy and Conceptual Traveling," 677–97 (694–95), in Alagappa, ed., *Asian Security Practices: Material and Ideational Influences* (Stanford, CA: Stanford University Press, 1998). Whether the entity that identifies the threat is believed or not, and by whom, is a matter for empirical investigation. Obviously, the credibility of someone who cries wolf will be affected by the wolf's own existence and behavior.

socioeconomic, and political heterogeneity of Southeast Asia. Can we speak, in that context, of the security of diversity? We can. Anything that is valued can warrant concern for its "security" on the part of whoever values it.

I will not even try to inventory the myriad possible dangers and sources of danger that an authority might identify. Suffice it instead to highlight two different targets and two different sources of threat that are especially relevant to the discussion of security in this book: state versus human security on the one hand, and external versus internal threats on the other.

Some quick definitions are in order. In this book, "the state" is an institutional structure of official authority with sovereign jurisdiction over a particular territory.[6] A "society" encompasses the totality of persons living within that jurisdiction. A "country" incorporates both the state and the corresponding society. Sometimes, here and elsewhere in this book, if only to avoid repetition, "state" may be used interchangeably with "country," but the intended meaning should be clear from the context. Finally, a "government" consists of a specific set of more or less temporarily incumbent officials speaking and acting on the state's behalf by virtue of holding positions of authority in it. In the Kingdom of Thailand, for example, the monarch heads the state, while a prime minister leads the government. In Indonesia, on the other hand, the president plays both roles. When for stylistic reasons "state" and "government" are used synonymously, the context should clarify the difference.

Threats to the security of the state may come from outside the borders of a country. In 1975 Indonesia invaded and occupied East Timor. In 1978 Vietnam did the same thing to Cambodia. In 1979 China briefly avenged its Cambodian ally by attacking Vietnam. But not since then—some thirty years ago—has a war between two or more states or governments broken out inside Southeast Asia or along its perimeter.[7]

Far more relevant than interstate wars in Southeast Asia today, and hence in the pages of this book, are external or cross-border threats that do not involve troops intentionally transgressing borders but implicate dangers that ignore borders altogether. Perils of this sort include environmental degradation, ranging from air and water pollution to global warming; natural disasters such as the deadly Indian Ocean earthquake and tsunami of 2004, or the already

---

[6] For a state to exist, it need not exercise sovereignty across its territory fully, uniformly, or effectively—or even legitimately in the eyes of the population it ostensibly rules. In extremis, of course, the state may be so degraded or challenged that it no longer exists as a singular noun. In 2007–08 the boundary between the presence and absence of the state could be located somewhere between grossly mismanaged but sovereign Zimbabwe and the polycentric near-anarchy of Somalia.

[7] These borders have not always been conflict-free, however. Most notably, in the mid-to-late 1990s, incursions from Myanmar into Thailand by the armed forces and armed opponents of the junta resulted in the deaths of "several" Thai nationals, according to Amnesty International, "Myanmar: The Kayin (Karen) State: Militarization and Human Rights," 1 June 1999, <http://www.amnesty.org/en/library/info/ASA16/012/1999/en>.

mentioned and also lethal Bay of Bengal cyclone of 2008; maritime abuses, from piracy to overfishing; transnational crimes, from money laundering and "phishing" for identities in cyberspace to trafficking in persons and drugs; externally aided insurgencies and terrorism; perceived threats associated with unrestricted or illegal immigration; damage to cities and crops from floods and droughts; illnesses from infectious disease; sudden economic downturns of global or regional scope, including the financial crisis that swept parts of East Asia beginning in 1997; and the list goes on. In this book, along with Caballero-Anthony and Tay, Dosch also considers such "nontraditional" threats to human security. Unconventional, too, are the risks of shifting toward nuclear energy noted by Michael S. Malley in his chapter.

A disturbing aggregate assessment of threats to states and societies appears annually in the Failed States Index compiled by The Fund for Peace and *Foreign Policy*. The Index sums a dozen indicators of social, economic, and political insecurity, and then uses these to score and rank countries according to their vulnerability to "state failure," including "violent internal conflict and societal deterioration." Of the 177 countries whose risk was assessed for 2006, 20 were judged by *Foreign Policy* to be in "critical" condition. Another 20 were said to be "in danger," and 20 more were placed on the "borderline" between stability and instability. By this evidence, sustainable internal security in that year had eluded one-third of all the world's countries.[8]

Among the ten countries traditionally said to make up Southeast Asia, Myanmar was "critical," while the "borderline" group, listed in declining order of vulnerability to failure, included Laos, Cambodia, Indonesia, and the Philippines. By this measure, fully *one-half* of all Southeast Asian states were said to be at risk of "state failure." Timor-Leste was also deemed "critical," and if that turbulent case is included in Southeast Asia, an actual if bare majority of the region's constituent countries were internally insecure or at serious risk of such insecurity.

These judgments err on the side of alarmism. State failure in the sense of outright collapse is an extreme and rare condition. Yet the empirical data summarized by the Index do show that the insecurity of states and societies is a serious problem worldwide, and one from which Southeast Asia is hardly immune. The demonstrations that broke out inside Myanmar in August 2007, followed by their violent suppression in September, and the shooting of the prime minister of Timor-Leste in February 2008, in the aftermath of earlier strife, certainly confirmed the "critical" status of those countries.

---

[8] For a list of the rankings, see The Fund for Peace, "Failed States Index 2007 [for 2006]," <http://www.fundforpeace.org/web/index.php>. For explanations and interpretations, including the quoted phrases, see "The Failed States Index 2007 [for 2006]," *Foreign Policy*, July–August 2007, <http://www.foreignpolicy.com/story/cms.php?story_id=3865&print=1>.

When it comes to asking Lenin's question—"What is to be done?"—cross-country aggregations and rankings are not enough. If by "the state" we mean to distinguish the ruling apparatus of a sovereign country from the society that it subsumes, one can easily picture a state whose brutality or indifference has left its people to contend with poverty, illness, exploitation, crime, and political violence, and yet for all that, remains itself relatively durable and secure. To the extent that the apparatus itself is responsible for such appalling conditions, it may be necessary to threaten or even disrupt state security in order to improve human security. But is this realistic? Even if it is, who can guarantee that coercion in a good cause will not simply breed chaos, that interference will not merely enlarge insecurity, leaving both the state and the society worse off than they were before?

Looking ahead to our next concept, what of democracy? Will democratization ensure an *effective* state—or merely an elected one? Are democratic procedures a necessary and universal prerequisite of human security? Or are there circumstances in which the introduction of democracy is likely to disrupt the capacity of the state to protect society? Is welfare a function of liberty, or is it the other way around?

Starkly phrased, these questions raise some of the hard choices implied by the title of this book. How should Myanmar's Southeast Asian neighbors deal with the malign regime in charge of that state? Should they intervene? Are conditions inside the country bad enough to warrant violating Myanmar's sovereignty for the sake of civility? Or are there softer choices between invasion and indifference, ways of nudging a misgoverned country toward a better future? In their chapters, Kyaw, Jones, and Kuhonta offer usefully diverging answers to these questions.

Democracy

In the 1990s Muthiah Alagappa wrote that the word *"security* is now used with more than thirty different adjectives," and listed thirty-seven examples. Fresh qualifiers have been popularized in the decade since he wrote, including two that recur in the present volume—"nontraditional" and "human" security.[9] Yet this variety of understandings of security cannot compete with the expansion of *"democracy* with adjectives" to include not dozens but "hundreds of subtypes."[10]

---

[9] Alagappa, *Asian Security Practices*, 11 (quote), and 694–95 (taxonomy). "Nontraditional" and "human security" roughly update his "non-conventional" and "individual security," respectively.

[10] David Collier and Steven Levitsky, "Democracy with Adjectives: Conceptual Innovation in Comparative Research," *World Politics* 49, no. 3 (1997), 429–30, my italics.

There are several reasons for this lexical explosion. In contemporary discourse, by and large, "democracy" *as a term* is a good thing.[11] Some politicians, however, want the legitimacy that the word confers without the constraints that the reality can imply. Adjectives result, including Ayub Khan's "basic democracy" in Pakistan, Sukarno's "guided democracy" followed by Suharto's "Pancasila democracy" in Indonesia, Vladimir Putin's "managed democracy" in Russia, and Than Shwe's "discipline-flourishing democracy" in Myanmar. Typically, these adjectives are meant to prevent a more or less subjugated population from thinking that the noun "democracy" should necessarily imply and require a different qualifier, namely, "liberal" as in "liberal democracy."

Conversely, activists and analysts who are committed to liberal democracy as the only form of government worth seeking or having may insist on "democracy without adjectives,"[12] by which they most often mean the liberal kind, traditionally distinguished above all by the proposition that individuals have innate rights and freedoms that the state must respect. Such a commitment explains, for example, why the American organization Freedom House considers Laos, a self-described "people's democracy," to be the second *least* democratic country in Southeast Asia (after Myanmar).[13]

Related to a liberal democracy is an electoral one—a country whose people can "choose and replace their leaders in regular, free, and fair elections." If the incidence, degree, and risk of state failure are hard to quantify, so too are the regularity, freedom, and fairness of elections. Nevertheless, in the last decades of the twentieth century, according to Freedom House data as interpreted by Larry Diamond, the proportion of all countries that were electoral democracies more than doubled—from 26.7 percent in 1973 to 61.3 percent in 1995.[14] But the figure then leveled off. A decade later, in 2006, at 62.6 percent, the global proportion of electoral democracies had barely changed. And if the celebrated global "third wave" of democratization[15] that had begun in the mid-1970s had petered out, democrats had reason to be concerned.

By 2008, a growing number of observers were indeed rethinking the answer to Diamond's implicitly optimistic query, "Can the whole world become

---

[11] This is true despite the views of a small, extremist fringe, including radical Islamists who explicitly reject democracy as atheistic.

[12] A Latin American example is Enrique Krauze, *Por una Democracia sin Adjetivos* (Mexico City: Joaquin Mortiz/Planeta, 1986).

[13] "Freedom in the World 2008," <http://www.freedomhouse.org/uploads/fiw08launch/FIW08Tables.pdf>. The country's official name is the Lao People's Democratic Republic.

[14] For the definition and the data in this and the next paragraph, see Larry Diamond, *The Spirit of Democracy: The Struggle to Build Free Societies throughout the World* (New York: Times Books, 2008), 22 and Appendix (Table 2).

[15] Samuel P. Huntington, *The Third Wave: Democratization in the Late Twentieth Century* (Norman: University of Oklahoma Press, 1991).

democratic?"[16] Among the drivers of rising demo-skepticism were the deadly quagmire in Iraq, resulting from U.S. President George W. Bush's experiment in democracy-by-invasion; the reversal of democratization in Russia under Vladimir Putin; and the durability of authoritarian rule in China despite the contrary predictions of demo-optimists who expected economic growth to foster political pluralism in that country.[17] But more than these cases were involved. According to the annual surveys of all countries by Freedom House, freedom worldwide suffered successive net declines in 2006 and 2007—the first two-year slippage since 1994 and the worst ratio of improvement to deterioration since the fall of the Berlin Wall in 1989.[18]

As with the evidence of insecurity in the Failed States Index, this ebbing of democracy's "third wave" may have been interpreted with excessive dismay. Freedom House classifies each country as "Free," "Partly Free," or "Not Free." These judgments aggregate the answers to a lengthy checklist of questions regarding different aspects of political rights and civil liberties. It is entirely possible for a country to retain or even raise its summary status while losing ground on one or more of these component dimensions of freedom. Despite net global declines in these finer gradations of freedom in 2006 and 2007, the distribution of countries across the "Free," "Partly Free," and "Not Free"

---

[16] Larry Diamond, "Can the Whole World Become Democratic? Democracy, Development, and International Policies," University of California-Irvine Center for the Study of Democracy, 2003, <http://repositories.cdlib.org/csd/03-05>. The question was optimistic because the scope of what *can* happen is so much greater than the chance that a particular phenomenon actually *will* occur. Buoyed by the "third wave," Diamond argued by extrapolation ("most states can become democratic, because most states already are") and by example (since democracy had arrived and survived in Mali, "in principle" it could develop "in most other very poor countries"). But he added some challenging provisos: "Virtually every country in the world may be[come] democratic," he wrote, but only in the long run, and only *if* global, integrative economic growth and American support for democratization could be sustained.

[17] Admittedly, the Bush administration stressed democratization as a rationale for its invasion of Iraq only *after* weapons of mass destruction were not found. By adding insincerity to ineffectiveness, however, that sequencing discredited freedom as foreign policy even more. As for disappointment at the longevity of autocracy in China, in 1996 Henry S. Rowen asked, "When will China become a democracy?" and answered "around the year 2015." A decade later, acknowledging that by Freedom House standards China had "remained deep in Not Free territory," he reset his deadline to 2025. Compare Rowen, "The Short March: China's Road to Democracy," *The National Interest* 45 (Fall 1996), 61, and "When Will the Chinese People Be Free?" *Journal of Democracy* 18, no. 3 (July 2007), 38, 50.

[18] Larry Diamond, "The Democratic Rollback: The Resurgence of the Predatory State," *Foreign Affairs* 87, no. 2 (March–April 2008), 39.

categories in 2007, as compared with 2005, actually improved, albeit to a very small degree.[19]

This book is focused, however, on Southeast Asia, and there the trends have been more discouraging. Corruption and coercion in the Philippines, including reportedly massive electoral fraud and official intimidation of the opposition to President Gloria Macapagal-Arroyo's government, caused that country to be downgraded for 2005 from "Free" to "Partly Free," a label it kept through 2007. Meanwhile in Thailand, the coup d'état that overthrew the elected government of Prime Minister Thaksin Shinawatra in September 2006 dropped his country from "Partly Free" to "Not Free" for that year.

Thailand regained "Partly Free" status thanks to the junta's willingness to allow elections to take place in December 2007, which the opposition won. But the lesser shifts along finer gradations across the region were not encouraging. Of the component trends for 2006 and 2007 that were not large enough to lift or lower a Southeast Asian country from one to another of the three summary rungs—trends in Malaysia, Myanmar, and the Philippines (and Timor-Leste)—all pointed downward.[20] Nor did Southeast Asia look better compared with other areas. Among all nine world regions as of the end of 2006, only the one spanning the Middle East and North Africa was more authoritarian than Southeast Asia.[21]

The relevance of democracy for this book lies in this contrast between the global "third wave" of political reform and the regional "recalcitrance" that persists in Southeast Asia.[22] The discrepancy poses a broader version of the question, already introduced, as to whether Myanmar's neighbors can or

---

[19] For the list of 27 questions and 131 subquestions, see "Methodology," *Freedom in the World 2007* [for 2006], <http://www.freedomhouse.org/template.cfm?page=351&ana_page=333&year=2007>. From 2005 through 2007, the percentages of "Free," "Partly Free," and "Not Free" countries shifted from 46 to 47, 30 to 31, and 24 to 22 percent, respectively. See "Historical Country Ratings," *Freedom in the World 2008* [for 2007 and earlier], <http://www.freedomhouse.org/uploads/fiw08launch/FIW08Tables.pdf>.

[20] For the data, see "Table of Independent Countries," *Freedom in the World 2008* and *2007*.

[21] This comparison relies on Diamond's analytic categories and country assignments— "liberal democracy," "electoral democracy" (including Indonesia, the Philippines, and Timor-Leste), "competitive authoritarian[ism]" (including Malaysia), "electoral (hegemonic) authoritarian[ism]" (including Cambodia, Singapore, and Thailand), and "politically closed authoritarian[ism]" (including Brunei, Laos, Myanmar, and Vietnam). To single out Southeast Asia on Diamond's list of world areas, I divided his "Asia" into its three constituent regions: Northeast, Southeast, and South Asia. Even if Timor-Leste's "electoral democracy" is included as Southeast Asia's eleventh state, varieties of authoritarian rule characterize eight (or nearly three-quarters) of the countries in that region. See Diamond, *Spirit of Democracy*, Appendix (Table 5).

[22] See my "Region and Recalcitrance: Rethinking Democracy through Southeast Asia," *The Pacific Review* 8, no. 2 (1995).

should try to impel its junta toward reform. If the Southeast Asian region itself has not democratized—not fully or sustainably, notwithstanding the (so far) "Free" status of Indonesia—is there a role for regionalism to play in trying to facilitate more open, competitive, and accountable rule, not only in Myanmar but in other ASEAN states as well? Or would such an effort, if it were attempted, either founder for lack of agreement or trigger conflicts that would, in the end, render Southeast Asia neither democratic nor secure?

Regionalism

Regionalism is a process. It is the intentional bringing together of physically more or less proximate states, societies, or economies, in various ways and to varying degrees, for ostensibly common purposes and activities—forming or nourishing a shared identity, improving conditions and solving problems, or projecting influence beyond the region whose nature is thereby purposely created or shaped.[23] Like democracy, regionalism can be the business of governmental or nongovernmental organizations (NGOs) or actors. And if "waves" of democratization have spread variations on that form of rule around the world, so too has the evidence of regionalism become ubiquitous.

An obvious way to estimate the incidence of regionalism is to ask how many regional organizations there are. The question is answered annually by the Union of International Organizations. The 2007–08 edition of their *Yearbook of International Organizations* identified 7,759 "conventional international bodies" (CIBs)—"membership organizations" that were "genuinely international in character" and operated in "at least three countries." Of these CIBs, no fewer than 6,138, or 79 percent, were "regionally oriented" as opposed to global or near-global in scope and purpose. Striking, too, was the overwhelming preponderance of *non*governmental entities among these regionalist bodies—5,963 or 97 percent of the 6,138. Merely 175, or 3 percent, of these regionally focused CIBs were official—intergovernmental—in nature. Yet these 175 official regional organizations constituted 72 percent of all 242 intergovernmental CIBs.[24]

To the extent that "regionally oriented" CIBs have regionalist intentions or potentials, in contrast to their presumably more globalist counterparts, one may infer from these comparisons that regionalism is far more common than globalism. The sheer prevalence of regional associations, compared with their

---

[23] Regionalization is, in contrast, a process whereby transactions and interactions across national borders, undertaken without the intent of forming a region in its own right, of and for itself, nevertheless facilitate that result. Decisions by firms in one country to invest in, import from, or export to one or more neighboring countries may thus be regionalizing without being regionalist.

[24] Union of International Organizations, ed., *Yearbook of International Organizations: Guide to Global and Civil Society Networks* (Munich: K. G. Saur Verlag, 2007), vol. 1B, 2995.

larger-scale globalist or potentially globalist counterparts, argues for a focus on regions. Compared with the world as a whole, regions are already well equipped with resident associations that could—if they are not already promoting security, democracy, prosperity, or some other value in their respective neighborhoods— be encouraged or given incentives to do so. At the same time, the near-totally *non*governmental character of these regional associations warrants the attention that Caballero-Anthony, Dosch, and others in this book pay to regional NGOs and the growth of civil society in Southeast Asia.

Abundance and influence are two different things. It does not follow merely from the large number of regional organizations, and their almost wholly nongovernmental character, that private-sector or civil-society regionalism— regional cooperation outside the state—is necessarily more effective than globalism, or than regionalism spearheaded by governments. As the *Yearbook* data show, nearly three-quarters of all intergovernmental CIBs are regional in character. In view of the largely regional (rather than global) contexts in which governments do choose to cooperate, official regionalism is hardly a spent force. And for all the talk of globalization erasing the sovereignty of states, they remain essential to the furtherance of security, democracy, and regionalism, and for that matter globalism as well.

These organizational patterns favor the approach adopted in this book: to acknowledge the intergovernmental Association of Southeast Asian Nations as the legitimate exponent and embodiment of official regionalism in Southeast Asia, yet also to recognize that ASEAN acting alone, without help from civil society, may not be able to prevent state failure, to improve nontraditional security, or to reduce what might be termed the "democratic deficit" in Southeast Asia compared with most of the rest of the world.

ASEAN is by far the most often recurring acronym used in this book. Every chapter deals with the Association—its background, organization, performance, members,[25] or prospects, including its past or future relevance for security and democracy in the region. As I will argue later in this introduction, ASEAN is hardly synonymous with Southeast Asia. But it is practically impossible to think or write about regionalism there without referring to the Association. If the region as a region is to cope with new and complex challenges to security and democracy, action by ASEAN will be necessary. ASEAN's actions are unlikely to be sufficient, however, unless they are deepened and strengthened by unofficial regionalism—commitments, proposals, and actions by regional NGOs. Indeed, success in achieving human security, competitive elections, accountable government, and respect for individual and minority rights in Southeast Asia is

---

[25] ASEAN was founded in 1967 by five Southeast Asian states—Indonesia, Malaysia, the Philippines, Singapore, and Thailand. By mid-1999 the grouping had doubled its membership to include Brunei, Cambodia, Laos, Myanmar, and Vietnam as well. For a detailed review of ASEAN's organizational development, see chapter 3, by Termsak Chalermpalanupap, in this book.

likely to require initiatives on all three of the "tracks" that policymakers like to cite: "Track I" where governments operate; "Track III" where NGOs are active; and the intermediate "Track II," where both kinds of actors meet and interact, informally and (one hopes) creatively, to address problems whose regional scope and local complexity exceed the ability of either set, by itself, to resolve.

As noted at the outset of this essay, the interactions of regionalism with security and democracy around the world are an understudied subject. Books on regionalism and democracy are especially rare. I say this based on a June 2008 search of the titles of books in English in WorldCat, a global catalog of more than 100 million bibliographic records in some 60,000 libraries around the world. As referenced in this database, book titles that include one or more of the "critical terms" in *Hard Choices* form a sequence of ever smaller circles (with the number of titles noted in parentheses). There is a vast literature that represents itself as being about "security" (104,773), one about "democracy" roughly one-third as large (31,554), and a much smaller one on "regionalism" (2,358). Far fewer are books whose titles include both "regionalism" and "security" (50), yet they are nearly twice as common as titles on "regionalism" and "democracy" (15). Surprisingly, only one book in English has a title that spans all three of these critical terms—"regionalism," "security," and "democracy"—and that book is *Hard Choices*.[26]

If the case for this book's focus is strengthened by its novelty, however, it certainly does not follow that its authors have begun from scratch. As the citations in their chapters attest, ideas and propositions relevant to the study

---

[26] It follows from this that no other book has all three of these key words and "Southeast Asia" in its title. Nor do "regionalism," "democracy," and "Southeast Asia" occur in any other book title. A search of article titles yielded comparable results. These key word frequencies are approximations that change as the database is updated, and they understate the actual-content coverage of these topics. One cannot, for example, conclude from the absence of the word "regionalism" in its title that Amitav Acharya's *Constructing a Security Community in Southeast Asia: ASEAN and the Problem of Regional Order* (London: Routledge, 2001) is not about that phenomenon; it most certainly is. Nor can one say that it makes no mention of "democracy"; it does.

Electronically scanning all the words in all the books listed in WorldCat is of course not feasible. But I did expand the search beyond a book's title to scan other information on its bibliographic record, which could include subject classifications and a table of contents. The results of these wider searches did not alter the *ordinal* sequence of the sets of titles enumerated here. Nor did they weaken the distinctiveness of *Hard Choices*. An inspection of the six books (other than *Hard Choices*) whose records referred to all four critical terms (even though their titles did not) revealed that none was about security, democracy, *and* regionalism in even roughly equal measure, and all six relegated Southeast Asia to brief treatment as part of a larger area such as the Pacific Rim, Asia, or East Asia. All searches of <http://www.worldcat.org> were performed on 13 June 2008. The precision of numerical results is less reliable than the orders of magnitude they reflect, especially with a database as large as this one.

of regionalism, security, and democracy in Southeast Asia may be found in a variety of existing works, whatever their titles may be.

Economy?

This book does not give equal treatment alongside security, democracy, and regionalism to a fourth topic—economy. Analyzing three chosen themes and the dynamics between them was challenging enough. Most of the chapters do, nevertheless, deal with economic variables. Termsak reviews the ASEAN Economic Community. Kyaw and Kuhonta write of economic sanctions against Myanmar. Tay conveys the economic consequences of "the haze" in Indonesia. Several authors, including Dosch, Malley, and Jones, discuss the possibly material basis of security advanced in the well-known argument that expanding commerce among countries makes them more interdependent and thus more likely to enjoy the comforts of a "liberal peace." That said, however, none of the contributors pictures the economy as the primary driver of interstate security or intrastate democracy in Southeast Asia.

In 2005, an estimated 26 percent of all trade by ASEAN's member economies was conducted with one another. In that same year, twice as much, or 53 percent, of all trade by the economies of East Asia—the ASEAN ten plus China, Hong Kong, Japan, South Korea, and Taiwan—took place among themselves. Nor has the ASEAN Free Trade Agreement, signed in 1992, turned Southeast Asia into a trade bloc by enlarging the proportional extent of intraregional trade. Since 1995, that figure has stayed within a narrow range of 22 to 26 percent.[27]

One may argue that threats to the security of Southeast Asia are less likely to come from within its own region than from Northeast Asia, especially given the geographic, demographic, and military imbalances between the ASEAN states on the one hand and China on the other. One could assess the materialist argument that intra-*East* Asian trade promotes interdependent prosperity and therefore peace, not to mention democracy, within that much larger zone. One could ask to what extent such effects, if real, have resulted from regionalization—the economic activities of millions of firms and entrepreneurs on Track III—or regionalism—including the ASEAN Plus Three (China, Japan, South Korea) framework for economic cooperation on Track I that ASEAN initiated in 1997. However, that far wider research agenda would have meant writing a different—and much longer—book. Moreover, inside a Southeast Asian rather than an East Asian frame, the case for interpreting commercial

---

[27] The data for 2005 are from Siow Yue Chia, "Whither East Asian Regionalism? An ASEAN Perspective," *Asian Economic Papers* 6, no. 3 (October 1997), 3 (Table 1), <http://www.mitpressjournals.org/doi/pdfplus/10.1162/asep.2007.6.3.1>. The range since 1995 is from the ASEAN Secretariat as reported by Denis Hew, *Brick by Brick: The Building of an ASEAN Economic Community* (Singapore: Institute of Southeast Asian Studies / Canberra: Asia Pacific Press, 2007), 211 (Fig. 10.1).

interdependence and material prosperity as drivers of security and democracy is harder to maintain.

The resource endowments of many Southeast Asian countries are more competitive than complementary. The needs of the hypermodern, high-income city-state of Singapore do mesh well with those of its immediate neighbors— vast, agricultural, low-wage, mineral-rich Indonesia, and the intermediate case of middle-income Malaysia. But this long-standing commercial nexus at the strategic southern end of the Strait of Malacca is exceptional in the larger context of Southeast Asia. As for a liberal peace, in the early-to-mid 1960s, for political reasons, the relative complementarity of these three economies did not stop Indonesia's then-president Sukarno from infiltrating Singapore and trying to "crush" Malaysia. Neither did it restrain Malaysia, which at first included Singapore, from expelling that island state.

Nearly half a century later, despite the further meshing of these countries' economies and the firmly established peace among them, nationalist tensions continue periodically to mar their political relations, as I shall later illustrate. That Indonesia, Malaysia, and Singapore enjoy interstate peace reflects the record of cooperation among their political elites in an ASEAN context at least as much as, and certainly more directly than, it expresses the structural fit between their different economies. As for democracy, were it a function of either rates or levels of economic growth, Singapore would be a bastion of freedom and accountability, and Indonesia's poverty would have kept it autocratic. The reverse is true: Prosperous Singapore's illiberal polity incorporates "calibrated coercion," while far-lower-income Indonesia is by Freedom House measures the lone liberal democracy in Southeast Asia.[28]

Materialist theorists have been puzzled by the paucity of democracy in a region whose socioeconomic progress has been so remarkable. Worldwide, among all thirty countries and one territory ranked highest on the Human Development Index (HDI) for 2005, only three had not been designated "Free"

---

[28] See Cherian George, "Calibrated Coercion and the Maintenance of Hegemony in Singapore," Working Paper Series No. 48, Asia Research Institute, National University of Singapore, September 2005, <http://www.ari.nus.edu.sg/docs/wps/wps05_048.pdf>; and Freedom House, "Freedom in the World 2008 [for 2007]," <http://www.freedom-house.org/uploads/fiw08launch/FIW08Tables.pdf>. For 2007, Singapore and Indonesia ranked 8th and 156th respectively in per capita GDP at purchasing power parity (PPP) among the economies of the world, according to *The 2008 World Factbook* (Washington DC: Central Intelligence Agency, 2008), <https://www.cia.gov/library/publica-tions/the-world-factbook/rankorder/2004rank.html>. An evaluation of just how liberal Indonesia's democracy is lies beyond my limited space and scope. For a skeptical view, see Richard Robison and Vedi R. Hadiz, *Reorganising Power in Indonesia: The Politics of Oligarchy in the Age of Markets* (London: RoutledgeCurzon, 2004), esp. ch. 10.

for that year by Freedom House, and they were all East Asian: Hong Kong ("Partly Free"), Singapore ("Partly Free"), and Brunei ("Not Free").[29]

Do these exceptions "prove the rule" that prosperity ensures democracy? Believers in that rule could dismiss the case of Hong Kong by noting its subordination to China, which is still poor and therefore still, in their view, "Not Free." Brunei can be set aside because crude oil and natural gas account for so much—just over half—of its GDP. When prosperity pours out of the ground, rather than from a population's own efforts, economic growth is likely to reinforce autocratic rule by whoever controls the flow, other things being the same.[30]

The Singapore exception is harder to handle, but arguments can be made to explain its uniqueness as a materially flourishing autocratic state: Its perilous location between potentially hostile countries encourages Singaporeans to let their leaders do what they think is best. Capitalism has not yielded freedom in Singapore because market forces have been too constrained by government to play their natural role. Confucian culture has blunted the otherwise democratizing force of economic growth. Uniquely talented patrician leaders—who will not be easy to replace—have kept political pluralism at bay. Among these and other explanations, some imply permanent or only slowly changing barriers to the arrival of liberal democracy in Singapore. Other arguments, particularly those with a focus on leadership succession, could be used to predict major reform soon. What is noteworthy about all of these explanations, however, is that by stressing the causal power of noneconomic phenomena, they undermine the materialist argument in the act of rescuing it.

Rather than confirming a necessary or unilinear progression from economic development to liberal democracy, this book's treatment of economic factors highlights their political ambiguity and the historical contingency of their political effects. Several chapters, for example, deal with the Asian financial crisis (AFC) that struck Southeast Asia in 1997. If we believe in straight-line fashion that economic miracles promote democracy, it should follow that economic debacles spawn the opposite—autocracy. Instead, the 1997 crisis, to varying extents from one more or less affected country to another, worked

---

[29] For each jurisdiction covered, the HDI annually averages measures of "three dimensions of human development: a long and healthy life; access to knowledge; and a decent standard of living." The component indicators are "life expectancy at birth[;] adult literacy and combined gross enrolment in primary, secondary, and tertiary education[;] and gross domestic product (GDP) per capita in Purchasing Power Parity US dollars (PPP)." See Human Development Report Office, *Human Development Report 2007/2008* (New York: United Nations Development Programme, 2007), 225 (definition) and 229 (data). The Freedom House designations are from <http://www.freedomhouse.org/uploads/Chart83File137.pdf> and <http://www.freedomhouse.org/uploads/Chart84File136.pdf>.

[30] They are not the same in Norway, whose oil-and-gas-rich political economy sustains a liberal democracy that earned the second-highest HDI in the world in 2005. See *Human Development Report 2007/2008*, 229.

to delegitimate *any* incumbent government that appeared passive, indifferent, or incompetent in the face of the crisis. In Indonesia, that delegitimation, in tandem with other conditions and events, did speed the shift from an existing authoritarian format to a new and democratic one. It would be unfair, however, to infer from this particular transition that economic downturns, regardless of initial political conditions, are conducive only to democratization—or that they are, for that matter, inherently despotic in political effect.

I have introduced this book's three analytic themes, and noted a foregone fourth. It is time to ask the next critical question: Why this particular region?

Why Southeast Asia?

Why focus on Southeast Asia? The answer is threefold: because the challenges that security and democracy pose for regionalism in that part of the world are, on balance, attractively *difficult*; because conditions there are creatively *diverse*; and because a book about these challenges in 2008 is especially *timely*.

Difficulty

Southeast Asia is an attractively *difficult* site for analyzing how regionalism can affect security and democracy.

It is helpful to picture a spectrum of instances drawn from different parts of the world. At one extreme, in Europe, security and democracy have already been achieved, and regionalism has been institutionalized. One can debate how much credit should be given to the entity now known as the European Union (EU) for achieving security and democracy (not to mention prosperity) in its neighborhood, and whether these historic gains are likely to be jeopardized in future. The Union remains, nevertheless, the single most successful instance of regionalism in the world.

At the opposite end of the spectrum of regionalist experiences, farthest from Europe, lie the countries of the Middle East and North Africa. There, Europe's accomplishments are more or less absent, and security has been a sometime thing. Since 1980, major violence—often prolonged and in some cases ongoing—has occurred across and/or within the borders of Algeria, Iraq, Israel, Kuwait, Lebanon, Morocco, Palestine, and Yemen. Democracy, too, has proven elusive. Of the region's seventeen states, only Israel and Turkey are democratic.[31] As for regionalism, disunity has long bedeviled both of the larger official organizations in this part of the world—the African Union (AU) and the Arab League.[32]

---

[31] See Diamond, *Spirit of Democracy*, Appendix (Table 5).

[32] Nor is such disunity a thing of the past. Half of the twenty-two heads of state or government entitled to attend the Arab League's summit in Damascus in March 2008 chose not to do so, and one (Lebanon) was not represented at all. See "A Snub for Syria," editorial, *The Boston Globe*, 29 March 2008, <http://www.boston.com/bostonglobe/editorial_opinion/editorials/articles/2008/03/29/a_snub_for_syria>.

Political splits have also thwarted the ability of smaller-scale regionalisms in the area, such as the Arab Maghreb Union and the Gulf Cooperation Council, to foster security or democracy in their vicinities. Only in the AU has democracy been even a rhetorical priority for these organizations, which is not surprising in light of the mostly authoritarian make-up of their constituent states.

As a locale for scholarly analysis and policy prescription, Southeast Asia is an engaging mixed case between these European and North African–Middle Eastern extremes.

I noted earlier that since the birth of ASEAN in 1967, war has never broken out between any of its member states. This is striking circumstantial evidence that the Association has helped its members to achieve and maintain interstate peace. If non-ASEAN states in Southeast Asia had been as successful as ASEAN members in avoiding war, the grouping's edge in peaceability would disappear. In reality, when Vietnam overran Cambodia in 1978, neither belonged to ASEAN. Nor was Vietnam a member when China attacked it in 1979. Indonesia did belong to ASEAN when the Suharto regime seized East Timor in 1975, but with that exception no ASEAN state has so far invaded, or been invaded by, a nonmember. Looking still farther back in history yields ample additional evidence of warfare in Southeast Asia—between its polities, or between them and outsiders. This record of prior turbulence belies the idea that regional peace incubated ASEAN, rather than the other way around.

Nevertheless, even if the danger of outright invasion has been durably overcome and ASEAN is one reason why, there is still room for improvement along security's other key dimensions:

- "Human security," including the protection of individuals and minorities from official predation, discrimination, and neglect
- "Nontraditional security (NTS)," at risk from environmental and other novel hazards that ignore national borders
- *Intra*state security, as endangered by the rise and the repression of movements against central authority
- Better governance, including the rule of law and the reduction of corruption
- Effective democracy, including the protection of human rights and civil liberties

It is security in these senses that is featured in this book, and it is in these contexts that Southeast Asia is an attractively difficult case.

The difficulty lies in the challenges to ASEAN to adopt and address this new agenda—challenges the Association may well fail to meet. The difficulty is attractive for study and advice because the record of regionalism and its achievements is neither so fulsome as to ensure success, nor so abject as to preclude it. If official or Track I regionalism has managed to facilitate security at the level of states, can that achievement be extended to include the security of societies and persons as well, including the diminution in Southeast Asia of opaque, abusive, and unaccountable rule? It is the surface plausibility of arguments on *both* sides of this question that recommends Southeast Asia as the spatial focus of this book.

Diversity

Another reason for exploring security, democracy, and regionalism in Southeast Asia is the region's creative *diversity*. It would be hard to imagine a more heterogeneous place. From Kachin in northernmost Myanmar to Papua in extreme southeastern Indonesia, from Aceh in far-western Indonesia to the easternmost Philippine island of Mindanao, the topographies and ecologies of Southeast Asia—subcontinental, peninsular, maritime—are spectacularly varied. The region's peoples speak some 1,500 languages, and all of the world's major and many minor religions are represented there. Southeast Asian countries differ greatly in their demographic size, from 235 million in Indonesia—the world's fourth most populous country—to a mere 375,000 in Brunei as of 2007. Per capita GDPs (at purchasing power parity) also ranged widely in that year, from US$ 48,900 in Singapore—above the U.S. figure of $ 46,000—to a scant $ 1,900 in Laos.[33]

Dissimilar, too, are the historical experiences and political systems of Southeast Asia's countries. Ten of the region's arguably eleven states were colonized prior to World War II, for varying lengths of time and in differing ways and degrees, by Britain (Brunei, Malaysia, Myanmar, Singapore), France (Cambodia, Laos, Vietnam), the Netherlands (Indonesia), Portugal (Timor-Leste), and Spain followed by the United States (the Philippines). One country (Thailand) was not colonized in a formal sense at all.

In mid-2008 in Southeast Asia one could find a military junta (Myanmar), an absolute monarchy (Brunei), two ostensibly communist one-party states (Laos, Vietnam), a dominant-party parliamentary monarchy (Cambodia), a dominant-party parliamentary republic (Singapore), a restored (post-coup) multiparty parliamentary monarchy (Thailand), a dominant-party parliamentary federation with a rotating king (Malaysia), a presidential republic of multiple but weak parties (the Philippines), a multiparty presidential republic (Indonesia), and a nascent and mainly parliamentary but also presidential multiparty republic (Timor-Leste).

---

[33] These estimates, which incorporate Timor-Leste, reflect Cliff Goddard, *The Languages of East and Southeast Asia: An Introduction* (Oxford: Oxford University Press, 2005), 44, 47; "Languages of Indonesia (Papua)" in Raymond Gordon, Jr., *Ethnologue: Languages of the World* (15th ed., Dallas, TX: SIL International, 2005), <http://www. ethnologue.com/show_country.asp?name=IDP>; and *2008 World Factbook*, <https:// www.cia.gov/library/publications/the-world-factbook/rankorder/2119rank.html> (populations) and <https://www.cia.gov/library/publications/the-world-factbook/ rankorder/2004rank.html> (per capita GDP).

Southeast Asia is not democratic by Freedom House standards. Of the region's eleven states (including Timor-Leste) in 2007, only one was "Free." But that exception was Indonesia, by far the largest, most populous, and potentially most influential state in the region. The rest were evenly distributed between "Partly Free" (Malaysia, the Philippines, Singapore, Thailand, and Timor-Leste) and "Not Free" (Brunei, Cambodia, Laos, Myanmar, and Vietnam).

Diversity is not a synonym for deadlock, any more than homogeneity implies harmony. But in conditions of such prodigious variety, how amenable to *regional* promotion are security and democracy as objectives? Is Southeast Asia's variegation so daunting in this context that regionalism's prospects look *un*attractively difficult?

It is roughly true that, compared with markedly similar states, highly diverse ones are more likely to have diverse outlooks, and that what it means to be "secure" or "democratic" is likely to vary depending on who, what, and where you are. Another look at the adjacent but very different states bordering the Malacca Strait will illustrate not only these points regarding the subjectivity of "security" in Southeast Asia, but also how, in this instance, a divergence that was attributable to diversity has been largely overcome.

Singapore is small, rich, mainly non-Muslim, and mostly ethnic-Chinese. Malaysia is much bigger, much less rich, and majority Muslim-Malay. Indonesia is huge, poor, largely Muslim, and overwhelmingly non-ethnic-Chinese. As Dosch notes in his chapter, the late Southeast Asianist Michael Leifer, drawing on some of these differences, portrayed Singapore's foreign policy as a mini-state's response to vulnerability and showed how Indonesia's outlook projected that vast country's sense of regional entitlement.[34]

In ASEAN circles during the Cold War, different visions of regional security and how to achieve it competed for approval. Singapore's sense of vulnerability led its leaders to define regional security in *strategically inclusive* or balance-of-power terms. The city-state's rulers wanted major players such as China, Japan, Russia, and especially the United States to be present inside the region, where they could not only check one another but could also potentially restrain any local would-be hegemon—the most worrisome of which was Indonesia.

Malaysia championed a *strategically exclusive* concept of regional security, in which Southeast Asia would declare its neutrality in the Cold War, the United States would withdraw its forces from Vietnam, and outside powers would abstain from further interference in the region. Indonesia for its part felt entitled to recommend the *strategically privileged* concept of "regional resilience" as a larger version of the "national resilience" it had itself pursued, in which regional security would ultimately depend not on outside powers but on the strengths of Southeast Asians themselves. Viewed from Jakarta, not least among those

---

[34] See Michael Leifer, *Singapore's Foreign Policy: Coping with Vulnerability* (New York: Routledge, 2000), and *Indonesia's Foreign Policy* (London: Allen & Unwin, 1983).

strengths were Indonesia's own assets and authority as the region's largest and therefore most entitled member.

Regionalism, however, far from being undermined by these differences, bridged them. In 1971, Singapore, Indonesia, and the rest of ASEAN humored Malaysia by jointly stating a desire to turn Southeast Asia into a Zone of Peace, Freedom and Neutrality (ZOPFAN).[35] But the strategic abstention implied by ZOPFAN was never implemented on the ground, and eventually the end of the Cold War retired neutrality as a posture. Meanwhile, ASEAN's success in fostering comity among its diverse members helped to moderate both the vulnerability felt by Singapore and the entitlement felt by Indonesia.

In 2008, there was still no uniform view of regional security to be found across all of ASEAN's diverse members. Versions of strategic inclusion had, nevertheless, become conventional in the region. ASEAN's confidence in its ability proactively to engage outside powers had grown as fear that they would interfere receded, the ongoing phobias of Myanmar's junta notwithstanding. From worrying about foreigners destabilizing Southeast Asia, ASEAN had progressed to attempting to help foreigners stabilize the rest of Asia. A case in point was the 1994 launching of the ASEAN Regional Forum (ARF), whose twenty-six members (as of mid-2008) included all the major powers.

When he was Indonesia's president (1998–99), B. J. Habibie, while addressing some foreign journalists, directed their attention to a map. "All the green is Indonesia," he said—and added dismissively, if not derisively as well, "That red dot is Singapore." Habibie's successor, Abdurrahman Wahid (1999–2001), made headlines by remarking, "Basically Singaporeans underestimate the Malays. They think we do not exist." Added Wahid, "If we hold the water for a moment, they will have no water to drink." By "we" he meant Indonesia acting jointly with Malaysia, for it was Malaysia on which Singapore—the "red dot"—relied for half or more than half of all its fresh water.[36] What is important about this contretemps, however, is how little it mattered to the actual security of the countries involved.

---

[35] "Freedom" in this context meant that the region should be "free of any form or manner of interference by outside powers." The text of the declaration is in K. S. Sandhu et al., *The ASEAN Reader* (Singapore: Institute of Southeast Asian Studies, 1992), 538–39.

[36] See Michael D. Barr, "The Little Red Dot Speaks," *Asian Analysis* [Canberra], January 2001, <http://www.aseanfocus.com/asiananalysis/article.cfm?articleID=345>, and Vaudine England, "Singapore Greets Wahid Outburst with Silence," *South China Morning Post*, 28 November 2000, <http://www.singapore-window.org/sw00/001128sc. htm>. On Singapore's quarrels with Malaysia over fresh water, including disputed estimates of the city-state's dependence on its Malaysian supplier, see "Water: The Singapore-Malaysia Dispute—The Facts," *New Straits Times* [Kuala Lumpur], 21 July 2003, <http://www.singapore-window.org/sw03/030721ns.htm>.

ASEAN's Way

Strategic inclusion is one thing; sovereignty is another. If Cold War–derived neutrality has been superseded in Southeast Asia, ZOPFAN's emphasis on noninterference has not. That declaration committed ASEAN's founding states to a region freed of meddling by outsiders. Since ASEAN's founding, intraregional intervention—intrusion by one member in the affairs of another—has also been taboo. The defense of member-state sovereignty was critical to building confidence and reducing suspicion, especially in ASEAN's early years. In effect, the ruling elites overcame the conflictive risk of diversity by underpinning regional security not only positively, with proactive cooperation, but also negatively, with mutual assurances that no one member would fish in the troubled waters of another.

When "national sovereignty rules," to cite Dosch's argument in this book, national sovereigns are essentially told they can stop worrying about what a neighboring sovereign might say publicly about them or plan privately to do to them. ASEAN's aversion to interference sustained a reciprocal kind of impunity: Each member regime could do what it wished behind its own borders, provided it gave the same leeway to other member regimes. In an abusively ruled country such as Myanmar, the arrangement fostered tolerance of repression—the region turning a blind eye. Yet the external security of all member states—as opposed to human security inside them—was thereby upheld, as was regional security defined in minimalist terms as the absence of interstate war.

In and of itself, the prohibition of interference was—and is—neither pro- nor antidemocratic. Observing this rule protected every member regime, despotic or democratic, from ouster through subversion or invasion by any other member, or by ASEAN itself. Whether an ASEAN country became more or less democratic, or prolonged its status quo, was left to the changing balance of power between the regime and its opponents. Noninterference in this respect supported the autonomy of political change.

ASEAN has always been and remains an intergovernmental body—an incumbents' club. To the extent that belonging to the Association bestows legitimacy, the direct beneficiary is not society but the regime that rules it—however civil the society and uncivil the regime might be. But if in the course of locally driven events society does somehow manage to "civilize" the state, replacing despotism with democracy, the principle of noninterference obliges ASEAN to accept the results—and seat the reformist leader of the new regime at the regional table. When democracy replaced autocracy in Indonesia in 1998–99, the country's new leaders were welcome to represent their country at ASEAN events. By the same token, none of ASEAN's leaders who gathered in the Philippines for a week of summitry in January 2007 demurred when the junta that had recently overthrown its elected predecessor in Bangkok arrived to speak on Thailand's behalf.

As these examples illustrate, the diversity of Southeast Asia's countries at a given point in time has been conducive to diverse changes inside them over time. If, back in 1967 when the Association was born, its originating states—Indonesia, Malaysia, the Philippines, Singapore, and Thailand—had all been manifestly democratic, the new grouping might have followed Europe's model and required all future members to be democratic as well. Conversely, had ASEAN's founding members all been extremely and equally repressive, they might have used their creation to inoculate the region against democratization. Instead, the sheer heterogeneity of the region, the lack of trust among ASEAN's first leaders, and their wish to develop their respective economies in conditions of interstate peace led them to rest their cooperation on national sovereignty and its corollaries: noninterference and consensus.

These principles—flagstones of what became known as the ASEAN Way—impeded the ability of the grouping explicitly to advocate, let alone require, any one political format for its members. Noninterference meant limiting the drivers of domestic political change to events and actors inside state borders. Consensus gave each member state the right to veto the regional promotion of any particular type of regime. The doubling of ASEAN's membership since 1967, by further diversifying the grouping, has enhanced the restraining effect of these impediments.

It follows from this that if Southeast Asia's variegation inhibits *regional* action for or against democracy, the ASEAN Way is compatible with a range of *national* developments from reaction through reform to rebellion—and even, however unlikely, revolution. ASEAN's members are ten different experiments-in-progress. What happens to them will necessarily affect the organization to which they belong, including its future ability and inclination selectively to encourage, or discourage, any one kind of change.[37]

Is ASEAN Losing Its Way?

Alongside attractive *difficulty* and creative *diversity*, the twists and turns of current events have made the study of security, democracy, and regionalism in Southeast Asia unexpectedly *timely* as well.

Writing *Hard Choices* was an idea conceived in 2006 in the knowledge that 2007 would be a watershed year for official regionalism in Southeast Asia. Forty years would have elapsed since ASEAN's birth in 1967. The onset of its middle age seemed a good time to reflect on where the Association stood, and might stand in the future, on matters of security and democracy.

But more than a birthday was involved. As Termsak relates in his chapter, it was already clear in 2006 that ASEAN hoped in 2007 to crown the celebration

---

[37] A book is sorely needed in which each chapter investigates how much and in what ways a particular member of ASEAN has influenced the Association, and considers consequences of the Association's ability, in turn, to influence the states that comprise it.

of its fortieth anniversary with the signing of an ASEAN Charter. Optimistic advocates of stronger regionalism began looking to the Charter as potentially a breakthrough text that, in putting the Association on a firmer institutional basis, might even amount to, or later evolve into, a regional "constitution" of sorts. Not surprisingly, such a term was too provocative for sovereignty-minded governments to entertain. A genuinely supranational institution was neither realistic nor desired. A "charter" sounded less intrusive, and more congenial to the ASEAN Way of noninterference and consensus.

Despite these qualms, however, the Charter's planners—Keng Yong notably among them—did not wish merely to decorate the upcoming anniversary with cosmetic rhetoric. The drive to charter ASEAN, as Termsak explains in his essay, was motivated in no small measure by a perceived need to equip the Association with a legal personality. No one involved had the slightest intention to charter a Government of Southeast Asia. That was—is—a preposterous idea. But the plan for the Charter to include language that would render ASEAN a more fully and explicitly legal authority, with more clearly juridical rights and responsibilities, did reflect an intention to make the organization more "sovereign" *in its own right*, quite apart from the acknowledged sovereignty of its member states.

Some of the ways in which ASEAN would benefit by having a legal personality were minor. The Association would, for instance, be entitled to change the domain name of its Internet address from ".org" (for organizations in general) to ".int" (for organizations that are international, intergovernmental, and established by treaty). But other possibilities raised intriguing questions that some of the authors of this book discussed among themselves while writing it. For example, if ASEAN were to acquire a legal personality, and it agreed but failed to do something, could it be sued for breach of promise? Less fanciful would be the likely enhanced ability of the organization to raise money all by itself for its own budget, including funds endowed for use in perpetuity, thereby reducing its dependence on contributions by member states. As for the question underlying these and other possibilities, it was neither minor nor chimerical: How much authority should and would ASEAN have in relation to the authority enjoyed by each of its member states?

At ASEAN's anniversary summit in Singapore in November 2007, the Charter was unveiled and signed by the leaders of all ten member governments. The text appears at the back of this book. In mid-2008 it was too soon to know whether the document would weaken or strengthen the ASEAN Way, or prolong, on balance, the status quo. All ten members must first ratify the document before it can come into force, and it will have to be interpreted and applied before its effects can be known.

I will return to the Charter at the end of this essay. For now, I will merely suggest a few of its implications. Once in effect, the document will allow ASEAN, as a legal personality, to reach agreements with comparable entities such as the EU, agreements that will be, in theory, binding under international law. Possessing legal status will also, though again only in principle, make it easier for the Association to ensure that member states actually comply with its agreed-upon rules and decisions. The Charter will not transform ASEAN into a body with fully executive authority including the power to force its members to carry out its decisions. But the Charter could open at least some room for making the Association less allergic to interference, depending on the nature of the issue and the perceived danger of doing nothing. Reforming the ASEAN Way could, as a matter of practice, become marginally less difficult. National sovereignty as a barrier to regional action could become more conditional, albeit to a still unknown and possibly only modest degree.

The rule of consensus will not be abandoned, but it could be replaced by voting in certain circumstances—for efficiency to resolve an issue that does not elicit strong feelings or, conceivably and only in extremis, for effectiveness in overcoming a debilitating deadlock. These incremental shifts may not occur, but if they do, ASEAN could wind up stepping away from its prior emphasis on informal understandings and toward a more formal-legal or "European" way of doing regional business. Between noninterference seen as complicity in repression and interference feared as triggering division, between consensus at the risk of inaction and voting at the risk of splitting, what will the Association do? Hard choices indeed.

I have noted that this book was conceived in the knowledge that Southeast Asia on its fortieth anniversary might be on the cusp of change. What I did not know was that dramatic political events would break out in Myanmar to stain the celebration, embarrass the Association, and render this book even timelier than I had imagined it to be.

The Junta Cracks Down

The year 2007 in fact involved two anniversaries for ASEAN. Alongside its own would-be happy fortieth birthday was the distinctly less happy tenth anniversary of its 1997 decision to admit Myanmar to membership. That decision had benefited the generals in Yangon (formerly Rangoon)—and in Naypyidaw after a new capital was built there beginning in 2005—rather more than it had served the image of ASEAN in the capitals of democratic states outside Southeast Asia.

The Association had been turned into a tainted shield. Observance of the ASEAN Way protected Myanmar from intramural criticism while making the Association seem complicit in tyranny. Meanwhile the United States, the EU, and ASEAN's other democratic partners faced hard choices of their own: to uphold human rights by downgrading relations with the Association insofar as they involved Myanmar at all, to work with ASEAN but attend its events only if the junta was absent or was represented by a lower-level functionary, or to cooperate fully with a successful regional organization in an economically attractive, strategically important part of the world.

In 2005 and 2006, as planning proceeded for the commemorative summit in Singapore, the political situation inside Myanmar was basically in stasis between the intransigence of the generals and the resistance of their nemesis, Aung San Suu Kyi. Detained and harassed, she remained unbowed. Her National League for Democracy (NLD) had won the 1990 elections by a landslide, but to no avail when the ruling generals canceled the result. The NLD could not achieve political reforms, but neither would it give up and go away. Since 1992 the regime had been pursuing at a glacial pace a "roadmap" toward a constitutional "democracy." As noted earlier to illustrate "democracy with adjectives," however, the sort of democracy Senior General Than Shwe had in mind was not just "disciplined" but "discipline-*flourishing*"[38]—a format that would entrench the military's political role and deny such a role to Suu Kyi.

In August 2007, with the Singapore summit barely three months away, alumni of an uprising that had failed nearly two decades earlier reignited public opposition to the Myanmar regime. What started as a protest against suddenly higher prices for energy and transportation, triggered when the junta cut fuel subsidies, became explicitly political in character. Soon Buddhist monks were leading mass demonstrations against the junta. In September the regime cracked down. Peaceful protesters were beaten and dispersed. Hundreds were arrested. Some were killed. Media reports and images of these brutalities triggered outrage not only in the West, but in parts of Southeast Asia as well.

ASEAN as an organization was eloquently silent in the face of these blatant violations of human security by a member state. The ASEAN Way of keeping quiet while turning a blind eye was on full display. The secretary-general of ASEAN had no authority to criticize the junta; his job definition was to manage policy, not make it. The doctrine of noninterference, in any case, implied nonresponsibility. Requiring ASEAN to keep its hands off the junta allowed the Association to wash its hands of the junta's behavior.

ASEAN's public indifference to events in Myanmar seemed to reveal the organization as nothing more than the sum of its sovereign parts. In reformist circles, this was all the more reason for a Charter that could transform the Association from a mere political arena into a legal personality capable of speaking and acting on its own. Conservatives, in contrast, endorsed organizational silence as preferable to polarizing the Association over an internal matter and setting a precedent that could haunt other states when in the future they too had to quash domestic opposition.

Of any ASEAN country other than Myanmar, Singapore had the most at stake. It occupied the chair of ASEAN's Standing Committee. As host of the imminent anniversary summit, its image was most clearly at risk. News circulated at the end of September that the city-state's leaders had been working

---

[38] "Junta Wants 'Discipline-Flourishing Democracy' in Myanmar," Islamic Republic News Agency, 5 January 2007, <http://www2.irna.ir/en/news/view/menu-239/0701058175140530.htm>.

behind the scenes to persuade the leaders of Brunei, Indonesia, Malaysia, the Philippines, Thailand, and Vietnam to join Singapore in "urging the Myanmarese authorities to exercise restraint" and peacefully to seek a "political solution for national reconciliation."[39] Other international organizations, including the United Nations (UN) and the EU, had already made public statements and taken public actions regarding the crisis in Myanmar.

In New York on 25 September 2007, the UN General Assembly began its annual ritual of listening to speeches by leaders from around the world. All ten of ASEAN's foreign ministers, including Myanmar's, were in town for the occasion. They met in private on 27 September to review plans for the ASEAN Charter. The crisis in Myanmar came up, and a rancorous discussion ensued.

The result of this meeting buoyed the reformist position that ASEAN needed to speak out. Singapore's Foreign Minister George Yeo, in his capacity as the ASEAN chair and on behalf of his fellow foreign ministers, described in strong language the chagrin that he and his colleagues felt about events in Myanmar. They were, he said, "appalled" at "reports of automatic weapons" being used against demonstrators. Reports that the protests had been forcibly suppressed, with fatalities, had led his colleagues to voice their "revulsion" to the foreign minister of Myanmar. They had insisted that the government of Myanmar stop using violence. They had "strongly urged" a "political solution," including the release of Suu Kyi and all other political detainees, and efforts to achieve "national reconciliation" and "work towards a peaceful transition to democracy."[40]

The ministers were concerned, said Yeo, that "the reputation and credibility of ASEAN" had been seriously impacted by the crackdown. He then added a remark whose ironic significance would only become clear at the summit in Singapore in November: ASEAN's foreign ministers had urged Myanmar's government "to cooperate fully and work with" Ibrahim Gambari, the special envoy for Myanmar appointed by UN Secretary-General Ban Ki-moon.

Never before had a chair of the Standing Committee of ASEAN criticized more vehemently the actions of a member state, and done so in public and on behalf of "the ASEAN foreign ministers"—Myanmar's own minister in this instance presumably excluded.

There is much to be said about Yeo's remarks, including the unprecedented expression of "revulsion" at an ASEAN member's behavior.[41] What matters

---

[39] Gamar Abdul Aziz, "ASEAN Cannot Remain Silent over Myanmar Unrest: PM Lee," *Channelnewsasia.com* [Singapore], 28 September 2007, <http://www.channelnewsasia.com/stories/singaporelocalnews/view/302532/1/.html>.

[40] The quotes in this and the next paragraph are taken from "Statement by ASEAN Chair, Singapore's Minister for Foreign Affairs George Yeo in New York, 27 September 2007," <http://app.mfa.gov.sg/2006/press/view_press.asp?post_id=3125>.

[41] See, for example, my "ASEAN's 'Black Swans,'" *Journal of Democracy* 19, no. 3 (July 2008).

most in the present context is the extent to which Yeo contravened the ASEAN Way by appearing to violate its cardinal principle of noninterference. As for the principle of consensus, it has two different faces. It can imply a need for *unanimity* that empowers a minority to disagree, thus preventing action. Or it can, on the contrary, imply a norm of *solidarity* that encourages that same minority to acquiesce, thereby enabling action.

In New York in September 2007, solidarity trumped unanimity. It is my understanding that none of the foreign ministers knew in advance exactly what Yeo would say. (Had he told them, some might have objected.) Again to my knowledge, none later chose to contradict what he actually did say. By claiming to speak on behalf of all ten ministers, Yeo disguised interference as consensus. By not refuting him, the ministers went along. Arguably they did so to maintain an appearance of harmony. In this admittedly extreme instance, the consensus principle did not embolden Myanmar's foreign minister to object. He neither vetoed Yeo's statement in advance nor denounced it afterward. Consensus in this case did not slow ASEAN down to what its least willing member would allow. Instead, one part of the ASEAN Way—consensus operating not as an invitation to exercise one's veto but as a disincentive to doing so—was used to hide the violation of another: the principle of noninterference erected as a barrier to criticism.

Did the Singaporean chair's revulsion violate Myanmar's sovereignty? Only the paranoid would define sovereignty as the right not to be criticized in private, and it is hardly less extreme or naive to argue that the principle confers immunity from being criticized in public as well. ASEAN's rulers, including the junta, are more realistic than that. When Indonesian presidents Habibie and Wahid disparaged Singapore, the latter's leaders could not and did not claim that their sovereignty had been transgressed. Propriety perhaps, but not sovereignty. Revulsion is not invasion.

Yeo's criticism put Myanmar's generals on notice that they could not expect intra-ASEAN collegiality to let them off the public-relations hook whenever they behaved as egregiously as they had in suppressing the nonviolent "saffron revolution" (so named after the colors of the robes worn by the protesting monks). The junta's dilatory behavior in the wake of Cyclone Nargis in 2008, however, showed once again that in a crisis the generals would not subordinate their desire to remain in power to the niceties of regional public relations. Nor, in 2007, did ASEAN follow up Yeo's statement with action in the sense of taking the initiative to facilitate reconciliation, let alone democracy, in Myanmar. Instead, the Association urged the junta to deal with the UN, knowing that in the Security Council, China would veto intervention. In this respect, despite appearing to interfere, ASEAN continued to deflect responsibility for what its most reviled member was up to. In retrospect, Yeo's words resembled substitutes for deeds more than deeds themselves.

The Chair Backs Down

The junta itself, of course, resisted a role for ASEAN, but the Association could hardly use that as an excuse for regional inaction. Yeo had, after all, been able to criticize the junta while acting as the ASEAN chair and representing "the ASEAN foreign ministers," who had themselves "agreed" to his speaking publicly on the matter. What was there to prevent Singapore from moving from words toward deeds by proposing actual steps to be taken in ASEAN's name to help bring about security, or even democracy, in the errant state? If the junta refused to receive, for example, a good auspices mission seeking Aung San Suu Kyi's release from detention, publicly offering to mediate would at least have limited the damage to "the reputation and credibility of ASEAN" about which the foreign ministers had been so concerned.

Southeast Asian rulers had already applied an "ASEAN Minus X" formula to boost economic cooperation. A subset of the ten members could decide to do something without having to involve reluctant states. The Myanmar issue was more controversial, of course. Yet a single member state could have organized a subset group—"minus X"—to encourage reform in ASEAN's most problematic state. As a large democracy with a history of military rule, Indonesia was a logical candidate to play such a role. Conversations I had with relevant actors in Jakarta in December 2007 suggested, however, that Indonesia did not want to rock the ASEAN boat, but hoped instead to work in tandem with non-Southeast Asians: Ban Ki-moon's Special Envoy Gambari on the one hand, and China on the other.

Kyaw notes in his chapter that China, too, may have encouraged the junta to engage with the UN. He favors trying to encourage China to play a more positive role in Myanmar. I agree. Unfortunately, in March 2008, a version of Myanmar's "saffron revolution" broke out in Tibet and triggered a crackdown comparable to what the junta had done. The parallel between the two cases cannot have been lost on Chinese leaders. In March 2008, it was not easy to picture them trying to persuade Myanmar's strongman Than Shwe to accommodate Aung San Suu Kyi, any more than they themselves were willing to reconcile with the Dalai Lama. (Chinese policy on one or both of these fronts could, of course, change.)

Also noteworthy is the evidence that Kyaw reports, based on interviews with nearly a dozen active or retired officials, that only if an effort were made to overthrow their regime would the generals actually cancel Myanmar's membership in ASEAN. On a bleak horizon, this amounts to good news, inasmuch as it implies useful room for creative regional initiatives that would not cause the generals to quit the Association and thereby terminate whatever modest collegial leverage ASEAN might have. The bad news is that despite being revolted and appalled, Southeast Asian leaders showed no interest in creative *regional* diplomacy along "minus X" lines.

Any discussion of roles for regionalism to advance security and democracy must address the question of who: Who will represent the region in pursuing such goals? On this score what Foreign Minister Yeo said in New York was less important than who he was. As the 2008–09 occupant of the rotating chair of ASEAN's Standing Committee, he could speak bluntly on controversial matters *and* represent the Association at the same time. Also at the same time, however, as foreign minister of Singapore, he represented a government alleged to enjoy close ties to the junta—ties representing leverage that Singapore was apparently unwilling to use in an effort to nudge the regime toward reform, or ties that existed partly because of that unwillingness and the generals' knowledge that Singapore's leverage would not be so used.[42]

The ASEAN Charter signed in Singapore in November 2007, if and when it is ratified by all ten member states, will not only give the grouping a legal personality. It will also strengthen the position of the annually rotating ASEAN chair. The member state holding that position in a given year will host and chair two ASEAN summits, and will also chair nearly all of the Association's other organs—a Coordinating Council, three Community Councils, relevant Sectoral Ministerial Bodies and meetings of senior officials ("where appropriate"), and a Committee of Permanent Representatives as well (see Charter, Art. 31.2).

According to the Charter, the chairing state "shall ensure an effective and timely response to urgent issues or crisis situations affecting ASEAN, including providing its good offices and such other arrangements to immediately address these concerns" (Art. 32.c). It is hard to read this mandate and not think of what George Yeo said as the ASEAN chair in New York in September 2007—and of what a future ASEAN chair might more legitimately be able to *do* to help resolve a crisis that endangers human security and implicates authoritarian rule in Southeast Asia.

I have argued that ASEAN's diversity both limits and enables what the organization can accomplish. Its diverse members have upheld regionalism as

---

[42] See Eric Ellis, "Singapore, a Friend Indeed to Burma," *Sydney Morning Herald*, 1 October 2007, <http://www.smh.com.au/news/business/singapore-a-friend-indeed-to-burma/2007/09/30/1191090945019.html>; Andrew Seith, *Burma's Secret Military Partners*, Canberra Papers on Strategy and Defence, No. 136 (Canberra: Australian National University Strategic and Defence Studies Centre, 2000); and Leslie Kean and Dennis Bernstein, "The Burma-Singapore Axis: Globalizing the Heroin Trade," *Covert Action Quarterly*, Spring 1998, <http://www.thirdworldtraveler.com/Global_Secrets_Lies/BurmaSingapore_Drugs.html>. The authorities in Singapore might of course respond that nothing could reform the junta, and therefore that maintaining personal, financial, and military relations with it, insofar as these even existed, yielded no leverage at all. Or perhaps the response would be that using and thereby jeopardizing such leverage was simply less important than serving Singapore's own economic and security interests, which had to be kept separate from, not used to advance, any ideology—indeed, that an ideological foreign policy was not something a vulnerable city-state, so unlike the United States, could afford.

a barrier to interference in their affairs—not a means of promoting, let alone imposing, any one kind of rule. But that same variety harbors the potential for political change, and if those changes are democratizing, they could increase resistance to using noninterference as an excuse to look the other way whenever state predation occurs. As different members succeed each other in the ASEAN chair, under the Charter's provisions, the ASEAN Way could be, at least intermittently, revised.

Apart from the chair of ASEAN, could its secretary-general (SG) help orient the Association toward reform? The answer is yes, and the Charter does modestly strengthen that office. In 2007, the gap in authority and capacity between the ASEAN Secretariat and the heads of states or government gathered in summits was still far too great to expect the SG to lead ASEAN in a policymaking sense.[43] In 2008, however, the opportunity for leadership created by Nargis gave some reason to reconsider such a judgment, as discussed later in this chapter.

What of the ASEAN chair? Could a future occupant proactively help to pilot the region toward reform? Democracy's proponents should not expect too much. The line-up of chairs to come does not inspire hope for future regional pressure for reform in Myanmar, for example. As of mid-2008, following the English-alphabetic rotation of member-state names, Singapore was set to be succeeded by Thailand, Vietnam, Brunei, and Cambodia before the lone democratic member in 2008, Indonesia, could take over the chair for 2013. Thailand was reckoned by Freedom House to be "Partly Free" as of 2007. But the government that emerged from the December 2007 elections was sufficiently pro-Thaksin to indicate that it would continue his policy of appeasing the junta for the sake of Thai access to Myanmar's resources.[44] As for Vietnam, Brunei, and Cambodia in 2007, they were all "Not Free." If they are still in that category when the time arrives to sit in ASEAN's chair, they are not likely to ask Myanmar to accept political pluralism—not when they themselves refuse to do so.

Things could change in the meantime. In 2005 Myanmar was persuaded not to take its scheduled turn to occupy the chair in 2006, but it did not give up its right to take that turn later on. In 2008 the junta announced that multiparty elections would be held in 2010. Conceivably, the junta might use the ostensible legitimacy to be gained by that exercise, however manipulated by the regime the balloting might be, to claim the chair in 2010 or 2011. If ASEAN consented to Myanmar's insertion, Indonesia's turn would be postponed until 2014.

These potential developments notwithstanding, it is likewise possible that the situation on the ground in Myanmar could deteriorate, notably along its long border with Thailand. The case for democracy could be "securitized" in

---

[43] See my "Challenging ASEAN: A 'Topological' View," *Contemporary Southeast Asia* 29, no. 3 (2007), 424–46.

[44] The Associated Press, "Thailand's New PM Defends Myanmar," MercuryNews.com, 16 March 2008, <http://www.mercurynews.com/breakingnews/ci_8592938>.

the sense that spillover effects from repression and misrule by the junta could endanger its neighbors enough to alienate them.[45] Worsening externalities, measurable in flows of drugs, pathogens, and refugees, could eventually justify ASEAN support for political reform in Myanmar, or conceivably even for regime change, as a means of reducing human insecurity in the region. In that strictly pragmatic context, one would not need to be a democrat to encourage democratization. A comparably instrumental logic had been evident in ASEAN's motivation in persuading Myanmar's generals not to take the chair, namely, to limit its own guilt by association with the junta in the eyes of democratic states outside the region.

One might have hoped that the generals, having passed up the chance to lead ASEAN in 2006 and having let the Singapore chair upbraid their government publicly in New York in September 2007, would have been similarly acquiescent at the anniversary summit two months later. They were not.

Singapore had invited the UN's envoy for Myanmar, Gambari, to give a short briefing on Myanmar to all sixteen heads of state or government assembled in the city-state for an East Asia Summit (EAS) on 21 November, the day after ASEAN's own summit. Just two days before Gambari's scheduled appearance, Myanmar's prime minister put his foot down. At a dinner with his ASEAN colleagues he insisted that Singapore cancel the invitation. Gambari was already in the air en route to Southeast Asia, but Myanmar's prime minister was firm: What had happened in his country was his government's own internal concern and the business neither of ASEAN nor the EAS. He invoked the principle of noninterference—and he won. To the embarrassment of Singapore as the host state, and by implication ASEAN as well, the invitation to the UN envoy merely to brief the EAS was withdrawn. This time, consensus showed its other face: not solidarity as pressure on Myanmar to go along, but unanimity as license for Myanmar not to do so.

From the outside looking in, a single government appeared to have held all nine of its co-members hostage to its wish to hide its misdeeds. The reality was less clear-cut. Some members complained that Singapore had not cleared the invitation with them first. Others did not want Gambari to air Myanmar's dirty linen in front of Australia, China, India, Japan, New Zealand, and South Korea—the non-ASEAN members of the EAS. Some at the dinner were likely thinking to themselves that the invitation could come back to haunt them if and when they too had to quell dissent within their borders. The fact that, in his remarks in New York, George Yeo as the ASEAN chair had specifically urged the junta to work with Gambari surely added to Singapore's discomfort, and to the sense that Myanmar's generals had brazenly won the day.

---

[45] On this concept, see Barry Buzan, Ole Wæver, and Jaap de Wilde, *Security: A New Framework for Analysis* (Boulder, CO: Lynne Rienner, 1998).

We are left, in retrospect, with a vivid if sobering illustration of what makes Southeast Asia such an intriguingly difficult case of regionalism in relation to security and democracy. In New York, the ASEAN chair had been able to skirt the ASEAN Way of noninterference and consensus-as-unanimity. Speaking on behalf of his fellow foreign ministers, Yeo had gone so far as to support a "transition to democracy" in a member state. In his *words*, in effect, state security had been superseded by human security, autocracy by accountability. Scant months later in Singapore, however, the ASEAN Way had staged a comeback. As a matter not of words but *deeds*, diplomatic propriety in the service of state security—Myanmar's—had obliged that same chair to rescind an invitation, to back down. The clarity of the first outcome had been compromised, if not actually reversed, by the complicity of the second.

A charter, by definition, is all words. What deeds might the words in the ASEAN Charter sustain? Do its provisions, on balance, reaffirm or reform the ASEAN Way? I now turn to these questions.

Chartering ASEAN

Whatever its ultimate result, drafting the ASEAN Charter was a unique experiment. Never before had the Association tried to codify its goals and methods in what some hoped would be a legally binding blueprint for the future of regionalism in Southeast Asia.

Proponents of a charter for ASEAN were well aware of the ill-fated effort of European leaders to establish a constitution for the EU—an organization long thought to represent the gold standard of successful regionalism. What a feather in ASEAN's cap it would be if a grouping mainly of developing Asian ex-colonies of Europe could manage to "constitutionalize" itself, and thus succeed where its older, richer, and institutionally more advanced Western counterpart had failed.

EU governments had signed the treaty to establish a European Constitution in 2004. Like the ASEAN Charter, it had to be ratified by all member states in order to come into effect. In referenda held for that purpose in mid-2005, absolute majorities in France and the Netherlands voted the document down. A less ambitious version, less presumptuously named the Treaty of Lisbon, was signed in that city in December 2007. Supporters of the latter text hoped for its ratification by all twenty-seven EU members in 2008 so that it could enter into force on 1 January 2009. In parallel fashion, advocates of the ASEAN Charter hoped for its prompt ratification by all ten of the Association's states, so that it could become effective no later than December 2008, shortly before the planned activation of the EU's Treaty of Lisbon. The race between regionalisms was on.

The Lisbon Treaty was to be ratified by all EU members "in accordance with their respective constitutional requirements," which were not specified.[46] Fearing another debacle if voters were again allowed to have their say, member governments preferred to submit the text to their parliaments for approval. By 12 June 2008, France, the Netherlands, and sixteen other states had ratified, none of them by referendum. On that day, however, the Irish government did consult the voters, who rejected the treaty by 53 to 47 percent.[47]

Compared with the Lisbon Treaty, the ASEAN Charter was even more vague on the method of ratification. Member states were free to approve the text "in accordance with their respective internal procedures."[48] Consensus on method proved easier among ten relatively undemocratic governments than among twenty-seven relatively democratic ones. ASEAN rulers quietly agreed not to consult their populations. Singapore, the first to ratify, did not even bother to consult its parliament. Its prime minister simply declared his government's endorsement. The next to ratify was Brunei. There the Charter could not be approved by the legislature because the country—a sultanate—lacked one. In other authoritarian states, such as Laos, legislative approval amounted to rubber-stamping what the rulers had decided to do.

By mid-June 2008, Brunei, Cambodia, Laos, Malaysia, Singapore, and Vietnam—six of the ASEAN ten—had ratified the document. But further sailing looked less smooth. Myanmar's intransigence at the anniversary summit had sufficiently angered Philippine President Gloria Macapagal-Arroyo for her to warn that the Senate in Manila might not ratify the Charter unless the junta first freed Aung San Suu Kyi from confinement. Six months later, however, she was urging Senate ratification despite Suu Kyi's detention having been renewed for another year.[49]

If the Philippine Senate's approval was not assured, neither was ratification by the People's Representative Council (DPR) in Indonesia. In Jakarta, soon after the Charter was signed, an Indonesian colleague privately described it to me as "garbage" because it lacked strong provisions for human rights. Another Indonesian colleague, also privately, characterized the Charter's content as a

---

[46] Treaty of Lisbon Amending the Treaty on European Union and the Treaty Establishing the European Community, Final Provisions, Article 6.1, <http://europa.eu/lisbon_treaty/index_en.htm>.

[47] "EU Sees No Quick-Fix after Irish Reject Treaty," AFP [Agence France-Presse], 16 June 2008, <http://afp.google.com/article.ALeqM5iunsxJK71tQi1A93m206mCUQqlSQ>. The referendum was required by Ireland's constitution.

[48] ASEAN Charter, Art. 47.2.

[49] "Arroyo Urges Congress to Ratify Asean Charter," GMANews.TV, 13 June 2008, <http://www.gmanews.tv/story/101019/Arroyo-urges-Congress-to-ratify-Asean-Charter>.

victory for some of the least democratic states in the region.[50] (Four of the six early ratifiers—Brunei, Cambodia, Laos, and Vietnam—were "Not Free" in 2007.) Nevertheless, as of mid-2008, and barring the unforeseen, there was a good chance that ASEAN could have all ten approvals in hand, as planned, by the next summit in Thailand in December 2008. Failing that, since the Charter specifies no deadline for completing the endorsement process, it could simply continue.

The vicissitudes of ratification in Europe and Southeast Asia highlight the ambiguity of democracy's relationship to regionalism. Ireland's referendum illustrated democracy at work, but the outcome did not. One percent of the EU's 490 million people live in Ireland. By democratically rejecting the treaty and thereby ensuring its defeat, in effect, that one percent dictated to the other ninety-nine percent, including the citizens of the eighteen member countries whose democratically elected legislatures had all voted to approve it.

Like the Lisbon Treaty, the ASEAN Charter was drafted by elites. The Charter's authors were not about to expose a consensus reached behind closed doors to the vagaries of public opinion. The Charter's enthusiasts sought to deflect objections to the text by arguing that its critics should support ratification anyway, because only after coming into effect could it be amended. As specified in the Charter, however, the amendment process is a gauntlet of consensuses. Any change that a member state might propose must gain a consensus in favor among the foreign ministers of the member states. Only then would they pass the amendment up the ladder to the heads of state or government gathered in a summit, who would then have to reach their own consensus in favor. Only then would the proposed change be submitted for ratification by all member states, and only if that third and necessarily unanimous consensus was achieved would the change be made.[51] In the light of this obstacle course, a state that ratifies the Charter is, upon doing so, more likely to lose leverage than to gain it.

The case for a more "people-centered" ASEAN is argued in several of this book's chapters. To the extent that the Association does try to become more widely participatory, it may face a trade-off between regionalism as predictable cooperation managed by states and democracy as institutionalized uncertainty involving societies. Meanwhile, to the extent that the EU's experience with regionalism by referendum has any influence on ASEAN insiders, it is likely to make them more elitist, not less.

If all ten ASEAN states do ratify the Charter, will it be a milestone of reform that invigorates the organization to do more and do it better? Or will it be a

---

[50] Interview, Jakarta, 8 December 2007. "Consensus," said this person, "is at the heart of the Charter—and it kills the Charter." A third Indonesian source, Jusuf Wanandi of the Jakarta think tank CSIS, called the Charter "a real letdown" and urged the DPR not to ratify it. See his "ASEAN's Charter: Does a Mediocre Document Really Matter?" *The Jakarta Post*, 26 November 2007.

[51] ASEAN Charter, Art. 48.

millstone of reaction, weighing the Association down to its lowest common denominator? Will the Charter help ASEAN to step up, as its chair did at the UN in New York, to defend and promote human security and political accountability in its region? Or will it incline ASEAN to back down, as that same chair did at the summit in Singapore, and wrap itself ever more tightly in the ASEAN Way of sovereignty, noninterference, and consensus-as-unanimity? Or are the Charter's contents sufficiently vague and varied to point in most or all of these directions?[52]

Expectations that the text's provisions would orient ASEAN toward liberal reform were raised in January 2007 by the publication of the *Report of the Eminent Persons Group (EPG) on the ASEAN Charter*.[53] ASEAN's leaders had asked the EPG to review where ASEAN had been and should be going, and to recommend what the proposed Charter should say. As they read the report, democratically minded observers were surprised and heartened by the liberal-reformist tenor of the EPG's advice.

Far from endorsing a continuation of the state-centered ASEAN Way, the EPG spoke up for human security. Noting the damage done to the region by border-jumping calamities such as the AFC, the epidemic of Severe Acute Respiratory Syndrome (SARS), and the 2004 Indian Ocean tsunami, the EPG argued that the ASEAN Way should be revised. The well-being of the populations living in various ASEAN member countries had become "more intertwined." The unstated implication was that globalization, having shrunk the difference between domestic and foreign affairs, had weakened excuses for the sovereign impunity of irresponsible regimes. In the diplomatic language of the EPG Report, member states would need "to calibrate their traditional approach of non-interference in areas where the common interest dictates closer cooperation."[54]

More remarkably still, at the top of the EPG's list of recommendations for the ASEAN Charter was

Promotion of ASEAN's peace and stability through the active strengthening of democratic values, good governance, rejection of unconstitutional and undemocratic changes of government, the rule of law including international

---

[52] Directly or indirectly, this book deals at length with these and related concerns regarding the Charter. See especially the essays by Dosch, Termsak, Sukma, Kyaw, Caballero-Anthony, and Jones. My comments here merely open the debate.

[53] This and the next few paragraphs draw on a draft of my article "ASEAN's Black Swans." *The Report of the Eminent Persons Group on the ASEAN Charter*, hereafter the EPG Report, may be accessed at <http://www.mfa.gov.sg/internet/press/16012007/ReportOfTheEminentPersonsGroup(EPG)OnTheAseanCharter.pdf>.

[54] EPG Report, 12 (par. 18).

humanitarian law, and respect for human rights and fundamental freedoms.[55]

Other striking innovations in the EPG Report included the idea that a "serious breach of ASEAN's objectives, major principles, and commitments to important agreements" by a member state could result in the "suspension" of its membership rights; that in making decisions, if "consensus cannot be achieved, decisions may be taken through voting"; and that ASEAN needed "to shed its image of being an elitist organisation comprising exclusively diplomats and government officials" and become more "people-centred," including allowing "civil society" and "human rights groups" to play larger roles in ASEAN affairs.[56]

Unfortunately for the fate of these proposed reforms, the EPG's role was purely advisory. In addition, its ten members, though drawn from all ten ASEAN states, were mostly *former* officials. Having retired from public service, they were free to think creatively. But they did not necessarily represent and certainly could not commit their home governments to whatever the EPG might recommend.[57] The actual text of the Charter was drafted by a High-Level Task Force (HLTF) whose ten members were all sitting officials with the authority to represent, and presumably also to commit, their respective governments.

Table 1.1 counts and compares references to the "ASEAN Way" and "liberal reform" in the EPG Report and in the ASEAN Charter.[58] The comparison may serve to indicate how much the liberal-reformist tone of the first document was diluted in the second. In the EPG Report, favorable mentions of items on an agenda for liberal reform outnumbered favorable mentions of components of the ASEAN Way by a ratio of 2.5 to 1. At 0.8 to 1, the comparable ratio in the Charter ran in the opposite, conservative direction. The Charter does favorably cite "human rights" and "democracy." But in the Charter, compared with the EPG Report, these references are balanced by more conservative language.

---

[55] EPG Report, 1 (Executive Summary [EC], par. 3); see also 15 (par. 27).

[56] These references are drawn, respectively, from the EPG Report, 16 (para. 31) and 5 (EC, par. 8 and 9).

[57] The EPG member from Myanmar was a sitting official. However, in addition to the Group's being merely advisory, his low-ranking position (as chair of the Civil Service Selection and Training Board) left the junta even freer to ignore the EPG Report, which the EPG members were not even asked to sign. The members are listed in Termsak's chapter.

[58] For fuller quotations from these texts, see the comprehensive table in Dosch's chapter.

Table 1.1 A Comparison of References to "Liberal Reform" versus the "ASEAN Way" in the EPG Report and the ASEAN Charter

References favoring	Frequency of references in EPG Report	Frequency of references in ASEAN Charter
A. Liberal Reform		
1. "Human rights"	16	7
2. "Civil Society"	15	1
3. "[Un]constitution[al government]"	11	1
4. "Rule of law"	6	3
5. "Democracy"/"[un]democratic"	5	4
6. "Fundamental freedoms"	4	4
Total references favoring Liberal Reform	57	20
B. The ASEAN Way		
1. "Consensus"	5	9
2. "Sovereignty"	5	3
3. "[Non-]interference"	6	3
4. "Territorial integrity"	4	3
5. "Right[s]" of member states	1	5
6. "Harmonious environment"	2	1
Total references favoring the ASEAN Way	23	24
Ratio of "Liberal Reform" references to "ASEAN Way" references within each text	2.5 : 1	0.8 : 1

Note: All references were read in context to ensure that the core concept was presented in a positive light. For example, a reference that criticized "unconstitutional" or "undemocratic" government or "interference" in a member state's affairs was coded as favoring, respectively, "constitutional" or "democratic" government or "non-interference." References that merely conformed to official usage, such as the "Lao People's Democratic Republic," were excluded.

Sources: *Report of the Eminent Persons Group on the ASEAN Charter* (EPG Report), <http://www.mfa.gov.sg/internet/press/16012007/ReportOfTheEminentPersonsGroup(EPG)OnTheAseanCharter.pdf>, and the ASEAN Charter, <http://www.aseansec.org/21069.pdf>.

The contrast should not be overdrawn. Where the EPG Report, for example, merely stated that creating an "ASEAN human rights mechanism" was a "worthy idea" deserving further study, the Charter says flatly that "ASEAN shall establish" such a body.[59] Looking ahead from mid-2008, the nature and mandate of that promised entity and the timeline for creating it could become an early topic of controversy between those in ASEAN who favor liberal reform and those who oppose it. Of particular interest in this regard will be Indonesia, not only because of its uniquely "Free" ranking for 2007, but also because it is ASEAN's largest and thus potentially most influential member.

Nargis and Noninterference

On 2 May 2008, Cyclone Nargis swept in from the Bay of Bengal and spiraled across the Irrawaddy Delta to devastating effect. An estimated 130,000 people died and some 2.4 million lost their homes or were otherwise seriously affected.[60] In the wake of the earthquake and tsunami that struck northwestern Indonesia in December 2004, killing around 170,000 people, the government in Jakarta had welcomed foreign assistance. In Myanmar in the aftermath of Nargis, the junta downplayed the emergency and refused, limited, or obstructed foreign efforts to provide relief, to the chagrin and fury of international observers.

As if this behavior were not deplorable enough, the regime then shifted priorities from lessening misery to stuffing ballots. The generals had long planned to draft and impose a constitution that would entrench their rule. A national referendum on the text had been set for 10 May 2008. Rather than postpone the vote until the victims of Nargis had been able to recover from the disaster, the junta held the referendum in two rounds: on 10 May in unaffected areas, and on 24 May in the delta. International observers were not allowed to observe the proceedings, and reports of manipulation were widespread. In announcing the results, the junta did not even bother to come up with two different numbers for the "yes" majority in each round, claiming instead that the constitution had been approved by 92 percent of those who voted in the inland areas on 10 May and by the same percentage in the delta two weeks later.[61]

In these depressing contexts, voices were raised in favor of violating Myanmar's air and sea space—parachuting in needed water, food, and medicine, or delivering them on small craft to the delta's villages. The largely Western proponents of such drastic action, notably French Foreign Minister Bernard Kouchner, argued that the generals had failed so egregiously to fulfill their

---

[59] EPG Report, 21 (par. 47); ASEAN Charter, Art. 14.1.

[60] "Burmese Enduring in Spite of Junta, Aid Workers Say," *New York Times*, 18 June 2008, 1A and 10A.

[61] Compare "Burma 'Approves New Constitution,'" BBC News, 15 May 2008, quoting the junta, <http://news.bbc.co.uk/2/hi/asia-pacific/7402105.stm> with Commission for Holding the Referendum of the Union of Myanmar, "Announcement No. 12/2008," Ministry of Foreign Affairs, Naypyidaw, 26 May 2008, <http://www.mofa.gov.mm/news/Announcements/26may08.html>. In the BBC item, Human Rights Watch and an opposition group are respectively quoted as calling the referendum an "insult to the people of Burma" and "full of cheating and fraud."

responsibility to look after their own people that humanitarian intervention was justified.

As Kuhonta notes in his chapter, this doctrine—the "responsibility to protect" (R2P) had been analyzed, defined, and proposed by an International Commission on Intervention and State Sovereignty (ICISS) in 2001. In 2005, at a World Summit, the UN General Assembly endorsed R2P. In 2006, the Security Council followed suit. A liberal optimist could believe that R2P was on its way to becoming a recognized part of international law, and that the UN might pioneer the doctrine's implementation. In that scenario, the international community would cite the junta's criminal neglect of the devastated and vulnerable victims of Nargis as justification for authorizing humanitarian intervention to save their lives—with or without the generals' consent. If there was ever a time when other Southeast Asian governments would have to jettison, or at any rate revamp, the ASEAN Way of putting sovereignty above suffering, surely this was it.

The ICISS's composition and approach were similar to those of the EPG. Like the members of the EPG, the Commission's members—retired officials, ex-diplomats, former politicians, professors, a businessman—were on the fringes of the policy world, not on active duty at its center.[62] Like the EPG Report, the ICISS Report was venturesome in its willingness to question the use of sovereignty to rationalize impunity. The R2P, wrote the ICISS, is "the idea that sovereign states have a responsibility to protect their own citizens from avoidable catastrophe," and that "when they are unwilling or unable to do so, that responsibility must be borne by the broader community of states." The catastrophe could involve "large scale loss of life, actual or apprehended, with genocidal intent or not, which is the product either of deliberate state action, or state neglect or inability to act, or a failed state situation." "The substance of the responsibility to protect," asserted the Commission, "is the provision of life-supporting protection and assistance to populations at risk" including the responsibility "to respond to situations of compelling human need."[63]

Read in retrospect, this language seemed written to fit the junta's criminal neglect of the victims of Nargis and its inhumane thwarting of humanitarian efforts to help them. The ICISS Report was not the last word on its subject, however. The R2P idea was weakened as it traveled from the reformist intellectual ambience of the Commission on Track III in 2001 to the UN resolutions endorsed by incumbent governments on Track I in 2005–06. At the UN, the list of dangers from which governments had the "responsibility to protect" their populations was pared down to include only the most horrific:

---

[62] There was even a small overlap in membership between the EPG and the ICISS; former Philippine President Fidel Ramos belonged to both.

[63] See *The Responsibility to Protect: Report of the International Commission on Intervention and State Sovereignty* (Ottawa: International Development and Research Centre, December 2001), XI ("large-scale loss of life" and "compelling human need") and 17 ("populations at risk"), <http://www.iciss.ca/report-en.asp>.

"genocide, war crimes, ethnic cleansing and crimes against humanity."[64] The generals' wrongdoing in responding slowly to Nargis and hampering efforts to assist its victims was not on the scale of these atrocities.[65] ICISS co-chair Gareth Evans raised the possibility that the junta's actions might constitute a crime against humanity,[66] but the suggestion was not taken up. Myanmar's generals escaped any comeuppance for violating the R2P principle, which remained on paper, awaiting implementation.

From Words to Deeds?

It is vital for students of regionalism in Southeast Asia to distinguish words from deeds. Even if the UN's sovereign governments had not raised R2P's threshold to a judgment—mass murder—more horrendous than what the junta plausibly deserved, ASEAN would still not have intervened in Myanmar without the junta's permission. What, then, did the Association actually do?

At first glance, ASEAN's response to Nargis can be summarized as "too little, too late." Not until 9 June 2008, a full month and a week after the cyclone's landfall, were full-scale teams finally assembled on ASEAN's initiative to *assess* the damage and given a send-off in Yangon to *begin* their work. According to the announced schedule, the findings of these teams would only be published in *mid-July*—two-and-a-half months after Nargis touched down.[67]

A fuller account of ASEAN's actions, however, yields a more nuanced view. The Association moved quickly to make up for lost time. Preliminary findings from the assessment teams' work were reviewed on 24 June, three weeks before

---

[64] UN General Assembly, "World Summit Outcome," 15 September 2005, par. 138–39, <http://www.responsibilitytoprotect.org/index.php/united_nations/398?theme=alt1>, and UN Security Council, Resolution No. 1674, 28 April 2006, Art. 4, <http://domino.un.org/UNISPAl.NSF/361eea1cc08301c485256cf600606959/e529762befa456f88525 71610045ebef!OpenDocument>. The watering down of the ICISS Report at the final, official level recalled the blunting of the EPG Report's reformist thrust by the HLTF of sitting officials who actually wrote the ASEAN Charter.

[65] "Burmese Endure in Spite of Junta" offers evidence to this effect.

[66] Gareth Evans, "Facing Up to Our Responsibilities," *The Guardian* [London], 12 May 2008.

[67] See these ASEAN Secretariat press releases: "Myanmar Deputy Foreign Minister Sent Off 250-Person Post Nargis Joint Assessment Teams," Yangon, 9 June 2008, <http://www.aseansec.org/21630.htm>, and "SG Surin Assured of Smooth Aid Operations," 14 June 2008, <http://www.aseansec.org/21648.htm>. The teams were said in the first release to consist of personnel from ASEAN member states, the Myanmar regime, the UN, the World Bank, the Asian Development Bank (ADB), the Red Cross in Myanmar, and local and international NGOs.

their scheduled completion and publication. Other action-oriented steps were simultaneously underway.[68]

As for the reason why time had been lost in the first place, ASEAN had wanted to do something constructive by working with, not against, the junta. That meant first establishing a comfort zone within which the regime was willing to move. ASEAN also wanted to avail itself of the UN's resources and expertise. The assessment teams were in fact sent off by Kyaw Thu, Myanmar's deputy foreign minister, in his capacity as the chair of an ASEAN-Myanmar-UN Tripartite Core Group (TCG). Even as he presided over the ceremony, Kyaw Thu made sure to remind the 250 team members present that their assessments should have no political content.

Rather than criticizing the Association for delays that were attributable to Myanmar's leaders, and remembering the junta's adamant refusal to let the UN's envoy Gambari brief the EAS, one might instead admire ASEAN's success simply in coaxing the TCG into existence. As for the lag in bringing relief to the delta, other channels of assistance had already reached the victims of Nargis beginning in May, and the scale of the devastation and dislocation ensured the relevance of such aid for some time to come.

Nargis did not abate until 3 May 2008. ASEAN's first official response to the disaster came almost immediately thereafter, on 5 May. On that day at the ASEAN Secretariat in Jakarta, Secretary-General Surin Pitsuwan, in office only since the start of the year, called on "all other ASEAN Member States to provide urgent relief assistance" to the cyclone's victims. Three days later, at his initiative, the Secretariat launched an ASEAN Cooperation Fund for Disaster Assistance to raise resources for post-Nargis relief.[69]

The Fund's guidelines included two provisos that betrayed the tightrope on which the SG had to balance. On the one hand, to alleviate Myanmar's fears of political interference, donors were warned not to place any conditions on the use of their contributions. On the other hand, to assuage donors worried that the regime would misuse their gifts, donations were described as "solely intended" to alleviate the suffering of the cyclone's victims. The guidelines also included a curious avowal that "no legal actions and/or proceedings shall be taken against [the] ASEAN Secretariat in connection with" its effort to set up and fill the Fund.[70] Reading between the lines of this "disclaimer," one could

---

[68] ASEAN Secretariat, "Post Nargis Joint Assessment Teams Complete Assessment of Cyclone Nargis-Affected Areas," 21 June 2008, <http://www.aseansec.org/21679.htm>.

[69] Surin's appeal appears in ASEAN Secretariat, "ASEAN Members Urged to Support International Emergency Relief for Cyclone Victims in Myanmar," press release, 5 May 2008, <http://www.aseansec.org/21505.htm>. The Fund's 8 May start date appears in ASEAN Secretariat, "Guidelines on the ASEAN Cooperation Fund for Disaster Assistance," n.d., <http://www.aseansec.org/21532.htm>.

[70] The 8 May date is given in the Secretariat's "Guidelines on the ASEAN Cooperation Fund for Disaster Assistance," n.d., <http://www.aseansec.org/21532.htm>.

understand not only the intent to avoid possible wrath, but also a foreshadowing of the Association's legal and therefore liable personality that the Charter, once fully ratified, would bestow.

Additional moves by Secretary-General Surin quickly ensued. On 9 May he urged Myanmar's Foreign Minister Nyan Win (who had endured George Yeo's revulsion the previous September) to consider quickly allowing ASEAN to help. By "immediate assistance" Surin meant deeds, not words—not an assessment mission that would write a report for others to act on, but "ASEAN relief and rescue teams" tasked to save lives and lessen suffering straightaway.[71]

The generals declined Surin's offer. It was clear by this time that they had become part of the problem, unwilling as they were to open the country's doors to outsiders whose motives they suspected. Surin persisted. His goal was to form "a coalition of mercy for Myanmar relief, rehabilitation and reconstruction with ASEAN in the lead and [the World Bank] and the UN helping with their resources and expertise."[72]

A smaller and therefore less intrusive ASEAN Emergency Rapid Assessment Team was dispatched to Yangon with the junta's permission. The team's report struck a delicate balance between explicitly praising and implicitly criticizing Myanmar's regime. On the one hand, the junta was described as having "tried its level best to meet the demands" of the crisis. This was manifestly untrue. On the other hand, the report acknowledged that "the issue of access to the affected areas" was "the main overarching concern for the international community including other ASEAN Member States and international organizations." The critical term "other" accurately implied that access was not the junta's main concern, despite "the possibility of a potential second wave of deaths and morbidity due to diseases and nutritional deficiency which could be avoided through a more coordinated effort between the international community and the Government of Myanmar."[73]

On 19 May in Singapore, the ASEAN foreign ministers met and agreed to undertake three tasks. First, they would set up "an ASEAN-led coordinating mechanism" to facilitate international aid, including the expeditious deployment of relief workers; second, they would form a task force under Surin to pursue such coordination; and third, they would work with the UN to organize an aid-pledging conference for international donors six days later in Yangon. In announcing these results, George Yeo as the chair of the meeting offered the junta

---

[71] ASEAN Secretariat, "ASEAN Stands Ready to Help the Affected Population in Myanmar in Response to Cyclone Nargis," press release, 9 May 2008, <http://www.aseansec.org/21527.htm>.

[72] Surin Pitsuwan, personal communication, 13 May 2008, used with permission.

[73] "ASEAN Emergency Rapid Assessment Team Mission Report, 9–18 May 2008: Cyclone Nargis, Myanmar," <http://www.aseansec.org/21558.pdf>. As noted in the previously cited news item, "Burmese Enduring in Spite of Junta," later reports from the delta did not confirm these fears.

both a concession and a concern: Foreign assistance "should not be politicized," but Myanmar "should allow more international relief workers into the stricken areas."[74] At the 25 May donors' conference, more than fifty countries pledged nearly $50 million, but the United States and other major powers made their support contingent on the junta's giving aid workers access to the delta.

On 4 June, as if to illustrate ASEAN's ability to smooth the entry of aid, a thousand metric tons of relief supplies arrived in Yangon in a container ship filled and commissioned by France. Alongside the French ambassador to Myanmar, members of the TCG, including Singapore's ambassador, watched the material being off-loaded to boats that the World Food Program had chartered for transport to the delta.[75] Although ASEAN could not and did not claim sole responsibility for this success, it had played an important intermediary role between the suspicious junta and the frustrated donors. The occasion was all the more notable in light of the French foreign minister's argument only a month before that the UN would be justified in delivering aid by force, if force were necessary to override the generals' refusal to discharge their "responsibility to protect" their own citizens.[76]

Linkage versus Separation

I mention these details because the issues they raise illuminate the nexus of security, democracy, and regionalism featured in this book. It was not possible in mid-2008, with the crisis still ongoing, to know the full and ultimate implications of the handling of the cyclone's aftermath—for ASEAN, for Myanmar, or for the impact of each on the other. The following tentative conclusions were, nevertheless, already plausible.

The cyclone transformed Myanmar from ASEAN's embarrassment into its opportunity. The Association had long been challenged to disassociate itself from its blatantly antidemocratic member—enough to rescue its own reputation, but without splitting open its own ranks, divided as they were between more and less democratic states. Nargis changed ASEAN's intimacy with the junta from a liability into an asset. The disaster led to the opening of negotiating space between the outraged impatience of foreign donors and the obstructive suspicion of the regime—space that the Association, led by Surin, proceeded to fill.

---

[74] "Special ASEAN Foreign Ministers Meeting Chairman's Statement," Singapore, 19 May 2008, <http://www.aseansec.org/21557.htm>.

[75] ASEAN Secretariat, "Tripartite Core Group Witnessing the Unloading of Relief Supplies for the Cyclone Nargis-affected Areas," press release, 7 June 2008, <http://www.aseansec.org/21623.htm>.

[76] Steven Erlanger, "France Urges UN to Force Cyclone Aid on Myanmar," *International Herald Tribune*, Wednesday, 7 May 2008, <http://www.iht.com/articles/2008/05/07/europe/cyclone.php>.

ASEAN sought to make itself doubly indispensable, to Myanmar's generals as a friend who could help ensure that foreign aid workers did not foment regime change, and to international donors as a friend who could persuade the generals to allow aid in. On the one hand, the French supplies arrived on 4 June in a civilian (commercial) vessel while French, British, and American warships waited offshore for permission that never came, in line with the junta's fear of being overthrown. On the other hand, the supplies were off-loaded and sent directly to victims in the delta to avoid their misappropriation by the regime. Thus did ASEAN, through the TCG, simultaneously serve the desires of its two mutually mistrustful clients.

In the process, ASEAN also served its own interest. Events in 2007, especially the last-minute kowtowing to Nyan Win in Singapore, had made the Association look cowardly, irrelevant, or both. In contrast, post-Nargis, ASEAN could be praised for having saved lives by cajoling the regime into opening its country's doors wider than it would have done without the Association's good-neighborly pressure.

According to this felicitous narrative, the implications of ASEAN's vigorous go-between role were encouraging. The Association had co-opted the generals into finally exercising their responsibility to protect the cyclone's victims. Success in persuading the junta to open its doors wider to incoming aid represented a victory for liberal international norms and a defeat for the junta-shielding ASEAN Way. One could only admire Surin's skill in using the force of Nargis to dent the principle of noninterference.

Or, conversely, had Myanmar's leaders effectively co-opted the Association into helping to entrench their tyrannical rule? On 25 May in Yangon, at the donors' conference that ASEAN had helped organize, foreign governments and international organizations pledged material support for the cyclone's victims. No political support was forthcoming for those same victims, however, despite their having been pressed on 24 May—just the day before—into voting in a sham referendum for a constitution that would prolong military rule, and whose text the great majority of them had not even read. Nor did ASEAN's success in opening the door to more foreign aid stop the junta from keeping Aung San Suu Kyi's door firmly shut. On 27 May, the day after the pledging donors had gone home, the junta renewed her house arrest for an additional year. Rather than crediting Surin with clever diplomacy on behalf of R2P, perhaps one should "admire" the generals' skill in using the cyclone's sympathy-generating force to shield their own cruel reassertion of sovereign impunity and political noninterference—not breaching but actually reinforcing the ASEAN Way.

These opposing interpretations of what happened in the aftermath of Nargis imply contrary prospects of whether and how security, democracy, and regionalism can be related in the future. The first, more sanguine argument highlights a *linking* of this book's three critical terms—and holds out hope. By this reasoning, regionalism (ASEAN's diplomacy) can use insecurity (Myanmar's devastation) as leverage to encourage democracy (if not the junta's full-scale reform, at least a moderation of its behavior). The second, more skeptical argument features a *delinking* of security, democracy, and regionalism—and downplays hope. By this logic, unless insecurity is mainly and clearly attributable to autocracy (rather than to a natural disaster such as Nargis) and significantly worsens the well-being of the larger region (which Nargis did not), the provision of security (humanitarian aid) is unlikely to offer either an opportunity or a motivation to promote democracy (in Myanmar). The depoliticizing of intervention is instead likely to undercut the ability of a regional organization (ASEAN) to induce reform.

It is always risky to judge events while their repercussions are ongoing. Nevertheless, viewed in mid-2008 while the crisis was still under way, the story of Nargis and noninterference fit the second argument better than it fit the first. Rather than giving political leverage to ASEAN over the junta, Nargis changed the subject from politics to relief. That separation of politics from relief created an incentive for ASEAN and the foreign donors to censor themselves. How could one push to democratize the junta when people were suffering from an act not of Than Shwe but of God?[77] By resisting aid, the generals widened the distance between democracy and security. Emphasizing democracy in this context was made to appear inhumane. Reports of widespread starvation in the delta as a consequence of regime neglect could have reconnected politics and relief, possibly even making democracy appear to be a requisite for security. But conditions on the ground had not worsened to that degree as of mid-2008. International agencies engaged in relief operations were complaining of insufficient funds, but that implied criticism of ostensibly stingy foreign donors as much as it did of Myanmar's callous regime.

Reforming Regionalism

An important possible implication of the limits of linkage and the ease of separation is that ASEAN's energetic and creative post-Nargis diplomacy may turn out to matter more for the nature of Southeast Asian regionalism itself than for either security or democracy inside Myanmar. The tensions between ASEAN and Myanmar tended, on balance, to erode the ASEAN Way of consensus defined as unanimity. ASEAN managed to play an independent and proactive role in shaping events. Its statements and policies were not consistently limited to what Myanmar would allow. Despite successfully vetoing Gambari's briefing of the EAS in Singapore in November 2007, the junta could not prevent regional leaders from speaking critically and acting independently of its wishes. Especially intriguing in institutional terms in 2007–08 was the high-profile post-Nargis balancing act undertaken by Secretary-General Surin.

---

[77] The regime could have installed storm barriers and an early-alert system to warn the delta's residents of imminent danger, of course, but the cyclone itself was beyond human control.

ASEAN chairs come and go, but the Secretariat continues. The long-standing practice of recruiting SGs whose careers had been spent largely inside the civil services of their respective countries helped to ensure their deference, once in office, to the leaders of the Association's member states. Already comfortable with hierarchical discipline on Track I at the national level, these men had little difficulty keeping a low-to-fairly-low profile in ASEAN's regional hierarchy. Reporting to multiple bosses—the heads of state or government—further reduced the incentive to take independent initiatives. SGs were expected to manage and implement, not lead.

That said, the personalities of those who filled the position did matter. To cite a recent example, Secretary-General Ong Keng Yong's (2003–2007) roots in Singapore's civil service did not prevent him from making candid remarks about ASEAN, often disarmed with self-deprecatory humor, including his bemused self-description as "more secretary than general."

In the history of ASEAN, Surin Pitsuwan, who took over from Keng Yong on 1 January 2008, is unique. Surin is the first SG to have been recruited not from the civil service but from civil society. Although he has held bureaucratic positions in Thailand, and served as his country's foreign minister (1997–2001), in the course of his career he has also been a newspaper columnist, a university professor, an elected legislator, a party politician, a liberal activist, and a public intellectual.

Of particular relevance to this book's critical terms are Surin's experience as the founding chair of the Council of Asian Liberals and Democrats, his efforts as ASEAN chair to enlist member governments in the restoration of security to East Timor in 1999, his service on a UN Commission on Human Security, and his work on the Advisory Board of the ICISS that advanced the R2P idea and cited the failure to exercise it as a reason for humanitarian intervention. His degrees are not in economics but political science (BA, MA) and Middle Eastern studies (PhD, Harvard). As a Thai Muslim, he has a personal link to majority-minority relations in his Buddhist-majority country's shaky democracy. He is tall, handsome, energetic, articulate, and outgoing. If Keng Yong had been disarmingly realistic about the limitations of his position, Surin came across in his first months on the same job as charmingly idealistic about what ASEAN could accomplish. If ever an SG could turn his position into a bully pulpit for security, democracy, and regionalism, it was Surin Pitsuwan.

In May 2008, Surin told an audience in Washington DC, "I did not expect to be baptized by a cyclone, but that's exactly what is happening." Not only was he baptized as ASEAN's spokesperson; Nargis's destruction and the junta's obstruction galvanized him into rounds of intense activity. Unforeseen events had created "a defining moment for ASEAN" and "a transformative moment for the region." There were "long-term implication[s] for the region" that depended "on how we play our hand," "how we cooperate," and "how imaginative we are." [78] Wrapped inside the plural "we" one could discern as well a singular "I"—the sense in which what he himself did and did not do in that post-Nargis moment would define his own secretary-generalship for months or even years to come.

Once the crisis had abated, would Surin's high profile also subside? Would the SG stop rushing around Southeast Asia—indeed, around the world—trying to make regional policy? Would the Secretariat be returned full-time to its usual agenda of administrative service and coordination for the rulers and ministers of the member states? In June 2008, in mid-crisis, it was hard to say. Nevertheless, in view of the challenges on the horizon, including the Charter's ratification and implementation, and given Surin's personal background and style and the remaining four-plus years of his tenure, it was hard to ignore at least a modest potential for regionalism in Southeast Asia to change.

As he operates at the crossroads of security, democracy, and regionalism in Southeast Asia, however, Surin may prove least successful in using ASEAN to promote democracy in its member countries. As an intermediary between angry donors and stubborn generals in Myanmar, he tried to save lives. But in doing so he also helped save the junta's face, and to that extent his actions may have marginally prolonged its lease on life. Presumably, in view of the disaster's scale and the urgency of relief, that was an acceptable cost. At what point, however, would working with the junta begin to serve the generals' interest in survival more than that of the displaced people in the delta?

In any case, as a priority goal for ASEAN to implement throughout the region, democratization remains a nonstarter in Southeast Asia. Surin will have more success in pressing the Association to address human security, an issue that lay at the heart of the organization's post-Nargis moment, than he will in persuading it to promote political pluralism. Unless member states themselves, first, become more enamored of liberal democracy, he is unlikely to jeopardize their support on other matters by leading them in that ideological direction.

Future historians may remember Surin most of all for an organizational legacy internal to regionalism itself. When he retires from office at the end of 2012, he may leave ASEAN in somewhat less diffuse, modestly more coherent, and perhaps more centralized shape than it was five years before. By alphabetic rotation, his successor will be Vietnamese. It will be interesting to learn whether Vietnam, the region, and the Association will have changed enough by then to preclude the naming of an obedient Communist Party bureaucrat to the position.

---

[78] "A Conversation with Surin Pitsuwan," Council on Foreign Relations, 14 May 2008, <http://www.cfr.org/publication/16284/conversation_with_surin_pitsuwan_rush_transcript_federal_news_service.htm>.

In the meantime, Surin's tenure and the hard choices he makes in the course of it will illustrate, however unevenly, both the limits and the potentials of leadership in changing how regionalism interacts with security and democracy in Southeast Asia.

Summary with Interpretation

I began by elucidating security, democracy, and regionalism in Southeast Asia, the critical terms used in this book. I argued that, as a site for studying how regionalism can affect security and democracy, Southeast Asia is attractively difficult, creatively diverse, and remarkably timely as well. In discussing the ASEAN Way's two main principles, noninterference and solidarity, I noted that the first implies indifference to domestic political change and therefore impedes neither democracy nor autocracy as such. The second, however, comes in two versions with opposite implications: consensus as unanimity, catering to the slowest or least willing member, and consensus as solidarity, pressuring such a member to go along. A third principle is informality, but it is less durable than the other two; witness the legalistic provisions of the Charter and ASEAN's corresponding acquisition of a legal personality.

Having reviewed the book's critical terms, I examined in some detail three critical occasions in the history of ASEAN in 2007–2008. All involved Myanmar, and each illuminated in a different way the nexus of security, democracy, and regionalism in Southeast Asia. In September 2007, the junta cracked down, leading the ASEAN chair to excoriate state violence and urge a transition to democracy. Two months later, the junta put its foot down, and the ASEAN chair backed down. In the eyes of democratic observers, ASEAN gained face on the first occasion but lost it on the second.

These incidents showed that the ASEAN Way's principles could be stretched in practice. Consensus as reluctant solidarity enabled George Yeo to express collective revulsion. Consensus as necessary unanimity allowed the junta to reverse an invitation. Member-state sovereignty and noninterference were not barriers to be clearly respected or clearly breached. They were subjective matters of degree, context, and interpretation. The differing outcomes on these occasions illustrated how the balance between what a critic was willing to say and what a target was willing to withstand could change, depending on the situation, the issue, and the actors involved.

I then summarized the evolution of the ASEAN Charter and compared its fate, as of June 2008, with the rejection of the EU's Lisbon Treaty by Irish voters in that same month. In the first instance, the cautious and constrained bureaucrats in the HLTF diluted the private-citizen EPG's liberal ideas. In the second, a referendum challenged Europe's rulers and the EU's official bureaucracy in Brussels. The two cases illustrated the tensions, disappointments, and ironies that can arise when regionalist projects are transferred from Track III to Track I (in Southeast Asia, from the EPG to the HLTF for actual drafting and later signing by ASEAN's relatively illiberal governments)—or in the opposite direction, from Track I to Track III (in Europe, from the bureaucracy in Brussels for ratification by democratically elected legislators and the private citizens in Ireland who voted no).

The two cases illustrate the tensions and disappointments that can arise when regionalist projects are transferred back and forth between Tracks I and III. Comparable at the global level was the Track III-to-I narrowing of the scope of the R2P, as it was taken from the ICISS and filtered through the UN.

A main lesson to be drawn from the two-way turbulence between regionalist Tracks is that a "people-centered" ASEAN will be easier to advocate than to implement. Participatory regionalism will not split the organization apart,[79] but democracy is not a key that fits all locks. The challenge for participatory regionalists in Southeast Asia is not just to promote a fruitful intersection of Tracks I and III, but also to distinguish the extent to which solving a particular policy problem requires specialized knowledge or general consent—and what mix of expertise and participation should therefore be brought to bear on its solution. Implementing human security—defined as protection from infectious disease or violent weather—may call for the insulation of science from politics. Regular, free, and fair elections will be needed to sustain human security when it is defined as protection from state predation. With respect to referenda, the Irish "no" vote will not necessarily derail regionalism in Europe, any more than would such an outcome in Southeast Asia. Like the EU, in order to achieve regional goals, ASEAN is already accustomed to "minus X" arrangements and different deadlines suited to the differing capacities of its members.

On a physical and ethical scale unimaginably greater than the diplomatic incidents in New York and Singapore in 2007, a third critical moment for ASEAN arrived in May 2008, when deadly winds and surging waters smashed open Myanmar's delta and the junta tried to keep it closed. Led, in the full sense of that word, by its new SG, ASEAN interposed itself between foot-dragging generals who feared destabilization and frustrated foreigners who wanted to help the victims but not the regime. Nargis turned ASEAN's embarrassment into its opportunity. Surin planned, exhorted, cajoled. Words led to deeds, which answered—at least temporarily—the standard accusation that the Association was nothing but a talk shop.

---

[79] This judgment is in keeping with the implicitly incremental character of Amitav Acharya's definition of "participatory regionalism" as an arrangement in which officials take a "less rigid view of non-interference," become "more responsive to the demands of civil society," and thereby allow a "wider range of transnational issues" to be addressed. From a Track I perspective, of course, this argument could be reversed to suggest that two-way participation requires, on the part of civil society activists, a more realistic view of noninterference and of official constraints on meeting their demands, such that transnational issues are not only addressed but resolved. See Amitav Acharya, "Democratisation and the Prospects for Participatory Regionalism in Southeast Asia," *Third World Quarterly* 24, no. 2 (April 2003), 388.

A key question in this book is the extent to which security, democracy, and regionalism can be linked in ways such that movement along one dimension leverages movement on another. ASEAN's response to the aftermath of Nargis did link regionalism to the restoration of human security, but it required the separation of both regionalism and security from democracy. Future analysts may look back and ask, Who co-opted whom? They may also note the extent to which Surin's handling of the crisis represented a change, however modest, in the nature of regionalism in Southeast Asia. Surin placed the Secretariat at the center of fast-moving events. He showed how the SG's personality and proactivity could, at least marginally and for the time being, raise the status of that position. One could imagine a future backlash from unreconstructed champions of the ASEAN Way, who push Surin's secretary-generalship back toward the purely administrative "secretary" end of that compound noun, especially were he to try wielding regionalism as a tool for fostering democracy in Southeast Asia.

If regionalism is ever to play a democratizing role in the region, it will have to operate in some fashion through security. The kind of security best suited to inducing a linkage of regionalism to democracy is human security—not the realpolitik business of protecting the state, but the moralpolitik challenge to protect society, ultimately including the protection of society from the state itself.

The raising of ASEAN's profile to defend human security after Nargis is discouraging, insofar as it required an explicit separation of security from democracy. That was a victory for the junta and the defenders of a strictly Westphalian version of the ASEAN Way. What if, however, Surin's upgrading of his role, and that of the Secretariat, were to outlast the exigencies of a natural disaster and become institutionalized in a chartered organization with a legal personality as well? In that event, ASEAN could more easily evolve toward participatory regionalism.

Paradoxical though it may seem, an optimal degree of centralization inside ASEAN could increase its receptivity to democracy. A key question for participatory regionalism is, Who participates? The number and diversity of NGOs in Southeast Asia is daunting enough. But the question should also be asked on Track I. The *regional* interests of an emerging civil society are more likely to be ignored than engaged by an Association that is no more than the sum of its parts—a loose grouping without a regional center of gravity strong enough to counterbalance its ten sovereigns and their diverging *national* (not to mention personal and political) agendas. As for operationalizing a regional response to human security—including assigning the optimal mix of expert knowledge and popular legitimation needed to overcome a given threat—that task, too, will be more effectively discharged by an ASEAN whose Secretariat plays a more than administrative role.

The closing section that follows offers some necessarily and intentionally unfinal thoughts on the fate of the ASEAN Way. They are unavoidably incomplete because they will be read with hindsight that was unavailable when they were written. They are purposely so because they end only the beginning of a book whose remaining chapters greatly exceed in scope and detail my introductory assignment here.

Unfinal Thoughts

Is reform beyond ASEAN's grasp? In 2007, the retreat of the Charter's official drafters from the EPG's creative but purely advisory views paralleled the behavior of ASEAN's Singaporean chair in at first stepping up but then backing down. It does not follow from these reversals of direction, however, that ASEAN is in a long-term process of abandoning reform and reaffirming the ASEAN Way. The EPG Report is water under the bridge. If the Charter is ratified into effect, what will matter is the gap or fit between what it says and what ASEAN does.

Two key policy frontiers will continue to challenge the stewards of regionalism in Southeast Asia: (1) the extension of prior success in fostering interstate peace to encompass and improve human security; and (2) the even more venturesome broadening of regional authority and action to include the defense and nourishment of democracy—or of decency, at least, to use the term that Jones favors in his chapter.

Read in this forward-looking context, the 0.8-to-1 distribution of markers of liberal reform versus the ASEAN Way in the Charter's language reaffirms an argument I have tried to make in this essay: The prospects of movement toward these policy frontiers are notably difficult, and yet, at the same time, intriguingly open. To the obviously limited extent that words imply deeds, the nearly even balance between words of reform and retrenchment in the Charter suggests that it could be used to nudge ASEAN in either direction. There is, in short, no single way (or Way) ahead.

As for what will move regionalism down one path or another, I hope my discussion of Southeast Asia's diversity has made clear that potentials for political change on the ground could significantly affect how regionalism relates to human security and political accountability.

The surprising results of elections held in Malaysia on 8 March 2008 are potentially a case in point. The ruling National Front (NF) failed to win a two-thirds majority for the first time since 1969. From having lost control of only one of Malaysia's thirteen state legislatures in the previous (2004) election, the NF lost five in 2008.

Despite these casualties, the NF retained its parliamentary majority and the prime ministership that went with it. A resurgent opposition did not necessarily augur a more liberal political system, let alone stimulate official interest in human security or democratization as regional goals. An earlier instance of political change, the electoral restoration of civilian rule in Thailand in December 2007, did not yield a government with an interest in pressing the junta in adjacent Myanmar to reform. But it remains the case that if ASEAN is no more than the sum of its sovereign component parts, it is from developments inside those ten parts that pressures to revise or reaffirm the ASEAN Way will arise.

Democratic Indonesia is a particularly suggestive illustration of the possible regional implications of national political change. Within five years of its own democratization in 1998–99, Indonesia took the lead in planning an ASEAN Security Community (ASC)—renamed in the Charter the ASEAN Political-Security Community (APSC). Though not an official, Rizal Sukma, a contributor to this book, played a key role in the process. As he relates in his chapter, Indonesia made clear from the start that it wished, in this instance, to widen the meaning of security beyond the state. The ASC's Plan of Action explicitly defends democracy and human rights in this context. Indonesia never intended for the ASC to spread political pluralism around Southeast Asia, nor to threaten the ASEAN Way. But in this example a democratic government did, modestly but explicitly, help to legitimate reformist norms for the region.

To the extent that other member states *themselves* become more democratic, and Indonesia remains so, it is possible that the region's largest state will draw more support from fellow members for enlisting regionalism, carefully and cautiously, in support of democracy in a reasonably "liberal" form—or in support of human rights, better governance, and the rule of law without reference to the contentious "L" word.

The logic of this expectation may seem tautological. That is, that already existing, national-level democracy inside member states may be a key precondition for the regional-level pursuit of democracy inside member states. In extreme form, such an argument suggests that ASEAN will be able to reform its members only when they no longer need to be reformed. Understood as a historical sequence, however, the notion is quite plausible: that the democratization of each additional member state should, if other things are roughly equal, marginally increase the capacity and willingness of a regional organization to encourage those of its members that are still not democratic to become so, and to defend or improve democracy where it already exists.

That is my adaptation of the main conclusion reached by Jon Pevehouse in his unique study of the impact of major regional organizations on democracy inside countries around the world. "The more homogenously democratic a regional organization's membership," he wrote, "the more likely it will be to pressure autocratic governments to liberalize." At the same time, however, he found "little evidence that long-standing authoritarian regimes were effectively pressured to democratize by regional organizations. Rather, my cases indicate that only when a state suffers a breakdown of democracy is pressure from an IO [international organization] helpful in the emergence of democracy." Applied to ASEAN, this finding may be good news for the nascent and vulnerable democratic government of Indonesia, but it will also comfort the long-standing dictatorship in Myanmar.[80]

A policy implication that Pevehouse drew from these results is that already democratizing states could protect themselves against backsliding by forming their own regional clubs. He cited the Southern African Development Community (SADC) as having adopted this strategy. Pevehouse did not predict that Southern Africa would succeed in becoming such a club. But he noted that "such an outcome" was "certainly possible," *if* SADC's already democratic members continued to use SADC "as a forum to pressure neighbors to undertake and continue democratic reforms."[81]

They did not. Instead, the SADC stood by while Zimbabwe's President Robert Mugabe made a mockery of democracy by plunging that SADC member country into what by 2008 had become a bloody vortex of political murder and intimidation, electoral rigging, blatant corruption, and financial chaos. Not only that. Compared with ASEAN's ten members, SADC's fourteen were markedly *more* democratic. In contrast to the Association's 0.2-to-1 ratio of "Free" to "Not Free" states in 2007, the SADC's ratio was a *more* encouraging 1.3 to 1 in that year.[82]

In this instance, a contingent variable—leadership—mattered more than a systemic one—democracy—in explaining regional pressure for member-state reform. Like Indonesia inside ASEAN, South Africa in SADC is large, influential, and politically "Free." Yet South African President Thabo Mbeki, tasked by the SADC to deal with Mugabe, indulged him instead, disappointing observers who thought that South Africa's own democracy would incline its leader to support a similar system next door. If there was a lesson in this experience for democrats in Southeast Asia hoping for regional pressure toward reform in Myanmar, it was not to infer a democratizing foreign policy from the fact of democracy in Indonesia. It was, rather, to hope that a systemic incentive, if it did exist, would not be reversed by a leader in Jakarta more inclined to cater to Than Shwe and his generals than to try reforming their regime.

---

[80] Jon C. Pevehouse, *Democracy from Above? Regional Organizations and Democratization* (New York: Cambridge University Press, 2005), 3–4 ("homogenously democratic") and 213 ("little evidence"). Almost all of the fifty-five organizations, including ASEAN, still existed in his cut-off year, 1992; they are listed on 68–69 (Table 3.4).

[81] Pevehouse, *Democracy from Above?*, 212 and 213 (quotes).

[82] The proportions of members that were "Partly Free" were similar in ASEAN and SADC—respectively 35.7 and 40.0 percent. (Freedom House, "Freedom in the World 2008 [for 2007].") If ASEAN was privately divided over Myanmar, SADC was publicly split over Zimbabwe. If the ASEAN chair had expressed seemingly collective "revulsion" against Myanmar in September 2007, the SADC chair in June 2008 directed the word "scandalous" *at his own Community* for having "remain[ed] silent on Zimbabwe." (Zambian President Levy Mwanawasa as quoted by Peter Greste, "Fresh Dilemmas over Zimbabwe," BBC News, 22 June 2008, <http://news.bbc.co.uk/2/hi/africa/7468399.stm>.)

In the wake of World War II and its aggressive fascisms, Europe "securitized" autocracy as a threat to peace, and democracy as a requisite to peace, and proceeded to institutionalize that linkage in what became the EU. Southeast Asia's experience has been altogether different. The record of interstate security of which ASEAN is so proud had nothing to do with democracy. If the theory of democratic peace[83] argues for democracy as a precondition of security on the grounds that democratic states do not fight one another, one might even say that regionalism in Southeast Asia has vindicated the opposite doctrine: an "autocratic peace theory" in which authoritarian states jointly and wisely avoided war.

Theories are never immune from realities and their changing interpretation. The established banality of peace between states in Southeast Asia has made violent conflicts within states stand out even more sharply, and their resolution seem more urgent. Would-be global norms, including a state's responsibility to protect its population from harm,[84] have helped to limit regional patience with tyrannical misrule in Myanmar. Civil society has grown to the point where the state is less able to get away with conflating its own security with the security of its people.

Southeast Asian regionalism in the evangelical service of liberal democracy is political science fiction. A modest regional agenda on behalf of good governance, human rights, and the rule of law is not. The phrase "human security" appears nowhere in the ASEAN Charter. Regional efforts on its behalf, however, are not only feasible; they could also accelerate in the aftermath of the natural catastrophes of 2004 and 2008. Also missing from the Charter is any reference to the "ASEAN Way." Sovereignty, consensus, and noninterference will sooner be amended than omitted as guidelines of regionalism in Southeast Asia.

---

[83] See Bruce M. Russett, *Grasping the Democratic Peace: Principles for a Post-Cold War World* (rev. ed., Princeton, NJ: Princeton University Press, 1995 [1993]).

[84] See *The Responsibility to Protect: Report of the International Commission on Intervention and State Sovereignty* (Ottawa: International Development Research Centre, 2001).

Assessments

SOVEREIGNTY RULES: HUMAN SECURITY, CIVIL SOCIETY, AND THE LIMITS OF LIBERAL REFORM

Jörn Dosch
University of Leeds
United Kingdom

The Association of Southeast Asian Nations (ASEAN) came into being on 8 August 1967, some four decades ago. The founding of a regional organization among small- and medium-size states in Asia, without the involvement of a hegemonic power, was as unprecedented as it was path-breaking. If one discounts the earlier ill-fated attempt by the Philippines, Thailand, and the Federation of Malaya to form the Association of Southeast Asia (ASA), this was the first time that any of the newly independent Asian states had come together in a coordinated effort to weather the challenges of the international environment and to create a peaceful and stable regional framework for development. ASEAN has often been described as the most successful regional cooperation scheme outside Europe, second only to the European Union (EU). Indeed it has become the model for regionalism in many other parts of the world.[1]

ASEAN was the brainchild of an elite group of policymakers who responded to a clear and straightforward pattern in world politics. The Association was born of the Cold War, which had just been reinforced by the escalating Vietnam War. Although they did not officially say so, ASEAN's founders saw intensified regional cooperation as a way to strengthen Southeast Asia's position in the Asia Pacific area and thereby to reduce their region's risk of falling victim to global rivalry among the great powers.

While the Bangkok Declaration, ASEAN's founding document, stressed the importance of regional economic cooperation and cultural exchange among the nations of Southeast Asia—most of them only recently independent—the main objective was undoubtedly security. Washington had just revived President Eisenhower's "domino theory" of 1954, in which world communism was seen as aggressively expansionist. Southeast Asian leaders were well aware of this American perception. Having so recently gained their freedom from colonial

---

[1] See for example, Donald E. Weatherbee, *International Relations in Southeast Asia: The Struggle for Autonomy* (Lanham, MD: Rowman & Littlefield, 2005), 88.

rule, they wanted to avoid at all costs a situation of fresh dependence on outside powers. They did not want to see great-power rivalries repeatedly flaring up on their own doorstep. A second and also implicit security-related reason for ASEAN's founding was the perceived need to integrate the regional giant Indonesia into a framework for cooperation, with the aim of making Jakarta's international actions less bellicose, more transparent, and more predictable.

Over the ensuing decades, the Association successfully institutionalized a network of regular meetings among its member states, which enabled the governments of Southeast Asia to liaise on the problems and challenges faced by the region. ASEAN's reputation for success was burnished by its role in helping to orchestrate Vietnam's withdrawal from Cambodia and the subsequent Paris Peace Accords of 1991, which ended the Indochina conflict. One of the Association's most notable achievements was the ability of its member states to harmonize their foreign policies and to speak, more often than not, with one voice in international affairs. As time went on, ASEAN seemed more and more to fit Karl W. Deutsch's model of a pluralistic security community, a grouping of states in which the use of military force by one member against another is extremely unlikely.[2]

ASEAN worked well for many years because of the relative simplicity of its political process. Analytically speaking, the structure of the Cold War in general and the condition of anticommunism in particular were the independent variables, and regional cooperation was the dependent variable. Intervening variables hardly existed. Instead, the process of managing regional cooperation was the purview of tiny groups of politicians and government officials. Due to the autocratic, or at best, semidemocratic nature of the politics in the countries in which they maneuvered, these groups could follow and implement narrowly defined national interests, unconstrained and unchallenged by competing political actors, civil society groups, or critical media. Regional policy agendas tended to remain constant, and were hierarchically structured. Horizontally, foreign policy was separated from domestic politics. Vertically, security enjoyed the highest priority in foreign relations, and it was understood as hard security, achievable by managing threats to the integrity of the nation-state.

In the predominantly nondemocratic setting of Southeast Asian politics at the time, peace and stability prevailed not despite but because of two things: first, the relative insulation of policymaking; and second, well-defined international structures that endured over many years and required little policy adaptation. These were the two pillars of quick and overall effective intra-elite policy coordination and conflict management.

---

[2] Karl W. Deutsch, Sidney A. Burrell, and Robert A. Kann, *Political Community and the North Atlantic Area: International Organization in the Light of Historical Experience* (Princeton, NJ: Princeton University Press, 1957).

Since then, conditions have changed. In the post–Cold War era, manifold structural shifts in the global environment and political changes inside countries have moved the political process of regionalism in Southeast Asia toward a more complex, more pluralist, and less centralistic (though not necessarily decentralized) model. The number of political actors has grown, tendencies toward dispersed decision-making have increased, and global, regional, and national political dynamics have intertwined to an extent never seen before in the region. Political change and increasingly open and liberal political spheres across Southeast Asia have resulted in a broadening and deepening of security discourses, to which ASEAN now has to respond.

It is at this multidimensional juncture that security, democracy, and regionalism meet. To be sure, in an organization that still consists mainly of soft authoritarian regimes, governments cannot be expected to promote democracy. Some observers may ardently wish for ASEAN to commit its members to democratic values. Since many of these sovereign states do not believe that democracy is the best or most suitable form of government, it makes sense that they do not seek the Association's assistance in pursuing it.

This reticence is confirmed by the explicit but ultimately weak pro-democracy rhetoric in the charter that ASEAN adopted at its fortieth-anniversary summit in Singapore in November 2007. Nevertheless, international structural settings and how actors respond to and reshape them are constantly in flux. I do not support the idea that ASEAN's presumed failure to support democratic movements (such as the National League for Democracy, which opposes the junta in Myanmar [or Burma]) has strengthened authoritarianism in Southeast Asia.[3] There is no explicit consensus against democracy inside ASEAN. The few references to democracy in the ASEAN Charter are positive. ASEAN has not in fact hindered the development of democratic practices inside its member countries. ASEAN states might not have collectively and openly endorsed the agendas and activities of prodemocracy groups. But the picture changes substantially when we look at individual members such as Indonesia, the Philippines, Thailand, Cambodia, and Malaysia. To varying degrees in these nations, prodemocratic civil-society organizations have mushroomed and in most cases have been allowed to pursue their agendas. A priority item on many of these agendas is "nontraditional security," or "human security"—concepts that can be understood as broadening the scope of security to include respect for human rights.

This chapter begins with a short overview of Southeast Asia's changing discourse on security, and proceeds to consider the impact of political liberalization on the region's responses to security challenges. How have the dynamics of identifying and managing security-relevant issues (especially in the field of nontraditional security) changed under the condition of democracy? I

---

[3] As argued, for example, by Eric Martinez Kuhonta. See p. 40 of "Walking a Tightrope: Democracy versus Sovereignty in ASEAN's Illiberal Peace," *The Pacific Review* 19, no. 3 (2006), 337–58.

will argue that democratization, particularly in Indonesia and the Philippines, and even limited liberalization, as in Vietnam, have yielded new institutional frameworks for agenda-setting and policymaking in the security arena. These movements have likewise facilitated the participation of new groups of actors, such as civil-society organizations, in the policymaking process. This participation and the new understanding of security have changed the way the ASEAN states, both individually and collectively, perceive and respond to security challenges.

However, four decades of declaratory ASEAN solidarity have not eliminated the mutual suspicions and disputes among Association members. A main conclusion of this chapter is that *national sovereignty rules*. That it does still rule is the main reason why there is no shortage of security discourses in Southeast Asia but a clear dearth of effective and efficient regional measures to counter emerging security challenges, especially that of nontraditional security.

Security in Southeast Asia: A Changing Discourse

What exactly is security, and how does it come about? Security is not the predictable outcome of any one set of rules. What constitutes a threat to security varies from one perception to another. Views of security differ greatly according to an actor's location and status within the international system. Security is, in short, subject to interpretation.

Historically, security was understood in terms of threats to state sovereignty and territory. During the Cold War, and particularly after the Vietnam War, it was generally thought that any further serious armed conflict in Southeast Asia would likely result either from conflicts between the great powers or their clients, or from unresolved territorial and border disputes, such as the one between Malaysia and the Philippines over the status of Sabah. Although many territorial conflicts still remain unresolved, security-threat perceptions in the region have changed substantially since the late 1980s. Globalization has encouraged localization—a rising emphasis on subnational issues and a revival of traditional conflicts within countries. These fault lines had been suppressed by the ideological divide of the Cold War and global nuclear deterrence. In post–Cold War Southeast Asia, local tensions are expressed more freely, and with a necessarily greater impact on regional stability.

Among the most important innovations in the post–Cold War discourse on security was the concept of "human security." This idea offered not only a useful alternative to the traditional concept of security as military deterrence. "Human security" also helpfully supplied a wider context for the narrowly political debate on human rights that had unfolded in international relations in the immediate aftermath of the Cold War.[4]

---

[4] Juwono Sudarsono, *Surviving Globalization: Indonesia and the World* (Jakarta: Jakarta Post Books, 1996), 69–73.

As defined by the United Nations Development Programme (UNDP), "human security" usually means freedom from fear and want. As the UNDP's 1994 *Human Development Report* stressed:

> The concept of security has for too long been interpreted narrowly: as security of territory from external aggression, or as protection of national interests in foreign policy or as global security from the threat of nuclear holocaust. It has been related to nation-states more than people. ... Forgotten were the legitimate concerns of ordinary people who sought security in their daily lives. For many of them, security symbolized protection from the threat of disease, hunger, unemployment, crime, social conflict, political repression and environmental hazards.[5]

The United Nations (UN) deserves credit for promoting the concept of human security, but the idea behind the term was not new in 1994. A few years earlier, for example, Barry Buzan had noted the importance of "individual security."[6] Security in a traditional sense had been understood as a top-down approach based on protecting the state from physical assault or ideological subversion. "'Human security,'" wrote Gareth Evans in 1999, "is a bottom-up approach: what matters is the people and their well-being."[7] By then the notion of human security had come to occupy center stage in discussions of foreign policy, and had made its way onto the agendas not only of the UN but also of the EU and the Group of Eight (G8), and was also eventually featured in the discourses of international organizations and individual actors in the Asia Pacific.

During the late 1990s, Japan's then–foreign minister (and later prime minister) Keizo Obuchi mentioned human security in many of his speeches. He defined it as "the keyword" encompassing "the notion of arresting all the menaces" to human dignity and the daily lives of human beings.[8] Meanwhile, parts of Southeast Asia were swept by financial and environmental crises. Beginning in 1997, while currency values plunged, smoke from forest fires in Indonesia caused a haze that spread to neighboring Singapore and Malaysia. The haze alone caused up to US$ 9.3 billion in economic losses to the region. These crises highlighted the need to look beyond the traditional understanding of insecurity as a matter of one state militarily threatening another.

---

[5] United Nations Development Programme, *Human Development Report 1994* (New York: Oxford University Press, 1994), 22.

[6] Barry Buzan, *People, States, and Fear: An Agenda for International Security Studies*, 2nd ed. (Boulder, CO: Lynne Rienner Publishers, 1991), 19.

[7] Gareth Evans, "Human Security and Society," *The Asia-Australia Papers*, no. 2 (September 1999), 59.

[8] Shinyasu Hoshino, "How Can Human Security Be Placed on the Regional Collaborative Agenda?" *Asia-Australia Papers* no. 2 (September 1999), 43.

It can be argued that norms to protect individual human beings first arose in Southeast Asia in 1993. In that year the World Conference on Human Rights obliged ASEAN members to formulate a common stance on the topic. But the change in perspective on security was especially evident at the fifth meeting of the ASEAN Regional Forum (ARF), held in Manila in July 1998. The foreign ministers from ARF's member states discussed the Asian financial crisis in great detail, and concluded that poorly designed reforms could negatively affect less privileged sectors of society and have an "impact on the peace and security of the region."[9]

Critics have questioned the significance of addressing developmental agendas and problems of governance as security issues. They have argued that nontraditional or human security is too broad to be useful as an analytic tool. Be that as it may, an Indonesian analyst has defended the notion by noting that "it is precisely because of its broad definition and its stress on the well-being of humanity as a whole that the concept of human security has an important political appeal that can transcend national boundaries."[10] According to Amitav Acharya, human security, and in a broader sense nontraditional security, is "a distinctive notion, which goes well beyond all earlier attempts by Asian governments to redefine and broaden their own traditional understanding of security as protection of sovereignty and territory against military threats."[11] A nontraditional approach to security has significantly influenced policy discourses in Vietnam. A comprehensive study by the Institute of World Economics and Politics in Hanoi has defined that approach as a multidimensional expansion of earlier thinking about security to encompass the subjects and objects of security, threats to security, the power to threaten it, and the contexts in which such threats can occur.[12]

Scholarship and Securitization: A Conflict of Interest?

At the intersection of scholarly studies and government agendas, the contributions of academic institutions and think tanks to security discourses in Southeast Asia have given rise to a "normative dilemma of speaking and writing security."[13]

---

[9] Anthony Burke, "Caught Between National and Human Security: Knowledge and Power in Post-Crisis Asia," *Pacifica Review* 13, no. 3 (2001), 218.

[10] Dewi Fortuna Anwar, "Human Security: An Intractable Problem in Asia," in *Asian Security Order: Instrumental and Normative Features*, ed. Muthiah Alagappa (Stanford, CA: Stanford University Press, 2003), 541.

[11] Amitav Acharya, "Human Security: East versus West," *International Journal* 3 (2001), 459.

[12] Nguyen Xuan Thang, ed., *Development Gaps and Economic Security in ASEAN* (Hanoi: Social Science Publishing House, 2006), 42.

[13] Jeff Huysmans, "Defining Social Constructivism in Security Studies: The Normative Dilemma of Writing Security," *Alternatives: Global, Local, Political* 27 (2002), 41–62.

By declaring a given issue to be security-relevant, the analyst may become a securitizing actor, to use the terminology of the Copenhagen School.[14] By linking the issue to security, the analyst is implicated in the act of securitization. Depending on how persuasive the act is to decision-makers, the analyst's linkage could even materialize in the real world of policy as a self-fulfilling prophecy. A scholar who studies security and what does or does not threaten it "cannot escape from the fact" that his or her analytic decisions, in speech or writing, risk contributing to actual policy decisions to securitize this or that issue.[15]

Consider the valuable analyses generated by the ASEAN Institutes of Strategic and International Studies (ASEAN-ISIS), or even more notably by the Institute of Defence and Strategic Studies (now the S. Rajaratnam School of International Studies) at Singapore's Nanyang Technological University (NTU). It would probably not be going too far to suggest that the speaking and writing of scholars associated with these institutions have significantly affected the (changing) official perceptions of, and policy responses to, security challenges in Southeast Asia.

Analysis and advocacy have long converged in ASEAN studies.[16] Scholars such as Amitav Acharya, Carolina Hernandez, Mari Pangestu, Kusuma Snitwongse, Hadi Soesastro, Estrella Solidum, the late Nordin Sopiee, Jusuf Wanandi, and many others did important and stimulating work on the topic of Southeast Asian regionalism. They were—many still are—active in Track II networks and as consultants to their own and other governments and global and

---

[14] Barry Buzan, Ole Wæver, and Jaap de Wilde, *Security: A New Framework for Analysis* (Boulder, CO: Lynne Rienner Publishers, 1998). The Copenhagen School's securitization model has become one of the most influential tools for the study of security in a broad sense, comprising five general categories of security: military, environmental, economic, societal, and political. While the Copenhagen School has never gained much influence in American academia, discussion and use of the model is by no means limited to Europe, given the popularity of the approach in, for example, Asian security studies. The approach allows and encourages the comparative historical and empirical investigation of securitization and desecuritization practices in both democratic and authoritarian polities. To quote Buzan et al., "Security is about survival." Securitization occurs "when an issue is presented as posing an existential threat to a designated referent object (traditionally, *but not necessarily*, the state, incorporating government, territory, and *society*" (7–8, italics added).

[15] See Rita Taureck, "Securitization Theory and Securitization Studies," *Journal of International Relations and Development* 9, no. 1 (March 2006), 57. Taureck draws on Jeff Huysmans' "Language and the Mobilization of Security Expectations: The Normative Dilemma of Speaking and Writing Security," paper presented at the ECPR Joint Sessions, Mannheim, 26–31 March, 2006.

[16] Jörn Dosch, "The Post-Cold War Development of Regionalism in East Asia," in *Regionalism in East Asia: Paradigm Shifting?* ed. Fu-Kuo Liu and Philippe Regnier (London: RoutledgeCurzon 2003), 47–48.

regional organizations, including ASEAN. In these roles, they have advocated intensified regional cooperation on both security and economic issues.

One might even say that leading scholars in this field of study, who are in one way or another personally involved in actual policy processes, naturally have a strong self-interest in acting as ASEAN's cheerleaders. International relations (IR) theories and related schools of thought—such as neorealism, idealism, and liberal institutionalism—are seldom free of normative agendas. Nor do they merely explain observed reality and thereby serve an academic purpose. Very often they also gain importance as recipes for making foreign policy. IR theories are distinctive in this regard because scholarly interpretations and policy decisions are reciprocally intertwined. The more that scholars meet and interact informally with officials who speak, off the record, as private individuals, integrated in so-called epistemic communities or in Track II settings, the greater the influence of think tanks and academics on foreign-policy processes.

These linked aspects of theory—as an analytical instrument, a policy recipe, and even a self-fulfilling prophecy—are often ignored in the IR literature. But that is all the more reason to keep in mind the wisdom of Claudia Aradau's (much criticized) claim that it is simply not possible "to think [of] security only analytically, outside any political project."[17]

In such a "political project" it may even seem necessary to respond to clear threats to security with policies that do not refer to security at all, as the next section shows.

Elephants in the Room: Substituting Agendas

Both individually and collectively within ASEAN, Southeast Asian governments have mastered the use of substitute agendas when addressing security challenges. The best example of the elephant called security sitting in the regional room, while the diplomats present pretend not to notice, is the founding of ASEAN itself; in its early statements the Association rarely mentioned security. A more recent instance is the proposed China-ASEAN Free Trade Area (CAFTA).

In November 2000, the leaders of ASEAN and China agreed to strengthen economic cooperation and uttered the words "free trade" for the first time in an ASEAN-China context. Ever since, CAFTA has figured prominently in academic studies of relations between these two parts of East Asia.[18] Under the Framework Agreement on ASEAN-China Comprehensive Economic Cooperation, which was officially announced and signed in November 2002, ASEAN and China envision that 99 percent of their bilateral trade will be liberalized in two stages: by 2010 for China and the more developed ASEAN Six (Brunei, Indonesia,

---

[17] Claudia Aradau, "Limits of Security, Limits of Politics? A Response," *Journal of International Relations and Development* 9 (2006), 81.

[18] Also referred to as the ASEAN-China Free Trade Area (ACFTA).

Malaysia, the Philippines, Singapore, and Thailand), and by 2015 for the less developed ASEAN Four (Cambodia, Laos, Myanmar, and Vietnam).

Although most analyses of CAFTA have focused narrowly on its economic implications, a sizable number of academic observers have highlighted the fact that the scope of the proposal goes beyond trade facilitation and tariff reduction.[19] "CAFTA is not primarily an economic project," a prominent Vietnamese analyst has argued. "Free trade might never actually materialize. But CAFTA is very important in terms of its political and security effects."[20]

CAFTA is but one of several instances in ASEAN-China relations where regional security has come into play even in the absence of an explicit political discourse on security involving the two sides. The intensified building of economic institutions in Sino-Southeast Asian relations is expected to facilitate regional stability and security. States that trade with each other are thought less likely to go to war against each other. This "liberal peace" hypothesis is of course almost as old as the study of IR itself, and the ASEAN-China example seems to be just another illustration of its popularity. From this perspective, growing economic interdependence reduces the negative effects of anarchy and ultimately transforms the nature of international politics, moving the affected countries toward a peaceful "trading world." For this standpoint it is interdependence, not insecurity resulting from anarchy, that increasingly structures the behavior of states in the international system.[21]

Hopes for a "liberal peace"—security underpinned by trade—have also shaped ASEAN's relations with the United States. It was no coincidence that U.S. President George W. Bush unveiled his administration's Enterprise for ASEAN Initiative (EAI) at the Asia Pacific Economic Cooperation (APEC) summit in Mexico, almost immediately following the 12 October 2002 terrorist bombing in Bali. Modeled on the successful Enterprise for the Americas Initiative, launched in 1990 by the then president George H. W. Bush, the EAI envisioned a web of bilateral free trade agreements (FTAs) linking the United States to the economies of Southeast Asia. Under the EAI, the United States and individual ASEAN countries will jointly determine if and when they are ready to launch FTA negotiations. The Initiative allows each partnering country the flexibility to move at its own speed toward an FTA with the United States.

---

[19] See, for example, Lijun Sheng, *China-ASEAN Free Trade Area: Origins, Developments and Strategic Motivations*, ISEAS Working Paper: International Politics and Security Issues Series No. 1 (Singapore: Institute of Southeast Asian Studies, 2003), 6. For a more detailed discussion, see Jörn Dosch, "Managing Security in ASEAN-China Relations: Liberal Peace of Hegemonic Stability," *Asian Perspective* 31, no. 1 (2007), 209–36.

[20] Author interview with Do Tien Sam (director of the Institute of Chinese Studies, Vietnamese Academy of Social Sciences), Hanoi, 4 April 2007.

[21] See Richard Rosecrance, *The Rise of the Trading State: Commerce and Conquest in the Modern World* (New York: Basic Books, 1986).

Officially, the Initiative emphasizes trade liberalization and facilitation. But security is the other side of that same coin. The EAI is based on the idea of "countering terror with trade."[22] From this American perspective, freer trade is meant to bind the United States more tightly to the region in a shared struggle against terrorism.[23] This logic inspired Richard Higgott to write of the "securitization of economic globalization" in U.S. foreign policy.[24]

All of these examples—ASEAN's founding rationale, CAFTA, and the EAI—have one feature in common: Officially, they are all about economic progress. But their hidden agenda is security. Hiding that agenda makes sense because it is less controversial to declare the pursuit of prosperity than to assume or reach agreement about which contingencies threaten security the most, the least, or not at all.

Having introduced and characterized the security debate in Southeast Asia, this chapter can now explore how and to what extent political change has impacted both the security discourse and the way the region's individual governments and ASEAN collectively deal with security challenges within their respective institutional settings. It is beyond the scope of this chapter to explain why specific countries have or have not become more democratic. Instead, after briefly locating democratization in regional and global contexts, I will examine how political liberalization (as an independent variable) has affected the creation and management of security policy inside ASEAN and the actors involved in those activities (as a dependent variable).

Democracy and Liberalization: Security Policymaking in New Contexts

In the early 1990s a lively debate took place on "Western" versus "Asian" values. Asian voices in this discourse sometimes used *democracy* as a synonym for Western culture in general and, in effect, rejected it as unsuited to their own societies. In Northeast and Southeast Asia, some governments accused Western governments and organizations of trying to impose on Asians alien concepts drawn from liberal, post-Renaissance, Euro-American traditions.

In fact, there has never been a consensus among East Asian leaders and thinkers that democracy is a purely Western construct that does not apply to their region. A case in point is the Korean democrat Kim Dae Jung. He has consistently opposed the cultural relativism of Lee Kuan Yew in Singapore

---

[22] Robert Zoellick, "Countering Terror with Trade," *Washington Post* (20 September 2001), A35.

[23] See Julie Gilson, "Complex Regional Multilateralism: 'Strategising' Japan's Responses to Southeast Asia," *Pacific Review* 17, no. 1 (2004), 71–94; and Christopher M. Dent, "The Asia-Pacific's New Economic Bilateralism and Regional Political Economy," in *Asia-Pacific Economic and Security Cooperation: New Regional Agendas*, ed. Christopher M. Dent (Hampshire, UK: Palgrave Macmillan, 2003), 72–94.

[24] Richard Higgott, "U.S. Foreign Policy and the 'Securitization' of Economic Globalization," *International Politics* 41, no. 2 (2004), 147–75.

and Mahathir Mohamad in Malaysia. In Kim's view, Asians are heirs to a rich regional legacy of democratic ideas, goals, and institutions.

In his thoroughly stimulating deconstruction of the notion of an exclusively "Western" understanding of democracy, Edward Friedman has observed that "while the potential for democracy is universal, its practice is idiosyncratic. Every democracy is *sui generis*." For Friedman, no democracy could flourish were it not "indigenized to fit particularities of culture, history and society."[25] To be sure, democracies are diverse, and deeply rooted in specific cultural and historical experiences. In the mainstream European view, for example, the idea of democratic political rule is geared to the working of the welfare state. American conceptions of democracy emphasize pluralism, in processes of decision-making and the structures of political power. In Latin America, the concept of civil society has been a leading element in movements for and toward democratic order. In Northeast and even more in Southeast Asia, the notion of democracy has long been based on principles of harmony and consensus, as illustrated, for example, in Indonesia's so-called *Pancasila democracy*[26] under President Suharto.

For all this variety, however, all young democracies share one common experience, regardless of cultural background: the wave of democratization that has washed over the globe for more than three decades. This wave has opened both the conduct of international relations and foreign policymaking to a larger number of actors than were involved in these activities when most regimes were authoritarian.

The ASEAN states, too, have felt this wave. Its most obvious impact within the polities of Southeast Asia has been the broadening of institutional settings for political decision-making. Specifically in the security arena, the accountability of regimes has increased, and that has in turn allowed for the direct participation of a growing number of actors outside government, or inside the government but outside its executive branch, in the process of identifying relevant threats and risks and deciding how to respond to them.

As long as security was the domain of unaccountable autocratic regimes and their small political elites, one could analyze the foreign policies, including the security policies, of Southeast Asian states in isolation from the structures and dynamics of their respective political systems. In the early 1980s, for example, foreign ministries in the region would not have lost much sleep over the interests of domestic actors.

Times have changed. Counting from the year of the first democratic elections that followed the most recent authoritarian regime, foreign policy

---

[25] See Edward Friedman, "On Alien Western Democracy," in *Globalization and Democratization in Asia: The Construction of Identity*, ed. Catarina Kinnvall and Kristina Jönsson (London: Routledge, 2002), 59.

[26] This concept of democracy called for decision-making through deliberations, or *musyawarah*, to reach a consensus, or *mufakat*, as opposed to the Western idea of democracy as majority rule.

and foreign security arenas have been opened up in the Philippines since 1986, in Thailand since 1992 (interrupted since 2006), and in Indonesia since 1999. Groups from outside the executive branch have forced their governments to pay greater attention to a range of nontraditional or human security issues, such as human rights and the environment. They have blocked or significantly changed governmental initiatives toward other countries involving these matters. Regime accountability has constrained the latitude for executive decision-making.[27] Remarkably, despite the commonsense character of this finding, domestic politics are often completely neglected as a field of possibly causal variables in the explanatory study of regional security in Southeast Asia.

The political transformations that have taken place in Southeast Asia since the 1980s have been most far-reaching in the Philippines, Thailand, and Indonesia, and to a lesser extent in Cambodia, a democracy on paper that in 2007 was still caught in the vicious circles of inherited authoritarianism. Yet the political process has seen changes to some degree even in the states most resistant to reform. No political system in the region is entirely immune to structural alterations, and this has had major implications for both the institutional structures and the actions of governments as they have sought to identify and manage traditional and nontraditional threats to security.

Vietnam offers a case in point. Even in the absence of any substantive moves toward democratization, Vietnam's policymaking on security has been affected by inputs, including demands, from newly emerging social groups and shifting structures of influence within the state-party apparatus. Vietnam is still a unitary state, where a bureaucratic elite shapes policymaking.[28] Empirical evidence nevertheless suggests that the spectrum of actors that try to affect security policy has widened, notwithstanding the retention of an effective monopoly over political discussion and policy formulation by the government and the Communist Party of Vietnam (CPV). The right of the CPV to guide state and society alike has been codified in the country's constitution since 1980. Yet in 2007, decisions made by the CPV politburo that once had the power of law were authoritative only to a great extent, that is, not absolutely.

The influence of Vietnam's National Assembly in the policymaking process, including matters affecting the country's external relations and security, has grown. If this trend continues, legislators will increasingly hold the relevant

---

[27] Tong Whan Park, Dae-Won Ko, and Kyu-Ryoon Kim, "Democratization and Foreign Policy Change in the East Asian NICs," in *Foreign Policy Restructuring: How Governments Respond to Global Change*, ed. Jerel A. Rosati et al. (Columbia, SC: University of South Carolina Press, 1994), 173.

[28] Gareth Porter, *Vietnam: The Politics of Bureaucratic Socialism* (Ithaca, NY: Cornell University Press, 1993).

government ministers accountable for their performance.[29] Often, however, conservative circles and the army, as agents of restraint, have warned against too-rapid reform and premature opening that could derail socialism, undermine national security, and facilitate a "peaceful evolution" by so-called "hostile forces"—phrases that implicate the United States. The struggle between reformers and conservatives over the means and ends of renovation (in Vietnamese, *doi moi*) has spilled over into foreign and security policy as well. This is particularly true for the conduct of Vietnam's relations with its former adversaries China and the United States, in which economic and security interests need to be balanced.[30]

The successful transformation of the economy has given rise to internationally active Vietnamese entrepreneurs. They have begun to lobby the government and the party to integrate Vietnam rapidly into the world economy and to adopt trade and investment regimes favorable to the country's growing number of private enterprises. The more complex international structures in the post–Cold War era and the challenges they pose for the steering capabilities of foreign policy–makers have also resulted in the expansion of the policy-consulting sector.

In Vietnam the degree of information-sharing between government agencies and think tanks, together with the latter's role in helping to set foreign and security policy agendas, cannot yet compare with the access and influence that the well-established institutes for international and strategic studies enjoy in some other ASEAN states. These institutes have been able to improve their research profiles and capabilities significantly, and the government increasingly draws on this new source of expertise.

A good example is the Hanoi-based Institute of World Economics and Politics (IWEP). IWEP has been involved in an extensive consultative process with government agencies on such foreign policy–relevant topics as nontraditional security, the future of economic integration within ASEAN, Sino-Vietnamese relations, what should be done with the Greater Mekong Subregion, and Vietnam's external interests more generally. In a 2005 report on "Development Gaps and Economic Security in ASEAN Economies," for example, IWEP spelled out a broad range of specific policy implications and recommendations for Vietnam's foreign policy, including "a more flexible approach to security." These ideas were fed into the governmental decision-making process to an extent seldom previously seen in relations between government offices and academic

---

[29] Michael J. Montesano, "Vietnam in 2004: 'A Country Hanging in the Balance,'" *Southeast Asian Affairs* (Singapore: Institute of Southeast Asian Studies [ISEAS], 2005), 407–21; Martin Gainsborough, "Party Control: Electoral Campaigning in Vietnam in the Run-up to the May 2002 National Assembly Elections," *Pacific Affairs* 78, no. 1 (2005), 57–75.

[30] Jörn Dosch, "Vietnam's ASEAN Membership Revisited: Golden Opportunity or Golden Cage?" *Contemporary Southeast Asia* 28, no. 2 (2006), 234–58.

institutions.[31] Study centers such as IWEP have also rapidly multiplied their international links, and are increasingly involved in collaborative research with counterparts in the United States, Japan, and Europe.

Armed Forces and Nontraditional Security: A New Policy Frontier?

An especially evident effect of democratization in Southeast Asia has been the decreasing influence of the armed forces on the security policy domain. At the same time, while growing civilian supremacy over the military has diminished its former monopoly on the definition and management of security, the armed forces in ASEAN member states have opened themselves to discourses on new facets of the topic, including nontraditional security (or NTS). The region's military establishments have also begun to meet regularly within ASEAN's institutional framework to discuss and exchange information on security management.

Southeast Asia's defense establishments have not elevated NTS issues to the top of the regional security agenda. "NTS is a major concern," said a senior official of the Malaysian Ministry of Defence, "but we would not compromise on traditional security capabilities."[32] According to a high-ranking officer in Singapore's armed forces, the relative reluctance of Southeast Asian security elites to give NTS a higher priority reflects the "inflexibility of the military structure which was put into place to respond to military threats and nothing else."[33]

Yet both the awareness of NTS and the perceived necessity to respond to its challenges have grown. There is a tendency in the Malaysian military, for example, to cling to the view that "nontraditional security is not our job." The Indonesian armed forces are more open to nonmilitary security issues—as are their counterparts outside Southeast Asia, in India and Pakistan. According to an Australian officer, NTS is first and foremost a political issue. But if politicians labeled an issue as a threat to security, the military certainly would get involved. Australia offers a case in point, with the securitization of illegal migration.

NTS issues already figure prominently in discussions among military actors in ASEAN. In May 2006 in Kuala Lumpur, an ASEAN Defense Ministers

---

[31] Nguyen Xuan Thang, "Development Gaps and Economic Security in ASEAN Economies," draft final report of a research project funded by the Ford Foundation, "Non-traditional Security: Development Gaps and Economic Security in ASEAN Economies," Institute of World Economics and Politics, Hanoi, September 2005, unpublished.

[32] Author interview, Kuala Lumpur, 25 October 2005.

[33] This official's view and the views of those cited in the subsequent paragraph were gathered during a roundtable discussion chaired by this author on 25 October 2005 at the Malaysian Armed Forces Defence College. Senior officers from the armed forces of Malaysia, Singapore, Indonesia, Pakistan, Australia, and the United Kingdom attended. A second source was a seminar with members of the Malaysian military held at the same place on 17 April 2006.

Meeting (ADMM) was convened for the first time. Nine of the ten member states were represented; Myanmar alone chose not to take part. The ministers' agenda was dominated by NTS threats such as terrorism, piracy, natural disasters, and transnational crime.[34] Coordinated responses to terrorist acts and natural disasters were also among the subjects reviewed at the third ASEAN Air Force Chiefs Conference held in November 2006.[35]

The ADMM is expected to "bolster security ties" and even to "shelve historic tensions."[36] It does provide another institutional framework for the discussion of security challenges. But it is not designed to move beyond the level of political rhetoric. Malaysian Defence Minister Najib Tun Razak has acknowledged that "we want this ADMM ... to engage and be open with other countries which have interests in the region." However, he added, "This forum is not based on any threat perceptions. We shouldn't [get] ahead of ourselves. We will only move at a pace that is comfortable and within the true spirit of how ASEAN takes positions, on the basis of consensus."[37]

To date, the most progressive move toward institutionalizing defense cooperation was made by Indonesia in 2004. In the context of a prospective ASEAN Security Community (ASC), Jakarta proposed that ASEAN set up its own force to help maintain regional peace (after concerned parties had requested that it do so). At their annual meeting in June 2004 in Jakarta, the Association's foreign ministers endorsed the plan to establish the ASC by 2020, but they rejected the idea of an ASEAN peacekeeping force. Indonesia's idea would have entailed a radical departure from past practice, and its rejection was expected. In the former, more authoritarian days of ASEAN, however, such a bold proposal for the joint management of regional security would never have seen the light of day. Senior officials would have met and buried it behind closed doors.

In 2000, Singapore's Defence Minister Tony Tan had suggested a wider role for the region's armed forces.[38] His main if unspoken objective, however, had been to help the Indonesian authorities stabilize their own country, and thereby to prevent communal violence from spilling over into other parts of the region. Indonesian Defense Minister Jowono Sudarsono politely rejected the Singaporean idea.

The idea of an ASEAN contingent for peacekeeping, which Jakarta raised four years later, was more radical and more specific than Singapore's suggestion. But the Indonesian proposal, too, had an unspoken dimension. Jakarta's idea was part of a major foreign policy move to reestablish Indonesia as the driving force

---

[34] Carolyn Hong, "ASEAN Reaffirms Security Community," *Straits Times*, 10 May 2006.

[35] "ASEAN Air Force Chiefs Meet in Indonesia," *Thai Press Reports*, 23 November 2006.

[36] Hong, "ASEAN Reaffirms Security Community."

[37] Hong, "ASEAN Reaffirms Security Community."

[38] "ASEAN Views on a Regional Military," *Straits Times*, 14 August 2000.

in Southeast Asian regionalism, following a period of passivity that had begun with the economic crisis in 1997. In 2004, Jakarta offered a comprehensive plan for Southeast Asian security. It included, for example, provisions to improve legal cooperation and to create a commission for human rights that would address potential abuses in the fight against terrorism.[39]

Acknowledgment of Security as a Multidimensional Phenomenon

As a matter of national policy doctrine, traditional realism is still the lens through which most Southeast Asian governments view defense and security. De facto, however, and at least implicitly, the great majority of the region's authorities have long acknowledged the relevance of—and the trend toward—a multidimensional understanding of security. In 2007, there was still no political or military consensus on the ultimate importance of NTS. But one could already say that the ASEAN states had come around to thinking of traditional and nontraditional security as two sides of one coin—although this perspective might be, in some countries, more implicit than stated. As political spaces in the region have been opened up—liberalized—regional security discourses have broadened and deepened. Official candor on such a sensitive subject is still limited, however. The long-standing strategy of using what could be termed "substitute security agendas," as discussed earlier, remains a typical feature of the approaches to security preferred by Southeast Asian states.

Singapore provides a good example. Its national security culture spans military, socioeconomic, and political factors. The city-state is extremely—and to a significantly higher degree than most of its regional neighbors—concerned about its position and status within the international system. The perception of vulnerability crucially informs Singapore's view of the world. "That vulnerability," wrote Michael Leifer, "is a function of a minuscule scale, a predominantly ethnic-Chinese identity associated with a traditional entrepôt role and also a location wedged between the sea and airspace of two larger neighbours [Indonesia and Malaysia] with which Singapore has never been politically at ease."[40]

This deep security complex also drives Singapore's foreign economic policy. Its feeling of insecurity has pushed Singapore to pursue aggressively its own economic advancement, for self-protection, not simply to better the lives of its people. Singapore's initiatives to establish bilateral FTAs on a global scale have

---

[39] "Indonesia Proposes ASEAN Peace-keeping Force, Extradition Treaty to Bolster Regional Security," *Associated Press Worldstream*, 22 February 2004.

[40] Michael Leifer, *Singapore's Foreign Policy: Coping with Vulnerability* (London: Routledge, 2000), 1.

been very successful. By 2008, Singapore had concluded ten FTAs, with seven more under negotiation.[41]

Singapore offers one of the best illustrations of a Southeast Asian government's use of substitute security agendas. Alongside their economic purpose, Singapore's FTAs enhance the city-state's global recognition. In addition to raising Singapore's profile, these agreements also serve a direct security purpose. The FTA with the United States, for example, helps to keep that powerful outsider engaged in Southeast Asia. Singapore sees the local American presence as vital to the security and stability of the region.[42]

Nonsecurity objectives, in other words, do not fully replace security goals; the substitution is only partial. Nor is the choice between nontraditional and traditional security objectives a matter of either/or. Again Singapore offers a striking example. When the earthquake and tsunami hit the Sumatran coast of Indonesia on 26 December 2004 with catastrophic results, Singapore was the first ASEAN member to respond to the disaster by offering substantial humanitarian aid. Charitable motivation in an NTS situation aside, however, one could note that Indonesia was the giant country that Singapore had been most wary of during the city-state's history as an independent nation. "This was a message that could not be missed: the smallest ASEAN state helping the biggest one," noted K. S. Nathan about his government's quick response in 2004. "Singapore enhanced its security by providing human security assistance to Indonesia."[43] "Substitution" works both ways.

A comparable nexus between security and economic objectives may be illustrated with another example from Vietnam. Hanoi's foreign policy took a new course in December 1986 when the sixth National Congress of the Vietnamese Communist Party adopted *doi moi*, the country's previously mentioned strategy of reform or renovation. The new approach was aimed mainly at liberalizing the national economy. But it carried decisive implications for Vietnam's foreign policy and security outlook. The ruling elite had concluded that the international isolation of their country following its invasion and occupation of Cambodia beginning in 1978–79 had significantly disrupted and damaged the Vietnamese economy.[44] But *doi moi* was driven not by purely economic concern. It also reflected Hanoi's realization that Vietnam's main

---

[41] See Singapore's FTA network, International Enterprise Singapore, <http://www.iesingapore. gov.sg/wps/portal/!ut/p/kcxml/04_Sj9SPykssy0xPLMnMz0vM0Y_QjzKLN4g3CwkFSY-GY5oFm-pFoYo4YImah3lCxUF-4WEgYQszXIz83VT9I31s_QL8gNzQ0NKLcEQAenL7-/delta/base64xml/L3dJdyEvd0ZNQUFzQUMvNElVRS82XzBfNlRW>.

[42] Ramkishen S. Rajan, et al., *Singapore and Free Trade Agreements: Economic Relations with Japan and the United States* (Singapore: ISEAS, 2001), 76.

[43] Author interview, Singapore, 10 April 2006.

[44] Jörn Dosch and Ta Minh Tuan, "Recent Changes in Vietnam's Foreign Policy: Implications for Vietnam-ASEAN Relations," in *Rethinking Vietnam*, ed. Duncan McCargo (London: RoutledgeCurzon, 2004), 197–213.

security challenges could no longer be attributed to aggressive behavior on the part of foreign powers, but stemmed from poverty and other shortcomings in the local economy.[45] Economy recovery and development were therefore stepping stones not just to prosperity, but to security as well.

Perhaps the oldest explicit concept of a flexible and open approach to security in Southeast Asia is Indonesia's long-standing doctrine of "national resilience" (in Indonesian, *ketanahan nasional*). This concept was eventually upgraded to "regional resilience" as the "rhetorical centerpiece" of ASEAN's approach to Southeast Asian security, but without its being explicitly labeled as a regional security doctrine.[46] According to one understanding of this concept, a secure international environment requires regional resilience, in which ideology, politics, the economy, society, culture, and military strength are combined through socioeconomic and cultural cooperation.[47] Such a sweeping formulation inevitably spotlights the role that civil society might play in achieving regional security.

Civil Society and the Charter Process: Unwelcome Advice?

In 2007, civil society organizations still had limited salience and influence in ASEAN. But their impact had markedly grown as a result of political liberalization and the associated emergence of transnational networks with liberal agendas.

In December 2005 in Kuala Lumpur, the leaders of ASEAN's member states committed themselves to establish an ASEAN Charter that would "serve as a legal and institutional framework of ASEAN." A window of opportunity was thereby opened, in principle, for civil society actors to contribute to the process of drafting the document. The Kuala Lumpur Declaration on the Establishment of the ASEAN Charter did not provide for direct input from nongovernmental actors. But the leaders did agree to create an Eminent Persons Group (EPG) "comprising highly distinguished and well respected citizens from ASEAN Member Countries, with the mandate to examine and provide practical recommendations" on the Charter's "directions and nature."[48] Subsequently,

---

[45] Andrew T. H. Tan and J. D. Kenneth Boutin, "Introduction," in *Non-Traditional Security Issues in Southeast Asia*, ed. Andrew T. H. Tan and J. D. Kenneth Boutin (Singapore: Select Publishing, 2001), 3.

[46] Donald K. Emmerson, "Goldilocks's Problem: Rethinking Security and Sovereignty in Asia," in *The Many Faces of Asian Security*, ed. Sheldon W. Simon (Lanham, MD: Rowman & Littlefield, 2001), 95.

[47] James R. Ferguson, "New Forms of Southeast Asian Governance: From 'Codes of Conduct' to 'Greater East Asia,'" in *Non-Traditional Security Issues in Southeast Asia*, 124–25.

[48] "Kuala Lumpur Declaration on the Establishment of the ASEAN Charter," 12 December 2005, <http://webevents.bernama.com/events/aseansummit/speech.php?id=378>.

civil society groups were invited to convey to the EPG their ideas on what the document should say.

Among the groups that accepted this invitation, one of the most active was a transnational network called Solidarity for Asian People's Advocacy (SAPA). SAPA was formed in early 2006 to accommodate discussion and debate among civil society groups in Southeast Asia, particularly nongovernmental organizations (NGOs) with regional interests and concerns.[49] In April 2006, SAPA submitted detailed recommendations on security to the EPG. In this submission SAPA paid particular attention to NTS challenges. SAPA presented additional advice on the Charter to the EPG in June, and again in November 2006.[50]

Compared with the extent of SAPA's ideas on how security should be treated in the Charter, the input of think tanks on the topic was rather small. The contribution compiled by former ASEAN Secretary-General Rodolfo Severino, and conveyed to the EPG on behalf of the Singapore-based Institute of Southeast Asian Studies (ISEAS), for example, mentioned security only in passing. In its submission, the ISEAS did say that "ASEAN also has to address unprecedented nontraditional security challenges like SARS [sever acute respiratory syndrome], avian flu and environmental hazards that demand expedient cross-border solutions."[51]

The EPG finalized its own fifty-page report in December 2006. A month later, at their summit in Cebu (Philippines), ASEAN's leaders signed the Cebu Declaration on the Blueprint of the ASEAN Charter, endorsing the EPG's report and directing a High-Level Task Force (HLTF) to begin actually drafting the Charter.

Some civil society actors were unhappy with this process. One of them was Anil Netto, a Malaysian journalist and social activist, who remarked:

> The EPG says it has met civil society groups but many have not heard about the Charter ... Critics suspect the lack of public consultation over the Charter could be due to the real intention behind the blueprint. They see the Charter as giving a legal personality to ASEAN, paving the way for a regional economic framework that would facilitate investment and

---

[49] Alexander C. Chandra, *Southeast Asian Civil Society and the ASEAN Charter: The Way Forward*, Solidarity for Asian People's Advocacy/SAPA, 1 October 2006, <http://www.asiasapa.org/index.php?option=com_content&task=view&id=41&Itemid=50>.

[50] See the "SAPA Letter to the EPG on the ASEAN Charter Reiterating the Key Points of Its Submission," 24 November 2006, <http://www.asiasapa.org/index.php?option=com_content&task=view&id=34&Itemid=50>.

[51] Rodolfo C. Severino, compiler, *Framing the ASEAN Charter: AN ISEAS Perspective*, (Singapore: ISEAS, 2005), vii. The ASEAN People's Assembly also submitted thoughts on the prospective text of the Charter.

trade in the region, while the interests of ordinary people—workers, the poor and the marginalized—could come a distant second.[52]

Regardless of whether or not the EPG engaged in a regular exchange with societal actors in the course of writing its report to the ASEAN heads of government, the comparison of SAPA's submission and the EPG Report in Table 2.1 shows a striking convergence of core concepts. (Table 2.1 also compares these two documents with the Charter itself, as it was finally signed by the ten heads of government at their 13th summit in Singapore on 20 November 2007.) Although SAPA's wording and that of the EPG differ, the EPG addressed almost all of SAPA's security-related concerns. The notable exception is the absence in the EPG Report of any mention of the state as itself a source of insecurity, in contrast to SAPA's reference to "threats as risks produced by State policy."[53]

With this convergence in mind, Alexander Chandra, a research associate at the Jakarta-based Institute for Global Justice and a leading activist in SAPA, expressed satisfaction with what SAPA's lobbying had accomplished:

> The report of the EPG indeed corresponds with SAPA inputs. ... [T]he EPG was progressive, although in the "ASEAN sense" ... It is of course difficult for everybody to feel happy about [the EPG Report]. Even within SAPA, there is divergence of perspectives on the EPG report. ... This problem is mainly due to the fact that some [of the groups in SAPA] still have some reservations about engaging ASEAN. SAPA mainly [comprises] organisations with centre-left and left political orientation[s], and, at times, it is difficult to reach consensus even amongst these groups.[54]

In any event, both SAPA's submission and the EPG's report were important contributions to ASEAN's growing awareness of, and responsiveness to, NTS issues.

Democracy and Disappointment: SAPA, the EPG, and How the Charter Turned Out

Table 2.1 juxtaposes relevant portions of three consecutive texts: (1) SAPA's submission (April 2006), (2) the EPG Report (December 2006), and (3) the final text of the ASEAN Charter (November 2007). The table also addresses the four

---

[52] Anil Netto, "Charter for ASEAN Bloc Bypasses Civil Society," Inter Press Service, 2 November, 2006.

[53] Solidarity for Asian People's Advocacy, *Submission on Political and Human Security to the ASEAN EPG on the ASEAN Charter*, 17 April 2006, Ubud, Bali, <http://seaca. net/viewArticle.php?aID=945>.

[54] Author email conversation with Alexander Chandra, 28 March 2007.

key issue areas of democracy and good governance, human security, human rights, and NTS.

The comparison raises two distinct but linked questions. First, how liberal-democratic or nontraditional did the Charter turn out to be in its pronouncements on regional security? Second, to what if any extent did civil society organizations influence the process of drafting the Charter?

The full text of the Charter appears at the back of this book. Various readers of the document may reach varying conclusions as to how much the Charter marks a departure for ASEAN from its authoritarian past and its traditional commitment to the principles of national sovereignty and noninterference. SAPA's judgment on this point, however, is clear:

> The Charter is a disappointment. [It] falls short of what is needed to establish a "people-centered" and "people-empowered" ASEAN. It succeeds in codifying past ASEAN agreements, and consolidating the legal framework that would define the Association. However, it fails to put people at the center, much less empower them.[55]

The Charter, as it was actually drafted by the HTLF, fell considerably short of the liberal-democratic thrust of the EPG Report, not to mention the "people-empowering" hopes of SAPA, among other NGOs. The latter had lobbied for profound changes in ASEAN's approach to regionalism. They had reason to be disappointed by the result.

To be fair, the ASEAN Charter commits Southeast Asia to liberal norms and values that go significantly beyond anything that would have been possible merely a decade ago. But in contrast to the EPG Report, nowhere in the Charter is it stated that regional security should be promoted by actively strengthening democracy, international law, and "respect for human rights and fundamental freedoms." Nor, again unlike the Report, does the Charter acknowledge any "need to calibrate the traditional policy of nonintervention in areas where the common interest dictates closer cooperation" against security threats of a nontraditional kind.

In these respects, the Charter's bottom line is this: ASEAN is still a government-centered entity where national sovereignty rules.

---

[55] Solidarity for Asian Peoples' Advocacies (SAPA) Working Group on ASEAN (2007), "Analysis of the ASEAN Charter," <http://www.focusweb.org/analysis-of-the-asean-charter.html?Itemid=145>.

Table 2.1 A Comparison of References to Democracy and NTS in the 2006 SAPA Submission by SAPA, the 2006 EPG Report, and the 2007 ASEAN Charter

Issue	SAPA Submission	EPG Report
Democracy, good governance	*Section II*—"Regional monitors and regulatory mechanisms, and a progressive and democratic regional political and security system, are important elements of regionalism."	"Promotion of ASEAN's peace and stability through the active strengthening of democratic values, good governance, rejection of unconstitutional and undemocratic changes of government, the rule of law including international humanitarian law, and respect for human rights and fundamental freedoms."
Human security	*Section IV, Principle 3*—"The ASEAN Charter should broadly define human security, allocate a specific chapter addressing the issue, and contain provisions that will lead to the implementation of its values." (6)	"ASEAN is instrumental in mobilising international support and cooperation to tackle international terrorism, transnational crime, SARS, the 2004 Asian tsunami disaster, and now avian influenza. These transnational threats to human security cannot be handled effectively by any single country or government in this region alone."
Human rights	*Section III*—"Human rights and dignity are part of core values and guiding principles that ASEAN has sought to uphold. Promotion and protection of human rights and dignity should be the primary goal of all efforts for regional integration and cooperation undertaken by ASEAN."	"Member States should ultimately advance to form an ASEAN Union comprising the three pillars of security, economic, and socio-cultural integration, that are closely intertwined and mutually reinforcing, in which human rights and fundamental freedom of all shall be protected by the rule of law and regional integration, and human security is guaranteed to every ASEAN citizen. This would ensure enduring peace, stability, security, equitable prosperity and human dignity in the ASEAN region for every individual to enjoy and to pursue the worthy aspirations of human potential in the 21st century."
Non-traditional security (NTS)	*Section IV, Principle 1/i*—"The ASEAN Charter should have distinctive chapters that address conventional and non-conventional security issues with reference to the State as well as to the people." *Section IV, Principle 1/ii* "It is also important to conceive threats as risks produced by State policy. As such, the sources of threats to ASEAN security can be less external than internal."	"Promotion of ASEAN's timely and effective responses to non-traditional and transboundary challenges and crises through mutual assistance or regional and international cooperation. ASEAN may need to calibrate the traditional policy of non-intervention in areas where the common interest dictates closer cooperation." ASEAN should "strengthen regional cooperation to deal with the growing number of transboundary challenges ranging from terrorism, transnational crimes, and maritime security to natural disasters and humanitarian aid, pandemics, and energy cooperation."

(Table 2.1 continued)

ASEAN Charter

Art. 1.7—"The Purposes of ASEAN are: . . to strengthen democracy, enhance good governance and the rule of law, and to promote and protect human rights and fundamental freedoms, with due regard to the rights and responsibilities of the Member States of ASEAN."
 Art. 2.2—"ASEAN and its Member States shall act in accordance with the following Principles:"
      (a) "respect for the independence, sovereignty, equality, territorial integrity and national identity of all ASEAN Member States;"
      (e) "non-interference in the internal affairs of ASEAN Member States;"
      (h) "adherence to the rule of law, good governance, the principles of democracy and the constitutional government;"
      (i) "respect for fundamental freedoms, the promotion and protection of human rights, and the promotion of social justice."

Art. 1.4—"To ensure that the peoples of and Member States of ASEAN live in peace with the world at large in a just, democratic and harmonious environment;"   *Art. 1.6* —"To alleviate poverty and narrow the development gap within ASEAN through mutual assistance and cooperation;"   *Art. 1.12*—"To strengthen cooperation in building a safe, secure and drug-free environment for the peoples of ASEAN."
Art. 14.1—"… ASEAN shall establish an ASEAN human rights body."   *Art. 14.2*—"This ASEAN human rights body shall operate in accordance with the terms of reference to be determined by the ASEAN Foreign Ministers Meeting."
Art. 1.8—"To respond effectively, in accordance with the principle of comprehensive security, to all forms of threats, transnational crimes and transboundary challenges;"   *Art. 1.9*—"To promote sustainable development so as to ensure the protection of the region's environment, the sustainability of its natural resources, the preservation of its cultural heritage and the high quality of life of its peoples."

Sources: Solidarity for Asian People's Advocacy, *Submission on Political and Human Security to the ASEAN EPG on the ASEAN Charter*, 17 April 2006, Ubud, Bali, <http://seaca.net/viewArticle.php?aID=945>; *Report of the Eminent Persons Group on the ASEAN Charter*, <http://www.aseansec.org/19247.pdf >; and "Charter of the Association of Southeast Asian Nations," <http://www.aseansec.org/21069.pdf>.

Civil Society and the Charter: Influential or Not?

An answer to the question of civil society's influence on the Charter must begin by acknowledging the diversity of the nonstate sector in Southeast Asia. Broadly speaking, two sorts of civil society groups exist in the region: "traditional" organizations such as academic think tanks and private-sector businesses on the one hand, and so-called "alternative" groupings, such as NGOs and grassroots movements, on the other hand. Groups in the latter set tend to be fragmented. Unlike the more institutionalized traditional groups, they may not have developed efficient lobbying strategies.

SAPA belongs in the second category. Table 2.1 features its suggestions for the Charter—rather than those made by other such "alternative" or "people-centered" groupings—because of the sheer extent of SAPA's effort to lobby the Charter-drafting process. The size of its investment in the process may in part explain the intensity of SAPA's eventual disappointment with what the HTLF actually wrote and the heads of government actually signed.

In Myanmar (Burma) in August 2007, demonstrations broke out against the military junta there. They soon grew to a scale not seen in that authoritarian state for nearly twenty years. Beginning in September, the junta cracked down. Some protesters were killed; many more were arrested and imprisoned. Acts of repression by the state continued in October. Images of Buddhist monks being brutalized sped through cyberspace, triggering outrage.

It was in this highly charged context that on 7 November 2007 the final text of the ASEAN Charter was somehow "leaked"—nearly two weeks before it was due to be unveiled and signed by ASEAN's leaders at their summit in Singapore. The document was quickly posted on the Internet and emailed around the world.

SAPA read the text and, on the eve of the 20 November summit, issued a series of demands. "In view of the shortcomings of the Charter *and the lack of meaningful civil society participation in its drafting* (which are undeniably related)," SAPA's Working Group on ASEAN called "for the postponement of the signing of the Charter until political transformation can be realised in Burma."[56] Instead, the prime minister of Myanmar, General Soe Win, joined the other nine heads of ASEAN government in Singapore, where the Charter was duly signed. SAPA then insisted that the signed document should be ratified "through a process of popular referendum," and announced its support for "drawing up a 'People's Charter' in time for next year's ASEAN Summit in Bangkok."[57]

---

[56] Solidarity for Asian People's Advocacy, "Bloody Hands on the Charter: Shame!" 20 November 2007, <http://www.asiasapa.org/index.php?option=com_content&task=view&id=72&Itemid=43>, italics added.

[57] Solidarity for Asian People's Advocacy, "Civil Society Organisations Come Together to Criticise Failings of the ASEAN Charter," 23 November 2007, <http://www.asiasapa.org/index.php?option=com_content&task=view&id=74&Itemid=42>.

As if to confirm, from a very different perspective, SAPA's claim that the views of civil society were not taken into account in the drafting process, a high-ranking ASEAN official who had been closely involved in preparing the Charter went so far as to claim that no official consultations between state and nonstate actors had taken place. According to this person, any similarity of wording or substance between SAPA's input and the EPG Report was purely coincidental.

Observers with close links to the EPG claim that its report was mainly based on what was called the "Alatas paper," a draft presented by one of the group's most proactive and vocal members, Ali Alatas, who had been minister of foreign affairs in Indonesia. Like nearly all the members of the EPG, Alatas was a former official. The Task Force, in contrast, was made up entirely of then-current officials. This difference helps to explain why the final Charter failed to fulfill the liberal promise of the EPG Report. Retired officials could be creatively liberal; sitting ones could not. No longer required to toe the official line, EPG members could give bold advice. Under discipline by the state and beholden to its policies, HLTF members had to be realistic and to accept compromises for the sake of writing a text to which all ten member governments could, at least in principle, agree.

Policy Scholars and the Charter: Regional Effects of National Reform

This is not to say that civil society had no influence at all. Notable among NGOs in the "traditional" category, for example, was ASEAN-ISIS, the previously mentioned Track II network of security studies institutes. Unlike the "alternative" network represented by SAPA, the policy intellectuals in ASEAN-ISIS were on familiar terms with officials in their respective national governments. ASEAN-ISIS did sponsor the formation of an affiliated organization, the ASEAN People's Assembly (APA), in 2000. But although APA, like SAPA, wants ASEAN to be more relevant in the lives of ordinary Southeast Asians, the Assembly's positions have been somewhat more centrist and less radical—less clearly "alternative"—than those favored by Solidarity activists. And ASEAN-ISIS certainly has helped to shape ASEAN's visions for the future, including the idea of an ASEAN Community, which is featured in the final text of the Charter.

In its own input into the drafting process, ASEAN-ISIS urged that a key goal of ASEAN, one that "must be included" in the Charter, should be "to develop and consolidate democracy and the rule of law, and [encourage] respect for human rights and fundamental freedoms."[58] In effect, Article 1.7 of the Charter (as quoted in Table 2.1) did just that. Observers consulted in

---

[58] ASEAN Institutes of Strategic and International Studies (ASEAN-ISIS), The ASEAN Charter. Memorandum 1/2006 (Bali, Indonesia, 18 April 2006), unpublished.

the course of researching this chapter also agreed that ASEAN-ISIS had been instrumental in shaping the Association's NTS agenda.

In the run-up to the Charter, two ASEAN-ISIS members, the Centre for International and Strategic Studies (CSIS) in Jakarta and the Institute for Strategic and Development Studies (ISDS) in Manila, pushed hard for the document to support democratic values and a mechanism for human rights. The two think tanks managed to get at least silent consent from those institutes inside ASEAN-ISIS that were less than eager to insert such language into the Charter. Even those from institutes in Laos and Vietnam did not object. (Myanmar is not represented in ASEAN-ISIS.) Indeed, in May 2007 in Manila, at an ASEAN-ISIS conference to examine the establishment of a human rights mechanism in ASEAN, the Vietnamese and (to a markedly lesser extent) the Laotian delegates joined the discussion proactively, constructively, and with previously unknown openness.

CSIS and ISDS played key roles in these conversations. A Vietnamese who had been a frequent participant in ASEAN-ISIS meetings later said that the role of these two institutes had been decisive "for getting human rights in the ASEAN Charter."[59]

That CSIS and ISDS were located respectively in Indonesia and the Philippines was no coincidence. It is a logical consequence of domestic political change that the two most democratic states in Southeast Asia in 2007 should have been driving forces in the quest for a regional commitment to democracy and human rights. In the late 1990s, then-democratic Thailand had established itself as a champion of regional institutional reform. But the coup in Bangkok in 2006 curbed the ability and willingness of the Thai authorities to speak up for democracy in ASEAN. "Thailand, given its current political crisis, has been reluctant to speak out," wrote one informed observer, "even though it has stronger views on human security and the enhanced role played by civil society organisations."[60] Thailand's military junta even expressed opposition to the inclusion of democratic principles in the Charter because the EPG had disavowed transfers of power by undemocratic means, such as military coups.

The reformist pressure that the Indonesian and Philippine governments mounted on initially reluctant member states in the HLTF, and in other intergovernmental negotiations on the Charter, was probably unprecedented in ASEAN's history. Vietnam, Laos, and (obviously) the Myanmar junta in particular wished to avoid any reference to human rights in the Charter. Nor did they relish the prospect of the Charter mandating the creation of a body to protect human rights.

At first, the conservatives won. The first HLTF draft of the Charter made no reference to a human rights watchdog. On the eve of the ASEAN ministerial

---

[59] Author interview, Hanoi, September 2007.

[60] Kavi Chongkittavorn, "Limited Time to Salvage the ASEAN Charter," *The Nation*, 11 June 2007.

meeting in July 2007, however, Jakarta and Manila managed to achieve approval for the clause on the establishment of an "ASEAN human rights body" in a compromise linked to a different matter. The quid for this quo was an understanding that the Charter would not introduce majority voting as a way of making ASEAN decisions. Between a human rights mechanism and any departure from consensus-based decision-making, Hanoi, Vientiane, and Yangon (Rangoon) feared the latter prospect more.

The promotion of democracy and NTS has emerged as a major rallying point in Indonesian foreign policy. Rizal Sukma, a CSIS policy scholar and a co-author of this book, has been among the influential voices in his country's "traditional" civil society sector. "The inclusion of human rights and democratic principles in the charter is non-negotiable," he said in 2007. "Indonesia must fight for it because we will have no basis for protecting people's rights if the principles are not included in the charter."[61]

The director-general for ASEAN affairs in Indonesia's foreign ministry, Dian Triansyah Djani, backed Sukma by stressing that Indonesia was continuing to insist on the inclusion of articles on human rights and democratic values in the ASEAN Charter. "The substance of the ASEAN Charter," said Djani, "will not be far from the recommendation of the Eminent Persons Group, which has highlighted the importance of including human rights and democratic values in the charter." Ikrar Nusa Bakti, of the Indonesian Institute of Sciences, added that it was time Indonesia, the biggest country in the region, took the lead in fighting for values that it upheld and practiced. "I think Indonesia now is the most democratic country in ASEAN," he said. "We should not let ourselves be bogged down by other ASEAN members."

Clearly, democratic Indonesia's new approach to the conduct of foreign policy reflects domestic political agendas, and is less sensitive to ASEAN solidarity than it was when the country was under authoritarian rule. Long gone are the days of Suharto's New Order regime, when Indonesia's Department of Foreign Affairs was de facto subordinated to the armed forces, and senior ambassadorial appointments went to generals rather than career diplomats.

Large Ends, Small Means, Modest Results: National Sovereignty versus Regional Action

ASEAN has made impressive verbal strides in addressing security threats. The changing discourse on security has been evident particularly in initiatives aimed at counterterrorism and transnational crime. In May 2003, a long-standing taboo was broken when ASEAN adopted a road map to form a regionwide human rights commission. Despite its nonbinding nature (in customary ASEAN fashion),

---

[61] Statements quoted in this and the next paragraph were made at a roundtable discussion in Jakarta, as cited in "Indonesia Holds Ground on ASEAN Charter," *Jakarta Post*, 15 June 2007.

the road map seemed to mark the crucial first step toward addressing the issue of human rights in a regional context. Four and a half years later, however, the establishment of a "human rights body" was still, in the text of the Charter, purely exhortatory—at a time when the brutal repression of peaceful dissent in Myanmar had made the matter nothing short of urgent.

More than rhetorical is the Southeast Asia Regional Centre for Counter-Terrorism (SEARCCT) in Kuala Lumpur. It organizes training programs, workshops, and seminars to help the region implement actual measures against terrorism.[62] As yet, the practical impact on regional policy is modest. "This is a center for training[,] not intelligence-sharing," a senior SEARCCT officer has admitted. "The latter would be difficult to achieve because the national intelligence agencies of the ASEAN states sometimes refuse to share information."[63]

Having already agreed on a plan of action to combat transnational crime, ASEAN members signed a Convention on Counter-Terrorism in January 2007. In a drive against terrorism, drug trafficking, money laundering, and other cross-border crimes—all NTS threats—the agreement aimed to reduce legal impediments to cooperation in tackling such problems. Among the most successful examples of emerging cooperation on NTS issues is the coordinated fight against piracy, including multilateral efforts to ensure maritime security in the Straits of Malacca.

These efforts include an "eye in the sky" initiative. The program involves shared aerial surveillance of potentially criminal acts in the Straits by all three riparian states—Indonesia, Singapore, and Malaysia. "In practical terms," however, this simply means that "personnel from these three countries are in the same aircraft monitoring the security of the Straits," to quote a senior official in Malaysia's Ministry of Defence.[64] In addition to intra-ASEAN activities, ASEAN and China have identified priorities for cooperation against transnational dangers such as terrorism, sea piracy, human and drug trafficking, and cross-border economic crime.

As of 2007, all institutional agreements regarding NTS were still nonbinding in nature. Sovereignty issues continued to constrain implementation. It is telling in this context that ASEAN members usually avoid the word "joint" when referring to cross-border cooperation. They prefer the term "coordinated activities," because the term "joint" might hint at a supranational approach—which would be controversial—while "coordination" is safely similar to mere

---

[62] Initially, SEARCCT was presented not as a regional initiative but as a Malaysian one. According to a 2003 statement of Datuk N. Parameswaran, the Malaysian foreign ministry deputy secretary, "The centre is a 100 percent Malaysian effort. It does not involve other countries." Quoted in BBC Monitoring International Reports, "ASEAN Regional Forum in Malaysia Talks of Shared Intelligence to Fight Terror," 23 March 2003.

[63] Author interview, Kuala Lumpur, 25 October 2005.

[64] Author interview, Kuala Lumpur, 25 October 2005.

cooperation. Sensitivities of this sort inhibit ASEAN's ability to enforce policy decisions and to implement them successfully. "At an operational level," a Malaysian government official has admitted, "we [in ASEAN] are still not clear as to how we can effectively and efficiently address nontraditional security challenges in a coordinated fashion."[65]

If one is to believe the data circulated by the RAND Corporation, terror in Southeast Asia has increased significantly in frequency since the Cold War. The RAND terrorism chronology counts ninety international terrorist attacks in the region of Southeast Asia and Oceania during the period 1968–85. However, from 1986 to 2002, international terrorist attacks in the region more than doubled, to 194.[66] ASEAN has never played any role in response to violence in Mindanao, in Aceh, in Southern Thailand, or for that matter in any other conflict-damaged place in Southeast Asia.[67]

This may seem surprising. The Association has, after all, been rhetorically active against threats to NTS. For example, the fourth ASEAN Chiefs of Army Multilateral Meeting (ACAMM), convened in 2003 in Kuala Lumpur, called for solidarity among the armies of member countries to fight terrorism in the interests of the region. Nine ASEAN countries were represented, and all nine army chiefs agreed that the ACAMM should work to forge stronger ties among ASEAN armies, including networking among ASEAN military intelligence agencies and exchanging ideas about how best to combat terrorists. Yet no specific actions were agreed upon.[68]

This approach is typical of ASEAN. It reflects the organization's core norms and preferences: nonbinding decisions achieved by avoiding conflict and building consensus. The result could be called "soft institutionalization."

A good illustration of this "ASEAN Way" and its ineffectiveness in addressing NTS challenges can be seen in how the Association has dealt with perceived threats of terrorism. The 2001 "ASEAN Declaration on Joint Action to Counter Terrorism" committed the member states, in sweeping terms, "to counter, prevent and suppress all forms of terrorist acts in accordance with the Charter of the United Nations and other international law, especially taking into account the importance of all relevant UN resolutions."[69] But the

---

[65] Author interview, Kuala Lumpur, 17 April 2006.

[66] Niklas Swanström and Emma Björnehed, "Conflict Resolution of Terrorist Conflicts in Southeast Asia," *Terrorism and Political Violence* 16, no. 2 (2004), 329.

[67] On the dynamics of these conflicts, including the question of whether or not "terrorists" are at work, see Jörn Dosch, *The Changing Dynamics of Southeast Asian Politics* (Boulder, CO, and London: Lynne Rienner Publishers, 2007), chapter 3.

[68] "Armies Against Terror," *Asian Defence and Diplomacy* 10, no. 10 (October 2003), 47–49.

[69] ASEAN Declaration on Joint Action to Counter Terrorism," Bandar Seri Begawan, 5 November 2001, <http://www.aseansec.org/5620.htm>.

Declaration's comprehensive agenda prescribed no specific institutionalized way of implementing such a broad obligation.

To be fair, ASEAN has established a regional framework for fighting transnational crime, and has adopted an "action plan" that outlines a regional strategy to prevent, control, and neutralize that nonmilitary threat. Nevertheless, the Association's overall response to the more controversial matter of terrorism, especially insofar as Muslims may be involved, has mirrored its traditional policy of not operationalizing the responsibilities that it places on its members. The action in ASEAN's action plans depends on voluntary participation.

The cautious approach of some ASEAN states to anti-terror cooperation is also prominently reflected in the "U.S.-ASEAN Joint Declaration for Cooperation to Combat International Terrorism."[70] Its text includes a paragraph that Washington was initially unwilling to accept because it committed the United States, as well as ASEAN, to "recognizing the principles of sovereign equality, territorial integrity and non-intervention in the domestic affairs of other states." The paragraph was added to the text at the request of Indonesia and Vietnam, whose governments feared that, absent such language, the Declaration could lead to the eventual basing of American troops in Southeast Asia.

In sum, ASEAN's insistence on consensus ultimately reduced both of these declarations against terrorism to the lowest common denominator—what the Association's least eager member was willing to accept. Lacking a consensus on how exactly to define terrorism, and because the issue touched on the sensitive matter of national sovereignty, ASEAN could not in these texts bind its membership to follow through on the commitments they declared. Nor is this pattern unique to counterterrorism. In rhetoric, ASEAN has never failed to address the latest NTS issue—the 1997 Asian financial crisis, the persisting haze from Indonesia, illegal migration, and so on—but not one of these verbal initiatives has been fully implemented.

Worth noting here is another instance of this pattern: avian influenza. On the one hand, the ASEAN states generally agree that bird flu can be tackled only through close cross-border cooperation. The states accordingly signed a regional action plan that was supposed to define a policy framework to contain the disease. They even began setting up a regional surveillance and alert network. But serious concerns about the effectiveness of the scheme soon came to the fore. In diplomatic language, ASEAN's secretary-general at the time, Ong Keng Yong, acknowledged that "it will still take some time to perfect the system," and "there are still pockets of inadequacy, especially in terms of getting bureaucracy in all different departments mobilized."[71]

---

[70] "U.S.-ASEAN Joint Declaration on Combating Terrorism," Washington DC, August 1, 2002, <http://www.state.gov/p/eap/rls/ot/12428.htm>.

[71] Ong Keng Yong, address to an Asia Society luncheon, Hong Kong, 1 November 2005, quoted in "ASEAN Sees Close Cooperation on Bird Flu, Disaster Relief, Crime," *Voice of America,* 1 November 2005.

Ong expressed confidence that ASEAN would ultimately be able to overcome these difficulties. But he also admitted that some member states were not being transparent in releasing information about the evidence of bird flu, and that outbreaks in remote areas were not being reported quickly enough.[72] Most crucially, ASEAN lacked funds to compensate farmers whose poultry flocks were being killed as a precaution. As a result, many farmers in affected areas were reluctant to report outbreaks, and even hid sick chickens because their livelihood depended on them.

Few objective observers would challenge the assessment that ASEAN lacks substance. Beyond the political rhetoric and the admirable but nonbinding declarations and agreements, ASEAN has neither the political will nor the institutional means to complete the sequence whereby concerns are translated into strategies, strategies into policies, and policies into actual practice.

Conclusion

Security, democracy, and regionalism are interdependent. During the first two or even three decades of ASEAN's existence, Southeast Asia's small political elite operated within autocratic or, at best, semidemocratic environments. Hence, they were able to follow and implement narrowly defined national interests in a manner largely unconstrained and unchallenged by competing political actors, civil society groups, or critical media.

Political liberalization and democratization have fostered greater openness and also more complexity in the making of foreign and security policy. Electoral competition, the stepped-up influence of parliaments and nonstate actors such as NGOs, greater transparency, and wider access to more independent sources of information all now play a part. In consequence, in nearly all the ASEAN states (Myanmar being the key exception), security agendas and discourses have broadened and deepened in scope and participation. Nontraditional or human security has become a legitimate topic for discussion and debate.

These liberalizing changes in the institutional setting for political decision-making have made the region's regimes more accountable in the previously restricted realm of security policy. A growing number of governmental actors not in the executive branch and of actors not in government at all are identifying and responding to security challenges. New liberal spaces have been opened—windows of opportunity for nonstate actors to lobby for more democracy and greater attention to NTS inside ASEAN. These involvements would have been unthinkable only a decade ago.

But not everything has changed. Most national security doctrines in Southeast Asia still rest on traditional, realist, state-based assumptions. The

---

[72] Ong Keng Yong, quoted in "ASEAN Sees Close Cooperation on Bird Flu, Disaster Relief, Crime."

political role of civil society organizations remains limited. And four decades of ASEAN solidarity have not fully erased lingering tensions and sensitivities among member states. Such obstacles have hindered the implementation of almost all regional security agreements. The abundance of security discourses in ASEAN is matched only by the absence of effective measures to implement them.

In short, in Southeast Asia, national sovereignty still rules.

INSTITUTIONAL REFORM:
ONE CHARTER, THREE COMMUNITIES,
MANY CHALLENGES

Termsak Chalermpalanupap[1]

ASEAN Secretariat
Indonesia

The Association of Southeast Asian Nations (ASEAN) was born in Bangkok, Thailand, in the heart of Southeast Asia, in 1967, more than four decades ago. Since then the organization has doubled its membership from five to ten Southeast Asian states.[2] It has, in effect, expanded to match the region. As of December 2007, Timor-Leste—which only gained full independence in May 2002—was the only Southeast Asian nation that remained outside ASEAN. In 2007 it was actively preparing to join ASEAN within five years, by 2012.

ASEAN celebrated its fortieth founding anniversary in 2007. The celebration presented an opportunity to look back on the extraordinary evolution of both the region and the organization, including the latter's remarkable growth. But it was also an opportunity for introspection about current conditions and future challenges. One could thus credit ASEAN's past success in expanding its membership to encompass the "SEA" in its name, while at the same time highlighting the need for the organization to deepen its role in solving regional problems and to strengthen its ability to meet the new demands of the twenty-first century.

ASEAN's pivotal achievement in 2007 was the ASEAN Charter, which was signed by the heads of state or government in all of its member states, at the Thirteenth ASEAN Summit, in Singapore on 20 November. How should we understand this unprecedented event? From what concerns did it arise? What challenges does ASEAN face? What organizational priorities should animate the Association on the threshold of its next forty years of evolution, if indeed it survives to celebrate its eightieth anniversary in 2047?

---

[1] Views expressed in this paper are the personal opinions of the author in his capacity as a "citizen" of ASEAN and do not necessarily reflect those of the Association or any of its members or employees.

[2] Indonesia, Malaysia, the Philippines, Singapore, and Thailand founded ASEAN on 8 August 1967. Brunei Darussalam joined in 1984, Vietnam in 1995, Laos and Myanmar in 1997, and Cambodia in 1999.

This chapter addresses these questions. The chapter opens with an overview of ASEAN's historical development as an organization for regional cooperation. It proceeds to explore rationales for, and steps undertaken toward, building an ASEAN Community and adopting the ASEAN Charter. Particular attention is paid to three key organizational projects: (1) an ASEAN Political-Security Community, related to questions of diversity and democracy; (2) an ASEAN Economic Community, focused on the member economies' linkages with one another and with the rest of the world; and (3) an ASEAN Socio-Cultural Community, to tackle both the limited awareness of the organization among ordinary Southeast Asians and the region's security. The chapter then reviews a series of challenges that the Association faces, including organizational overload, resource scarcity, and how ASEAN should balance the principle of nonintervention in member states' affairs with its collective regional "responsibility to cooperate" in tackling transnational issues that affect people throughout Southeast Asia. A concluding section revisits and assesses the ASEAN Charter in the light of these priorities and concerns.

My argument is this: ASEAN's fortieth anniversary is a time for celebration—but not complacency. ASEAN needs to reinvent itself. The Association is on record as planning to build an ASEAN Community by 2015. Yet in 2007 its "operational software" and "organizational hardware" were not up to that task. ASEAN was designed for confidence-building, not community-building.

ASEAN urgently needs to do three things: (1) to make sure that its visions and plans for the future are sufficiently clear, specific, and feasible to ensure effective cooperation and timely implementation by its member states; (2) to reform its organizational structure and procedures so that it can effectively and efficiently foster a genuine regional community in Southeast Asia; and (3) to strengthen its material and human resources on behalf of that same community-building task. It is in this context that an ASEAN Charter can help the Association prepare itself to develop, by 2015, a meaningful ASEAN community.

Before elaborating on this argument, it will be helpful to review briefly ASEAN's evolution, and thereby set the stage for a consideration of the ASEAN Community and Charter as manifestations of regionalism in Southeast Asia.

Forty Years and Counting: ASEAN Evolves

Although a full history of ASEAN is beyond my purpose here, four aspects of its evolution are worth highlighting: the increasing use of summits to raise ASEAN's profile and commit member states to cooperation programs and plans of action from the top leadership down; the expansion of the Association beyond foreign relations to encompass virtually all sectors of government policy; the birth and growth of the ASEAN Secretariat; and the development of bilateral and multilateral relations with a widening range of countries outside Southeast Asia.

For nearly its first decade, no summits were held. But in the wake of ASEAN's inaugural summit in 1976, meetings among the top leaders of the member states grew more frequent and more formal. Meanwhile, the Association innovated summits in various formats with non-Southeast Asian heads of state or government as well. By 2007 these arrangements included summits of ASEAN Plus One (with Japan, South Korea, and India); ASEAN Plus Three, or APT (with China, Japan, and South Korea); and since 2005, an East Asia Summit (EAS) comprising ASEAN, Australia, China, India, Japan, New Zealand, and South Korea, has also been convened.[3]

In ASEAN's early years, the Association conducted its business mainly at periodic meetings of the foreign ministers of the member states. By 2007, however, the scope of regionalism had been enlarged across entities, spanning

---

[3] After gathering for the first time in Bali in 1976, ASEAN's leaders met in Kuala Lumpur at the Second Summit in 1977 to celebrate the Association's tenth anniversary. In 1987, they met in Manila at the Third Summit to mark the twentieth anniversary. At their Fourth Summit, in Singapore in 1992, the leaders agreed to meet every three years. At their Fifth Summit, in Bangkok in 1995, they agreed to convene an informal summit in each of the two years between formal summits. Accordingly, the 1st Informal Summit was held in Jakarta in 1996; the 2nd Informal Summit in Kuala Lumpur in 1997; the Sixth Summit in Hanoi in 1998; the 3rd Informal Summit in Manila in 1999; and the 4th Informal Summit in Singapore in 2000.

At the 4th Informal Summit, ASEAN leaders agreed to meet annually in summits that would no longer be distinguished as informal or formal. To encourage free-flowing and fruitful discussion, summit ceremonies, preparatory meetings, and paperwork were to be kept to a necessary minimum.

Summitry with non-ASEAN leaders dates from 1977. With increasing frequency and coverage, ASEAN leaders met, in conjunction with their own summits, with their extraregional counterparts. These included Australia, Japan, and New Zealand in 1977; Japan in 1987; and Cambodia, Laos, and Myanmar (then not yet members) in 1995 and again in 1996.

The ASEAN Plus Three framework has evolved rapidly since its inception at ASEAN's 2nd Informal Summit, in Kuala Lumpur in 1997. On that occasion the leaders of China, Japan, and South Korea were invited collectively to join their ASEAN counterparts in the first-ever summit of APT, and separately in the ASEAN Plus One format. Both formats were used again at ASEAN's Sixth Summit, in 1998. At these ASEAN summits the Association's leaders announced, respectively, ASEAN's Vision 2020 in 1997, and a Hanoi Plan of Action in 1998 toward realizing the Vision.

APT summits were held annually thereafter through the eleventh such gathering in Singapore, on 20 November 2007, held in conjunction with that year's Thirteenth ASEAN Summit. By then the APT framework had become active across various domains, and especially on matters of regional economy and finance. At the Singapore summit, APT leaders issued their Second Joint Statement on East Asia Cooperation to chart the future direction of the APT for the next ten years.

The youngest such arrangement is the EAS. As of December 2007 its sixteen participating states had met annually three times in conjunction with ASEAN summits, including their third gathering in Singapore, on 21 November 2007. Russia and the European Union (EU) are known to have a keen interest in joining the EAS.

twenty-eight distinct ministerial sectors, including economics, finance, culture, society, and the environment. In 2006, for example, ASEAN ministerial meetings were inaugurated on defense and education.[4] In support of ASEAN's summit-level and ministerial agendas, member-state officials regularly gather in senior-officials meetings (SOMs), committees, subcommittees, and task forces, among other formats. In 2007 ASEAN had 110 such official bodies, not including those of an ad-hoc or project-specific nature.

The expansion from five to ten member states and the proliferation of official organizations, committees, and meetings have multiplied and intensified demands for leadership and coordination within ASEAN. The 1967 Bangkok Declaration that established ASEAN laid down only a modest structure: an annual gathering of foreign ministers, called the ASEAN Ministerial Meeting (AMM); an ASEAN Standing Committee, chaired in rotation by a member-state foreign minister and comprising the member-state ambassadors to that chairing country; an ASEAN National Secretariat in each member state, headed by an official at the director-general level (an ASEAN DG); and the possibility of forming specialized committees on particular topics.

Turbulence in Southeast Asia in 1967 and the failure of previous attempts at regional organization[5] clouded the future of another such experiment. Accordingly, those who signed the Bangkok Declaration that created ASEAN were only cautiously optimistic, and they did not establish a Secretariat for the new grouping they had just founded. Only nine years later, at the First ASEAN Summit, in Bali in 1976, hosted by Indonesian President Soeharto, did the members agree to create an ASEAN Secretariat. Philippine President Ferdinand Marcos at first suggested Manila as the location for the Secretariat, but then deferred to Soeharto's offer to host it in Jakarta. The First ASEAN Summit agreed on the latter site.

In Jakarta from 1976 to 1981, the ASEAN Secretariat was housed in a building belonging to Indonesia's Department of Foreign Affairs. Since 1981 the Secretariat has had its own seven-story building, inaugurated and given to the Association by Indonesia in a ceremony led by the then president Soeharto.

---

[4] One purpose of the inaugural ASEAN Defense Ministers Meeting in 2006 was to plan for an ASEAN Political-Security Community. Prior to that year's ASEAN Education Ministers Meeting, the ministers of education had met informally on the sidelines of their participation in the Southeast Asian Ministers of Education Organization (SEAMEO). SEAMEO was formed in 1965, two years before ASEAN's birth. As of 2007, SEAMEO's members consisted of all ten ASEAN states plus Timor-Leste, with Australia, New Zealand, and several European countries as associate members and Japan as a partner.

[5] Malaya, the Philippines, and Thailand formed the Association of Southeast Asia in 1961, but it was never more than embryonic. In 1963, Indonesia, Malaya, and the Philippines launched another grouping, Maphilindo, but it soon fell prey to conflicts between its members.

Indonesian officials like to cite this history as proof of their country's strong commitment to ASEAN.

The Secretariat's staff started small: a secretary-general (SG) and seven officers seconded from the five member governments and assisted by a staff of 26 Indonesians. The head of the office was not the chief of the Association, but merely the "Secretary-General of the ASEAN Secretariat."[6]

In 1992 the Secretariat was restructured. Its chief officer was renamed Secretary-General of ASEAN and given ministerial status. Henceforth, in principle, the SG would be selected by ASEAN foreign ministers at their annual AMM and appointed by the heads of state or government on the basis of merit, for a tenure of five years, renewable by them should the AMM so recommend.

In practice, there is an unwritten understanding among ASEAN foreign ministers—the AMM—that the member governments, in alphabetical rotation by country name in English, will take turns nominating one of their own citizens to become SG for one five-year term. In keeping with this practice, from 1993 through 2007, ASEAN had three SGs: Dato Ajit Singh, Malaysia (1993–97); Rodolfo C. Severino Jr., Philippines (1998–2002); and Ong Keng Yong, Singapore (2003–07). The fourth, as approved by the 2007 AMM and appointed at the Thirteenth ASEAN Summit, is former foreign minister Surin Pitsuwan, Thailand (2008–12).

Dr. Surin's tenure as SG marked the first time that a veteran politician with international stature held the post. He received his M.A. and Ph.D. in political science and Middle Eastern studies from Harvard University. He was deputy foreign minister of Thailand between 1992 and 1995, and foreign minister from 1997 to 2001. He was deputy leader of the Democrat Party, Thailand's oldest political party. His international experience included serving on the UN Commission on Human Security until 2003; advising the International Commission on Intervention and State Sovereignty between 1999 and 2001; and participating on the Advisory Board of the International Crisis Group and the International Advisory Board of the Council on Foreign Relations in New York.[7]

---

[6] The men who held this office in 1976–92 were H. R. Dharsono, Indonesia (1976–78); Umarjadi Notowijono, Indonesia (February–June 1978); Datuk Ali bin Adbullah, Malaysia (1978–80); Narciso G. Reyes, Philippines (1980–82); Chan Kai Yau, Singapore (1982–84); Phan Wannamethee, Thailand (1984–86); Roderick Yong, Brunei Darussalam (1986–89, a three-year term); and Rusli Noor, Indonesia (1989–92, a three-year term).

[7] Mr. Ong Keng Yong, prior to his own appointment as the ASEAN SG, had been press secretary to the prime minister of Singapore. He received his M.A. degree in Arab studies from Georgetown University. Mr. Severino had been the undersecretary for foreign affairs of the Philippines before he retired to become the ASEAN SG. He received his M.A. in international relations from Johns Hopkins University. Prior to his own retirement to take up the position, Dato Ajit Singh (now Tan Sri Ajit Singh) had been DG of ASEAN-Malaysia and ambassador to Germany. He received his B.A. in history from the University of Malaya.

Also for the first time in the national selection of a nominee to become ASEAN SG, Dr. Surin was chosen by the Thai government in an open recruitment exercise. The other shortlisted candidates were retired veterans of the Thai foreign ministry, so the choice of Dr. Surin was certainly deliberate. (Singapore had been the first to send a senior bureaucrat still on active duty.)

The growth of ASEAN fueled the growth of its administrative hub. The larger and more complex the administration of ASEAN became, the more essential it was that the Association be led by a dynamic person with a good knowledge of information technology. The SG must possess exceptional intellectual capability and mental acuity in tracking key decisions and developments while remaining sensitive to the delicate nuances of national positions on a multitude of issues before ASEAN at any given time.

In the Secretariat's fiscal year 2007–08, its personnel consisted of SG Ong Keng Yong; two deputy SGs (one Indonesian, one Cambodian); sixty officers (recruited from all member states except Brunei Darussalam);[8] and some 160 locally recruited and mostly Indonesian staff.

The final aspect of ASEAN's organizational evolution worth noting here is the multiplication of its relations with the rest of the world. Extraregional summitry accounts for only a small, if prominent, portion of these interactions. Participating countries in the APT process, for example, meet periodically at ministerial and senior official levels to consider a variety of sectoral concerns. As of 2007, ASEAN maintained regular engagements around the world with eleven designated Dialogue Partners (Australia, Canada, China, the EU, India, Japan, New Zealand, Russia, South Korea, the United Nations Development Program (UNDP), and the United States) and one Sectoral Dialogue Partner (Pakistan).

Noteworthy, too, in this context is the ASEAN-China Free Trade Area. In 2008, various comparable trading arrangements were under negotiation with China, India, Japan, Australia and New Zealand, South Korea, and the EU, and plans were being made to explore the possibility of opening such talks with the United States and Canada as well. Further evidence of ASEAN's near-global presence could be found in the ASEAN Regional Forum (ARF) and the Asia-Europe Meeting (ASEM), in which the ASEAN ten interact with seventeen and thirty extraregional countries, respectively, on security and interregional affairs.[9]

ASEAN members, together with their counterparts from China, Japan, and South Korea, engage Latin American countries in the annual meeting of foreign ministers under the Forum for East Asia and Latin America Cooperation

---

[8] Nationals of Brunei Darussalam seldom apply for any job in the ASEAN Secretariat. Two senior foreign affairs officials from the tiny sultanate (whose population numbers about 370,000) have served as deputy SG; and one was openly recruited to serve as an assistant director in economic affairs.

[9] Sri Lanka became the twenty-seventh participant to join the ARF in August 2007, enlarging the Forum's non-ASEAN membership to seventeen states.

(FEALAC). ASEAN members, led by Indonesia, also interact with African countries in the Asia-Africa Summit framework. Last but not least is the Asia Cooperation Dialogue (ACD), which Thailand initiated with strong support from ASEAN, China, Japan, and South Korea.

At the secretariat-to-secretariat level, ASEAN has good working relations and cooperation with its counterparts in various regions: the Economic Cooperation Organization (ECO, based in Tehran), the Shanghai Cooperation Organization (SCO, based in Beijing), the Gulf Cooperation Council (GCC, based in Riyadh, Saudi Arabia), the South Asian Association for Regional Cooperation (SAARC, based in Kathmandu, Nepal), and the Pacific Island Forum (PIF, based in Suva, Fiji).

It is no exaggeration to say that ASEAN and its members are engaging virtually the whole world in dialogue and cooperation.

Forming an ASEAN Community: Six Reasons Why

Since the early 2000s, creating an ASEAN Community has been a priority item on the Association's agenda. Why do the member states want to do this? At least six related reasons—priorities—come to mind.

First, although no ASEAN member has ever gone to war against another member, ASEAN's leaders—the heads of state or government—cannot take that happy condition for granted. They know that regional peace and security are not self-generating. They want therefore to intensify their cooperation to ensure ongoing stability in the region. They know that if ASEAN is allowed to weaken, its members are likely to seek security guarantees elsewhere, in alliances with outside protectors. Southeast Asian states would become again, as they were in the Cold War, the pawns of bigger powers. An ASEAN Political-Security Community[10] can help prevent such a predicament.

Second, an ASEAN Community would encourage economic competitiveness. Individually, the member economies are mostly small and developing. Collectively and cooperatively, they can become a sizable regional entity capable of dealing on a more equal footing with major economic powers. As Table 3.1 shows, the combined GDP of ASEAN members in 2005 was about four-fifths the size of China's GDP, slightly larger than India's, about one-fifth of Japan's, and about one-fifteenth that of the United States.

An ASEAN Economic Community with a single regional market would benefit all of ASEAN's members and peoples by enlarging the economic pie. Without such a regional economic entity, most of Southeast Asia's national economies would remain small, uncompetitive, and disadvantaged in this age of global competition.

---

[10] This pillar of the ASEAN Community was originally called the ASEAN Security Community, or ASC, and is referred to as such elsewhere in this book. In effect, however, the ASEAN Charter that was signed in November 2007 renamed the ASC the ASEAN Political-Security Community, or APSC. The latter term and abbreviation are therefore used throughout this chapter.

Table 3.1 Economic Indicators for ASEAN Members (Individually and Collectively), China, India, Japan, the United States, and Timor-Leste

	GDP (US$ billions) 2005	GDP in PPP (US$ billions) 2005	Exports (US$ billions) 2003	Net FDI inflows (US$ millions) 2003	Competitiveness ranking (by WEF) 2007
Brunei	6.4	17.5	4.6	289	not ranked
Cambodia	6.2	38.4	5.0	381	110th
Indonesia	287.2	847.6	93.6	6,107	54th
Laos	2.9	21.1	0.5	28	not ranked
Malaysia	130.3	275.8	188.5	3,965	21st
Myanmar	11.2	not available	6.3	72	not ranked
Philippines	99.0	426.7	73.7	1,133	71st
Singapore	116.8	128.8	296.1	20,081	7th
Thailand	176.6	557.4	156.2	4,008	28th
Vietnam	52.4	255.3	20.0	2,021	68th
ASEAN	889.0	—	844.5	38,085	—
China	2,234.3	8,814.9	974.0	72,406	34th
India	805.7	3,779.0	112.0	6,598	48th
Japan	4,534.0	3,995.1	590.3	2,775	8th
United States	12,416.5	12,416.5	1,869.0	99,443	1st
Timor-Leste	0.3	not available	0.1	102	127th

Sources: ASEAN Statistical Yearbook 2006 (ASEAN Secretariat); Human Development Report 2007/2008 (United Nations Development Programme [UNDP]); World Economic Forum (WEF).

Third, an ASEAN Community would help to reduce material disparities between member states. So long as a significant "development gap" separates advanced from less developed economies, the promise of equitably sharing regional prosperity will remain unmet. An ASEAN Community can help remedy this imbalance, both among its members and within each member. As shown in Table 3.2, Brunei Darussalam and Singapore enjoy high standards of living, comparable to those in many developed countries in the West, while Cambodia, Laos, Myanmar, and Vietnam lag far behind in their stage of development.

Fourth, in a globalized environment, no government can, by itself, assure complete human security for all its people, and for this reason, too, an ASEAN Community is worth building. Southeast Asians today face a range of transboundary threats. Examples include environment degradation and disasters, notably the Indian Ocean tsunami in December 2004 and the recurring haze from forest fires in Indonesia; infectious illnesses such as avian influenza, malaria, dengue fever, and HIV/AIDS; cross-border trafficking in drugs and persons; and international terrorism. Effective regional cooperation and active international support are required for tackling these transboundary threats to human security.

Fifth, a Socio-Cultural Community that would develop as part of an ASEAN Community could bring the Association's diverse peoples closer together, help render them more aware of belonging to one regional family, and thereby foster meaningful regional security. To support such activities, the Association has been promoting people-to-people contacts and cultural exchanges, including establishing an ASEAN Foundation in 1997.

But there is more to be done. For example, Cambodia and Myanmar are exceptions to the rule that ASEAN nationals enjoy visa-free travel to other member states. ASEAN-country visitors to Cambodia are charged visa fees of US$ 20–30 per person upon arrival. Cambodia is still a poor country and relies on the revenue. For security reasons, all visitors to Myanmar are subject to strict immigration controls. Despite these local priorities, visa-free travel for all ASEAN nationals within the ASEAN Community remains a goal worth pursuing.

A related challenge for ASEAN, particularly in the context of the ASEAN Economic Community, will be to reduce barriers to the freer movement of entrepreneurs, professionals, students, workers, and others from one part of the region to another. As ASEAN's peoples come to know one another better, they may better understand and appreciate what ASEAN has been trying to do for them, and for the region. Active popular support for the building of an ASEAN Community could follow.

Sixth and finally, an ASEAN Community will be more cohesive, with a stronger Secretariat, and thus better able to develop productive relations between Southeast Asia and the wider world, including managing more effectively the Association's extraregional offshoots such as the ARF, APT, and EAS.

Table 3.2 Spatial, Demographic, and Human Development Indicators for ASEAN (Individually and Collectively), China, India, Japan, the United States, and Timor-Leste

	Area (1,000 sq. km)	Population (millions) 2005	Human Development Index ranking 2005	Gender Gap Index ranking (by WEF) 2007	Life expectancy at birth (years) 2005
Brunei	5.8	0.4	30th	not available	76.7
Cambodia	181.0	14.0	131st	98th	58.0
Indonesia	1,891.0	226.1	107th	81st	69.7
Laos	237.0	5.7	130th	not available	63.2
Malaysia	330.0	25.7	63rd	92nd	73.7
Myanmar	677.0	48.0	132nd	not available	60.8
Philippines	300.0	84.6	90th	6th	71.0
Singapore	0.697	4.3	25th	77th	79.4
Thailand	513.0	63.0	78th	52nd	69.6
Vietnam	330.0	85.0	105th	42nd	73.7
ASEAN	4,466.5	556.8	—	—	—
China	9,596.0	1,313.0	81st	73rd	72.5
India	3,287.0	1,134.4	128th	114th	63.7
Japan	378.0	127.9	8th	91st	82.3
United States	9,826.0	299.8	12th	31st	77.9
Timor-Leste	16.0	1.1	150th	not available	59.7

Sources: ASEAN Statistical Yearbook 2006 (ASEAN Secretariat); U.S. Census Bureau; *Human Development Report 2007/2008* (UNDP); World Economic Forum (WEF).

Backboning the Body: A Charter for ASEAN

The ASEAN Community and the ASEAN Charter are complementary. In the anatomy of regionalism, if the Community is the body, the Charter is its backbone. The Charter is an international treaty, signed on 20 November 2007 by the heads of state or government in all ten member countries, and requiring ratification by all ten before going into effect.[11] It is, in effect, a constitution for ASEAN. It creates an explicit framework within which member states can work together. In that rules-based environment, agreements and decisions are legally binding.

The "birth certification" of ASEAN was the two-page ASEAN Declaration, better known as the Bangkok Declaration, signed in Bangkok on 8 August 1967, by four foreign ministers and a deputy prime minister.[12] It needed no further approval. Strictly speaking, it was a political, not a legal, document. It merely stated its signers' intention to cooperate under the ASEAN name.

The Charter is different. Depending on the country, the Charter may be ratified by an elected legislature, or by a formal act of the executive branch if there is no elected legislature or if the government does not require legislative ratification. Eventually the Charter will be registered with the UN Secretariat as an international agreement.

By drafting and signing the Charter, member states have for the first time agreed to confer on ASEAN the status of an intergovernmental organization with a legal personality that is separate from their own respective national identities. The Charter requires that the signatory states take steps to give the Association full legal standing under their own domestic laws. When this process is complete, ASEAN will become a formal institution whose members are legally bound, under its rules, to fulfill their obligations to one another and to the Association.

This is not a new idea. As far back as the early 1970s ASEAN's founding members considered underpinning their creation with a constitution. But those discussions led not to a Charter but to the signing of the Treaty of Amity and Cooperation in Southeast Asia, at the First ASEAN Summit, in Bali in 1976, and the issuing of a Declaration of ASEAN Concord. In the latter document, the members acknowledged the need to improve ASEAN's machinery, and promised in that context to study the desirability of "a new constitutional framework" for the Association. But it was not until the early 2000s, when

---

[11] Singapore deposited the instrument of its ratification of the Charter with the Secretary-General of ASEAN on 7 January 2008, Brunei Darussalam followed suit on 15 February 2008; Malaysia and Lao PDR on 20 February 2008; Vietnam on 19 March 2008; and Cambodia on 18 April 2008.

[12] Of the five founding ministers, the only one still alive in April 2008 was Thanat Khoman. He had signed the 1967 Declaration in his capacity as foreign minister of Thailand. Texts of this and all other ASEAN documents mentioned in this chapter may be accessed at <http://www.aseansec.org>. The Charter itself appears at the end of this book.

plans for an ASEAN Community were drawn up, that such a constitutional framework became necessary and the idea of providing the Association with a charter finally resurfaced.

The Ninth ASEAN Summit, in Bali in October 2003, agreed to begin preparing for a three-pillared Community for political-security, economic, and sociocultural cooperation in Southeast Asia. In 2004, at their Tenth ASEAN Summit, in Vientiane, Laos, the leaders issued the Vientiane Action Program (VAP), which listed steps to be taken between 2004 and 2010 that would establish the Community's three pillars of cooperation. These steps included working "towards the development of an ASEAN Charter" and "setting up relevant mechanisms" for that purpose. At their Eleventh ASEAN Summit, in 2005 in Kuala Lumpur, Malaysia, the leaders established an Eminent Persons Group (EPG) that would examine ASEAN's situation and recommend changes, including possible contents for an ASEAN Charter. The EPG comprised prominent Southeast Asians, one from each member state. Nearly all of them were former government ministers, but they were to act in their private capacity as individuals.[13]

The EPG submitted its report to the Twelfth ASEAN Summit, in Cebu, the Philippines, on 12 January 2007. By then enough momentum had developed for the leaders to anticipate launching the ASEAN Charter later that year and to reschedule the target date for completing the ASEAN Community from 2020 to 2015.

Although the EPG did make suggestions as to what the Charter should say, the Group was not empowered to write a draft Charter for the leaders to consider. That task was given to a High-Level Task Force (HLTF) set up by the ASEAN foreign ministers and made up of officials from the ministry of foreign affairs,

---

[13] The members of the EPG were Pehin Dato Lim Jock Seng, second minister of foreign affairs and trade (Brunei Darussalam); Dr. Aun Porn Moniroth, economic adviser to the prime minister and chairman of the Supreme National Economic Council (Cambodia); Ali Alatas, former minister for foreign affairs (Indonesia); Khamphan Simmalavong, former deputy minister of commerce (Laos); Tun Musa Hitam, former deputy prime minister (Malaysia); Dr. Than Nyun, chairman of the Civil Service Selection and Training Board (Myanmar); Fidel V. Ramos, former president (Philippines); Prof. S. Jayakumar, deputy prime minister, coordinating minister for National Security, and minister for law (Singapore); M. R. Kasemsamosorn Kasemsri, former deputy prime minister and former minister of foreign affairs (Thailand); and Nguyen Manh Cam, former deputy prime minister and former minister of foreign affairs (Vietnam). Tun Musa Hitam chaired the EPG, while ASEAN Secretary-General (SG) Ong Keng Yong served as its resource person.

acting in their official capacity.[14] In drafting a Charter, these officials were asked to take into account not only the EPG's ideas, but also directives from ASEAN leaders, existing commitments in milestone documents in ASEAN since 1967, and guidance from the foreign ministers who had appointed them.

The drafting process was consultative; decisions were made by consensus. From January to October 2007 the HLTF held thirteen formal meetings in the ten member states, and also met with a range of stakeholders and interested parties, including the ASEAN foreign ministers; bodies planning ASEAN Community's political-security, economic, and sociocultural pillars; the ASEAN Inter-Parliamentary Assembly (AIPA); and representatives of the civil society organizations and national human rights institutions of Indonesia, Malaysia, the Philippines, and Thailand.

Of particular interest on this list is AIPA. Established in 1977 as an Organization (AIPO), in 2006 it renamed itself an Assembly. The new designation implies a conceivable future for AIPA as an ASEAN-linked parliament for Southeast Asia, perhaps even comparable to the European Parliament associated with the EU.

In 2007, however, such a speculation was entirely premature. One of the AIPA members called ASEAN Parliament a "sweet dream." Only eight ASEAN states belonged to AIPA. Brunei Darussalam and Myanmar lacked legislatures and were only special observers. Despite the "ASEAN" in its name, AIPA remained outside the Association's organizational structure. AIPA was, nevertheless, recognized as a "partner in government" in building the ASEAN Community.

In March 2007, in Siem Reap, Cambodia, the foreign ministers of ASEAN met to review key sensitive issues that had arisen during the Charter-drafting

---

[14] The Task Force members were Pengiran Dato Paduka Osman Patra, permanent secretary, ASEAN senior officials meeting (SOM) leader, Ministry of Foreign Affairs and Trade, Brunei Darussalam; Dr. Kao Kim Hourn, secretary of state, ASEAN SOM leader, Ministry of Foreign Affairs and International Cooperation, Cambodia; Dian Triansyah Djani, director-general, ASEAN-Indonesia, Department of Foreign Affairs, Indonesia; Bounkeut Sangsomsak, deputy minister, ASEAN SOM leader, Ministry of Foreign Affairs, Laos; Tan Sri Ahmad Fuzi Haji Abdul Razak, ambassador-at-large, Ministry of Foreign Affairs, Malaysia; Aung Bwa, director-general, ASEAN-Myanmar, Ministry of Foreign Affairs, Myanmar; Rosario Manalo, president's special envoy for the drafting of the ASEAN Charter, Philippines; Tommy Koh, ambassador-at-large, Ministry of Foreign Affairs, Singapore; Sihasak Phuangketkeow (a member from December 2006 to March 2007), then–deputy permanent secretary, ASEAN SOM leader, Ministry of Foreign Affairs, and Pradap Pibulsonggram (a member from April 2007), deputy permanent secretary, Ministry of Foreign Affairs, Thailand; and Nguyen Trung Thanh, assistant minister, ASEAN SOM leader, Ministry of Foreign Affairs, who was succeeded by Mr. Pham Quang Vinh, SOM leader, Vietnam. Chairing the HLTF were Rosario Manalo (until August 2007) and Tommy Koh (from August 2007), while SG Ong Keng Yong served as resource person, as he had on the EPG. The author assisted SG Ong during both the EPG and the HLTF processes.

process and to guide the HLTF accordingly. Later that same month, at a meeting with civil society representatives in Manila, the chair of the Task Force, Ambassador Rosario Manalo of the Philippines, shared five key points of guidance from the ministers:

(1) The preamble to the Charter would not state that an ASEAN Community should eventually evolve into an "ASEAN Union." In the EPG, former Philippine president Fidel Ramos had advocated including this long-term goal, but he did not specify what it would mean.

(2) The Charter would contain no provisions whereby an ASEAN member could be suspended, expelled, or allowed to withdraw from the Association. Inside the EPG, in contrast, Ramos and another member, Tun Musa Hitam of Malaysia, had argued that ASEAN should preclude neither suspension nor expulsion as ultimate measures that might be needed to address a serious breach or noncompliance by a member state.

(3) Voting would not replace consensus-seeking in the Charter as a normal procedure in ASEAN. Voting would be available only to the member heads of state or government, and only if necessary—after failing to achieve consensus—on a case-by-case basis. Consultation to achieve consensus would remain the basic principle of decision-making inside the Association.

(4) In the case of disputes involving member states, any mechanisms that the ASEAN Charter might provide to settle such disputes would not affect the right of any member state to seek redress through other peaceful means, as provided by Article 33 of the UN Charter.[15]

(5) The foreign ministers advised the Task Force that the Charter could include a provision to establish an ASEAN instrument to address human rights issues in Southeast Asia.

The foreign ministers' resolution of these contentious issues made more realistic the HLTF's intention to produce a draft of the Charter in time for the same ministers to review at their 40th AMM, in Manila in late-July 2007. ASEAN's leaders would then sign the Charter at their Thirteenth ASEAN Summit, in Singapore in November.

Various observers can interpret differently the ministers' five guidelines.

---

[15] Article 33 appears in chapter VI of the UN Charter, which deals with the "pacific settlement of disputes." Article 33 makes the following two points: "(1) The parties to any dispute, the continuance of which is likely to endanger the maintenance of international peace and security, shall, first of all, seek a solution by negotiation, enquiry, mediation, conciliation, arbitration, judicial settlement, resort to regional agencies or arrangements, or other peaceful means of their own choice. (2) The Security Council shall, when it deems necessary, call upon the parties to settle their dispute by such means."

In my view, at this critical stage in ASEAN's evolution, it is vital to resist the temptation to continue business as usual and linger in the status quo. Passivity is not an option. Conditions have changed too much, and the challenges are too many and too urgent. Now is the time to move forward, accelerating ASEAN's momentum and enabling the Association to deliver more concrete results that will benefit all Southeast Asians.

The fifth guideline, which suggested the possible establishment of an ASEAN human rights body, was especially contentious. Among those who drafted the document, no satisfactory compromise could be reached on the nature of the proposed body, nor about the scope of its influence. They sought further guidance from the foreign ministers. The solution worked out at the 40th AMM, in Manila in July 2007, was simply to state the following two points in the Charter:

(1) In conformity with the purposes and principles of the ASEAN Charter relating to the promotion and protection of human rights and fundamental freedoms, ASEAN shall establish an ASEAN human rights body.

(2) This ASEAN human rights body shall operate in accordance with the terms of reference to be determined by the ASEAN Foreign Ministers Meeting.[16]

At their retreat in Singapore on 20 February 2008, ASEAN Foreign Ministers agreed to establish a high-level panel to draft the terms of reference of the ASEAN human rights body. The panel was formally appointed during the 41st ASEAN Ministerial Meeting in Singapore, 20–24 July 2008, and commenced work thereafter. As of this writing, it is still unknown what the ASEAN human rights body can or cannot do. But the agreement to establish such a new organ within ASEAN was in itself a significant step forward. For the first time, ASEAN had agreed to create an official regional organ to handle the promotion and protection of human rights in Southeast Asia at the regional level.

Human rights were not, however, an entirely novel topic for ASEAN, which had earlier contemplated forming a "commission" to promote and protect the rights of women and children in Southeast Asia. Indeed, ASEAN included the idea in the VAP. A regional human rights body was also in line with existing national commitments under the 1979 Convention on the Elimination of All Forms of Discrimination against Women, and the 1989 Convention on the Rights of the Child, to which all ten ASEAN states were parties.

---

[16] ASEAN Charter, Art. 14.1–2. At first, the foreign ministers wanted those drafting the document to try to draw up terms of reference for the ASEAN human rights body. But when they made little headway, due to lack of time and the sensitivity of the assignment, the second point had to be added to Article 14.

A closely related issue is respect for the rights of migrant workers. In January 2007, at their Twelfth Summit, in Cebu in the Philippines, ASEAN's leaders signed an ASEAN Declaration on the Protection and Promotion of the Rights of Migrant Workers. Subsequently in 2007, a high-level official committee was established to implement the Declaration. An ASEAN Forum on Migration was convened in Manila, 24–25 April 2008, to discuss further regional cooperation on the protection of migrant workers' rights.

It was expected that the ASEAN Charter would be fully ratified within a year of its signing, that is, by late 2008. Success in drafting, signing, and ratifying the Charter will amount to a paradigm shift in the geopolitical landscape of twenty-first-century Southeast Asia. Such a shift, when complete, will overshadow even the historic 1995 admission of Vietnam into ASEAN, which ended the Cold War in Southeast Asia.

In the ensuing sections, I examine the ASEAN Political-Security, Economic, and Socio-Cultural Communities that the Charter is meant to support, including their backgrounds and the issues at stake in their implementation.

A Political-Security Community: From Turbulence to Confidence and Beyond

Southeast Asia in the mid-1960s was a turbulent place. Indonesia was engaged in border clashes with Malaya before 1963, and also with the Federation of Malaysia after its creation that year in the face of vehement Indonesian objections. In 1965, Indonesian commandos—who were later caught and hanged—exploded a bomb in downtown Singapore. Also in 1965, Singapore, which had joined Malaysia in 1963, broke away from the Federation in acrimonious circumstances. The Philippines, rejecting Malaysia's claim of sovereignty over Sabah on Borneo's northern coast, refused until 1966 even to recognize the Federation. Meanwhile on mainland Southeast Asia, the Vietnam War raged on, with the Philippines and Thailand siding with the United States and South Vietnam.

An indigenously Southeast Asian community in these conditions could be no more than a fantasy. The Philippines and Thailand had already chosen to rely on U.S. protection against communist aggression by joining the Southeast Asia Treaty Organization (SEATO), in which they were the only Southeast Asian members.[17]

In 1965 and 1966 in Indonesia, the government of President Sukarno gave way to emergency rule by General Soeharto, who dismantled his predecessor's policy of "confrontation" against Malaysia and thereby facilitated the founding

---

[17] SEATO's other members were Australia, France, New Zealand, Pakistan, the United Kingdom, and the United States. Headquartered in Bangkok, SEATO was disbanded in 1997. However, bilateral Philippine-U.S. and Thailand-U.S. agreements for security cooperation were still in effect a decade later, and the United States counted both Southeast Asian states among its "non-NATO allies."

of ASEAN in Bangkok in 1967. The five founders had decided to work together, as best they could, to change Southeast Asia from a strife-ridden tropical archipelago into a coherent region in which regional peace would allow member states to concentrate on national development. It was this goal that helped to shape ASEAN's strong emphasis on "non-interference" and "self-determination" in its early years.

In 1971 the Vietnam War dragged on. Small contingents of Philippine and Thai troops were still in the country, helping U.S. forces to fight communism. Nevertheless, in that year, the five ASEAN-founding member states, including the Philippines and Thailand, announced their desire to make Southeast Asia a "Zone of Peace, Freedom and Neutrality" and to intensify regional cooperation.

The nature of such cooperation was made clearer in the Treaty of Amity and Cooperation in Southeast Asia (TAC) that was issued at ASEAN's First Summit, in Bali in 1976. Among the TAC's points, the principle that attracted the greatest attention was Article 2C, that of "non-interference in the internal affairs of one another." This principle became an important element of the non-intrusive, consensus-based "ASEAN Way."

Seldom noticed, however, is another and very different tenet in the treaty: that its signatories should engage in "*effective* cooperation among themselves" (emphasis added). In this sense, the establishment of a Charter-bound Community that can more effectively address regional problems is not novel but fulfills a commitment of more than thirty years' standing.

Nor is the Charter's legally binding character entirely unprecedented in this context. In launching the TAC in 1976, ASEAN's signatory states created a code of conduct that was legally constraining under international law for states willing to sign on to it.

The TAC has been amended to open it to accession by non-Southeast Asian states, so long as all of its Southeast Asian signatories—ASEAN's ten members—consent to each such addition. As of April 2008, fourteen nonregional states had signed on.[18] The United Kingdom at first planned to accede to the TAC on the sidelines of the ASEAN-EU Commemorative Summit, in Singapore on 22 November 2007. But London decided (reportedly in "sorrow rather than in anger") to postpone signing the TAC due to the violent suppression of Buddhist monks and other protestors in Myanmar in September 2007. At least prior to

---

[18] These fourteen states were Papua New Guinea (5 July 1989); China (8 October 2003); India (8 October 2003); Japan (2 July 2004); Pakistan (2 July 2004); Republic of Korea (27 November 2004); Russian Federation (29 November 2004); Mongolia (28 July 2005); New Zealand (28 July 2005); Australia (10 December 2005); France (13 January 2007); Timor-Leste (13 January 2007); and Sri Lanka and Bangladesh (30 July 2007). The Democratic People's Republic of Korea (DPRK, or North Korea) could be next; the ten Southeast Asian High Contracting Parties to the treaty have already given their formal consent to the DPRK's proposed accession.

that crackdown, the EU was also very interested in accession to the TAC, while the United States and Canada were still studying the possibility.[19]

In 1995, ASEAN bolstered its commitment to regional security and to Southeast Asia as a Zone of Peace, Freedom and Neutrality by signing the Treaty on the Southeast Asia Nuclear Weapon-Free Zone (SEANWFZ). This treaty, which all of the ten ASEAN heads of state or government signed, went into force on 27 March 1997. In July 2007, during their 40th AMM, in Manila, ASEAN's foreign ministers undertook a ten-year review of the implementation of the treaty's provisions. They reaffirmed their commitment to keep Southeast Asia free of nuclear weapons and to continue to encourage the world's original five nuclear-weapon states (NWSs) to support them by recognizing and respecting SEANWFZ.

Attached to the treaty is a protocol that is open to signature and subsequent ratification by these acknowledged NWSs—China, France, Russia, the United Kingdom, and the United States. Adherence to the protocol by any of these NWSs would oblige each of them to respect the treaty, including neither using nor threatening to use nuclear weapons against any of the Southeast Asian parties to the treaty.

As of 2007, only China had expressed support for SEANWFZ and readiness to sign the protocol. France, Russia, the United Kingdom, and the United States still had objections. One sticking point is the scope of the Zone's application, which includes the treaty states' continental shelves and two-hundred-mile exclusive economic zones (EEZs). These four NWSs have also been unwilling to provide "negative security assurance" not to use or threaten to use nuclear weapons in the Zone's area, especially since it includes these continental shelves and EEZs.

There also remains one important point of difference among the ten Southeast Asian signatory states. The difference concerns the rights of foreign ships and aircraft to move through the Zone and to visit ports and airfields within it. Every party to the treaty—that is, every ASEAN state—retains the prerogative to allow foreign ships and aircraft into its own territory and waters. But some of these governments are unclear about how to interpret or implement this prerogative without violating the provision in the treaty that requires any treaty state "not to allow, in its territory, any other State to develop, manufacture or otherwise acquire, possess or have control over nuclear weapons."[20]

---

[19] The TAC will have to be amended to open it to accession by intergovernmental entities such as the EU.

[20] The SEANWFZ Treaty established a Commission and an Executive Committee to oversee its operation, and authorized these bodies to make decisions by a two-thirds majority vote, but only in the event of failure to reach a consensus. In practice, however, the proposed sequence has been reversed: The lack of consensus to use voting to resolve disagreement over allowing foreign ships and aircraft into the Zone has prevented that procedure from being used to settle the matter.

In keeping with this concern for relations with outside powers, ASEAN has, in the course of its evolution, widened the geographical scope of its approach to regional security. For example, in the "Concert of Southeast Asian Nations" that ASEAN's leaders envisaged in their Vision 2020 and unveiled at their informal summit in Malaysia in 1997, the Association was projected to become "an effective force for peace, justice and moderation in the Asia-Pacific and in the world."[21]

This more inclusive frame was evident, too, in the Declaration of ASEAN Concord II adopted at the Ninth ASEAN Summit, in Bali in 2003, which looked forward to an ASEAN Community whose political-security pillar would elevate political and security cooperation in Southeast Asia "to a higher plane to ensure that countries in the region live at peace with one another and with the world at large in a just, democratic and harmonious environment."[22] At the same time, the Declaration reiterated "the sovereign right" of ASEAN members to pursue their own "individual foreign policies and defense arrangements," and their common commitment not to turn the security pillar—the ASEAN Political-Security Community (APSC)—into a "defense pact" or a "military alliance," and not to pursue "a joint foreign policy."[23]

In 2007 the ASEAN Economic Community was given its own Blueprint, and the Association's leaders told their ministers and officials to prepare one for the APSC in time to be considered at the Fourteenth ASEAN Summit, in Thailand in 2008. A Blueprint for the ASEAN Socio-Cultural Community was also envisaged.

The next section explores the several contrasting elements in this vision of Southeast Asian security within an environment that not only is "democratic" and "harmonious," but also respects the "sovereign" diversity of member states.

A Democratic Club? The Challenge of Political Diversity

In 2007 it was too early to discern exactly what the member states wanted to achieve by building an ASEAN Political-Security Community. Nor was this uncertainty surprising in the light of the striking diversity of Southeast Asia's political systems. In this respect, arguably no regional organization in the world has a more varied membership. The politics of Southeast Asian states range widely from "left" to "right," and include various sorts of democracy in between. Unlike the EU, ASEAN has never required a prospective member to possess a functioning pluralistic democracy with a good record on human rights.

---

[21] Declaration of ASEAN Concord II (Bali Concord II), Bali, Indonesia, 7 October 2003, <http://www.aseansec.org/15159.htm>.

[22] Declaration of ASEAN Concord II, <http://www.aseansec.org/15159.htm>.

[23] This and the preceding quotation appear in the Declaration of ASEAN Concord II, <http://www.aseansec.org/15159.htm>.

Membership in ASEAN was and still is open to any independent state in Southeast Asia willing to subscribe to the principles and purposes of the group. The ASEAN Charter further specifies the criteria for affiliation. Essentially, a new member must agree to abide by the Charter, enjoy diplomatic recognition by all the existing members, and all those existing members must support the new member's entry into the Association. Once inside the Association, every member state is entitled to be treated as a sovereign equal. To quote the Charter: "Member States shall have equal rights and obligations under this Charter" (Art. 5.1). Nor has ASEAN ever tried to change any member's political system. The Charter reaffirms this principle of "respect for the right of every Member State to lead its national existence free from external interference, subversion and coercion" (Art. 2.2 [f]).

Because of their political diversity, the member states have wanted neither to engage in collective defense nor to forge a common foreign policy. Their respective perceptions of real and potential enemies and friends diverge too much. The members also differ in the extent and nature of their reliance on outside powers for national security assurance and protection. Although the ASEAN Defense Ministers Meeting is an innovation, its basic assignment is to support whatever the leaders and foreign ministers have already put in place. Likewise, it has been careful to avoid giving any impression that ASEAN is turning into a military alliance.[24]

Challenges to security can arise suddenly and require a quick response. Yet the principle of consensus that underlies the ASEAN Way requires consultation, and that takes time. Dr. Surin Pitsuwan tried to address this gap when he was foreign minister of Thailand in the late 1990s. He proposed an "ASEAN Troika," whereby three member states selected for the purpose might respond to an emergency on the Association's behalf. Several foreign ministers thought this was a good idea; others were more cautious and wanted to ensure noninterference by such a troika. Thus, in the concept paper advancing Dr. Surin's idea, as adopted at the 33rd AMM, in Bangkok in 2000, consensus was required before every important step to be taken in the course of activating an ASEAN Troika.

A year later, on September 11, 2001, terrorists suddenly struck the United States. Thailand called for an ASEAN Troika to be convened, but there was no consensus to do so. Some member states argued that the 9/11 attacks did not

---

[24] At their inaugural gathering in 2006, the defense ministers said that their meetings would have four goals: (1) to promote regional peace and stability through dialogue and cooperation; (2) to offer guidance to already existing dialogues and cooperation involving senior defense officials and military officers; (3) to promote mutual trust and confidence through improved understanding of challenges to defense and security, including enhanced transparency and openness; and (4) to help establish an ASEAN Security Community as already stipulated in the Bali Concord II and the VAP. Of these objectives, only the reference to greater transparency and openness could be said to encourage a fresh initiative.

vitally threaten Southeast Asian security. So no Troika was formed then, nor has Dr Surin's idea been implemented since.

This does not mean, of course, that ASEAN can have no common foreign-policy positions. Consensus does exist on a range of matters, including the need for constructive engagement and mutual confidence-building with China regarding disputed areas in the South China Sea; the need to settle peacefully the nuclear issue on the Korean peninsula; and the need for the UN to play the central role in maintaining international peace and security, particularly in promoting national reconciliation in Myanmar and the reconstruction of Iraq.

Does its commitment to consensus make ASEAN a democratic club? Yes, if democracy means that consulting is preferred to voting and members are assigned equal rather than differentiated status. ASEAN can make no major decision without a prior consensus across all member states, and they all have equal responsibilities and obligations. Rich or poor, big or small, every member contributes the same amount to the Secretariat's budget. Sovereign equality is strictly upheld, and the notion of voting to end a deadlock is not accepted.

Procedural questions aside, however, ASEAN could and should aspire to be more democratic in the sense of fostering fundamental freedoms and human rights throughout Southeast Asia. In three separate parts of its text (Preamble, Purposes, and Principles), the Charter does mention democratic values, including human rights, fundamental freedoms, the rule of law, and good governance. The drafters of the Charter did not dispute the intrinsic merits of these democratic values. Nevertheless, they felt it was beyond their mandate to try to overcome the political diversity of ASEAN's members.

The question of how to reconcile promoting democratic values with building an ASEAN Community remains unresolved. "Caring and sharing" is the theme of the ASEAN Socio-Cultural Community. Caring and sharing should mean feeling the need to help all Southeast Asians enjoy basic freedoms and human rights. Without such empathy, there would be nothing to bind the region's peoples into a *community* of any kind. Yet ASEAN as an organization has yet to become seriously involved in promoting fundamental human freedoms and rights in the region. In this context, the Charter's mandate to establish an "ASEAN human rights body"—its exact name will be determined in the course of drafting its terms of reference—is a significant new initiative.

Equality of formal status and equality of actual influence are not the same. A case in point is the influence of the largest country in the region, Indonesia. Largely inspired by the democratization of Indonesia since the Soeharto era ended in 1998, ASEAN has begun to embrace democratic values as regional norms of conduct within the proposed Political-Security Community. At the Bali Summit in 2003, the Plan of Action adopted to implement this security pillar of the ASEAN Community went so far as to state that the Association's members "shall not condone unconstitutional and undemocratic change of government."[25]

Fortunately, the Plan of Action did not prescribe any punitive action to be taken if one or more members *did* condone such a change of government. Otherwise, ASEAN would have found itself in a serious dilemma following the coup against the government of Prime Minister Thaksin Shinawatra in Thailand on 19 September 2006. Leaving aside the question of how democratic his administration was or was not, the coup itself certainly was neither constitutional nor democratic. Yet ASEAN had to accept it as *fait accompli*. (In fairness one should note that the coup was not unpopular inside Thailand, and that His Majesty the King of Thailand also accepted the coup, without objection.)

In any event, the first two priorities identified in the Plan of Action for the ASEAN Political-Security Community to pursue are "political development"—the "highest political commitment" on which political cooperation in ASEAN should be based—and the "shaping and sharing of norms" that could help build "a democratic, tolerant, participatory and transparent community in Southeast Asia." As if to reinforce these ideas, the Charter states that, "ASEAN and its Member States shall act in accordance with . . . adherence to the rule of law, good governance, the principles of democracy and constitutional government" (Art. 2.2[h]).

One can hope that in these seeds lies the future growth of democracy across Southeast Asia.

An Economic Community: Plans Plus Priorities

The ASEAN Community's second pillar is economic. It is tempting to compare this modest initiative with the full-blown economic integration in the EU. But there is no plan in ASEAN to integrate the economic agencies of the respective member governments, nor to transfer power over economic matters to any central authority. ASEAN has no intention of erecting a "Southeast Asian Commission" comparable to the European Commission that the EU's members have empowered to manage the their region's economic integration. Nor is a customs union planned, since that would threaten the basically free-port status of Singapore and (to a slightly lesser degree) Brunei Darussalam. In 2007, the member economies of ASEAN were still at far different development stages. The Association was not yet ready to strive for any common external tariff, let alone a common external economic policy.

The Blueprint for cooperation under the ASEAN Economic Community until 2015, signed by the leaders during the Singapore summit on 20 November 2007,

---

[25] The statement went on to preclude the use of ASEAN Community territory by any member for "actions undermining peace, security and stability" in another member country. Read in context, that injunction arguably ruled out intervention to reverse a coup.

includes the promotion of five core elements: the free flow of goods, services, investment, and skilled labor, and the "freer" flow of capital.

The ASEAN Economic Community is also not a monetary union. The existing Roadmap for Monetary and Finance Integration, agreed to in 2003, focuses instead on financial-services liberalization, capital-markets cooperation, capital-accounts liberalization, and currency cooperation. ASEAN continues to study the idea of a common currency. But all in all, the region in 2008 was still very far from a monetary union.

This is not to deny progress already made. An ASEAN Free Trade Area (AFTA) has been in operation since 1993. The ASEAN Economic Community Blueprint will give more concrete prescriptions and a precise timetable for transforming AFTA into a Single Market and Production Base. Two important steps scheduled for 2008 involved drafting a new trade-in-goods agreement to tackle nontariff barriers, and a new comprehensive investment agreement to kick-start the largely moribund ASEAN Investment Area.

Back in 2003, in the AFTA context, member governments embarked on what they hoped would be the "accelerated integration" of nearly a dozen priority sectors.[26] By 2007, however, little progress had been achieved. The problem seems to be a lack of clear agreement on what the accelerated market integration of these sectors really means. There is no clear mandate for any ASEAN body to tackle issues that cut across two or more of these sectors, nor to drive the integration process within any one sector, especially if doing so could lead to *full* freedom of movement of services and investments, let alone capital, in that sector.

Other problems exist. Inside member-state governments, economic ministers and trade officials tend not to control customs officials, who are typically under the ministries of finance. The trade side has little say about service liberalization and investment cooperation. The national board of investment is usually not under the purview of the ministries of trade or economic affairs. Services and investment, too, are domains of numerous other bureaucrats and politicians who may have vested domestic interests to protect. Ministers and officials in agriculture, industry, transport, public health, tourism, and information and communication technology, among other departments, must be consulted and their cooperation secured before integration can be accelerated in or across "their" particular sectors.

This is not an easy task for ASEAN. No central authority is directly responsible for building the ASEAN Economic Community. No one in the

---

[26] In 2003 these sectors (and their country coordinators) were approved: wood-based products and automobiles (Indonesia); rubber-based products and textiles and apparel (Malaysia); agro-based products and fisheries (Myanmar); electronics (the Philippines); "e-ASEAN" (information and communication technology) and health care (Singapore); and air travel and tourism (Thailand). Subsequently, logistics (Vietnam) were added to the list.

Association seems prepared to empower any ASEAN body to take up this responsibility. Any hint of central supranational authority is anathema. A similar lack of coordination exists within individual member governments, causing occasional inconsistencies in the "national" positions that officials from different ministries will take. Policy coordination without any central regulator may no longer be sufficient to ensure compliance and meaningful progress in building the ASEAN Economic Community.

A different but equally serious complication arises from the eagerness of some member states to develop ASEAN's external economic linkages too fast and too soon, at a time when the ASEAN Economic Community remains rudimentary. Was it premature of ASEAN to plunge into signing the 2002 Comprehensive Economic Cooperation Framework Agreement with China, which included a subsequently initiated free trade agreement (FTA)? For members that could immediately benefit from closer economic linkages with China, the answer was, of course, no. It made sense to seize without hesitation the unprecedented opportunity that China (for largely political reasons) had offered.

Similarly, one could argue that negotiating with China and the other extraregional trading partners on a range of topics—including trade in goods, rules of origin, services liberalization, investment cooperation, and a dispute settlement mechanism—could stimulate ASEAN to work faster on such matters within its own regional market. One could also ask, however, whether ASEAN might be biting off more than it can chew.

Since its FTA with China, the Association has entered into similar comprehensive economic cooperation agreements and negotiations with India (2003), Japan (2003), and Australia, New Zealand, and South Korea (2004). In November 2005, ASEAN and the United States consented to work together to conclude a regionwide ASEAN–United States Trade and Investment Framework Agreement. In May 2007 in Brunei Darussalam, ASEAN's economic ministers agreed with the EU trade commissioner to plan talks toward an interregional FTA, including a joint commission to tackle procedural questions known as "modality" issues.

These are exciting breakthroughs. They have kept ASEAN on the radar of the international economic media. But to the extent that ASEAN does not have its own regional economic house in order, it may not be able to derive full benefit from these deals with economically powerful outsiders. In fact, each ASEAN member state, acting as a single economy, negotiates its own linkages individually with each external partner. These bilateral deals tend to decrease the interest that such external partners might otherwise have in pursuing regional agreements with ASEAN, especially while the ASEAN Economic Community itself is still under construction.

Will these bilateral external trade agreements help to enhance the competitiveness of the ASEAN Economic Community? Time, perhaps, will tell. What is clear is that trade talks with multiple dialogue partners will easily add at least another thirty to forty meetings a year to the already jam-packed

ASEAN calendar. Inevitably, these external trade meetings will cut into the time and sap the energy of largely the same groups of member-state officials who are supposed to implement, in their respective countries, ASEAN economic decisions and the Blueprint. On both of these initiatives, timely action is needed to realize the ASEAN Economic Community.

A Socio-Cultural Community: Caring and Sharing

The third and final pillar of the ASEAN Community is sociocultural in nature. In the 2003 Declaration of ASEAN Concord II, this pillar was meant to create "a Southeast Asia bonded together in partnership as a community of caring societies." To achieve this goal, existing functional cooperation on various matters related to human security and well-being was to be intensified. As of 2007, building this Community was entrusted to ministerial bodies in member governments in the following policy sectors: culture and the arts, education, health, social welfare, labor, antipoverty measures (including rural development), the environment (including measures against the regional haze, discussed later in this book), disaster management, youth, and information. Although these multiple agencies share a common concern for human security and well-being, it will be difficult to coordinate them in a common effort to build the ASEAN Socio-Cultural Community (ASCC).

Plans for this Community advocate not only "caring" but also "sharing" within and between Southeast Asian societies. However, ASEAN as an organization has few resources to share, including resources that might be used concretely to encourage greater empathy—more "caring societies"—across the region. Narrowing the development gap, for example, will require massive investments in economic infrastructure, especially in the newer member states such as Cambodia, Laos, Myanmar, and Vietnam. No significant long-term positive impact can be expected, for example, from the modest resources that ASEAN has managed to raise on behalf of the Initiative for ASEAN Integration (IAI), which are insufficient to fund more than low-cost capacity-building projects.

Caring and sharing within an expressly ASEAN Community also presupposes wide awareness of what the Association is and does. Yet after more than four decades of existence, ASEAN's profile and activities remain largely unknown to most of the peoples who live in its region. A low level of public awareness means, in turn, a lack of public interest. And interest, when it does exist, need not imply approval. Businesspeople in the member states may be more or less aware of AFTA and of ASEAN's external economic agreements. But many operators of small- and medium-sized firms in ASEAN countries feel threatened by the increased foreign competition resulting from AFTA and external linkages, and therefore do not support ASEAN. This lack of support stands in contrast to the enthusiasm among European entrepreneurs for EU-fostered economic integration.

Scholars in Southeast Asia's think tanks are also interested in ASEAN. But they tend to dismiss the Association for allegedly moving too slowly and trying to do too little. Often, at conferences and in publications, such scholars wonder why the Association is not doing more to tackle concrete problems in the region. All too often they conveniently overlook the fact that in order to take action on a specific issue, ASEAN needs a consensus sufficient to generate a mandate, and in turn, a mandate accompanied by sufficient actual resources to accomplish a given task. This disability affects all three Community pillars, but it could prove especially daunting in the difficult creation of "caring and sharing societies."

Caring and sharing require communication. The use of English as the only working language in ASEAN is a wise choice, and Article 34 of the ASEAN Charter reaffirms it. But the choice of English also limits the Association's ability to communicate with the estimated 560 million people who live in the region, of whom perhaps only 10 percent can read and write in that language. To overcome this obstacle, the national secretariats of ASEAN must reach out to their populations in their respective national languages.

A Socio-Cultural Community needs appropriate symbols to embody and promote its identity. ASEAN has its own flag and emblem. The EPG on the ASEAN Charter also recommended adopting an ASEAN anthem and an ASEAN motto—"One Vision, One Identity, One Community." Without public awareness, however, and even with such symbols, it will be hard to promote a "we" feeling throughout Southeast Asia. The EPG's recommendation in this matter has been incorporated into the ASEAN Charter (see Chapter 11, which addresses identity and symbols).[27]

One quick way to raise public awareness of ASEAN would be to make ASEAN Day, which falls on 8 August—the date on which the founding Bangkok Declaration was signed in 1967—a public holiday in every member state. If this were done, many Southeast Asians would want to know why they were being given a break from work on that day, and would then learn about ASEAN.

Important objectives in the ASCC—such as alleviating poverty, promoting education, and preserving national art and cultural heritage—are mostly under the direct responsibility of each government. Regional cooperation and international support can play only supplementary roles. Nevertheless, in 2007–08 the Blueprint for the ASCC was being drawn up, with a focus on helping the less-developed member states meet the Millennium Development Goals, and on narrowing the development gap.

Beyond the specifics of each of the three pillars in the ASEAN Community lies an additional challenge: Is the Association, as an organization, capable

---

[27] ASEAN can at least claim to have outdone the EU in three respects: in using only one official language, in having a motto, and in having an anthem. As of mid-2008, an ASEAN-wide composition contest was planned by Thailand's Ministry of Foreign Affairs to select the best entry for use as the ASEAN anthem.

of successfully stimulating, facilitating, and overseeing efforts to build these pillars in tandem to form one unified ASEAN Community? I now turn to that challenge.

ASEAN as an Organization: Time for Reform

ASEAN has grown and continues to grow. As of 2007, the total number of Association meetings at all levels exceeded 700 per year. (In the EU, there were about 3,500 meetings a year.) The number of meetings in ASEAN continues to rise steadily. Sooner or later new ASEAN ministerial bodies will emerge. Officials dealing with women's affairs want to establish a regular ASEAN ministerial meeting on their subject. Development planners feel entitled to a comparable vehicle for their own specialty and ideas. Forestry officials want their own ministerial body, independent of the ASEAN Ministers of Agriculture and Forestry (AMAF), which met for the twenty-sixth time in 2006. At the working level, Malaysia has advocated setting up a periodic ASEAN Heads of Town Planning Department Offices Meeting.

Already the lack of coordination is a serious problem, between ministerial meetings, between the meetings of ministers and those of senior officials within the same Community pillar, and between meetings at each of these levels across all three pillars. In the past, an attempt was made to bring the foreign affairs, economic, and finance ministers together in a Joint Ministerial Meeting (JMM) prior to an ASEAN summit. But when these ministers met, they had hardly anything to say to one another. The three ministers from the country hosting the JMM ended up talking among themselves.

Senior officials do gather in a Joint Consultative Meeting (JCM) chaired by the ASEAN SG. The JCM brings together upper-level administrators from the senior officials and senior economic officials meetings (SOMs and SEOMs). When these delegates are convened in the JCM along with the member states' foreign-ministry director-generals charged with ASEAN affairs, the entire ASEAN bureaucracy is meant to be represented at the working level. But the JCM, too, is ineffective. Most of its participants lack a mandate to speak for ASEAN committees beyond their immediate purview. Most also lack the time to study the key issues that these other committees are considering.

This being the case, ASEAN leaders, assisted by their ministers and the SG, have been expected to pull together all parties concerned in time for the summit. But this, too, has been difficult. Summits have occurred only once a year, typically unfolding over two hectic days packed with too many meetings. Priorities can get lost in the shuffle. For instance, the growing number of extraregional relations has meant that when the ASEAN leaders have finally gathered in a summit, they spend more time meeting their external partners than consulting among themselves on important intraregional issues.

To reduce the pressures on the summit, the ASEAN Charter calls for the heads of state and government to gather at least twice a year. In addition to holding their usual summit, including ASEAN Plus One sessions (with, as of 2007, China, Japan, South Korea, and India), and back-to-back with the APT and the EAS, the leaders convene a second summit among themselves to focus on ASEAN Community affairs. This second summit has become a necessity, as ASEAN leaders face more and more serious policy decisions, including cases of serious breach of the ASEAN Charter or noncompliance with major ASEAN agreements.

The full text of the ASEAN Charter is available at the back of this book. In the rest of this chapter I highlight and comment briefly on some of its more important provisions for institutional reform.

When the Charter comes into effect and the details are worked out in a new agreement, ASEAN will, for the first time, have a legal personality as an intergovernmental organization. Hitherto, only ASEAN member states have been able to enter into agreements and contracts with other legal entities such as governments and international organizations. This reform will enable ASEAN to do the same. ASEAN will be able to own properties and hold assets in its own name, to sue and be sued, and generally to behave as a legal personality can. The Association will not, however, be empowered to enforce any ASEAN agreements, nor to take punitive action against any member state that has violated such agreements.

In another effort to improve coordination, the Charter establishes a council for each of the three communities that make up the ASEAN Community: an ASEAN Political-Security Community (APSC) Council, an ASEAN Economic Community (AEC) Council, and an ASEAN Socio-Cultural Community (ASCC) Council. Each member state will send its own national delegation to each council meeting. But concerned ministries in each member state will need to coordinate their priorities, with one another and with their counterparts from other member states, within each council. The APSC Council, for example, will bring together foreign ministers, defense ministers, law ministers, and interior (home affairs) ministers to implement the ASEAN Political-Security Community.

The composition of the AEC Council will be more complex. Delegates to its meetings will be drawn from a dozen distinct ministerial bodies that focus on economic affairs in each member country. The mainstream economic ministers have always wanted to be the "coordinating ministers" for the AEC, but as of 2007 they had not won full recognition from the rest of their ministerial colleagues in the AEC. The ASCC also spans a dozen ministerial bodies in each member government, and there too the question of leadership will need to be resolved. On socio-cultural matters there is no clear leading position or portfolio, though the education minister in most member states is quite influential. But historically in ASEAN, education ministers have been relative newcomers, since their ministerial body in the Association has existed only since 2006. Undoubtedly, in this and related contexts, a number of ministers in ASEAN harbor doubts about the merit of these new Community councils.

In a further move toward better management, the Charter calls for the foreign ministers of the member states to form an ASEAN Coordinating Council (ACC)[28] to help the ASEAN leaders prepare for their summits, with support from the SG and the ASEAN Secretariat. This means that the foreign ministers will retain their prominent role in the Association. Their AMM will be renamed the "ASEAN Foreign Ministers Meeting" and will be one of the four ministerial bodies within the APSC Council. The foreign ministers will continue to participate in the ARF and will remain members of the SEANWFZ Commission. They will also most likely be on the High Council—a body provided for in the TAC to help settle disputes, but never activated—should it ever be brought into being.

Among the Charter's other reforms are steps to enhance the roles of the SG and therefore the Secretariat in advancing the interest of ASEAN and its legal personality; in monitoring the implementation of summit decisions and ASEAN agreements; in ensuring compliance with economic commitments, especially those in the ASEAN Economic Community Blueprint; in interpreting the Charter if and when requested; in reporting to the summit on important issues requiring the ASEAN leaders' decision; in representing ASEAN's views in meetings with external parties; and in supervising the ASEAN Foundation.

To help the SG fulfill these added responsibilities, the Charter has doubled the number of deputy secretaries-general (DSGs), from two to four. Two of the four will be chosen through the usual process of national nomination by member governments in alphabetical country-name order, and each will serve a single three-year term. The other two, however, will be recruited openly, and each of these DSGs will serve for up to two three-year terms. To ensure an equitable geographic distribution, the four DSGs and the SG will have to come from five separate member states.[29]

Another provision in the Charter will further enhance the Secretariat's role—the establishment of a Committee of Permanent Representatives to ASEAN, in Jakarta. In due course this new Committee will replace the ASEAN Standing Committee and handle meetings with ASEAN's external partners. The

---

[28] The ASEAN foreign ministers will participate in the ACC chiefly because most of the drafters of the Charter, all of whom were officials in ministries of foreign affairs, believed their ministers were best suited to perform such a coordinating role. Ideas that were suggested but not adopted included allowing each member government to designate the most suitable minister to sit on the ACC, or instead staffing it from a higher level—senior ministers, deputy prime ministers, or vice presidents—so that it would command greater respect.

[29] One of the DSGs will serve each of the three ASEAN councils—the APSC, the AEC, and the ASCC. The economic ministers have let it be known that they, too, want an openly recruited DSG for the ASEAN Economic Community. The fourth DSG may concentrate on Secretariat administration affairs and on narrowing the development gap among ASEAN member states.

latter will be encouraged to appoint their "Ambassadors to ASEAN"[30] to work directly with the Permanent Representatives in Jakarta. This reform will save the member states time and money. Instead of all ten members having to travel to a meeting hosted by a distant external partner, the event can take place in Jakarta. The Permanent Representatives will also address issues concerning the ASEAN Secretariat and support the ACC in preparing for ASEAN summits. This will reduce the ASEAN DGs' need to travel to numerous overseas meetings and enable them instead to concentrate on national coordination and implementation.

In line with the hopes of several ASEAN leaders, the Charter also appears set to make ASEAN a more "people-oriented" organization. More than two-thirds of ASEAN's fifteen stated purposes relate directly to human well-being and security, including one particular goal that commits the Association to promoting "a people-oriented ASEAN in which all sectors of society are encouraged to participate in, and benefit from, the process of ASEAN integration and community building [Art. 2.1]."

In recent years, ASEAN leaders have reached out beyond official circles to hold dialogues with the business sector, with legislators, and with civil society organizations. Foreign ministers and senior officials have also consulted with human rights activists in the informal Working Group for an ASEAN Human Rights Mechanism, and with think-tank scholars in the network of ASEAN Institutes of Strategic and International Studies (ASEAN-ISIS). Economic ministers and senior economic officials are in regular contact with the ASEAN Business Advisory Council (ABAC) and the ASEAN Chamber of Commerce and Industry (ASEAN-CCI). The Charter acknowledges these contacts by stating that the Association "may engage" with such entities, provided they support the Charter, and lists them in its Annex 2.

Reaching out to these groups is one thing, but involving them directly in ASEAN decision-making is quite another. ASEAN will and should remain an intergovernmental organization in which decisions are made by officials and ministers and their leaders—the heads of state or government. The notion that AIPA could someday become an ASEAN Parliament is still a long-term vision. Some in civil society would like to form an ASEAN Economic and Social Advisory Council. But that idea has attracted little official attention, and the Charter's drafters did not favor it.

Incorporating a multitude of private actors in decision-making roles will not necessarily make ASEAN more "people-centered," nor render its agenda and policy decisions more "people-oriented." Such external output would only further dilute the Association's already overstressed and underfunded capacity for action. After all, ASEAN is not a supergovernment; it is only an

---

[30] These "ambassadors to ASEAN" are not required to reside in Jakarta. But they can be more effective if they are based in Jakarta, where they can meet regularly, face-to-face, with the ASEAN Permanent Representatives as well as with the ASEAN SG.

intergovernmental organization. Rather, ASEAN will succeed by developing a capacity for action that will help its peoples enjoy happier lives in a freer, more equitable, safer, and healthier political, economic, social, and natural environment.

Relevant in this connection are the material constraints to which I have already referred. ASEAN has no structural adjustment fund to assist its weaker members. It lacks a development bank to mobilize funds to invest in needed infrastructure. This paucity of resources reflects an old mindset in the Association: that cooperation amounts mainly to consultations and policy coordination. But that was before ASEAN's leaders agreed in the early 2000s to include among the Association's ambitions a narrowing of the development gap between richer and poorer member societies and a promotion of equity alongside growth. Herein arises a chicken-and-egg dilemma. ASEAN needs a larger economic pie before benefits can be channeled to its weaker economies, yet closing the gap to strengthen the latter is crucial to that expansion.

In its present form and with its current funding, ASEAN cannot accomplish this nor tackle its many other complex tasks. For all its organizational extensions, the Association has few institutions of a brick-and-mortar nature with long-term staff. Its central Secretariat and its ten national secretariats are the only real, live organs in its machinery. The rest consists of summits, meetings, dialogues, committees, subcommittees, task forces, and so on—events, not agencies, and periodic occasions, not permanent offices.

A few affiliated centers of specialized excellence do exist. The ASEAN Foundation, the ASEAN Centre on Energy (ACE), and the ASEAN Earthquakes Information Centre are located in Jakarta. Los Banos, in the Philippines, is home to the ASEAN Centre for Biodiversity (ACB). The ASEAN University Network Secretariat is in Bangkok, and the ASEAN Specialized Meteorological Centre is in Singapore. Also worth noting are entities in cyberspace, among them a virtual secretariat for ASEM that the ASEAN Secretariat in Jakarta maintains, and a Virtual Institute of Science and Technology, run by the Asian Institute of Technology, in Pathumthani, Thailand.

ASEAN's external links have also engendered several bodies outside Southeast Asia. In Tokyo, an ASEAN-Japan Centre promotes trade, investment, and tourism. Ninety percent of its operating budget comes from Japan, while the ten ASEAN states supply the remaining 10 percent in equal, 1 percent contributions. In 2009, the 9:1 proportional sharing of contributions to the Centre budget will be changed to a new formula of 7:1, with Japan contributing 7 and ASEAN contributing 1. An ASEAN-China Center to promote trade, investment, tourism, education, and culture was being planned in Beijing, while a similar joint center between ASEAN and South Korea was scheduled for an early opening in Seoul in August 2008. Last but not least is the Economic Research Institute for ASEAN and East Asia (ERIA), temporarily housed at the ASEAN Secretariat pending agreement on a permanent site. Yet these are not core agencies of the Association.

If ASEAN member states are to strengthen its central administration, actual resources are needed to back their expressed faith in regionalism. Annually the member states contribute some US$ 8–9 million to fund the ASEAN Secretariat. In the 2007–08 financial year, which began in June 2007, the Secretariat's operating budget was US$ 9,050,000. In its budget proposal, the Secretariat had requested an increase of about 25 percent from its FY 2006–07 budget, but the actual increment was only 7 percent. A Secretariat budget barely larger than US$ 9 million is miniscule when viewed against the combined nominal GDP of the member states—more than US$ 1 trillion in 2007. Likewise in 2007, the EU's annual operating budget exceeded 125 billion euros.

To the Secretariat's US$ 9,050,000, each member state contributed an equal share of US$ 905,000. The ASEAN Charter has reaffirmed the practice of equal contributions, based on the principle of equal rights and equal obligations. The Secretariat's budget will remain effectively hostage to whatever the least able or least willing member is able or willing to pay.

An ASEAN Development Fund does exist outside the Secretariat's budget. Each member state has contributed US$ 1 million for a total of US$ 10 million. Interest earned on this amount can be used to fund specific projects. At around 5 percent per annum, however, the return on principal generates a mere US$ 500,000 per year—hardly a meaningful sum to support cooperation across a region of nearly 600 million people. The member states did agree to lift the principal to US$ 11 million, with additional contributions of US$ 100,000 per country by the end of 2007. But the disparity between means and ends remains.

Without its own resources, ASEAN as an organization cannot widen the range of feasible regional action. The idea to supply the ASEAN Political-Security Community with an ASEAN force to keep regional peace was shot down, ostensibly from concern that ASEAN could not afford to pay the bill for any peacekeeping operations that might result. Members argued that it was better to let the United Nations handle, and pay for, peacekeeping worldwide, including in Southeast Asia. Had adequate resources been available to ASEAN for a purpose such as peacekeeping, the decision could have been made on more clearly substantive grounds.

ASEAN was similarly unable to respond when its assistance in postconflict peacebuilding was directly solicited, as in East Timor after the 1999 referendum and in Aceh in 2005. Whatever other considerations may have led ASEAN to say no to these requests, it was financially unable to say yes. Malaysia, the Philippines, Singapore, and Thailand did participate in peace operations in East Timor and Aceh, but they did so as individual countries, not under any ASEAN arrangement.

Between Indifference and Interference: The Responsibility to Cooperate

Historically basic to ASEAN's credo, but increasingly controversial, is the belief that the domestic affairs of any member need not and should not be subject to interference from ASEAN or any other member state. The principle remains useful, so long as invoking it does not violate the common interest of ASEAN as a whole.[31]

Noninterference should not and cannot be abandoned, because it is part of international law and a logical corollary of sovereign equality. But it should be complemented with a second principle, that of fulfilling one's responsibility to ASEAN. I call this the *responsibility to cooperate*. This additional principle would oblige every member state to participate in ASEAN to the best of its ability and to support enhanced cooperation by promptly implementing ASEAN decisions and agreements. Every member state must avoid hurting ASEAN's common interest, and cooperate with fellow members in efforts to resolve all situations, domestic or bilateral, that disturb regional peace and harmony or disrupt the Association.

Indeed, one can argue that the responsibility to cooperate not only can prevail over the principle of noninterference, but has already done so. For example, several times Myanmar has decided—or has been persuaded by the other nine ASEAN foreign ministers to agree—to skip its turn to chair the Association for a year according to the normal alphabetic rotation. In 2006–07, the chairmanship therefore passed from Malaysia to the Philippines, and Singapore succeeded the Philippines for 2007–08, leaving Thailand next in line to chair ASEAN during 2008–09. Myanmar was also "persuaded" to skip its turn to chair the ASEAN Economic Ministers Meeting. This abstention enabled the economic ministers, under a Philippine chair, to conclude an agreement with the EU trade commissioner to start FTA talks, since the EU would almost certainly not have made that agreement had Myanmar been chairing the ASEAN side.

After forty years, ASEAN should have built up enough mutual confidence among its members to be able to rely on its members' responsibility to cooperate in building the ASEAN Community. The time has come to develop a more ambitious long-term political vision for the Association and the region. If the ideas of an "ASEAN Union" and promotion of democratic values are still thought to be too far-fetched, what creative but more realistic steps can be taken "to bring ASEAN's political and security cooperation to a higher plane," as envisaged in 2003 in the Declaration of ASEAN Concord II? In 2008, this was still an open question. But it was an important question, and it was time for ASEAN ministers and officials to tackle it in drawing up the Blueprint for the ASEAN Political-Security Community.

---

[31] The Charter refers to this condition—the common good—in committing member states to engage in "enhanced consultations on matters seriously affecting the common interest of ASEAN" and to acknowledge "collective responsibility" for regional security (Art. 2.2[g] and 2.2[b], respectively).

Consider the shortcomings of dispute settlement in ASEAN. The conventional wisdom among the region's diplomats has always been that bilateral disputes should be settled by the two parties concerned, without involving ASEAN or anyone else. Not every dispute, after all, disturbs or seems likely to disturb regional peace. Also, if necessary and with mutual agreement by the parties, a bilateral dispute can always be referred to the High Council provided for in the 1976 TAC.

Yet as of 2007 the High Council still existed only on paper. No two bilaterally disputing ASEAN states had ever agreed to refer their disagreement to the High Council. The possibility did arise in connection with rival Indonesian and Malaysian claims to sovereignty over Sipadan and Ligitan islands. Indonesia wanted to submit that dispute to the High Council. But in the end the two governments agreed to go instead to the International Court of Justice (ICJ) in The Hague, where Malaysia won in 2002.

A more recent instance of joint recourse to the ICJ involves Singapore and Malaysia's agreement to have the Court resolve their competing claims to an islet that they respectively call Pedra Blanca and Batu Puteh (and over still smaller features called Middle Rocks and South Ledge). In May 2008 the ICJ awarded Pedra Branca/Batu Puteh to Singapore, Middle Rocks to Malaysia, and did not explicitly assign the ownership of South Ledge. Neither the dispute nor its outcome distracted the two governments from cooperation in ASEAN.

As specified in the TAC, the High Council can only "*recommend* appropriate measures for the prevention of a deterioration of the dispute or the situation" (emphasis added). Even if such a Council were convened, it would have no authority to render a binding judgment. Its advice might cool things down, but the High Council's purely advisory status means that it cannot be used to *settle* a dispute.

The already low likelihood that any two ASEAN members would ever activate the High Council was lowered further in 2001. In that year it was agreed that High Contracting Parties located outside Southeast Asia could send observers to a High Council meeting, unless the Council decided otherwise.[32] (As noted earlier, fourteen such nonmembers of ASEAN had signed the treaty by 2007.) Knowing that they could end up quarreling in front of outsiders may make ASEAN members even less inclined to bring their disputes with each other before the Council.

Nor is it likely that any of the nonregional states that have signed the TAC would want to refer to the High Council their own bilateral disputes with any Southeast Asian states. Because the latter's membership in ASEAN automatically entitles them to sit on the High Council, an outside state in a bilateral dispute with an ASEAN state might well doubt that it could get an objective hearing there.

---

[32] As stated in Rule 14 in the Rules of Procedure of the High Council of the Treaty of Amity and Cooperation in Southeast Asia, adopted in Hanoi on 23 July 2001.

Meanwhile, many bilateral disputes between states in Southeast Asia remain unresolved, despite the intent of the ASEAN Political-Security Community to settle them expeditiously. It is time to think of new and better ways of addressing this problem on ASEAN's intramural agenda. The APSC may need a new dispute settlement mechanism for ASEAN members only.

Among disputes involving states both inside and outside Southeast Asia, competing claims to ownership of maritime space in the South China Sea have been especially intractable. The Spratly Islands and other parts of the sea have been claimed variously by Brunei Darussalam, China, Malaysia, the Philippines, Taiwan, and Vietnam. In 1992, hoping to defuse this potentially explosive issue, ASEAN issued a Declaration on the South China Sea that called for the resolution of "all sovereignty and jurisdictional issues pertaining to the South China Sea by peaceful means, without resort to force."[33]

At first, China was not prepared to rule out the use of force and did not subscribe to the 1992 Declaration. But as ASEAN continued to engage China on the matter, the Chinese position softened. In 1996, China became a Dialogue Partner of ASEAN. In 1997 in Malaysia, the then Chinese president Jiang Zemin met his Southeast Asian counterparts on the sidelines of ASEAN's 2nd Informal Summit. In their joint statement, they agreed to settle their differences peacefully, and specifically "to resolve their disputes in the South China Sea through friendly consultations and negotiations in accordance with universally recognized international law, including the 1982 UN Convention on the Law of the Sea."

In 2002 this understanding and related confidence-building ideas were developed further in a formal Declaration on the Conduct of Parties in the South China Sea. A year later, ASEAN and China became "strategic partners." In 2006 their respective leaders marked the fifteenth year of ASEAN-China consultation at a Commemorative Summit in Nanning, China, near its border with Vietnam.[34] By 2007, media references to the South China Sea as a "flash point" in Southeast Asia had become rare. These developments notwithstanding, in December 2007, in the wake of China's establishment of a symbolic administrative region of Sansha—its office is located on Hainan Island, and its jurisdiction is supposed

---

[33] ASEAN Declaration on the South China Sea, Manila, Philippines, 22 July 1992, Operative Paragraph 1.

[34] Normally, a commemorative summit with an ASEAN dialogue partner would occur on the thirtieth anniversary of their relationship. Examples of such thirty-year timing include ASEAN's summits with Japan in 2003, with Australia and New Zealand in 2004, and with the EU in 2007. Celebrating the fifteenth year of China's dialogue with ASEAN was special in this context. An ASEAN-U.S. commemorative summit had been planned for early September 2007, but was canceled because U.S. President George W. Bush could not attend. Subsequently, President Bush extended an invitation to all ASEAN leaders to gather at his Texas ranch for a commemorative summit in early 2008, but by the end of 2007 that meeting, too, had been called off.

to include the disputed islands of the Paracels and the Spratlys—Vietnamese marched to the Chinese Embassy in Hanoi to protest.

Balancing National and Regional Interests: The Need for Reciprocity

If ASEAN has been relatively successful in dealing with non-Southeast Asian states, and if no two of its members have fought each other during its existence, regionally significant conflicts occurring inside an ASEAN state have remained almost wholly outside the Association's purview. If and when the leaders of one country have asserted that a disturbance or difficulty inside its borders was strictly a domestic and not a regional concern, the other member governments have normally gone along and avoided even considering the issue, let alone acting on it. East Timor was a case in point for most of the prolonged Indonesian occupation of that half-island. Ongoing violence in southern Thailand is a more recent example. In such instances the lack of consensus among members has precluded forming an ASEAN Troika even for the purpose of sending a fact-finding mission to the country in question.

Given this context, in 2007, an ASEAN court of justice remained out of the question. ASEAN-ISIS did at first recommend that the Charter include an ASEAN court of justice, but subsequently withdrew the idea, and the Charter's drafters never looked seriously into the matter.

If corrective measures are to be taken for disputes that arise when members do not implement, or delay implementing, ASEAN agreements and decisions, they will have to be fashioned piecemeal through state-to-state diplomacy. The ASEAN Economic Community does incorporate an enhanced dispute settlement mechanism (DSM), agreed to in 2004. But the DSM is not available to private businesses or individuals claiming to have been financially damaged by such non- or delayed implementation. Nor have member states been willing to submit their bilateral trade or economic disputes to the DSM, preferring instead to address such problems quietly and bilaterally.

The ASEAN Charter does deal with the settlement of disputes. Three innovations are particularly significant. First, parties to a dispute may ask "the Chairman of ASEAN or the Secretary-General of ASEAN, acting in an ex-officio capacity, to provide good offices, conciliation or mediation" (Art. 23.2). Second, should a dispute remain unresolved despite such recourse, or the application of any other instruments or mechanisms cited in the Charter, it "shall be referred to the ASEAN Summit, for its decision" (Art. 26). The Charter also states that member states "shall endeavour to resolve peacefully all disputes in a timely manner" (Art. 22.1). This implies, in effect, that a dispute should not remain forever unresolved. Third, any member state that is "affected by non-compliance with the findings, recommendations or decisions resulting from an ASEAN dispute settlement mechanism, may refer the matter to the ASEAN Summit for a decision" (Art. 27.2). This legalistic provision is a clear departure from the ASEAN Way, in that it opens the possibility of redress to any member that suffers from another member's noncompliance with what the Association has said it should do.

Many of the existing domestic conflicts or crisis situations involve the alleged violation of citizens' rights by government and military authorities. Already in 1993, at the 26th AMM, in Singapore, ASEAN's foreign ministers agreed to consider establishing "an appropriate regional mechanism on human rights." As of 2007, only Indonesia, Malaysia, the Philippines, and Thailand had formed national commissions on human rights; these bodies had in turn set up their own network for mutual support. (Cambodia was in the process of formalizing its national human rights commission.) The ASEAN human rights body called for by the Charter will be a welcome addition. Unfortunately, the ASEAN Charter does not go as far as recognizing "ASEAN citizenship," unlike in the EU, where European citizenship is both recognized and protected by both the EU and its member states.

ASEAN should not abandon consultation and consensus in decision-making, nor scrap sovereign equality among member states. ASEAN's unity has been well served by these principles. But they can be adapted to reduce both the inordinate time that may be spent making a decision and the likelihood that what results is merely the least objectionable—as opposed to the most desirable—outcome for the Association.

ASEAN's leaders have come around to the view that if a bold decision is needed, they themselves need to take it, bypassing the chance of delay in deliberation at lesser levels of authority. This is what happened when the leaders agreed at their January 2007 summit to accelerate building the ASEAN Community despite lingering doubts among some ministers and senior officials. Yet passing responsibility to the very highest level has its drawbacks. Ministers and senior officials should also be able to make more decisions at their own levels. Waiting for a summit triggers its own delay. Under the Charter, the leaders will meet twice a year, but only one of those summits will be spent entirely on intraregional business.

Some flexibility does exist in the "minus X" formula used in the ASEAN Economic Community, whereby members that are unable or unready to join a particular cooperation scheme can opt out without stopping the scheme from going forward. "In the implementation of economic commitments," the Charter states, "a formula for flexible participation, including the ASEAN Minus X formula, may be applied where there is a consensus to do so" (Art. 21.2).

Comparable in purpose are the staggered deadlines and multispeed timelines that accommodate the more limited capacities of less developed members. Yet even these arrangements require a consensus before they can be put in place, as do the projects to which they apply. Flexibility is desirable in principle, but when a member state tries to maximize that condition for itself, to keep its own options open, rather than for ASEAN as a whole, implementation can suffer. Delays have been especially common in the ASEAN Economic Community, despite its provisions to prevent them.

The Charter does not provide for sanctions, suspension, or expulsion in the event of noncompliance. The reason is simple: If ASEAN expels any member, sooner or later there will be no Association to speak of. If ASEAN suspends any member, the atmosphere for dialogue and cooperation will deteriorate. The existential value of keeping every member within the ASEAN fold and of doing things step-by-step at a pace comfortable to all remains paramount.

What then will ASEAN do to ensure that its decisions are implemented? In the AEC, members could use the DSM to retaliate against one another for delays and noncompliance. But this will only further slow the AEC's formation. As already noted, the Charter does provide for a member state adversely affected by delays and noncompliance ultimately to refer its case to the ASEAN summit. But it is unclear what ASEAN leaders could or would do in such a situation.

ASEAN needs something positive to reward prompt implementation—an incentive more potent than appealing to a member's presumed desire to enjoy a reputation for cooperation. But first ASEAN needs its own income, so that it will have resources to offer as an incentive, or to withhold as a form of punishment.

National ego and ASEAN interest often conflict. After more than four decades, a serious disconnect remains between national policies and regional priorities. The Association must explore ways to make the national and the regional less competitive and more complementary. Just as ASEAN can help each member's national development, so can each member help ASEAN build a regional community by incorporating regional priorities into its own national preferences and actions.

Meshing interests in this way is a win-win arrangement. But it will take time before every Southeast Asian state has learned to accept the Association as something more—and more valuable—than the mere sum of its parts. Members will need to work more closely with the ASEAN SG, for example, according him or her greater respect and more confidence in his or her impartiality.

It is not coincidental in this context that during his secretary-generalship Ong Keng Yong liked to quip that he was more a "secretary" than a "general."

Conclusion: Looking Forward

At forty-nine wide-margined pages, including annexes, the ASEAN Charter is a mere one-tenth the length of the EU's ill-fated Treaty Establishing a Constitution for Europe. Ideally, in the eyes of some ASEAN leaders, the Charter should have been as bold as it was brief. But drafting it proved an unprecedented challenge.

Instinctively and sensibly, the officials on the HLTF exercised extreme caution in doing their job. They were in a difficult position. Though politically diverse and nationally constrained, they were expected to produce a Charter that would add significant fresh value to ASEAN—a document that everyone in the Association could be proud of. They were asked to reorganize a burgeoning family of bodies, meetings, and initiatives. Yet there would be no questioning the leadership role of the heads of state and government. Indeed, insofar as the frequency of summits will increase from once to twice a year, that role could increase.

As always, decisions made in drafting the Charter were based on consultation and consensus. What made its way into the text was not necessarily what was most desirable. More often than not, it was what no one could object to.

ASEAN needs clearer lines of authority. Inside the Association as of mid-2008, at the level immediately beneath the summit, there were twenty-eight separate ministerial bodies, served by a rapidly growing ASEAN bureaucracy. Most of the ministers want to report directly to the summit. The finance ministers, for example, prefer not to report through the economic ministers, although the latter are the formal AEC coordinators. Some of the finance ministers (in Malaysia and Brunei Darussalam, and until December 2007, in Singapore) serve simultaneously as heads of government. A clear reporting line is required to resolve and prevent disputes over turf.

Efficient resource mobilization to meet ASEAN's growing needs is another key challenge. At a minimum, the Association should be provided with its own reliable sources and steady flows of income. In the long run, ASEAN must aim at self-sufficiency, increasingly relying on its own resources to undertake cooperative activities in pursuit of its stated purposes. The Charter falls short in this respect. It does promise that "the ASEAN Secretariat shall be provided with the necessary financial resources to perform its functions effectively" (Art. 30.1). But what are "its functions"? The Secretariat's operating expenses are one thing. So far they have amounted to less than US$ 10 million a year. But resources to help narrow the development gap between ASEAN's economies and to fund its numerous projects are an entirely different matter. Resources for regional cooperation in the EU come from assessed contributions by all member states. Each amount is based on the size of that member's GDP and is augmented by a share of the value-added taxes and import tariffs that it collects. In this manner, the EU raises over 100 billion euros every year to fund its activities.

In ASEAN, the Charter has made this priority both more urgent, by enhancing the SG's mandate and the Secretariat's responsibilities, and more difficult, by reaffirming the practice of equal contributions, which renders the Secretariat's operating budget hostage to what the least wealthy or generous member is able or willing to pay.

The challenge is to explore more creative ways and means of mobilizing supplementary income for the Secretariat. But first the SG and/or the Secretariat, or other relevant ASEAN bodies, should be authorized to raise funds for ASEAN. A "Support ASEAN Fee" of US$ 1 per airfare, for example, could easily raise US$ 20–30 million a year for the Association—two or even three times the Secretariat's operational costs as of 2007. There would then be no need to rely on member-state contributions to fund the Secretariat. Time and

129

energy would no longer be wasted in the ASEAN Budget Committee in painful annual scrutiny and debate.

As for the broader building of the ASEAN Community, several ideas have been broached. An ASEAN Bond Market has already been implemented. Finance officials and the Asian Development Bank have been studying a possible investment-financing scheme for infrastructure in the region. But more must be done to mobilize the considerably greater resources that are necessary to realize the ASEAN Community.

With the Charter duly signed in November 2007, the immediate challenge is now to ensure its timely and full ratification so that it can come into effect as soon as possible. The Charter is not cast in stone, and it can be improved. In fact, upon the document's coming into force, any member state may propose an amendment immediately. Amendments aside, the entire Charter may be reviewed five years after its entry into force, or sooner, if the leaders want to do so.

The Charter is certainly not an end in itself. It cannot—nor was it meant to—radically revamp ASEAN in a "big bang" way. It does provide a new legal and institutional framework for the member states to use in building on the past forty years of ASEAN experience.

One should therefore not make too much of the fact that the Charter falls short of the most desirable outcome that many had wished for. What counts is that ASEAN leaders have declared their common determination and commitment to build the ASEAN Community, whose promising details this chapter has tried to convey, and to apply the Charter to that vital goal.

ASEAN's first four decades showed that it was capable of changing for the better. The gestation time of big new ideas usually took about one decade from inception to fruition. Back in 1967, the five founding fathers did not even bother to call for any central office to sustain their Association. Only in 1976, after nearly ten years of getting to know one another in regional meetings, did these founding members decide to establish the ASEAN Secretariat in Jakarta. And the Secretariat was deliberately kept to a low profile, with a small seconded staff to provide some meeting services and institutional memory.

By the early 1990s, the member states realized that ASEAN could do more than merely facilitate confidence-building meetings and piecemeal projects on technical matters. ASEAN's real potential, and its comparative advantage, was and remains in economic cooperation and market integration. When the member states wanted to launch the ASEAN Free Trade Area in 1993, they *first* had to strengthen the Secretariat. They did so in 1992, by openly recruiting its professional staff, renaming the chief officer Secretary-General *of ASEAN*, and giving that role ministerial status. Ten years later, in 2003, the member states took another big step forward by launching programs to build a three-pillared ASEAN Community. And again, the Association's rules and organization were upgraded to support that historic endeavor.

That upgrading is what the fortieth anniversary Charter, despite its limitations, is all about. The new legal and institutional framework that the Charter will put into place will enable ASEAN to intensify cooperation among its members and thereby become politically more cohesive, economically more competitive, and institutionally more capable of responding to challenges within and outside the region. The only crucial element still missing from the new format is the systematic mobilization of resources. That will have to be tackled sooner or later, but certainly not later than 2015—when the first phase of ASEAN Community-building is scheduled to end.

All in all, in my view, the history of ASEAN is an encouraging story of regionalism in Southeast Asia. The Association's members have gained enough experience over the past forty years to move beyond building confidence among Southeast Asian governments to building a community of Southeast Asians. With their Charter now in place, the members should be able to move forward at a faster pace to do many more important things together.

This is a historic mission. ASEAN cannot fail. The future of nearly six hundred million Southeast Asians is at stake.

ISSUES

POLITICAL DEVELOPMENT: A DEMOCRACY AGENDA FOR ASEAN?

Rizal Sukma

Centre for Strategic and International Studies
Indonesia

Four decades since it was established in August 1967, the Association of Southeast Asian Nations (ASEAN) continues to draw both criticism and admiration. In the eyes of its harshest detractors, ASEAN is a futile venture in useless regionalism. To many of its supporters, the Association is the most successful instance of regional cooperation outside the European Union (EU). In between these judgments, numerous analysts have acknowledged ASEAN's shortcomings while also noting its strengths. In the aftermath of the 1997 economic crisis that swept parts of Southeast Asia, however, the balance tipped toward more and more vigorous criticisms. Critiques intensified even within the Association. Participants and observers alike began calling for ASEAN to strengthen its relevance by revitalizing or even reinventing itself.[1]

The most important innovations that ASEAN has undertaken in response to such calls for change have been an ASEAN Security Community (ASC) and an ASEAN Charter.[2] These projects have evolved at the intersection of all three of the themes of this book: security, democracy, and regionalism. Whether the ASC should include democracy alongside security as a main regional principle or goal has been a key topic for discussion ever since the idea of such a Community was first approved in October 2003. Applied to ASEAN as a whole, the same themes

---

[1] See, for example, Simon SC Tay, Jesus Estanislao, and Hadi Soesastro, eds., *Reinventing ASEAN* (Singapore: ISEAS, 2001).

[2] A clarification of terms is in order. When the ASEAN Community was first proposed, it was to consist of three "pillars" that were themselves called communities: an "ASEAN Economic Community" (AEC), an "ASEAN Socio-Cultural Community" (ASCC), and an "ASEAN Security Community" (ASC). The names of the AEC and the ASCC have not changed. The Charter that the ten heads of government signed on 20 November 2007, which provided for the management of these three component communities by community councils, did name the one for the ASC "the ASEAN Political-Security Council" (APSC)—and thus by implication renamed the ASC the APSC. However, the ASC exists independently of the Charter, and was given its own "ASEAN Security Community Plan of Action" in 2004, three years before the Charter was signed. This chapter therefore uses the pillar's original name and abbreviation: the ASEAN Security Community, or ASC.

have animated debate in preparations for the Charter, since the organization first decided, in December 2005, that it needed to have one.

In view of ASEAN's aversion to taking stands that might imply passing judgment on the domestic political systems and practices of its member states, it is remarkable that the ASC Plan of Action includes and even emphasizes the promotion of democracy as a legitimate goal of the Association.[3] The Charter also makes a reference to the need for ASEAN member states to adhere to democracy and to promote and protect human rights.[4] This development raises important questions about the relationship between democracy and security in Southeast Asia. Can ASEAN promote democracy in the region? Even if it can, should it? And how would the promotion of democracy affect security in Southeast Asia? Would regional security be enhanced? Or would it be undermined?

This chapter argues that the relationship between democracy and security is problematic for ASEAN. Democracy is one way, among others, to attain and maintain security. Yet imposing democracy on a member state and intrusively spreading it throughout the region would trigger interstate tensions harmful to security. Therefore, democracy as envisaged in the ASC and the Charter is not meant to be the only instrument for ensuring or strengthening regional security. Nor is ASEAN being mandated to inculcate democracy directly inside member states. Forcing democracy onto the region is something the Association has not done, cannot do, and should not try to do.

The agreement to include democracy in the rationales for the ASC and the Charter is hardly a license to intervene. It is less a basis for policy than an attempt, in effect, to encourage and remind ASEAN's members that they need to embrace democratic values—but in the long run, at each state's own pace, and depending on its own political will to reform. Democracy promotion inside ASEAN will, in other words, take place within the limits of, and in line with, its long-established commitment to noninterference and conflict-avoidance. Nor should the new visibility of democracy on its agenda imply that the Association believes it to be the sole road to security in the region.

For these reasons, simply acknowledging democracy in this limited and normative context is unlikely in the future either to advance or to impede security in Southeast Asia.

This chapter does not pursue the abstract question of whether democracy is conducive or inimical to security in general. Nor will that question be taken up with reference to the ten individual countries of Southeast Asia. The chapter focuses, instead, on ASEAN—as it has dealt with, and as it may be affected by, the addition of democracy to security as a rationale for regionalism in Southeast Asia. I will pay particular attention in this context to the promises

---

[3] For the Plan and its Annex, see respectively, <http://www.aseansec.org/16826.htm> and <http://www.aseansec.org/16829.htm>.

[4] See Art. 1.7. The text of the Charter is located at the back of this book.

and pitfalls of a democracy agenda for the ASC and the Charter, and to its possible consequences for building a regional community.

The discussion is divided into several sections. The first sections trace the origins of the ASC, its relationship to the Charter, and the thinking and process behind the inclusion of references to democracy within the two initiatives. Next, the chapter reviews ten limits on ASEAN's ability to advance democracy. A final section reintroduces security as a possible benefit of democracy in Southeast Asia and recommends how, within the ASC and through the implementation of the Charter, democracy might be encouraged in a way that need not endanger security in the region.

Initial Failure (2003): "Political Development" Sidetracked

The ASC began as an Indonesian idea. Indonesia first officially proposed such a Community at an ASEAN Senior Officials Meeting in June 2003 in Phnom Penh. According to the proposal, one of the ASC's five key tasks would be "political development," and Indonesia understood that as committing the Community to encourage the democratization of Southeast Asia. The other four ASC duties that Indonesia listed were setting norms, preventing conflict, resolving conflict, and building peace after conflict.

Indonesia strongly argued that security in the region could not be attained and guaranteed unless member states paid attention not only to security in a narrow sense but also to the imperative of political development. Indonesia contended that even though political development had traditionally been understood as a domestic affair inside a given state, there was in fact room for future cooperation among ASEAN member states on this topic. And even if such cooperation were not yet possible, there should nonetheless be a collective commitment by the member governments to undertake and encourage political development inside their respective countries. A regional effort to transform ASEAN into a "democratic entity" was needed if ASEAN were to revitalize itself in response to the new and complex challenges of the twenty-first century.

Indonesia did not, at this early stage, openly advocate a "democracy agenda" for ASEAN, preferring instead to recommend that the ASC concern itself with "political development"—a more vague and thus less controversial term. The details of the proposal as these were spelled out, however, clearly registered the spirit if not the letter of an ASEAN "democracy agenda." What Indonesia meant by "political development" was that member states should, for example, "promote people's participation, *particularly through the conduct of general elections*"; "implement good governance"; "strengthen judicial institutions and legal reforms"; and "promote human rights and obligations through the establishment of the [previously proposed] ASEAN Commission on Human Rights."[5]

That Indonesia took this step was no coincidence. Since the resignation of President Soeharto in 1998 and the end of his authoritarian regime, ASEAN's largest member had been undergoing its own political development to become the third largest democracy in the world. In this respect, in calling for democracy in Southeast Asia, Indonesia was projecting its own experience onto the region.

In proposing, without using the words, a "democracy agenda" for ASEAN, Indonesia broke new and controversial ground. Unsurprisingly, most of the rest of the Association's members were at first skeptical about the value of such a regional endeavor. Questions were raised regarding the possible damage that such a "democracy agenda" might do to ASEAN's cardinal principles of noninterference, national sovereignty, consensus, and quiet diplomacy. The prospect that ASEAN might intervene in a member's domestic affairs triggered deep concern. Some feared that Indonesia's proposal could altogether doom the so-called "ASEAN Way" in which these principles had been enshrined. Most of the members understood that democracy could be one foundation of security. But they failed to see how the norm of noninterference in a member's "internal" affairs could be reconciled with the idea of promoting democracy inside that member by external intervention—ASEAN acting as an institution, for example, or other members acting alone or in coalition.

In the months following Indonesia's proposal, these and other objections to tasking the ASC with a de facto "democracy agenda" were raised repeatedly inside ASEAN, and especially in Senior Officials Meetings convened to prepare for the 9th ASEAN Summit, planned for October 2003 in Bali, Indonesia. The summit did commit ASEAN to building the Security Community. But the Declaration of ASEAN Concord II that formally approved the ASC listed only four necessary steps toward creating it: norms-setting, conflict prevention, conflict resolution, and post-conflict peace-building. Missing from the document was any reference to "political development," the fifth measure that Indonesia had proposed.[6] Instead, in its Concord II, ASEAN committed itself to upholding the principles of noninterference and national sovereignty,[7] in their own right and as underpinnings of the ASC. In this respect, despite hosting the summit, Indonesia failed to carry the day.

---

[5] Indonesian Department of Foreign Affairs, "Towards an ASEAN Security Community: Indonesia's Non-Paper," June 2003; italics added. At ASEAN Senior Officials Meetings, compared with a "paper" that conveys a fixed official view, a "non-paper" is not yet official, and is meant to stimulate responses from other member states.

[6] The text of this and other ASEAN documents mentioned in this chapter may be accessed at <http://www.aseansec.org/15159.htm>. The complete text of the ASEAN Charter appears at the end of this book.

[7] Donald K. Emmerson, "Security, Community, and Democracy in Southeast Asia: Analyzing ASEAN," *Japanese Journal of Political Science* 6, no. 2 (2005), 180.

Symbolic Success (2004–2005): Toward a "Democratic" Security Community

How, then, did democracy become an element in the ASC? Their inability in Bali to insert "political development" into the rationale for an ASC did not stop Indonesian officials from moving on to the next phase: operational planning for the actual creation of the Security Community to which ASEAN's leaders had just agreed. Fortunately for Indonesia, beyond the already mentioned four steps, the ASEAN Concord II did not specify how the ASC would be formed or what exactly it would do. Although ASEAN had fallen back on familiar norms, such as noninterference, sovereignty, and consensus, these general principles were usefully ambiguous as to the concrete actions they did or did not rule out.[8]

The Concord II did, nevertheless, provide some guidance regarding the ASC. First, in launching the ASC the Association went on record as wanting to strengthen political and security cooperation by institutionalizing it. To the extent that this priority implied giving more authority and leeway to ASEAN, it allowed for second thoughts on the sanctity of national sovereignty. Second, the ASC was intended to ensure "comprehensive security" in Southeast Asia. That phrase could be construed as an argument for linking domestic security to regional security in view of the former's impact on the latter. Third, setting norms, preventing conflict, resolving conflict, and building peace following conflict—all mentioned in the Concord II—were at least compatible with democracy as a means of peacefully institutionalizing disagreement and thus avoiding outright conflict.[9] In November 2004, at ASEAN's 10th Summit, in Vientiane, Laos, these guidelines were included in a Vientiane Action Program (VAP).[10]

In the run-up to the Vientiane summit, Indonesia managed to persuade other ASEAN states to reinsert the deleted imperative of "political development" in the language used to describe the ASC. Accordingly, the summit restored the phrase in two senses: as a "strategic thrust" in building the Community (in the VAP), and as an eventual activity of the Community itself (in the ASEAN Security Community Plan of Action, or ASCPA).

This victory for the Indonesian position was in some ways more apparent than real. Both the VAP and the ASCPA watered down Indonesia's original "democracy agenda" for ASEAN. Neither document referred, for example, to general elections as a key ingredient of democracy, or to the need to widen political participation by holding them. The ASCPA did, however, make democracy an objective of ASEAN when it called on member states to promote

---

[8] See Jurgen Hacke, "'Enhanced Interaction' with Myanmar and the Project of a Security Community: Is ASEAN Refining or Breaking with Its Diplomatic and Security Culture?" *Contemporary Southeast Asia* 27, no. 2 (August 2005), 202.

[9] See Declaration of ASEAN Concord II (Bali Concord II), <http://www.aseansec.org/16826.htm>.

[10] The text of the VAP is available at <http://www.aseansec.org/Publ-VAP.pdf>.

"political development" in order to "achieve peace, stability, *democracy* and prosperity in the region" (emphasis added). It also stated that "ASEAN Member Countries shall not condone unconstitutional and undemocratic changes of government" and included promoting "human rights" as one strategy for political development, although the full phrase used was "human rights and obligations." However imperfect this result, it did give ASEAN a democratic agenda to work on.

The ASC was planned as one of three pillars of an eventual ASEAN Community, the other two being an ASEAN Economic Community and an ASEAN Socio-Cultural Community. There is a growing awareness among the Association's past and present leaders that if it is to succeed in building such a complex and comprehensive regional community, ASEAN will need to change the way it operates.[11]

Enter the Charter. At the 11th ASEAN Summit, in Kuala Lumpur in December 2005, the leaders decided to devise an ASEAN Charter that would serve as a "legal and institutional framework" for the Association, and thereby enable it to realize its objectives, including all three pillars of the ASEAN Community. This Kuala Declaration also established an Eminent Persons Group (EPG), with a mandate to make recommendations "on the directions and nature of the ASEAN Charter." The EPG was tasked, in drafting its advice, to consider the "principles, values and objectives" of ASEAN laid out in the Declaration, and these included "the promotion of democracy, human rights and obligations" and the "strengthening of democratic institutions."[12]

It is important to note that nearly all of the ten members of the EPG, one from each member country, were *former* officials. To that extent, they were freer in what they could propose than if they had been on active duty and thus more closely tied to government policy. That may help to explain their venturesomeness in stating flatly that ASEAN should adhere to the principles of "respect for and protection and promotion of human rights and fundamental freedoms" and "the rejection of unconstitutional and undemocratic changes of government," and that the Charter should list among ASEAN's goals "the strengthening of democratic values" and "respect for human rights."[13]

The EPG was not asked to write the Charter. That task was entrusted to *sitting* officials in a High-Level Task Force (HLTF). Nor was it coincidental, given their active-duty status and necessary loyalty to incumbent governments,

---

[11] On this point, see, for example, Ali Alatas, "The ASEAN Charter," keynote address, conference on "Shaping ASEAN's Future: The Road Ahead," 4th ASEAN Leadership Forum, Jakarta, 17 April 2007, 2.

[12] Kuala Lumpur Declaration on the Establishment of the ASEAN Charter, Kuala Lumpur, Malaysia, 12 December 2005, <http://www.aseansec.org/18030.htm>.

[13] *Report of the Eminent Persons Group on the ASEAN Charter* (Jakarta: ASEAN Secretariat, December 2006), <http://www.aseansec.org/19247.pdf> pp. 28 (principles) and 15 (goals).

that the HTLF's members were distinctly cooler toward democracy than their counterparts in the EPG had been.

The actual Charter, adopted at the ASEAN's 13th Summit, in Singapore in November 2007, did retain "democracy" and "human rights" as legitimate goals of the Association. In the HLTF's closed-door deliberations, the case for omitting such references altogether had not prevailed.[14] Yet the Charter as finally revealed in Singapore was not an unalloyed instrument for the pursuit of democracy in Southeast Asia. In particular, "democracy" and "human rights" were retained in the Charter only in a general reference to the need for member states "to strengthen democracy, enhance good governance and the rule of law, and to promote and protect human rights and fundamental freedoms."[15] The Charter does not explain how these goals might be pursued, or what, if anything, will happen to members that do not pursue them.

Intention is one thing. Implementation is another. The key questions going forward are whether ASEAN will be able to put its rhetorical commitment to encouraging democracy into actual practice; how it might do so; and whether, if it does follow through, the effort will succeed. The EPG hit the nail on the head when it wrote that ASEAN's problem is not any "lack of vision, ideas, and action plans. The real problem is one of ensuring compliance and effective implementation of decisions."[16] Worth noting, too, is a journalist's still harsher description of the Association as "a hopeless powwow, meandering from one headline meeting to another" and leaving behind "a mile-long paper trail of declared intents with little effective follow-up."[17]

Based on its history of noninterference, and the lack and even fear of democracy on the part of some of its members, one may be forgiven for doubting whether ASEAN will in the future actually practice what its new democracy agenda has led it to preach.

ASEAN's Democracy Project: Ten Constraints

Will ASEAN vigorously and successfully pursue its democracy agenda? Conceivably, yes. But as of the end of 2007, an analyst trying to guess the future of the experiment was better advised to acknowledge constraints than to celebrate words. Despite the Charter's provisions for enforcement, modest in any case, member states remained basically free to belong to the Security Community without bothering to implement its democratic aspirations. That lack of institutional "muscle" was but one of a number of reasons not to hold

---

[14] Personal communication with a member of the HLTF, Manila, 6 May 2007.

[15] Preamble, ASEAN Charter.

[16] EPG Report, 20.

[17] Meidyatama Suryodiningrat, "Looking for Common Values: A Community Driven ASEAN," *The Jakarta Post*, 9 August 2004, <http://yaleglobal.yale.edu/display.article?id=4353>.

one's breath waiting for ASEAN to democratize Southeast Asia—as the following review of ten such constraints should make clear.

(1) **Noninterference principle.** ASEAN is constrained by the difficulty of promoting democracy while observing the principle of noninterference. As expressed in the 2005 declaration to establish an ASEAN Charter, member states must honor "the right of every state" to be "free from external interference," including "subversion or coercion," and thereby observe the Association's cardinal principle of "noninterference in the internal affairs of one another."[18] This principle has been interpreted to mean that the democratization of any member state can be accomplished only on that state's own initiative. Only with that state's acquiescence can any other ASEAN member, ASEAN itself, or any extraregional actor legitimately help the process along. To do otherwise would violate the principle of noninterference. Even the more democratic states in the region believe that democracy cannot and should not be imposed from outside.

(2) **Official regionalism.** ASEAN is still an intergovernmental association. It is rooted in the states and not, or at least not yet, in the societies of the region. The fact that its leaders want it to become a community indicates that it is not one yet. Unlike the EU, it cannot act in its own name with legal force, as opposed to mere persuasion, across a range of sectors. Strictly speaking, even the *Treaty* of Amity and Cooperation (TAC) is not legally binding, despite the emphasis I have added to its first word. While the Charter confers a legal personality on ASEAN, that will not become a reality until all members have ratified the document. As for the noncompliance of ASEAN members with its decisions, the Charter merely passes that problem to the heads of government to handle at a summit. ASEAN still lacks the supranational power to enforce its decisions, and there is no agreement among the members to give it that power any time soon. Every member, including Myanmar, supports "democracy," at least in theory. The problem is that no member can be obliged to practice it in reality.[19] Despite the evidence already introduced in this chapter that the balance of priorities has begun to shift toward societal regionalism in which democracy is valued, ASEAN in the post-Charter era is most likely to remain a case of official regionalism in which states are sovereign.

(3) **Comfortable inconsistency.** ASEAN's democracy project is further hampered by the gap between intention and implementation: saying

---

[18] ASEAN Security Plan of Action (ASCPA), <http://www.aseansec.org/16826.htm>.
[19] Emmerson, "Security, Community," 180.

one thing while doing another. Take the question of whether to accept a military coup in a member state as a fait accompli. In its plans for a Security Community and a Charter, ASEAN had vowed that member states "shall not condone unconstitutional and undemocratic changes of government."[20] The ink on this rule was, in effect, still fresh in September 2006 when a military junta seized power from an elected government in Thailand. Yet the new government was welcomed at the ASEAN summit in the Philippines in January 2007. Moreover, the ASEAN chair's statement on the summit made not the slightest reference to what had happened in Bangkok only a few months before. Nor did the statement express even mild misgiving over the lack of progress toward democracy in Myanmar. If ASEAN leaders were comfortable sitting down at a summit with Myanmarese junta, why shouldn't they do so with the Thai junta as well?

(4) **Nationalist feelings.** Narrower forms of nationalism still color the conduct of foreign relations in Southeast Asia. Despite habits of cooperation developed over more than four decades of intra-ASEAN collegiality—and notwithstanding recent pledges to turn the region into a sharing and caring community—suspicions and rivalries among Southeast Asian states have not entirely disappeared. Elements of competition and mistrust are still visible, for instance, in relations between Indonesia, Malaysia, and Singapore. Such tensions, even when merely latent, reinforce the salience of sovereignty and the corresponding fragility of regionalism. Permanently surrendering national prerogatives in whole or in part to a supranational body is out of the question in these conditions. Even giving in temporarily to external pressures, including pressures to democratize, could be politically costly—and not only in the less democratic states. From the progress toward political pluralism that Indonesians have already made, it does not follow that they would welcome foreign intervention, by ASEAN or any other outsider, to make their country even more democratic than it is.

(5) **Diverse regimes.** Southeast Asia's political heterogeneity amounts to a "reality check" for anyone who expects ASEAN to help democratize Southeast Asia. Inside the Association, a key fault line divides members with more open political systems from those whose politics are more closed.[21] In 2007, while Indonesia and the Philippines struggled to consolidate their fledgling democracies, Myanmar and Thailand were under military rule, although the junta in Bangkok had promised to restore democracy by the end of that year. Meanwhile, Malaysia and

---

[20] See ASCPA and Kuala Lumpur Declaration.

[21] Suryodiningrat, "Looking for Common Values."

Singapore continued to offer successful models of soft authoritarianism. Vietnam and Laos were still basically Leninist states. Cambodia, despite talk of reform, was still an experiment in one-man rule. As for the very different case of dynastic Brunei, its sultanate appeared quite stable—anachronistic perhaps, in the eyes of observers who associated democracy with modernity, but hardly ripe for liberalization. Scanning such diversity, an *official* and *regional* demand for political pluralism, judicial independence, and electoral accountability was nowhere to be seen.

(6) **Different motives.** ASEAN's leaders did not decide to include democracy alongside security and prosperity as a regional priority because they all believed in the superiority of democracy as a political system. The actual motives behind the decision differed from state to state. To illustrate: Unlike most of the other member states, Indonesia's support for democracy in a regional context reflected its new political identity. That support was also a tactical move to help deter antidemocratic forces inside Indonesia from reversing political reform.[22] Some of the other ASEAN members had a diametrically opposed reason for supporting democracy in the region: not to protect reform but to prevent it. These states were glad to equip the ASC with a "democracy agenda" if that meant preventing an "unconstitutional" change of regimes— "unconstitutional" in the sense that local or foreign democrats could stoke and use social and political unrest to overthrow an *autocratic* status quo. Not coincidentally, when faced with Indonesia's proposal to commit ASC members to holding general elections as the appropriate— "constitutional" in the sense of *democratic*—way to change regimes, it was officials of these same autocratic states who managed to delete this idea from the final document.

(7) **Problematic democracy.** The weaknesses of democratic transitions already under way are another constraint on efforts to help the rest of the region follow suit. Because democracy in the ASEAN countries is still nascent and fragile, it is hard for them to stand on solid ground as successful exemplars of that political choice. In 2007 the coup in Thailand showed not the success of democracy but its vulnerability. Indonesia and the Philippines were still relatively democratic, yet their political systems were rife with defects, including corruption. Other member states were accordingly less inclined to follow an Indonesian or a Philippine path. Some ASEAN states pointed to political turbulence in these countries as a reason *not* to repeat their experience. For the rulers of Malaysia and Vietnam, among other ASEAN countries, democracy à la Indonesia or

---

[22] Conversations with officials in the Department of Foreign Affairs, Jakarta, May 2007.

the Philippines was not a solution to be adopted but a set of problems to be avoided. Malaysia's recent crackdowns on demonstrations demanding free elections, and its handling of the demonstrations of its ethnic Indian community, are illustrative.

(8) **Stability first.** An eighth obstacle to regional democracy highlights this book's comparison of democracy with security. If ASEAN member states were more confident of their survival and stability, they might be more willing to risk political reform. Instead, in some parts of the region, the leaders feel insecure, for themselves and their regimes. Worried about opposition and infiltration, they are reluctant to initiate changes that could get out of hand. Historically, ASEAN has expressed and fostered a corresponding belief in domestic stability as crucial to regional security. In the competition for priority attention to democracy versus security, the former is thus easily sidelined or postponed in the name of the latter.

(9) **Disinclined neighbors.** The geopolitics of the wider world are another reason not to expect democracy to sweep Southeast Asia anytime soon. Take the growing influence of China and India in Myanmar. Burmese dependence on these huge neighbors creates leverage for them to use, if they wish, to nudge Myanmar away from authoritarian rule. But their rivalry for access to sources of energy in Myanmar, especially oil and gas, has had a far greater opposing effect—leading them to ignore the violation of human rights and the absence of democratic elections inside the country, lest doing so jeopardize their need to work with its regime. Although India is itself democratic, it has not been willing to encourage democracy in Myanmar for fear of pushing the Burmese authorities even deeper into China's embrace. Such conditions make it even less likely that ASEAN could, even if it wanted to, coax the junta into loosening its grip on the country.

(10) **Global backlash.** The decline of the moral legitimacy of the United States as a promoter of democracy also serves to undermine any suggestion within ASEAN that it should make democratization a top priority. The controversial U.S.-led war on terror has created a less hospitable global climate for democracy promotion. In Southeast Asia, some ASEAN members have cited Indonesia's "messy" democracy as a reason for Indonesia's difficulty in curbing the surge of terrorist threats in the country. It is much harder now for supporters of democracy to argue for the legitimacy and moral urgency of democracy promotion as a regional priority, either for ASEAN or its members.

The difficulty of democratizing the states of Southeast Asia through actions originating outside their borders should not be overstated. The preceding constraints could be lessened or removed. But it is highly unlikely that all of them could be diminished, let alone erased, by ASEAN in the near- or even the medium-term future.

Fortunately in this discouraging context, regional security does not require the prior establishment of regional democracy. The usefulness of the ASC and the Charter does not depend on the theory of democratic peace whereby, as more and more governments abandon autocracy for accountability, interstate conflicts become less and less likely, because democracies do not fight one another. ASEAN's members have avoided wars with each other for more than forty years without having first democratized themselves.

What will be interesting to watch, however, is the extent to which the operation of the Community and the observance of the Charter will, by explicit design or unintended effect, work to erode these limits on democracy as a regional priority for Southeast Asia.

Conclusion: What Should Be Done?

ASEAN is not so naive as to think that security is attainable only through democracy. In this respect, the limited nature of the Association's democracy agenda makes sense. Indeed, such an agenda can be advanced only by first divesting it of grandiose expectations. It is constructively modest of the ASC to plan on starting its democracy project by promoting good governance and respecting human rights among member states, not attempting—and then surely failing—to revamp their politics in a liberal image. ASEAN hopes to start not with grand gestures, but to attend to the more feasible business of instilling respect. Likewise, it seeks to promote human rights by facilitating, through its VAP, the adoption of a memorandum of understanding—not a "treaty"—to coordinate existing human rights mechanisms in a single network, and to launch a commission to promote and protect the rights of women and children. In this way, ASEAN should be able to pursue a portion of its democracy project without jeopardizing regional cohesion.

ASEAN can and should also pursue security through other means. Political development is, after all, only one of the priorities in the ASC. Impediments to regional democracy should not stop the Community from underpinning security by shaping and sharing other relevant norms, preventing and resolving inter-state conflict, and building peace in the wake of such conflict, should it occur.[23] Subscribing to "the principle of comprehensive security," as ASEAN does in its VAP, means that slow going on the democratic road to maintaining regional peace and comity is no reason for timidity on other roads. With or

---

[23] Additional regional security strategies are reviewed in Rizal Sukma, "Southeast Asian Security: An Overview," unpublished paper, 9th Asian Security Conference, Institute for Defense and Security Analysis, New Delhi, 9–10 February 2007. On "comprehensive security," see, e.g., the VAP, <http://www.aseansec.org/Publ-VAP.pdf>.

without promoting democracy. ASEAN can and should strengthen its resistance to conflict by using the Charter to institutionalize, step by incremental step, a nonpartisan, eventually enforceable, and regionally acceptable rule-of-law regime.

In moving toward such a regime, ASEAN can and should pioneer measures to reduce suspicion by building confidence between national defense establishments; by jointly combating nontraditional insecurity in the form of piracy, terrorism, and infectious disease; by using and linking peacekeeping institutions in ASEAN member countries on behalf of regional peace and security; and by taking the initiative to organize a regional capacity to respond quickly with emergency relief should a natural disaster strike any member country. Such ideas already exist on paper, as in the VAP, and a few modest successes have already been made in translating such rhetoric into reality. Notable among these moves was the first-ever ASEAN Defense Ministers Meeting, held in Kuala Lumpur in May 2006. ASEAN has stepped up cooperation against nontraditional threats to security such as terrorism. An ASEAN Convention on Counter Terrorism was agreed to in January 2007. That year, ASEAN members also signed a Treaty of Mutual Legal Assistance in Criminal Matters.

As for the principle of noninterference, it should not—indeed, cannot—be overthrown. But it should and can be interpreted in the context of member states' interdependence. If and as such a view gains ground, it will become harder to invoke noninterference in the name of sovereignty to veto cooperation that requires each country to adjust its policies in the name of interdependence. Whatever the fate of ASEAN's democracy agenda, its security agenda will continue to illustrate its members' vulnerability to spillover effects from violence, negligence, and other conditions and events inside a given member country. Other chapters in this book explore these nontraditional challenges to regional ingenuity.

Balancing the principle of nonintervention with the fact of interdependence will help ASEAN justify paying attention to such transboundary issues. As regional solutions to one-country problems are worked out, interdependence will become more acceptable as a basis for such action. In this evolving context, a range of crises and failings inside particular countries—natural disasters, terrorist activities, human trafficking, epidemic threats to health, and gross violations of human rights—could become fair game for regionally organized remedial action. Such an erosion of the Westphalian barricade between what is "domestic" and what is "foreign" has, indeed, already begun.

It would be naive to think, however, that this shift in ASEAN's operative principles—from rejecting "interference" to accepting interdependence—will unfold naturally, all by itself. The ASEAN Charter that the regions' leaders signed in November 2007 failed to provide the Association with the authority to ensure compliance by member states. All suggestions that ASEAN establish a legal regime in Southeast Asia that would punish noncompliance[24] fell on deaf ears. Without compliance, implementation is not possible. Without implementation, ASEAN will be all talk and no action. The Charter says nothing about sanctions, let alone suspension or expulsion, but leaves the matter to the discretion of the leaders of the member states. They could, in theory, sanction a noncompliant member. But by also reinforcing consensus as the main way of making ASEAN decisions, the Charter has made it highly unlikely that ASEAN's heads of government would ever agree to punish one of their own.

Last but not least, in order for ASEAN to become more effective, it will need to strengthen its organization. Here, the Charter does offer a window of opportunity for at least four key reforms. First, it has mandated the streamlining of formerly cumbersome ASEAN structures, including a reduction in the number of uncoordinated meetings. Second, the Charter has enhanced the role of the Secretary-General, which could encourage further reform and progress. The Secretary-General has been mandated, for example, to monitor the implementation of ASEAN decisions, and to report cases of noncompliance to the leaders. Even if the leaders do nothing in response to such a report, at least the case in question would be on record. Third, although the Charter refers only to the need to establish an unspecified "ASEAN human rights body," that provision opens the door for the Association to begin preparing to put into practice the Charter's support for democratic principles and human rights. As of December 2007, Indonesia had already promised to propose terms of reference to speed the formation of such a human rights body. Fourth, the Charter recognizes the importance of participation by nongovernmental organizations and actors in ASEAN decisions and programs, though the text does not stipulate how such involvement should occur. A separate, implementing agreement on this issue needs to be concluded soon.

As of the end of 2007, only modest headway had been made toward an ASC. That, however, is all the more reason to seize the limited opportunity provided by the Charter to reform and strengthen the Association, and thus keep it, and Southeast Asia, moving forward in this twenty-first century. Security is more likely than democracy to serve as a goal of such momentum. But as the Association copes, as it must, with nontraditional challenges to security—challenges that ignore the borders drawn neatly on maps—progress on a democracy agenda could become, over time, less controversial and more feasible.

An opportunity for progress on this score is more likely to be found in the ASEAN Security Community Plan of Action than in the Charter. The ASCPA will not be abandoned, even if and when the Charter is ratified and comes into

---

[24] Including the recommendation to this effect made by the ASEAN Institutes of Strategic and International Studies (ASEAN-ISIS), "The ASEAN Charter," Memorandum No. 1/2006, 18 April 2006 (revised), <http://www.siiaonline.org/uploads/693/AI-Memo-18April-ASEAN_Charter.doc> 11.

effect. The ASCPA provides a much better foundation for ASEAN to realize and exercise its commitment to democracy and human rights, as prescribed in principle by the Charter.

Whether the ASCPA is implemented will, of course, depend on many factors. Not least among these will be the willingness and the capacity of the Security Community's original promoter, Indonesia, to persuade the other members that the time has come for ASEAN to make meaningful room on its agenda for democracy and human rights.

ASEAN's Pariah:
Insecurity and Autocracy in Myanmar (Burma)

Kyaw Yin Hlaing
City University of Hong Kong

In the eyes of its many critics in Western democracies, the junta that rules Myanmar (Burma)[1] is an abomination. At a minimum, and partly for that reason, the country embarrasses the more democratic governments in ASEAN, to which Myanmar also belongs. No regime in the region has attracted more foreign opprobrium more persistently over a longer period of time. Yet Myanmar's State Peace and Development Council (SPDC)—formerly the State Law and Order Restoration Council (SLORC, 1988–97)—continues to survive and even, in its own way, to thrive.

Until 2007, the SPDC and its opposition were locked in a stalemate—the regime unable to destroy its critics, the critics unable to oust the regime. In September 2007, however, the government brutally cracked down on large protests, led by monks, which had taken place in many parts of the Buddhist-majority country. The junta's leader, Senior General Than Shwe, announced that he would personally meet the main opposition leader, Daw Aung San Suu Kyi, or Daw Suu for short,[2] if she stopped denouncing the government and calling for Western governments to impose economic sanctions on the country. The junta then appointed a minister to be a liaison between the government and Daw Suu. While having meetings with the liaison minister, Daw Suu announced that "in the interest of the nation, I stand ready to cooperate with the Government in order to make this process of dialogue a success."[3]

Nevertheless, as 2008 began, little if any progress toward reconciliation had been made. Daw Suu and the liaison minister had met a few times since November 2007, but with no apparent result. Than Shwe, known to be in declining health, did not appear in person when the sixtieth anniversary of Myanmar's independence from Britain was commemorated on 4 January 2008,

---

[1] In 1989, the government of Burma in the capital city of Rangoon replaced these two names with Myanmar and Yangon, respectively.

[2] Burmese people often refer to Daw Aung San Suu Kyi as Daw Suu, as will this chapter.

[3] AP Press, text of Aung San Suu Kyi's Statement, 8 November 2007, <http://ap.google.com/article/ALeqM5gyhLpt3U4pZY688FfNh8cTpuNBdgD8SPNP3G3>.

although a statement was read out in his name.[4] Daw Suu remained, meanwhile, under house arrest.

Myanmar's political future is, in a word, precarious. As of this writing, the junta has still not revealed what, if any, concessions it is willing to offer to its opposition. Nor has it revised its 2003 "roadmap" for Myanmar to become what Than Shwe has called a "discipline-flourishing democratic state."[5] I will examine that plan in this chapter.

This chapter scans and appraises the dynamics of Myanmar's situation—the efforts outside Myanmar and inside ASEAN to change it, and the ways in which ASEAN can and should wield its influence to effect such change. There are other key questions: Why has political deadlock persisted for so long? Why did the regime finally decide to have a dialogue with Daw Suu? How has Myanmar's membership in ASEAN affected both the country and the Association? Have Western sanctions worked? What roles have China and India played? What if anything can ASEAN do to enhance the prospects for security and democracy in Myanmar?

The charges leveled against Myanmar's junta have been comprehensive and severe: terrorizing its citizens through the use of rape, torture, forced labor, and arbitrary arrest; plundering the country's rich resources; failing to stop the spread of HIV/AIDS within its borders and in the wider region; and producing and distributing opium and methamphetamines. On the political front, the junta's actions have been blatantly antidemocratic. After organizing elections in 1990, it refused to hand over power to the political party that won the contests. By harassing, intimidating, and confining the opposition—including its leader, Daw Suu—the regime has made her iconic, especially in the West. Because of its actions, the junta has been accused of damaging stability and peace, both regionally and internationally.

Outsiders disagree about what should be done. The United States and the European Union (EU) have responded to the junta's intransigent behavior by imposing multiple sanctions on Myanmar. Their strategy has been to force the generals from power by isolating Myanmar from the international community, a policy known as "transformative isolation." But the regime's fellow members in ASEAN have rejected this Western approach. They have argued that only by engaging Myanmar can outsiders encourage democratic change. Based on that reasoning, they have mostly preferred to adopt a conciliatory stance toward the junta—a policy of "constructive engagement."

Neither approach—transformative isolation or constructive engagement—has worked. When Myanmar was admitted to ASEAN in 1997, many of the Association's leaders seemed to believe that participation in its activities would

---

[4] Joe Boyle, "Burma's Bittersweet Independence," BBC News, 4 January 2008, <http://news.bbc.co.uk/2/hi/asia-pacific/7171361.stm>.

[5] As quoted in "Burma Marks Independence Day," BBC News, 4 January 2008, <http://news.bbc.co.uk/2/hi/asia-pacific/7171008.stm>.

lead the generals in Yangon[6] to realize that the status quo was unacceptable, and that political reforms were required.[7] In 2007, the democratizing changes that the United States and EU had spent much of the preceding two decades trying to pressure into effect were still not in sight.

The Myanmar military is not a monolith, as this chapter will show. But it is determined to remain in power for many years to come. In order to establish what it euphemistically calls a "disciplined democracy," the SPDC has started a process, however prolonged and delayed, meant to deliver a constitution that will guarantee the military's continued role in politics.

Almost uniformly, Western governments, human rights organizations, and Burmese prodemocracy groups in exile have rejected this effort. They have called for outsiders to take stronger measures against the Myanmar military junta, including by Myanmar's ostensible partners in ASEAN. Some voices in some parts of Southeast Asia have likewise been raised in support of a harder line. Parliamentarians and the media in countries such as Cambodia, Indonesia, Malaysia, the Philippines, and Thailand, noting that Myanmar has become an embarrassment to ASEAN, have urged that it be expelled from the Association if the junta continues to refuse real democratic reform.[8] Western and especially American officials, politicians, and activists meanwhile have argued repeatedly that Myanmar's government is a menace to the region. As evidence that the junta is causing regional instability, they cite the circulation of opium and synthetic drugs coming from Myanmar and the inflow into neighboring countries of refugees escaping repression.

Leaders of the major ASEAN states understand that unless the political deadlock between the opposition and the generals can be resolved in favor of reform, tension over Myanmar will continue to mar the Association's relations with the United States and the EU. Rather than advocating "regime change," these Southeast Asian leaders have urged "national reconciliation." Compared with outright replacement, they argue, reconciliation is less threatening to the junta, and is thus more realistic, yet still holds out hope for reform that could mollify the international community.

Notwithstanding their drawn-out "constitutional" process, which in any case would entrench military rule, Myanmar's generals have countenanced neither reconciliation nor reform, much to ASEAN's rising frustration. Public

---

[6] In November 2005, the administrative capital was officially moved from Yangon to a previously undeveloped site roughly 320 kilometers to the north. In March 2007, the new capital was officially named Naypyidaw.

[7] Michael Richardson, "Voting for Burma, ASEAN Aims at Unity in Its Region," *International Herald Tribune*, 2 July 1997, <http://www.iht.com/articles/1997/06/02/asean. t.php>.

[8] See, for example, the website of the ASEAN Inter-Parliamentary Myanmar Caucus (AIPMC), a group dedicated to bringing about political change in Myanmar, at <http:// www.aseanmp.org>.

expressions of such frustration have multiplied in Southeast Asia since 2005. Yet aside from some modest collegial arm-twisting in closed-door settings, ASEAN has made no concerted effort to rescue Myanmar from its self-inflicted pariah-hood and thereby salvage the Association's international reputation.

In November 2007, all ten Southeast Asian states, including Myanmar, adopted an ASEAN Charter. Some of its provisions could someday allow the group to take punitive steps against members for noncompliance with ASEAN principles—including, in theory, democracy. As of this writing, it seems unlikely that the Charter will soon be used in this way.

Among other regional organizations, the EU can significantly influence its members' domestic policies. Even the materially weak and internally divided African Union (AU) has taken positions critical of the domestic political behavior of its members. In 2006, for instance, the AU's Commission on Human and People's Rights strongly condemned the Zimbabwean government for its violations of human rights.[9]

Far from exerting a comparable role with regard to Myanmar, ASEAN and its members have basically embraced the junta, and thereby helped to prolong its tenure. In the wake of the generals' brutal crackdown on the peaceful demonstrations of September 2007, the prime minister of Singapore, Lee Hsien Loong, as chairman of ASEAN, issued a statement condemning the junta for killing monk protesters. However, he and other ASEAN leaders refused to take any punitive action against the junta. When Myanmar Prime Minister Thein Sein said that his government wanted to work with the UN in trying to solve the country's internal political problems, ASEAN leaders took the comment at face value.

Worse still, these leaders agreed to honor the junta's last-minute objections and withdrew an invitation that had been extended to Ibrahim Gambari, the UN Special Envoy to Myanmar, who was scheduled merely to report his findings to Asian leaders gathered in Singapore in November 2007, in conjunction with the ASEAN Summit. ASEAN's leaders apparently thought that a rapid democratization of Myanmar might contribute to the country's disintegration, which would in turn destabilize the region. Therefore, even as they called for political reforms in Myanmar, the assembled Southeast Asian heads of state and government refused to take any measures that they felt might undermine the junta's ability to maintain law and order. Their inaction led one observer to conclude that "ASEAN cannot do anything for the Burmese people."[10]

---

[9] Andrew Meldrum, "African Leaders Break Silence over Mugabe's Human Rights Abuses," *The Guardian*, 4 January 2006, <http://www.guardian.co.uk/world/2006/jan/04/zimbabwe.andrewmeldrum>.

[10] Anselmo Lee, Executive Director of the Asian Forum for Human Rights and Development (FORUM-ASIA), as quoted by Wai Moe, "ASEAN Countries Vote against UN Resolution on Burma," 21 November 2007, <http://www.irrawaddy.org/article.php?art_id=9386>.

Why has ASEAN failed to influence the political development of Myanmar? Does that failure mean that the Association should join the United States and EU countries in sanctioning Myanmar? How should ASEAN deal with the junta? I will address these questions by examining how Myanmar's generals have interacted with the rulers of other ASEAN states; by assessing the efficacy of a policy of engagement compared with one of isolation; and, finally, by recommending steps that the Association could take that might help Myanmar to resolve its political deadlock in favor of reform. First, however, I will explain how the deadlock came about, and why it persists.

From Ne Win to Daw Suu: The Making of an Impasse

From its independence in 1948 until 1962, the nation then known as Burma had a parliamentary system styled after that of its former British ruler. In March 1962, a Revolution Council led by General Ne Win replaced the parliamentary format with military-dominated, one-party rule. The military has governed—or misgoverned—the country ever since.

On 8 August 1988, massive student-led opposition broke out against the military and its political monopoly, the Burma Socialist Program Party (BSPP). Soldiers fired at demonstrators; many were killed. But the protests, which came to be known collectively as the Four Eights Democracy Movement, had swept the country and virtually paralyzed the BSPP regime. On the verge of being overrun, the BSPP government offered to hold national elections in which multiple parties could compete.

The democracy movement's leaders called for an interim government to prepare the elections. Instead, the BSPP government allowed the commander-in-chief of the armed forces to take power, create the State Law and Order Restoration Council (SLORC), and use it to impose direct military rule. SLORC announced that it would hold multiparty elections, and asked the public to form political parties to contest them. More than two hundred such parties were formed. But activists in these parties distrusted SLORC, and vice versa. Controversies quickly arose over what the parties were permitted to do and how the elections would be held. Already fearing a repressive outcome, students began fleeing to border areas where they formed prodemocracy groups in exile.

The junta amply justified the students' fears. SLORC showed no mercy toward its challengers. When the elections were finally held, in 1990, the National League for Democracy (NLD) emerged the victor by a landslide, soundly defeating the National Unity Party (NUP), which, many thought, was backed by the junta. But despite having triumphed, the League was not allowed to rule. It was the biggest party, had been especially critical of the military government, and therefore received the harshest treatment at the hands of the regime. The leader of the NLD, Daw Aung San Suu Kyi, was detained in 1989. Many NLD members, too, have been detained and harassed.

155

From the very beginning of this ostensible experiment with democracy, the military regime and the civilian parties could find no basis for working together to liberalize the political system. It is no exaggeration to say that Myanmar has been politically deadlocked since 1988, when the generals took direct control.

Burmese prodemocracy groups and the international community, especially the United States and the EU countries, pressured the junta to honor the results of the 1990 elections, but to no avail. The junta promised instead to institute "disciplined democracy." Several opposition groups also called for a three-way dialogue between the regime, the NLD, and the country's ethnic minorities, whose rebellions had long bedeviled the central government. But that idea, too, fell on deaf ears. Instead, bypassing the League, the generals negotiated ceasefire agreements bilaterally with various ethnic insurgent groups.[11]

In the early 1990s the junta announced that it planned to convene a National Convention to discuss political issues with all groups in the country. The meeting was held in 1992, but the military showed not the least inclination to surrender power. Outnumbered by delegates handpicked by the regime, representatives of the opposition parties saw most of their proposals rejected. Spokespeople for ethnic minorities and persons involved in the ceasefire agreements also found it almost impossible to get their demands accepted by the junta.[12] Military leaders would not even specify a date by which the National Convention was expected actually to deliver a constitution. Opposition groups reasonably concluded that the junta would do everything it could to prolong the drafting of the document and thus enhance its own power relative to that of other groups while the process continued. As for the eventual outcome, it was clear that the military would settle for nothing less than a text that would guarantee its strategic political role for years to come—or as one veteran Burmese politician put it, "eternally."[13]

Yet hope sprang eternal in Myanmar. In 1995, when the generals released Aung San Suu Kyi from more than five years of house arrest, many of her supporters hoped that she and the junta would somehow end their standoff and reconcile sufficiently to be able to work together. But the regime did not have détente, let alone compromise, in mind. The economy had spurted forward thanks to economic reforms that the junta had undertaken in the early 1990s, and that success led military leaders to believe they no longer needed to worry

---

[11] Mizzima News Group, "Democracy Supporters Call for Tripartite Dialogue in Burma," 20 March 2001, <http://burmalibrary.org/reg.burma/archives/200103/msg00054.html>.

[12] Interviews with minority leaders and activists, 2004 and 2006–07.

[13] Interview, 12 December 2003.

about the opposition.[14] They had relaxed Daw Suu's confinement not because they wanted reconciliation, but because they were confident they could control the country without imprisoning her in her home. Nevertheless, immediately after the restriction was lifted, Daw Suu tried to reach out the junta. She made conciliatory comments and invited military leaders to engage in a dialogue with her party. The junta ignored her overture.

The NLD then asked the government to make the National Convention more democratic and transparent. In 1996, after the government had also ignored that request, the League decided to boycott the government's National Convention.[15] In 1998, in a similar challenge to the National Convention, Daw Suu and her colleagues formed a Committee Representing People's Parliament (CRPP), comprised of 250 members who had won the 1990 election representing various political parties. The government responded by outlawing the group and arresting many of the politicians involved.

It was then that Daw Suu came out flatly in favor of what I identified earlier as the "Western" strategy on Myanmar. "Economic sanctions are good," she proclaimed, "and necessary for the rapid democratization of Burma."[16] At about the same time, she began traveling to outlying areas to meet the general public. When the government moved to prevent her from making such trips, she protested by traveling as far as she could and refusing to return to Yangon. She was forced to go back, however, and in 2000, after several attempts to leave the capital, was again placed under house arrest.

In late 2000, news of a secret meeting between Aung San Suu Kyi and senior government officials again briefly stimulated hopes of reconciliation between the junta and the NLD. Hope flared yet again when she was released from her second period of house arrest, in May 2002. Yet ostensible moves toward reconciliation stalled once more, scant months after her release, and local and foreign observers were again dismayed. In late May 2003, in the wake of a clash between progovernment and pro-NLD groups, the junta cracked down. Daw Suu was put into so-called protective custody and many NLD members were detained.[17]

---

[14] After it took control of the country, the SLORC undertook some economic reforms, which included privatizing many economic sectors, such as export/import and border trade. Although the reforms were not undertaken systematically, they attracted some large foreign investments and spurred economic growth.

[15] Htet Aung Kyaw, "Road Map to Division," *The Irrawaddy Online Edition,* 17 September 2003, <http://irrawaddy.org/opinion_story.php?art_id=400>.

[16] BBC, "Pilger on Daw Suu's Standoff," 28 July 1998, <http://www.burmalibrary.org/reg.burma/archives/199807/msg00709.html>.

[17] Kyaw Yin Hlaing, "Myanmar in 2004: Why Military Rule Continues," *Southeast Asian Affairs* (2005), 239.

These events raise two obvious questions: Why does the political impasse between the NLD and the junta persist? and, Why are they unable to begin a productive political dialogue?[18]

Why Has the Junta Been Intransigent? Explaining the Impasse

Observers of Myanmar have tried to explain the deadlock in four ways. Of these, the first three focus on the military regime's obduracy, in the form of personal legacy, electoral shock, and reformist defeat.

The case for personal legacy traces the military's intransigence back to General Ne Win—his original prestige within the armed forces, as well as his subsequent prolonged direct and then presumed indirect control of the regime. Some political activists argue that Ne Win's long control of the junta from behind the scenes made dialogue between the junta and the NLD impossible.[19] The second argument, for electoral shock, in contrast, highlights the junta's determination, following the debacle of 1990, never again to allow circumstances to develop in which it might have to share power with its opposition.[20] Those who cite reformist defeat highlight the power struggle between the two groups of military officers, often referred to as soft- and hard-liners. They argue that proponents of a softer line lost a decisive struggle for power inside the regime that left hard-liners firmly and fully in charge.[21]

I will deal later with the fourth explanation for the deadlock—reciprocal obstinacy—which calls Daw Suu herself partly to account. According to this view, Myanmar's political impasse has resulted from the unwillingness of either side—the regime or the League—to meet the other halfway. For now, looking back on these events, assessing only the explanations that focus on the junta, and keeping in mind the often fragmentary and impressionistic nature

---

[18] This chapter does not explore the positions of a third possible partner in dialogue: Myanmar's ethnic minorities. The real stalemate is not between them and the junta, but between the junta and the NLD. I say this based on numerous interviews conducted in 2004–07.

[19] Kyaw Yin Hlaing, "Aung San Suu Kyi of Myanmar: A Review of the Lady's Biographies," *Contemporary Southeast Asia* 29, no. 2 (August 2007), 369; and interviews with political activists, 2004–05.

[20] Many political activists made this argument in the early 1990s. Interviews and personal communications with fifteen Burmese writers, political analysts, and activists, 2001–04 and 2007.

[21] Aung Zaw, "Aung San Suu Kyi: Between SLORC and a Hardline," *The Irrawaddy*, 13 June 1995, <http://burmalibrary.org/reg.burma/archives/199506/msg00059.html>; Maung Maung Oo, "Fall from Fortune," *The Irrawaddy* 9, no. 1 (January 2001), <http://www.irrawaddy.org/article.php?art_id=2107>; Bertil Lintner, "Signs of a Power Struggle within the Ruling Junta," *Far Eastern Economic Review*, <http://www.burmalibrary.org/reg.burma/archives/199703/msg00292.html>.

of evidence regarding a regime as secretive as Myanmar's, I find none of these arguments persuasive.

Personal Legacy?

Ne Win's tenure as head of state ran from 1962 to 1981, longer than any previous ruler since dynastic times. He played a key role in the emergence of SLORC, and wielded major influence over leading figures in the junta until the mid-1990s. But there is no evidence, direct or indirect, that he took an active part in post-BSPP domestic politics in Myanmar. Interviews I was able to conduct in 2002–03, 2005–06, and 2007, with several former Socialist government officials and a retired senior official who had served in SLORC, all confirmed that Ne Win did not involve himself in relations between the junta and its opposition. A retired general also noted that Ne Win had not exercised any formal power since the end of 1988.[22]

In 2002 the conviction of his son-in-law and three grandsons on possibly trumped-up charges of high treason—plotting to overthrow the SPDC—clearly indicated that Ne Win was not as powerful as the case for his personal legacy would require. If anything, by going after his younger relatives, members of the junta proved themselves more concerned with protecting their own interests than with serving their former commander or shielding his descendants. In March 2002, in the wake of the discovery of the supposed plot against the junta, Ne Win himself was put under house arrest. He died in disgrace at his home in Rangoon on 5 December 2002. In fact, Ne Win had ceased to be a key political player since a few months after the SLORC/SPDC took control of Burma in September 1988. Therefore, it is not reasonable to attribute the country's political impasse to him.

A variation on the legacy argument draws an influential line of continuity from Ne Win all the way to SLORC (via the BSPP and the National Unity Party, or NUP) and asserts that this historical lineage and momentum still sustains the intransigence of the regime. Ne Win's importance for the BSPP is beyond dispute. He took part in creating both the NUP, basically a new name for the Burma Socialist Program Party (BSPP), and the SLORC, which many assumed backed the NUP. It is true that the junta would have preferred the NUP to the NLD.

One should think twice, however, before labeling the NUP a mere extension of SLORC—as if the legacy from Ne Win were still intact and uncontested. Nowhere in the country did the military help NUP candidates win the 1990 elections. SLORC's first chairman, the late General Saw Maung, had an acrimonious relationship with some leading members of the NUP. Partly for

---

[22] Interview, 9 February 2007. Also see Kyaw Yin Hlaing, "Factional and Power Struggle in Post-Independence Burma," *Journal of Southeast Asian Studies* 39, no.1 (2008).

that reason, senior military officers were even ordered not to play golf with members of the NUP.[23]

Worth noting, too, is that initially, as election preparations got under way, the junta expected—and may even have hoped—that none of the contesting parties would gain a clear majority of the vote. Until late 1989, many senior military officers, especially Saw Maung, thought this would be the most likely outcome. It is not hard to see why the junta might have wanted the parties to split the vote more or less evenly. Such an outcome could have made them easier to manipulate, framing the military as a united and overarching institution without serious civilian rivals, rather than a military necessarily committed, because of its history, to the NUP as New Win's latest authoritarian creation.

Electoral Shocks

On 27 May 1990, the junta held elections, as it had promised. To the surprise of the international community, the elections were free and fair. To the dismay of the junta, however, the NLD won 392 of the 492 seats at stake. The NUP won only 11 seats. Immediately after the elections, the junta announced that it would not transfer power to the winning party until the country had a new constitution.

Although the election results were related to the political impasse, the NUP's electoral defeat was not the underlying reason. The NUP was never a vehicle for the junta to keep itself in power. Indeed, the junta knew in advance that the NUP could not win the elections. The junta announced a week before the elections that it would continue to rule the country even after the elections. Regardless of who won the elections, the junta was not going to give up power, and the political deadlock was bound to happen. Even if the elections had generated the kind of results the junta had wanted, many opposition groups would not have accepted them and disputes would still have arisen between the junta and opposition groups. The electoral outcome could well have contributed to the political impasse, but it was not the main reason why the junta and the opposition could not find a way to resolve their political differences.

Reformist Defeat?

If personal legacy and electoral shock give too much importance, respectively, to one actor and one event, the case for reformist defeat is similarly too focused on one particular internal struggle for power that the soft-liners lost, thereby supposedly entrenching the winning—harder—line. In fact, if indeed one can reliably identify and characterize personalities and factions inside the regime, those who supposedly favored reform were never stronger than those who

---

[23] See Kyaw Yin Hlaing, "Myanmar in 2004," 256.

supposedly opposed it. In this context, the outcome of any one factional clash could not have been significant.

Those who emphasize reformist defeat, and imply the counterfactual—that democratizers could have won—misunderstand the nature of Myanmar's regime. General Khin Nyunt headed the Directorate of the Defense Service Intelligence from 1984 to 2004. He was widely thought to be the leader of a supposedly reformist group within the junta. Many Myanmar watchers and probably most Burmese considered him to be more powerful than the hard-liners who were thought to oppose him.[24]

There were, to be sure, several reasons for thinking that Khin Nyunt was especially influential. He appeared on state television and was covered by state newspapers more than any other senior official, partly in the context of the inspection tours he made far more often than any of his colleagues. At state ceremonies he walked ahead of other senior officials and sat next to Saw Maung. In a country where most of the information conveyed by the media is about the activities of influential officials, General Khin Nyunt's frequent appearances on state television and in the newspapers made it seem as if he was the most powerful official in the government.

He was, of course, feared. Ostensibly to maintain surveillance of opposition elements, he dispatched his intelligence agents throughout the country. Yet many apolitical people thought that because of his power he could help them, if only they could make their material or personal needs or grievances known to him.

Most of the senior SLORC leaders were less impressed with Khin Nyunt's power. Indeed, they were indignant that such great influence could be attributed to a relatively junior intelligence officer with so little combat experience. Although the Council claimed to embody collective leadership, its members had risen to power through the hierarchy and were not about to abandon its distinctions. In both private and public settings, most senior officials tried to show that they were in fact at least as powerful as Khin Nyunt. When his proposals clashed with theirs, they objected less as a matter of substance than from suspicion that he was trying to put them down. In reality, most of the senior generals were more or less equally powerful, and the junta's internal modus operandi was not so much top-down as multipolar.[25]

In early 1992, SLORC revamped the government by expanding its military composition, making it even more blatantly martial in character. The cabinet was enlarged to include new ministerships. Every regional commander was given one, and retired military officers already serving in government departments and corporations received the rest. This move toward further militarization paved the way for the rise of General Than Shwe, in March, to the chairmanship of

[24] Aung Zaw, "Aung San Suu Kyi: Between SLORC and a Hardline," *The Irrawaddy*, 13 June 1995, <http://burmalibrary.org/reg.burma/archives/199506/msg00059>.

[25] See Kyaw Yin Hlaing, "Factional and Power Struggle in Post-Independence Burma."

SLORC, succeeding Saw Maung, who had retired due to poor health and a nervous breakdown reportedly brought on by overwork.

In the early 1990s, Than Shwe seemed an unprepossessing figure. He had been a lecturer at the Central Institute of Political Science back in the 1960s, which might have indicated his interest in statecraft. But his indifferent and reserved personality appeared to confirm the public perception that he was a weak leader, unlikely to make much of an impact on the junta or its strategy. The truth of the matter, noted later in this chapter, was altogether different.

Meanwhile, the perception that Khin Nyunt was becoming more powerful raised the question of who in the junta would move against him. In 1992, following the government shake-up, that role fell to the new vice chairman of SLORC, General Maung Aye, who disagreed with Khin Nyunt on many issues. From that disagreement there stemmed the misleading impression that Khin Nyunt was a moderate, even a liberal.

Maung Aye appeared less cosmopolitan and more inward-looking than Khin Nyunt. Maung Aye was said to have opposed Myanmar's application for membership in ASEAN and favored harsh actions against domestic political dissent. Accordingly, several Myanmar watchers branded Maung Aye a hard-liner and Khin Nyunt a moderate.[26]

The distinction was convenient but superficial. Maung Aye was not as tough as he was thought to be; Khin Nyunt was not as soft. Although Maung Aye appeared to believe that Myanmar could survive in isolation, he did not completely oppose improving relations with other countries. As for Khin Nyunt, although he preferred a flexible approach in dealing with foreigners and the domestic opposition, he was adamantly against offering any concession that would make him and his fellow officials look weak. Their determination not to give in to their opponents is in fact the only similarity between these two leaders. Further, even if Khin Nyunt was prepared to work with Daw Suu under some conditions, he could not easily pursue such a tactic in defiance of his army colleagues. The fewer than four hundred agents staffing his intelligence corps were miniscule compared to the three hundred thousand soldiers in the army's combat units.

Khin Nyunt's rivals were prominent among the ministers who lost their jobs in the revamping of the regime's top personnel in 1992. One might therefore view that event as a triumph for Khin Nyunt and a sign of his clout. In reality, the changes worked more in favor of his rival Maung Aye. The regional commanders who replaced the fired ministers were apparently closer to Maung Aye than to Khin Nyunt. It was Maung Aye's position in the regime and the

---

[26] Soe Win Nyo, "SLORC Power Struggle Intensifies," *DAB Newsletter*, January 1995, <http://www.burmalibrary.org/reg.burma/archives/199605/msg00027.html>. See also "The Fence between True Opinions and Lies," which provides examples of opinion papers about power struggles within the military regime, written by Burmese political activists and analysts, <http://laphilosophe.wordpress.com/category/burma/>.

armed forces that became more dominant than Khin Nyunt's, therefore, not the other way around.

Nevertheless, both men understood that any confrontation between them would topple the government, including themselves. Uneasily aware that they needed each other in order to keep their common enemies under control, they avoided a confrontation. Each one defined his respective interests clearly and tried to confine his activities within those limits. When their interests did conflict, the two generals turned to their respected senior, Than Shwe, to arbitrate and decide the matter.

The thesis of reformist defeat, like that of personal legacy, fails to fit this account. Khin Nyunt was not clearly more reformist than his rival Maung Aye, nor was he clearly defeated by him. Nor does the actual rise and significance of Than Shwe jibe with an explanation of regime obstinacy as an effect, and then an after-effect, of Ne Win's long reign.

The rivalry between Khin Nyunt and Maung Aye and their two contending factions strengthened Than Shwe's position. The departure of his contemporaries had left Than Shwe the most senior serving military officer in Myanmar. His role as an apparently nonpartisan arbiter between Khin Nyunt and Maung Aye allowed him to appoint his own loyalists to key official posts. The image of disinterested neutrality, which he cultivated, helped to garner acquiescence and respect from both camps. While using both groups to control the opposition to the regime, Than Shwe used each to check the other's influence, while his own influence grew.

In the years after 1997, when SLORC was reconstituted as the SPDC, Than Shwe became the most powerful figure in the regime. Already by 2000, knowledgeable observers and the junta's own inner circle had come to view him as a dominant leader, almost on a par with the former strongman Ne Win in the latter's heyday.[27] Two years later, discredited and under house arrest, Ne Win died—and no one could then be said to overshadow Than Shwe.

To summarize, then, neither the personal legacy of Ne Win, nor the electoral shock of 1990, nor the seeming reformist defeat of Khin Nhyunt explains the regime's intransigence in refusing to work with the NLD. These arguments are not flat-out wrong, but as sole or primary explanations, they are flawed, and they omit much. Not least among those omissions is Than Shwe's success in both concentrating power in his hands and using it to ensure the junta's survival—not only for now but, if he and his fellow generals can manage it, far into the future.

The Junta versus the NLD: The Dynamics of Impasse

Even if one could fully explain why Myanmar's regime has been so unyielding, such an account would ignore the possibility that the opposition to that regime

---

[27] Interview with a veteran politician, 1 May 2005.

has also been stubborn and therefore shares at least some responsibility for the stalemate. Such a possibility raises the fourth answer mentioned: the case for *reciprocal obstinacy*, in which Daw Aung San Suu Kyi and the NLD are found to have contributed, at least to some extent, to the stand-off between their movement and the regime.

Reciprocal Obstinacy?

Obviously, the NLD was not responsible for the 1998 crackdown, nor for the refusal to let the 1990 election decide who would lead the country. Likewise, it has not violated rights, stifled freedoms, or repressed dissent. Daw Suu did not put herself under house arrest and detain, harass, and intimidate her own followers. However, even keeping this imbalance firmly in mind, one must acknowledge the strength of the convictions on both sides.

Consider how the junta and the NLD tried to legitimize themselves. SLORC tried to acquire legitimacy for itself by denying legitimacy to the prodemocracy movement. From a physically much weaker position, the NLD pursued the same strategy in reverse. Throughout the 1990s, both parties spent more time and energy attacking each other than looking for ways to cooperate. As a result, mutual trust between the junta and the NLD remained essentially zero. One source close to the junta noted, for example, that many senior officers feared that if they ever lost power, they and their families and friends would be subjected to violent acts of revenge by NLD and other opposition groups. As a motivation to keep power at all costs, the possible existence of such a fear may have mattered more than whether it was realistic or not.

Another source of the stalemate was lack of clarity about each group's demands. When they did call for dialogue, neither the ruling generals nor the prodemocracy activists made clear what they could give in return for what they wanted from the other side. Each side emphasized mainly what it wanted from the other, and felt thwarted when those demands were not met. Frustration fed intransigence. Democracy groups blamed the deadlock wholly on the junta's refusal to honor the results of the 1990 election. By contrast, the junta considered democracy activists, especially Daw Suu, to be Myanmar's worst and most troublesome wrongdoers.

To be sure, there have been moments of thaw, démarche, and even incipient cooperation. Rumors circulated in late 2000, for example, that secret meetings had taken place between Daw Suu and senior military leaders. Two years later, following her release from house arrest, she went out of her way to reduce mistrust between the regime and the NLD, even declaring that the junta and her movement had established enough confidence in each other to allow for cooperation. As if to illustrate such confidence, she even visited several major infrastructure projects undertaken by the government. At about this time, according to well-placed sources, Khin Nynt approached Than Shwe and convinced him that in order to counter international pressure, the junta should talk to Aung San Suu Kyi and the NLD.[28]

This reduction of tension was, however, short-lived. Despite its willingness to talk with its opponents, the SPDC was not willing to risk real political reform. According to sources close to the regime, Than Shwe only wanted the NLD and other opposition groups to support the government and play the political game according to the government's own rules. Daw Suu's continued call on the international community to maintain economic sanctions rankled senior military leaders. Senior officers did meet with her, but no meaningful dialogue ensued between the League and the Council.

When the junta failed to comply with her requests to resume dialogue on mutually agreeable terms, Daw Suu reverted to a harder line, demanding that the SPDC release all political prisoners and honor the 1990 election. The League also renewed its commitment to the outlawed CRPP, whose members had won that election, and refused to call for the lifting of economic sanctions. Daw Suu and other leading NLD members then toured the country, mobilizing support. Between June 2002 and May 2003, she visited ninety-five townships.

People turned out in droves to see her and hear her speak. When she criticized the junta, sometimes fiercely, they applauded—clear evidence of her popularity. The generals responded by deploying members of the regime-backed Union Solidarity and Development Association (USDA) to distribute anti-League pamphlets and organize protests against her. But she continued to tour the country amid outpourings of public support.

At her rallies, the USDA grew increasingly aggressive. By early 2003, bloodshed seemed only a matter of time. Things came to a head on 30 May 2003, when USDA operatives attacked NLD members who were accompanying Daw Suu near the town of Depayin, in central Myanmar. The government said that four were killed and forty injured. But opposition sources reported some seventy deaths and over one hundred injured. Blaming the event on the unruliness of the NLD members and their supporters, the junta placed Daw Suu under "protective custody"—and in doing so threw her back into the limelight as perhaps the most famous political prisoner in the world. At the same time, a sweeping crackdown began against the League.

Could the Depayin incident have been avoided? What if, earlier that year, Daw Suu, the League, and other democracy groups had stopped supporting foreign sanctions on Myanmar's economy? Would the attack have occurred? Conversely, if the junta had been willing to make concessions to the NLD, might the democracy movement have taken a less provocative approach? It is hard to know. But even if Daw Suu had reversed her position on sanctions and the attack had not occurred, it does not follow that Than Shwe would have reciprocated by agreeing to share power with—let alone cede power to—the

---

[28] Interviews with retired government officers, 2004–06.

League. What is known is that neither party found a way to work with the other in what remained basically a zero-sum situation.

From the Roadmap to the Four Eights

In 2003, not long after the Depayin incident, the junta revived the long-stalled process of holding a National Convention (NC), this time in the context of a seven-step "roadmap" toward "democracy" in Myanmar.[29] The SPDC invited NLD leaders to drop their boycott and rejoin the Convention. The League agreed, but then changed its mind and said it would take part only if the generals first released from custody all of its detained leaders.[30]

When the government did not comply with their demand, NLD leaders resumed their boycott of the NC. Senior military leaders said the convention would go on without the League. NLD leaders responded by criticizing the junta in public statements and foreign media interviews. The Shan National League for Democracy, which had won the second-largest number of seats in the 1990 election, also decided not to attend the NC.

The NLD's statements called for the government to release political prisoners and to convene the parliament that had been formed by the popular elections of 1990.[31] The government publicly rejected these proposals as mere "fantasy." The League was disinvited from the sessions of the NC, which proceeded without its participation. Many delegates seemed frustrated with their inability to speak their mind at the convention, and some minority-group representatives openly voiced their unhappiness with the process. Even so, most of the minority groups wanted to stay inside the process, on the chance that it could conceivably offer an exit from deadlock. As one minority delegate put it, the convention was "a joke," but "better than nothing" at all.[32]

---

[29] The Seven Steps in the SPDC roadmap are as follows: (1) reconvening the National Convention that has been adjourned since 1996; (2) after successful reconvening of the National Convention, step-by-step implementation of the process necessary for a genuine and disciplined democratic system; (3) drafting of a new constitution in accordance with basic principles and detailed basic principles laid down by the National Convention; (4) adoption of the constitution through national referendum; (5) staging of free and fair elections for *Pyithu Hluttaws* (legislative bodies), according to the new constitution; (6) convening *Hluttaws*, attended by *Hluttaw* members, in accordance with the new constitution; (7) building a modern, developed, and democratic nation by the state leaders elected by the *Hluttaw*, and the government and other central organs formed by the *Hluttaw*. See Kyaw Yin Hlaing, "Myanmar in 2003: Frustration and Despair?" *Asian Survey* 44, no. 1 (January/February 2004), 87–92.

[30] The National League for Democracy, Statement for National Convention, 14 May 2004, <http://www.dassk.com/contents.php?id=757>.

[31] All NLD statements are available at <http://old.ncgub.net/NLD_Statements/NLD-Sta200602012_B.htm>.

[32] Interview, 15 January 2007.

In October 2004, Khin Nyunt fell from grace. He had been prime minister since August 2003. He was replaced in that position by Soe Win, a man known for his loyalty to Than Shwe. It was initially announced that Khin Nyunt had retired on grounds of health. Then, in a speech to government leaders and local businesspeople, General Thura Shwe Mann, the third-highest-ranking official in the SPDC, charged Khin Nyunt with corruption, insubordination, and attempting to split the Tatmadaw, as Myanmar's army is officially called.

The real story behind Khin Nyunt's removal, however, was rather different. Allegedly at the urging of Maung Aye and his supporters, Than Shwe had asked Khin Nyunt to move against certain corrupt intelligence officers on Khin Nyunt's own staff. Instead, Khin Nyunt had met in secret with his closest aides to gather information about the corrupt activities of certain ministers and regional commanders who were close to Maung Aye. Such a secret and unauthorized meeting of military officers would have been considered tantamount to mutiny.

The important point here is that Khin Nyunt was not fired for being a reformist. Had he obeyed the order to discipline his own subordinates and not moved secretly against Maung Aye, Khin Nyunt might well have kept his job. Khin Nyunt had also been willing to talk to opposition groups, so his dismissal was a setback for a possible junta-NLD reconciliation. But that was collateral damage from Khin Nyunt's fall, not sufficient cause for the fall itself. Khin Nyunt was placed under house arrest, and the NC went on.

In November 2004, mere weeks after Khin Nyunt was purged, further evidence was brought that he had not been fired for favoring reform. In the middle of that month the regime freed several student leaders, including Min Ko Naing, the most famous detainee in the country after Aung San Suu Kyi. Min Ko Naing had led the All Burma Federation of Students Unions before his jailing in 1989.

Soon after their release, many of these student leaders came together in an informal network, generally known as the 1988 generation students group. Because Min Ko Naing was the most popular political activist after Daw Suu, expectations were high that he and his comrades might be able to end the deadlock and set political reform in motion. But the '88 generation group confined its activities to issuing statements on Myanmar's sociopolitical and economic deterioration, giving interviews to foreign media, and organizing, among other events, an anniversary commemoration of the 8 August 1988 showdown between the army and the correspondingly named Four Eights Democracy Movement.

Despite its public appeal, the Four Eights group could not revive student activism in Myanmar. Most who took part in the movement's activities were from the 1988 generation, not current students, and the older cohort did not know quite how to mobilize the younger one. The Four Eights leaders were also under surveillance by the government. Facing a plethora of rules meant to quell dissent, they could not do anything political without breaking the law. If they remained active in politics, they were subject to arrest at any time.

In 2006, after one of the 1988 group's events drew over two thousand people, the junta rearrested Min Ko Naing and four other leaders of the group, but released them several months later. Rumors circulated in April 2007 that some 1988 leaders had been meeting with certain military officers. Hopes rose that perhaps the junta would work with the '88 generation after all. But knowledgeable sources said privately that the authorities' motivation in talking with '88 group members was only to make sure they would not create problems. According to these sources, the regime was bent on moving forward on the seven-step roadmap while continuing to dictate the terms of public participation in political life.[33]

On 3 September 2007, Myanmar's ruling junta finally concluded the NC, fourteen years after it had begun. The NC had adopted 104 principles for the new constitution. Most opposition groups, while rejecting the government's NC and its 104 principles, could not come up with any concrete strategy to cope with the situation. A leading political activist even said, "We are running out of ideas. We tried to do whatever we could, but we don't know exactly what we should do now. Maybe we should seriously think about doing something within the framework of the junta's roadmap."[34]

The situation changed in August-September 2007. In August, without prior warning, the regime sharply raised the price of fuel. Responding to the hardship caused by the sudden hike, the '88 generation returned to the streets to denounce the government's indifference to public welfare. Buddhist monks followed suit in September by organizing large protests of their own in major cities across the country. From the outside it looked as though the regime might fall at last, but that was not to be. Instead, the government forcefully cracked down on the demonstrations and arrested their leaders.

The Peaceful Demonstrations of September 2007

In mid-2007, no Myanmar-watcher anticipated the outbreak of any major protests, let alone the escalating opposition that would soon occur. Even when the government raised fuel prices, many residents of Yangon were resigned. Although they were very upset over the higher cost of fuel, they did not think they could do anything that would make the government change its mind.

Nevertheless, in August, within a few days after the fuel prices went up, '88 group members did protest in an effort to pressure the government to alleviate the people's economic difficulties. Small demonstrations took place in several cities and towns. The government allegedly used members of a "governmental

---

[33] Interviews with retired government officers, businesspeople, and political analysts, 2007.

[34] Interview, 14 September 2007.

nongovernmental organization" (or GONGO) known as Swan Arshin in trying to disperse the protests.[35] Many members of the Swan Arshin group beat up the protesters. When the protests did not die down after a few days, the government arrested several leading members of the '88 generation group. Sporadic protests continued to take place in various parts of the country. Most people at that time were merely spectators, however, and probably did not think anything would come of the protests.

In September 2007, a series of events changed public perceptions of the protests. On 5 September, a group of monks from Pakokku staged a peaceful demonstration against the higher fuel prices.[36] Local officials tried to disperse the protest, reportedly using members of two GONGOs—the Union Solidarity and Development Association (USDA) and Swan Arshin—to do so. Many were reported to have been beaten by supporters of the government, and three monks were arrested. Soldiers also tried to disperse the protests by firing guns into the air. On the following day, when local officials went to one of the main Pakokku monasteries to apologize for what had happened the day before, the monks, angered by the mistreatment of the peaceful demonstrators, held the officials hostage until the local government had agreed to release those who had been detained.[37]

Meanwhile, an underground organization known as the Alliance of All Burma Buddhist Monks emerged. The Alliance made its presence known by distributing leaflets asking the government to apologize for the mistreatment of monks in Pakokku.[38] The Alliance warned the government that if it did not issue a formal apology by 17 September, the monks would hold *patam nikkujjana kamma*, that is, they would boycott the receipt of alms from family members of the armed forces.[39] The junta ignored the Alliance's ultimatum. On 17 September 2007, several hundred monks staged peaceful protests. Although there was no central organization coordinating all protest groups from various parts of the country, the Alliance regularly issued guidelines for monks to follow. All the statements the Alliance issued were disseminated throughout Myanmar via the

---

[35] See Asian Human Rights Commission, "Asian Human Rights Commission: Burma: Dramatic Price Rises, Protests, and Arrests Oblige International Response," BurmaNet News, 22 August 2007, <http://www.burmanet.org/news/2007/08/22/asian-human-rights-commission-burma-dramatic-price-rises-protests-and-arrests-oblige-international-response>.

[36] See BBC News, "Q&A: Protests in Burma," 2 October 2007, <http://news.bbc.co.uk/2/hi/asia-pacific/7010202.stm>.

[37] Shah Paung, "Monks Take Officials Hostage for Hours in Upper Burma Standoff," *The Irrawaddy*, 16 June 2008, <http://www.irrawaddy.org/article.php?art_id=8524>.

[38] *The Irrawaddy*, "Burmese Monks Demand Government Apology," BurmaNet News, 10 September 2007, <http://www.burmanet.org/news/2007/09/10/irrawaddy-burmese-monks-demand-government-apology-yeni>.

[39] *The Irrawaddy*, "Burmese Monks Demand Government Apology."

Burmese-language programming of external media such as the BBC, the Voice of America, Radio Free Asia, and the Democratic Voice of Burma.

The junta blamed its political opponents and Western countries for the protests. Official media portrayed the former as power-mongers, and the latter as neocolonizers hoping to install satellite regimes in developing countries.

Some domestic political groups opposed to the junta did suggest privately that they had played a role in sparking the September demonstrations. But my interviews with several activists, and my observation of how the protests unfolded, indicated that the peaceful movement of September 2007 had virtually nothing to do with either opposition groups or Western countries.

Opposition elements, especially those in exile, have been trying to provoke mass demonstrations in Myanmar against the junta ever since it first seized power in 1998, but their efforts have consistently failed. Prodemocracy activists in exile did manage to provide some assistance to local opposition groups. But these recipients were lay actors, not monks. My interviews in 2007 with many activists in exile revealed that neither the Alliance of All Burmese Buddhist Monks nor any other monk associations received any financial assistance from any exile group.[40]

One activist, who had spoken both to exile groups and to members of the Alliance, noted that although some members of the Alliance had communicated with some opposition members in the past, the Alliance was formed independently of all other opposition groups, and the monks had organized the protests on their own initiative and of their own free will. Nor was there evidence to indicate that the Alliance or other networks of monks had interacted with any foreign embassies or governments.

The government had only itself to blame for the September 2007 protests. If the junta had publicly explained why it had raised fuel prices, many people, including many monks, would have understood. Indeed, after listening to an account of how burdensome the fuel-price subsidy had become for the state budget, fifty young people, many of whom had joined the protests, came to agree that considering how expensive oil had become on the world market, continuing the subsidy unchanged would have been difficult. But why, they asked, had the government, before raising fuel prices, chosen not to inform the general public of the need for it?[41] If the government had told people in a respectful manner why it had decided to increase fuel prices, much of the turmoil that occurred could have been avoided.

---

[40] Interviews, September 2007. For the safety of their comrades inside Burma, these informants did not specifically name the groups they had assisted or what kind of assistance they had offered.

[41] In fact, only people in Yangon could buy gasoline at a subsidized rate, even before the price hike. Very few outside the capital had access to subsidized gas. Most people had relied on black-market gas for many years.

Quite apart from their use of force, the junta and its local officials also mishandled the protests once they had begun. If, for example, following the violence in Pakokku on 5 September, local authorities had apologized to the monks and punished those responsible for the bloodshed, further violence might have been avoided. Before the protests had broken out and gathered steam, many opposition groups were willing to consider new strategies; reportedly some in the exiled activist community were even ready to explore some way of working with the government. Instead, on top of their overall mismanagement of the country, the generals' mishandling of the fuel-price rise and the ensuing protests gave the opposition good reason to stand firm for an obviously popular cause.

To the surprise of many inside Myanmar, the government did not immediately crack down on the protesting monks. As a result, the number of participants grew, from a few hundred to a few hundred thousand in less than a week. So did public sympathy for their cause. In the streets, lay supporters followed the monks to protect them from harm. The demonstrations grew larger but remained peaceful.

Originally, the monks had not planned to prolong their demonstrations. According to an activist monk from Yangon, many senior monks feared that the government would brutally repress the protests if they dragged on. Some monks therefore wanted to stop the demonstrations after a few days.[42] But growing public support swayed many younger monks toward continuing to protest until the government complied with their demands.[43] Some monks also wanted to enlarge the protests by allowing lay political activists to join in. The Alliance finally agreed on both counts: to continue the protests and let other citizens join, while insisting that they remain peaceful.[44]

Although there is no way of knowing how many came out onto the streets, the demonstrations in downtown Yangon were voluminous enough to persuade many residents that a large majority of the population had taken part. The protests elsewhere in the country were smaller, but also peaceful and orderly. In Mandalay, three main monasteries demonstrated separately and did not allow lay activists to join them. In Pakokku, however, monks from various monasteries and laypeople came together from the beginning.

The demonstrators' ultimate goal was to pressure the government into working for national reconciliation and genuine political reform. But the Alliance and other protest groups did not voice their political demands in a united manner. Protesters in Pakokku made more political demands than their counterparts in Yangon and other places. In Yangon, it was only after lay protesters began joining the demonstrations that the Alliance and other groups called openly for democratic reform. In Yangon, which until recently had been

---

[42] Interviews, 27 October 2007.

[43] Radio Free Asia (Burmese Language Program), "Burma's Fuel Protest," 19 September 2007, <http://www.rfa.org/english/news/social/2007/09/19/burma_fuelprotest>.

[44] Interview with a political activist, 28 October 2007.

the capital city where all foreign embassies were based, the protests quickly gained widespread domestic and foreign attention. As the size and momentum of the demonstrations swelled, the prospect of political change began to seem less impossible to many in Myanmar.

On 25 September 2007, the junta finally decided to stop the protests. First, a curfew was imposed in the cities where major demonstrations had taken place. Immediately thereafter, large contingents of soldiers burst into these cities. The soldiers initially ordered the protesting monks and laypeople to disperse. When the protesters did not obey these orders, the soldiers began to lob tear gas and fire guns. In some places the soldiers fired warning shots in the air before opening fire at the demonstrators. At other locations, however, soldiers allegedly shot at protesters without prior warning. Soldiers also beat monks and lay protesters with bamboo sticks.

It is clear that several hundred protesters were beaten in Yangon. The number who were killed outright became a matter of dispute between the generals and their opponents. The junta told a UN human rights envoy that fifteen people had been shot dead, but opposition groups claimed that soldiers had killed more than one hundred.[45]

As far as we know, no protesters were killed in the other cities. This was due in part to instances of cooperation between military officers and some senior monks. In Mandalay, for example, military officers asked senior monks to keep the young monks under supervision inside the monasteries, saying they did not want to shoot at them. These officers also warned that if the monks did go to the streets, they would have to obey orders and shoot at them. Realizing that the officers were serious, senior monks begged their juniors not to go out, and most of the junior monks listened to their seniors and stayed in.

The demonstrations did not stop right away, but around the country their size and number had diminished significantly by 27 September. On the following day, monk protesters who had not yet been arrested were interned in their monasteries. Security forces then raided the main monasteries in cities where major protests had taken place and detained the protest leaders they found there. By the end of September, most people in Myanmar knew that the monks' peaceful protests had been, at least for the time being, subdued.

The Internet and the Internationalization of Myanmar as a Political Issue

The advent of the Internet, and the access that many in Myanmar have recently gained to it, has transformed coverage of events in the country. During September 2007, hundreds of young people in Myanmar tried to share their firsthand knowledge about the protests with friends living in foreign countries. Some tried to share what they saw or heard about the protests with millions of people

---

[45] Thomas Fuller, "At Least 15 Died in Crackdown, Myanmar Tells Envoy," 17 November 2007, <http://www.nytimes.com/2007/11/17/world/asia/17myanmar.html>.

around the world through Internet blogs. While the protests were going on, there emerged a few dozen blogs dedicated to information and pictures about the demonstrations in various parts of Myanmar. Most of these young people had grown up after the Four-Eights Democracy Movement and were unaware of the brutal stance the government could take against its challengers. When the government did not take any prompt actions against the protests, young people who had initially been spectators began to walk with the monks and became a part of the protests. They told their friends from inside and beyond the country how exciting it was to be a part of the movement.

When they personally witnessed soldiers shooting at and beating up monks and other protesters, these same young people from various parts of the country were shocked and grew angry at the government. As a result, they began to behave like serious protesters, using the Internet systematically and globally to disseminate information about the military government's repression of the peaceful demonstrations. Thanks to these young activists, the international media came to realize the gravity of the situation in Myanmar.

The Internet activities undertaken by young protesters proved to be very effective. Thanks to the pictures and the information they circulated, the international community began to pay serious attention to Myanmar. The prime minister of Singapore, Lee Hsien Loong, as chairman of ASEAN, issued a statement condemning the junta for killing monk protesters.[46] Some ASEAN diplomats noted that the availability of photographs of the government's brutal repression of monks made it very difficult for ASEAN governments to remain quiet.[47]

Myanmar's military leaders also appear to have understood that their handling of the September protests had damaged their reputations. Even China, the junta's staunch ally, felt compelled to advise Myanmar's military to work with the UN. For the first time in its history, ASEAN harshly criticized the junta. Sources close to the Chinese government said that it was partly because the Chinese leadership had requested such cooperation that the Burmese junta decided to work with the UN in solving its political problems. Cooperation aside, the junta made it very clear that the NLD and its leader, Aung San Suu Kyi, would not be a part of its plan to institute so-called disciplined democracy in the country.[48] In less than two weeks after the protests were suppressed, the government announced that its leader Than Shwe would meet Aung San Suu Kyi if the latter stopped confronting the government and stopped calling for

---

[46] See Agencies, "Massacre of the Monks in Burma," 2 October 2007, <http://www.news.com.au/heraldsun/story/0,21985,22515138-661,00.html>.

[47] Interview, 11 November 2007.

[48] See Democratic Voice of Burma, "Burmese Democracy Party View Exclusion from National Convention," 3 February 2005, <http://www.burmanet.org/news/2005/02/03/democratic-voice-of-burma-burmese-democracy-party-views-exclusion-from-national-convention>.

the international community to impose economic sanctions.[49] As noted earlier, the junta even appointed a cabinet minister to deal with Aung San Suu Kyi directly. (Since then, some meetings between Daw Suu and representatives of the junta have taken place, and Daw Suu has also been allowed to see her party members.) For the first time in three years, the junta even allowed the UN human rights envoy to investigate Myanmar's human rights situation. Many people at the time thought that mounting international pressure—via the availability of pictures and information about repressive government activities—had made the junta realize that it could not remain in power without talking to the political opposition.

The Referendum, the New Constitution, and Cyclone Nargis

Despite the positive developments noted earlier, the junta made it clear that it would not revise the 104 principles. On 18 October 2007, the junta formed a committee, including retired and serving government officers, businesspeople, and some representatives of GONGOs and ethnic groups, in order to draft the new constitution. In February 2008, the junta announced that it would hold a referendum for the new constitution on 10 May 2008 and that the new elections would be held in 2010. Copies of the constitution were made available to the public in April 2007. Meanwhile, senior Burmese generals were reportedly unhappy with Daw Suu for releasing a statement to the international community through UN special envoy Mr. Gambari without first consulting with them.[50] Although a representative of the junta and Daw Suu have met a few times, true democratic changes were nowhere in sight. The government stated that it would work with opposition groups only so long as its rules were followed. For her part, Daw Suu seemed unwilling to abide by the government's parameters. While the junta was preparing for the referendum, some senior military officers publicly noted that Daw Suu would not be allowed to run in the 2010 elections.[51] In May 2008, the junta drove this point home by extending Daw Suu's house arrest.

Most opposition groups—unhappy that the junta had made amendments to the constitution very difficult—called for the public either to cast a "no" vote in the referendum, or to boycott it altogether. A survey of 350 people conducted in late March and early May indicated that many people remained indifferent to the referendum.[52] Only 28 percent of the survey participants said they would definitely cast a "no" vote, and 39 percent remained undecided. However, a

---

[49] See Sebastien Berger, "Aung San Suu Kyi: Leader Offered Meeting," 10 October 2007, <http://www.telegraph.co.uk/news/main.jhtml?xml=/news/2007/10/05/wburma105.xml>.

[50] Interview with a government official, 28 April 2008.

[51] "Democrat Banned from Myanmar Elections," *Manila Times*, 21 February 2008, <http://www.manilatimes.net/national/2008/feb/21/yehey/world/20080221worl.html>.

[52] A group of young Myanmar researchers conducted this survey under my supervision.

second survey, conducted in the same areas as the first, indicated that the number of people who would cast "no" votes had increased to 32 percent. More than 90 percent of the participants also believed that the government was prepared to do anything to get the desired results in the referendum. Most were also waiting to see how the government would manipulate the referendum.

On 2 May 2008, Cyclone Nargis devastated many areas in lower Myanmar, claiming the lives of more than one hundred thousand people and leaving about two million people homeless. The international community called for the junta to postpone the referendum, but the the junta rescheduled it only in the areas hardest hit by the cyclone. In the wake of the cyclone, the public ceased to care so much about the referendum, and focused instead on the disaster victims.[53] Suddenly, it became quite easy for the government to manipulate the referendum, and there were rumors of irregularities while it took place and after it had been completed.[54] In mid-May 2008, the government announced that more than 90 percent of the voters had supported the new constitution.[55]

Cyclone Nargis created problems for Myanmar, but the junta was determined to remain in power, despite harsh criticism from the international community and from opposition groups. At the time of this writing, Myanmar's general public was very unhappy with the way the junta had handled the Nargis disaster. Whether more large protests against the junta could be mobilized, taking advantage of growing public dissatisfaction, remained to be seen.

Myanmar and ASEAN: Expectations, Frustrations, and Outside Interests

Burma became a sovereign republic in January 1948. Burmese nationalists were among the first in Southeast Asia to argue that the region needed its own international organization in order to cope with life after independence. Burma's first prime minister, U Nu, was instrumental in creating the Non-Aligned Movement. Burmese student leaders traveled to international student meetings, while leaders of trade unions and political parties were active in their own international networks. But following Ne Win's coup in 1962, the country's foreign involvements declined. The government in particular became less engaged abroad, shunning global and regional meetings for fear of being dragged into the Cold War.

---

[53] More than fifty people I interviewed in the wake of Cyclone Nargis noted that they could not care less about the referendum.

[54] More than thirty voters to whom I spoke said they did not even see their ballots. After being asked to sign a sheet at their polling stations, officials there simply told voters to return home.

[55] "Announcement on Results of the Referendum Held in the Whole Country," The New Light of Myanmar, 27 May 2008, 1–2, <http://www.myanmar-embassy-tokyo. net/news/may/2008-05-27-NLME.pdf> .

In 1967, as they made preparations to launch ASEAN, the leaders of Indonesia, Malaysia, the Philippines, and Thailand invited the Burmese government to join as a founding member. Suspecting that ASEAN would be a pro-Western body akin to the Southeast Asia Treaty Organization, Ne Win declined the invitation, and Burma's relations with its eastern neighbors continued to be bilateral in nature.

As the years passed, attitudes toward ASEAN diverged within the regime. By the 1990s, some senior officers had concluded that membership in the Association could help to counter Western pressure, including the economic sanctions that Western countries had imposed. These officers understood the need to rely on China for that purpose, but they also wanted to improve relations with Myanmar's Southeast Asian neighbors, if only to gain more freedom to maneuver. According to one retired senior official, it was widely believed in the junta that Myanmar should not allow itself to become a mere satellite of China.[56] In that context, entering ASEAN could be seen as a counterbalancing strategy. Other members of the junta were less keen to join the Association, possibly because they were unconvinced that Southeast Asia's diverse governments would be as accepting of Myanmar's political status quo as China had been.

In the end, according to a diplomatic source, foreign ministry officials in several ASEAN countries, wanting Myanmar to join, managed to persuade Myanmar's ambassadors to these countries that it should do so. These ambassadors then passed the idea upward to the junta, through their foreign minister in Yangon.[57] Officers who favored affiliation then went to Senior General Than Shwe, the chairman of SLORC, and convinced him that joining ASEAN would elicit support from its members and help to offset the effects of Western hostility.

Most ASEAN countries paid little heed to developments in Myanmar in the late 1980s and early 1990s. But the withdrawal of Vietnamese troops from Cambodia and the establishment of an elected government there led the Association to invite Vietnam to join, which it did in 1995. ASEAN diplomats were encouraged to work to include all the remaining Southeast Asian states in the Association. In 1996, after consulting with the Chinese government and securing its support, Myanmar formally applied for membership.

Western critics of Myanmar and Burmese activists for democracy and human rights, including Daw Suu, opposed membership and called on ASEAN to reject the application. Reportedly, some ASEAN leaders, among them Singapore's Lee Kuan Yew, were reluctant to welcome Myanmar into the group, while others, notably Malaysian Prime Minister Mahathir Mohamad, insisted on allowing all of the region's countries to join. ASEAN officials held consultations on the matter, and between themselves and their American and European counterparts. ASEAN decided to admit Myanmar, and did so in 1997.

---

[56] Interview, 12 August 2006.

[57] Interview, 21 September 2005.

A former secretary-general of the Association would later list five reasons why Myanmar was allowed in. First, he wrote, Myanmar was clearly, as a matter of geography, part of Southeast Asia. Second, Myanmar had, for the first time ever, decided to become aligned, and had chosen ASEAN with which to align itself. Third, Myanmar was a fairly large country, "bigger than France" and "very strategically located between China, Thailand, India, Bangladesh and Laos." With a land boundary far longer than France's with Germany, and a history of conflict with adjacent states in three major wars from 1870 to 1945, he concluded that Myanmar was clearly "critical to its neighboring countries and to ASEAN" in terms of its "territorial integrity and political stability." Fourth, Myanmar was "located in the Golden Triangle" and was "the largest producer of poppy seeds" in that area. Fifth, were Myanmar to join ASEAN, "there would be better opportunities to influence" the country "to adjust its internal policies and move toward national reconciliation."[58]

Myanmar's government took a different view of the benefits of belonging to ASEAN. Far from nudging the junta toward reform, membership would provide a collective basis for meeting "the groups posing a threat" to the country. Joining the Association would create opportunities "to open the door wider politically and economically with the help, understanding and sympathy of fellow ASEAN members." That is, by facilitating inflows of investment from other ASEAN states, Myanmar's affiliation with ASEAN would help diversify the country's economy and thus mitigate the impact of the American embargo.[59]

Frustrations

Before reviewing the role of ASEAN in the light of these contrasting expectations, a brief note on the UN's involvement is in order. For five years, until his December 2005 decision to resign, a former Malaysian diplomat, Razali Ismail, served as the UN secretary-general's special envoy to Burma/Myanmar. In that capacity he tried and failed to end the stand-off between the NLD and the SPDC. One may therefore ask, rhetorically: If the UN as a global body could not succeed in Myanmar, how could ASEAN possibly do so?

Razali's mission was not a complete failure. Many political prisoners were released because of the pressure he applied. His Malaysian nationality and his diplomatic profession were assets in Yangon. Several senior members of the junta were willing to talk with him as a fellow Southeast Asian who had been closely associated with Malaysian Prime Minister Mahathir, one of the strongest supporters of Myanmar's admission into ASEAN. Razali failed to conciliate

---

[58] Rodolfo Severino, *Southeast Asia in Search of an ASEAN Community: Insights from the Former ASEAN Secretary-General* (Singapore: Institute of Southeast Asian Studies, 2006), 134.

[59] Quoted in Mya Than, *Myanmar in ASEAN: Regional Cooperation Experience* (Singapore: Institute of Southeast Asian Studies, 2005), 85.

the junta and its opposition not because he was incapable, but because he fell victim to internal rivalries beyond his control. Regular army officers, notably Than Shwe, were deeply suspicious of their counterparts in intelligence. The army faction came to associate Razali with individuals in the intelligence faction, notably Khin Nyunt, and with Daw Suu. After being barred from returning to Myanmar for nearly two years, Razali finally stepped down. (In May 2007, a Nigerian, Ibrahim Gambari, was appointed as special envoy to Burma/Myanmar, reporting to the UN's new secretary-general, Ban Ki-moon.)

While Razali was failing to budge the regime beyond releasing prisoners, ASEAN was coping with the consequences of its new member's odium in Western eyes. In 1997, soon after Myanmar's entry into ASEAN, the then British foreign secretary Robin Cook announced on behalf of the EU that the junta would be excluded from the second summit of the Asia-Europe Meeting (ASEM), scheduled to take place in London in 1998, unless the human rights situation in Myanmar improved. ASEAN leaders unanimously protested the British decision. Prime Minister Mahathir went so far as to warn that if Myanmar were barred from the summit, ASEAN as a bloc might boycott the event.[60] The problem was temporarily solved when the junta decided not to attend ASEM.[61]

If the deadlock within Myanmar did not go away, neither did the controversy over Myanmar between ASEAN and the EU. As ASEAN countries unanimously sided with Myanmar, EU countries finally gave in and allowed the junta to attend the EU-ASEAN ministerial meeting in 2000. When EU countries again insisted that Myanmar should not be represented at the ASEM in Hanoi in 2004, ASEAN countries unanimously responded that if ASEAN's new members could not attend ASEM, ASEAN would not agree to the participation of the EU's new members. A compromise was reached that allowed Myanmar to be represented in ASEM on the condition that the country's head of state would not lead the delegation. In 2005, all ASEAN countries sent junior officers to the meeting of the EU-ASEAN economic ministers in Holland to protest the Dutch government's refusal to grant a visa to Myanmar's minister.

ASEAN diplomats also defended Myanmar from its critics in the United States and the United Nations. An analyst close to the junta concluded that membership in ASEAN had lived up to the regime's expectations by providing "a diplomatic shield" against its adversaries outside Southeast Asia.[62] Myanmar, in turn, met the obligations of membership, such as paying annual dues and attending ASEAN meetings.[63] But the stalemate inside the country continued. Daw Suu and other Burmese political activists, the international media, and

---

[60] Mya Than, *Myanmar in ASEAN*, 105, 107.

[61] BBC News, "ASEM 2: Guide to the Issues," 4 April 1998, <http://news.bbc.co.uk/2/hi/special_report/1998/03/98/asem_2/71528.stm>.

[62] Maung Aung Myoe, *Regionalism in Myanmar's Foreign Policy: Past, Present and Future*, working paper (Singapore, Asia Research Institute, 2006), 18.

[63] See Mya Than, *Myanmar in ASEAN*, 88–90.

several Western governments chastised the Association for not pressuring the junta to reform and to respect human rights. In self-defense, ASEAN officials began discussing the matter, especially in ministerial meetings. One ASEAN diplomat recalled a sense of frustration in ASEAN circles at being criticized for the wrongdoing of a member they could not control. "We did not wish to intervene in the internal affairs of Burma," he noted. "But since we were not left alone, we had to do something." ASEAN diplomats were willing to defend Myanmar, but not to look like complete fools when doing so.[64] Another experienced source remarked that if the junta "wanted us to defend them," the diplomats wanted it to "prove that it was worth defending. ... We could defend the Myanmar government as long as we saw some progress."[65]

The leaders and officials of the major ASEAN countries regularly asked senior officials in Myanmar for updates on implementation of the junta's roadmap toward national reconciliation. ASEAN officials also asked their Myanmar counterparts on several occasions to release political prisoners and to speed up the constitution-drafting process. In these meetings, one informant recalled, "We expressed our frustration with the pace of the national reconciliation process." Often, in reply, Myanmar simply read back the official line. "They always said they were working on [reform]. They said things in their country were complicated and [they] had to effect changes gradually."[66]

Retired diplomats and policy scholars were also enlisted in such discussions. One ASEAN researcher recalled being asked by his boss to offer advice to Myanmar's leaders, especially Khin Nyunt, on political development and how to accomplish it. The researcher duly explained to Khin Nyunt how democratic reforms were carried out in other countries. Khin Nyunt listened politely, thanked him for his presentation, and did nothing. "All our efforts," the researcher concluded, "were futile."[67]

In this context, the junta won. Myanmar's generals used ASEAN to defend themselves against their critics, but ASEAN diplomats could not persuade the Myanmar to meet the criticism even partway. ASEAN ministers were reportedly frank with the regime behind closed doors, but in public communiqués their comments were invariably toned down. Most Burmese political activists came to view the Association as toothless—a paper tiger too timid to speak out against the junta's misdeeds, let alone do anything that might prevent them.[68] The junta did not even bother to keep its fellow member governments informed about political developments in the country.

Probably because of these frustrations, when legislators in several major Southeast Asian states were moved by conditions in Myanmar to form an ASEAN

---

[64] Interview, 15 April 2007.

[65] Interview, 20 April 2007.

[66] Interview, 28 April 2007.

[67] Interview, 12 April 2007.

[68] Interviews with more than twenty Burmese political activists, 2007.

Inter-Parliamentary Myanmar Caucus (AIPMC), their respective governments did not try to stop them. Established in 2004, the AIPMC joined the United States and the EU in accusing the junta of endangering regional stability, and called on ASEAN to encourage democratic reforms inside Myanmar.[69]

Each July the chairmanship of ASEAN has passed by alphabetic rotation to a different member. Laos held the position in 2005–06 and Myanmar was scheduled, for the first time, to take over for the 2006–07 year. That succession would have subjected ASEAN, in effect, to shame by even closer association with its most notorious member.

AIMPC campaigned against allowing Myanmar to occupy the chair. Some Caucus members, notably Indonesia and the Philippines, convinced their fellow parliamentarians to pass resolutions urging their respective governments to prevent Myanmar from assuming this role. In 2005, the junta decided to relinquish that opportunity. Emboldened by that success, AIMPC members urged ASEAN to take even harsher action against the regime—a view shared by other prodemocracy activists, scholars, and diplomats in the region.[70]

In March 2005, a Malaysian government spokesman had opposed giving the ASEAN chair to Myanmar before it undertook democratic reforms. In March 2006, Malaysia's foreign minister, Syed Hamid Albar, traveled to Myanmar as an ASEAN envoy, tasked with obtaining information on progress toward reconciliation and democracy. The junta refused to receive ASEAN's envoy. "Even when they allowed him to come to Burma," an ASEAN diplomat later observed, "Syed was invited as Malaysian foreign minister, not as an ASEAN envoy. Syed's attempt to meet Aung San Suu Kyi also proved to be futile. We are very frustrated with the Burmese government."[71]

Confronting Myanmar with Sanctions

Relinquishing the ASEAN chair is the sole action that the junta has taken that could be construed as a victory for ASEAN. But does that one action really constitute a success for ASEAN? If so, should ASEAN mount a still bolder campaign to isolate Myanmar inside Southeast Asia, just as Western states and international organizations have tried to sequester the junta from the larger world?

Both of these questions can be answered in the negative. First, although declining the chair may have saved ASEAN's face, it did not speed reform inside Myanmar. Second, as former ASEAN SG Rodolfo Severino has argued, ASEAN might have acquired more leverage against the junta had Myanmar been allowed to take over the chair. By this logic, knowing that, as the chair, it would be hosting meetings in Myanmar in mid-2007 to which the United States and the

---

[69] See the AIPMC website at <http://www.aseanmp.org>.

[70] Interviews with ASEAN diplomats and politicians, 2007.

[71] Interview, 1 April 2007.

EU would be invited, the junta might have had an incentive to, in Severino's phrase, "loosen up a bit." Such good behavior might have given Myanmar's critics a reason to relent and attend, and put ASEAN in its debt. Conversely, by passing up the chance to chair the Association, the junta robbed ASEAN of its leverage and left it with only the ability to thank the generals for their forbearance. Third, as Severino also rightly noted, if Myanmar had hosted the ASEAN summit and other ASEAN meetings, it would have had to grant visas to American, European, and other foreign journalists. Such reporters could have exposed more fully to the world the junta's wrongdoing and the suffering of ordinary citizens, which might in turn have intensified pressure for reform.[72]

By logical extension, even Myanmar's expulsion from ASEAN—a highly unlikely prospect—would not necessarily speed either reconciliation or democratization inside the country. ASEAN, for one, would lose all leverage. According to one senior military officer, expulsion would not weaken the regime, as long as it retained the support of China, India, and Russia.[73]

If the junta has disappointed some of its Southeast Asian neighbors, some of the latter have in turn disappointed Myanmar. The junta was annoyed, for example, when Indonesia abstained from the vote against Myanmar in the United Nations Security Council (UNSC) in 2007. But the generals were not ready to resign from ASEAN. Interviewed on this question, three serving and eight retired officials answered that the government wanted to remain a part of ASEAN as long as ASEAN governments did not actually take part in activities to topple it.[74]

Myanmar's military leaders did not relish being an entirely black sheep inside the Association. Sources close to the junta recalled that after their Southeast Asian colleagues began to discuss the Myanmar situation in ASEAN meetings, the junta handled its domestic opposition more carefully and less repressively. One source close to the junta also noted that ASEAN deserved some credit for the emergence of the seven-step roadmap to reconciliation. In his view, it was partly to avoid appearing overly retrograde in ASEAN's eyes that the junta had decided, in the context of the roadmap, to reconvene the stalled NC.[75] It is also worth noting that Myanmar's military leaders allowed the relief team from ASEAN countries to help Cyclone Nargis victims in the delta areas. They also permitted the ASEAN Secretariat to assess the damages in storm-hit areas, even as they denied similar access to most relief teams from Western countries. These two concessions indicate that the junta wants to remain on good terms with ASEAN countries.

---

[72] Severino, *Southeast Asia in Search of an ASEAN Community*, 144.

[73] Interview, 3 April 2007.

[74] Interviews, February and May 2007.

[75] Interview, 28 April 2007.

One option that is open to ASEAN, at least in theory, is to join the West in boycotting Myanmar's economy. Is this advisable? To answer the question, one must assess the impact of Western sanctions.

Western strictures on Myanmar date back more than two decades. In the wake of the junta's crackdown and takeover in September 1988, the United States and the EU suspended all technical and financial assistance and the sale of military weapons to Burma, although these sanctions were not legislated into law until 1990. In 1997, at the urging of Burmese prodemocracy groups and their foreign sympathizers, the Clinton administration restricted new investments by American companies in Myanmar and issued a visa ban on senior military officers and their families and associates. EU countries imposed similar sanctions. After the Depayin incident in 2003, Washington banned imports from Myanmar. European governments condemned the junta for the incident but did not introduce new sanctions. In September 2006 at the UN, acting on an American request, the Security Council debated whether to put Myanmar on its agenda. Ten of the fourteen members of the UNSC voted in favor of the U.S. proposal. However, although the UNSC did discuss the Myanmar issue, China and Russia vetoed the resolution that called for an end to human rights violations in Myanmar.[76]

The bitter fact is that these measures and the comprehensive and prolonged antijunta pressure they have sustained have failed to achieve their original goal—namely, to force democratic reform, and failing that, to bring down the regime. Not least among the reasons for this failure is Myanmar's prior isolation from the international community. Unlike, for example, the Philippines, Myanmar had never relied on any major Western power. No Western government, therefore, could change the minds of the country's generals. Unlike most East European nations, Myanmar had never belonged to any major political bloc. The collapse of the Communist bloc and the end of Cold War had little impact on the generals' confidence in their authoritarian format, still less the need to reform it. The country's long isolation—and its leaders' isolationism—had effectively insulated Myanmar from any meaningful engagement with the West. In this context of already minimal foreign leverage, sanctions were almost redundant.

Western economic restrictions did cause some problems for the regime. To the extent that its revenues were less than they would have been without the sanctions, the junta was less able to legitimate itself by funding development projects, and was correspondingly less able to take the credit for economic growth. Shortages of foreign exchange made it harder for state-owned factories to function properly. But none of these difficulties ever threatened the regime. As I will note later, Myanmar has been blessed—or cursed—with

---

[76] "Double Veto for Burma Resolution," BBCBurmese.com, 14 January 2007, <http://www.bbc.co.uk/burmese/highlights/story/2007/01/070114_doubleveto_burma_unsc.shtml>.

enough natural resources to enable its generals to keep themselves in power for some time to come.

Even in the highly unlikely event that Western sanctions do someday bankrupt the regime, the result could fall grievously short of the good intentions behind it. Were the junta to collapse in red ink, living conditions in Myanmar would already have grown even more dire. One can picture the country rife with poverty, disease, and drugs, its infrastructure neglected and its environment degraded. Moreover, there is no guarantee that a successor government would reverse the record of mismanagement compiled by the current regime.

No reliable research has been done on the impact of economic sanctions on Myanmar. Circumstantial evidence indicates, however, that sanctions have made more difficult the lives of ordinary citizens working in tourism, textiles, and agriculture. As a stimulus to reform, an embargo is effective when it both weakens the targeted regime and enables civil society to take advantage of that weakness by organizing for regime change. In Myanmar, although economic sanctions have hurt the junta, civil society has remained even weaker than the somewhat weakened state. Increasingly, American and European observers and officials have recognized that isolation has failed to produce the intended results, and question the value of its indefinite continuation.[77]

The Interests of China and India

Had the entire world rejected and isolated authoritarian Myanmar, after the example of the successful global campaign against apartheid in South Africa, the junta might have collapsed within a decade of seizing power. But the Southeast Asian states are not the only ones to have conducted business as usual with Myanmar. China is a major case in point. The Western arms embargo has not stopped Beijing from supplying the junta with an estimated US$ 2 billion in military hardware at "friendship prices."[78] China has helped the regime to build up its infrastructure—roads, railroads, ports, dams, sports stadiums, bridges, and radar stations. China extended interest-free and low-interest loans amounting to US$ 485 million to the junta in the period from 1998 through early 2006.

[77] See David Steinberg, Tsumori Shigeru, Andrew Selth, Pavin Chachavalpongpun, Peter Christian Hauswedell, and Kyaw Yin Hlaing, "Panel Discussion: Alliances and the Problems of Burma/Myanmar Policy: The United States, Japan, Thailand, Australia, and the European Union," Sasakawa Peace Foundation, Washington DC, 2006.

[78] David I. Steinberg, "Burma: Feel-Good U.S. Sanctions Wrongheaded," *YaleGlobal Online*, 19 May 2004, <http://yaleglobal.yale.edu/display.article?id=3901>.

In June 2006, Beijing promised an additional US$ 200 million "for five unspecified government ministries" in Myanmar.[79]

The Chinese government has allowed its citizens to invest freely in Myanmar—as have Myanmar's co-members in ASEAN. Because most Chinese investment has entered the country indirectly, through the overseas Chinese, its total value is hard to estimate. Some local analysts and businesspeople have surmised that China has become the largest foreign investor in Myanmar, as well as its largest trading partner.[80] Of Myanmar's 2005 total trade of US$ 5 billion, China accounted for $1.5 billion.[81] These figures are doubly revealing: first, that nearly one-third of Myanmar's trade is with China, but second, that a far larger share of Myanmar's commerce with the world involves other countries. Apparently, even if China dropped its trade with Myanmar to zero, the junta could survive.

Unlike autocratic China, democratic India initially supported the movement for democracy in Myanmar. But the government in New Delhi changed its mind when it realized that China's assiduous cultivation of Myanmar and its burgeoning presence there could become a strategic constraint along India's politically turbulent eastern flank. In the early 1990s, India stopped criticizing the junta and began providing the government with economic and technical aid. In the early 2000s, the Indian and Myanmar armies jointly mounted operations along the India-Myanmar border to quell insurgent groups fighting Indian rule.[82] The 2003 discovery of large reserves of natural gas off the Arakan coast in western Myanmar prompted New Delhi to make large investments in building a pipeline to carry the gas from Myanmar to India. In short, Myanmar has become a key trading partner that India can ill afford to alienate.

In contrast to their Chinese counterparts, Russia's top leaders have kept some personal distance from the junta. But that has not prevented Moscow from selling several million dollars' worth of weapons to Myanmar, including MiG 29 fighter jets. Russia has also offered to train Myanmar's civilian and military technicians and officers, and has reportedly agreed to build factories

---

[79] Nyi Nyi Lwin, *Economic and Military Cooperation between China and Burma*, September 2006, <http://www.narinjara.com/Reports/BReport.ASP>. The reference to unspecified ministries reflects testimony by Jared Genser before the U.S.-China Economic and Security Review Commission on 3 August 2006.

[80] Interviews, 2005–07. Because most Chinese investments originating from Yunnan province were made through local connections, it is difficult to know the exact amount of Chinese investment in Myanmar, but available figures do support the statement that China is the country's biggest foreign investor. See Nyi Nyi Lwin, *Economic and Military Cooperation between China and Burma*.

[81] Lwin, *Economic and Military Cooperation*.

[82] Sudha Ramachandran, "India Presses Burma over Insurgents," *Asia Times*, 20 September 2006, <http://www.yuyu.net/burmanet2-l/archive/1238.html>.

for repairing and upgrading arms that Myanmar had previously acquired from the Soviet Union.[83]

In these ways, China and Russia, and prospectively India as well, have helped to prolong the SPDC's tenure. It is hardly coincidental that in early 2007 both China and Russia used their vetoes to stop the UNSC from taking punitive action against the Myanmar junta.

Myanmar and ASEAN: Recommendations

Is there a role for ASEAN to play in pursuing reconciliation and democratization in Myanmar?

As of this writing, the facts on the ground were not propitious. Turning deaf ears to the appeals of AIPMC legislators, all nine of ASEAN's other member governments still refused to impose any sanctions on, let alone expel, their most controversial co-member. Thailand and Singapore, respectively, are still the second- and third-biggest investors in Myanmar. Thailand, sharing as it does a lengthy land border with Myanmar, is especially concerned that economic sanctions on its neighbor could unleash a destabilizing flood of refugees, for which Bangkok might become responsible. In addition, roughly one-fifth of the natural gas needed by Thailand comes from Myanmar, and plans are under way for Thailand and China jointly to develop and import hydroelectric power from Myanmar.

The sale of its rich natural resources continues to alleviate many of the problems the junta faces. Such resources are being depleted, of course. Eventually they will run out, or their further exploitation will become uneconomical. However, new finds are also being made that may extend the junta's ability to resist Western sanctions. The vast Shwe ("Gold") underwater gas reserve, discovered off the Arakan coast, is a case in point. That field is thought to be large enough to generate anywhere from US$ 800 million to US$ 3 billion annually, once production begins.[84]

In 2007, the other ASEAN governments still did not see the status quo in Myanmar as a threat to the stability or security of their region. Five Southeast Asian diplomats told me that Myanmar had been discussed in ASEAN circles from time to time only because the junta's behavior gave the Association a bad image in the eyes of outsiders, not because the situation inside the country was thought to endanger the region.[85]

ASEAN has never specified criteria for membership, beyond physical location in Southeast Asia. The absence of any threshold that every member

---

[83] Åshild Kolås and Stein Tonnesson, "Burma and Its Neighbors: The Geopolitics of Gas," *Austral Policy Forum* (7 September 2006), 10, <http://www.nautilus.org/fora/security/0674KolasTonnesson.html>

[84] Kolås and Tonnesson, "Burma and Its Neighbors."

[85] Interviews, April–May 2007.

must meet helps protect Myanmar from being singled out. As for democracy, Brunei, Laos, and Vietnam were long-standing autocracies. Thailand was at least temporarily under military rule following a coup in 2006. Governments in Cambodia, Indonesia, Malaysia, the Philippines, and Singapore have continued, in various ways and to different degrees, to resort to undemocratic methods of keeping themselves in power. In contrast to the explicitly democratic EU, the members of ASEAN lack both the moral authority and the political will to advocate democracy in Myanmar.

As of this writing, ASEAN still had no clear and common idea as to how it should handle the Myanmar question—or even what exactly the question was. ASEAN's leaders did feel pressed to do something to limit the damage that the junta's behavior had caused the Association. They were in this respect reactive, not proactive. Further curtailing their ability to deal with political issues involving their newer and less democratic co-members—not only Myanmar but also Cambodia, Laos, and Vietnam—were the "principles of tolerance, restraint, accommodation, consensus, consultation, equality and national resilience" that had come to pave the "ASEAN Way."[86]

A Promising Charter?

At their summit in Singapore in November 2007, the leaders of Southeast Asia signed an ASEAN Charter. In the run-up to this event, an Eminent Persons Group (EPG) advised ASEAN "to develop democracy, promote good governance and uphold human rights and the rule of law."[87] They called for the "rejection of unconstitutional and undemocratic changes of government."[88] According to the EPG, membership in ASEAN should have not only benefits, but consequences as well. Accordingly, "any serious breach" by "any Member State" of ASEAN's "objectives, principles, and commitments," including its "norms and values," the EPG argued, should put the offending state at risk of having its "rights and privileges" as a member suspended.[89]

The final text of the Charter was not as bold as the EPG wished it to be. But the document did provide for a regional commission for human rights, and it contains language to strengthen the Association's ability to enforce compliance by member states. As always with ASEAN, however, the devil is in the details, and even if agreement can be reached on these details, will full implementation necessarily follow?

---

[86] Phar Kim Beng, "The Problems of a Two-tiered ASEAN," *Asia Times*, 20 February 2003, <http://www.atimes.com/atimes/Southeast_Asia/EB20Ae03.html>.

[87] *Report of the Eminent Persons Group on the ASEAN Charter*, December 2006, 22, <http://www.aseansec.org/19247.pdf>.

[88] *Report of the Eminent Persons Group*, 29.

[89] *Report of the Eminent Persons Group*, 31.

The Charter does not define democracy, leaving open a wide variety of possible understandings. In one of the meetings held to discuss the Charter's possible contents, a Vietnamese delegate noted that although his country was not a multiparty democracy in the Western sense, it still deserved the title because it practiced democracy *within* its one-party system.[90] Nor does the Charter specify precisely what actions constitute violations of human rights. I interviewed an official from Myanmar who wondered whether ASEAN would consider the Singapore government's unfair treatment of its political opposition a violation of human rights. Championing human rights, he seemed to imply, could become a slippery slope for the whole region.[91]

Another official from Myanmar who attended meetings on the Charter called it a veiled attempt to prosecute his country. Even though delegates from Myanmar had agreed to most of the Charter's contents, he said, the text's potentially disturbing implications for the government appeared not to have been made clear to the junta's top echelon.[92] If he was right about this, Myanmar may well raise objections if and when the Charter is enforced.

It is likewise unclear how decisions will be reached under the Charter's terms. For example, if consensus is to give way to voting, will measures be adopted by a simple or an absolute majority? As for the punitive suspension of a member's rights and privileges, this provision will be very difficult to enforce. Even if it is applied to Myanmar, the junta is more likely to renounce ASEAN than to acquiesce in suspension. In either case, will renouncing ASEAN moderate—or on the contrary, reinforce—the regime's errant behavior?

The media has described the Charter as the toothless tiger. Philippine President Gloria Arroyo has threatened that her country's parliament will not ratify the Charter if Myanmar's government does not undertake democratic reforms. In fact, if parliaments in some ASEAN countries do not ratify the Charter, the junta will benefit, since such abstention will only delay any effect the Charter could have on Myanmar's political development.

An Agenda for ASEAN

Charter or not, the long-suffering people of Myanmar cannot afford to wait for ASEAN to act. The situation is dire and requires urgent remedies. While waiting for the Charter to be ratified, ASEAN should consider doing several things to facilitate a constructive political transition. These steps will not transform Myanmar—anything so radical would be impractical—but they are both feasible in principle and could be at least modestly helpful in practice.

First, ASEAN should convince the junta to grant amnesty to all political prisoners and all blacklisted political activists who are currently exiled in foreign

---

[50] Interview, 28 April 2007.

[51] Interview, 29 April 2007.

[52] Interview, 25 April 2007.

countries, and allow them to return to Myanmar if they want to compete in the 2010 elections. ASEAN should likewise pressure the junta to grant greater political space to the opposition so it can prepare for the 2010 elections.

In 2007, the roadmap seemed an unlikely route to meaningful democracy in Myanmar. Nevertheless, the mere existence of a formal constitution and its rules could, however modestly, reduce the junta's ability to act on its whims and enlarge the space for political activities—activities that could in turn create more opportunities for further work toward the country's eventual democratization.

Second, ASEAN could and should ask the junta specifically what sorts of roles nonstate actors will be able to play in the "disciplined democracy" that it envisages for Myanmar, including the future of the country's current and former political prisoners. In pressing these questions, ASEAN leaders should not argue from abstract norms or moral values but should instead appeal to the regime's own self-interest. ASEAN could point out, for example, the advantage of cooperation over repression as a path to stability, and the benefits of creative endeavor, including entrepreneurship and innovation. ASEAN or a subset of its members could sponsor educational activities, such as seminars and exchanges, in and with Myanmar, to drive home this point.

Third, ASEAN could and should encourage the junta to create a formal role for Daw Suu and other leading political activists in the political process of the country. In so doing, ASEAN might advise the junta to permit the SPDC to establish a political advisory committee with prominent political leaders like Daw Suu and Min Ko Naing.

Fourth, ASEAN could and should encourage China to facilitate actively a smooth political transition in Myanmar. As many ASEAN leaders have directly or indirectly stated, there is very little ASEAN can do to effect political changes on its own. However, several sources revealed that it was mainly because of China that the junta finally agreed to allow the UN special envoy to come to Myanmar. ASEAN governments should work more closely with their Chinese counterparts to contribute effectively to Myanmar's political transition.

Fifth, ASEAN could and should help the growth of Myanmar's still-nascent civil society by promoting cooperation between nongovernmental organizations in Myanmar and other Southeast Asian countries. One ASEAN researcher acknowledged that such cooperation was currently "very limited" and "very elitist," and that it took place mainly among intellectuals in the region's institutes for strategic and international studies (ASEAN-ISIS). These meetings, he said, had become occasions for a long-standing coterie of "old friends" to gather again and again, repeating to each other "whatever they [had] said in previous meetings." At such events, he had found the participants from the five original—founding—members of the Association especially "patronizing." ASEAN, he concluded, should look beyond and below its jet-setting policy scholars to encourage civil-society organizations at the grass-roots level, across all of the region's countries.[93]

I agree. Mutual back-patting by the region's status-quo elites will not better the lives of Myanmar's citizens, nor restrain their rulers. Rather than assume its own blamelessness when it comes to the need for political change, ASEAN itself needs to follow the democratizing advice that some of its members would have it dispense to the junta. The more the other nine members practice what their Charter preaches, the better the chance that regionalism will be able, after all, to expedite security and democracy in Myanmar.

---

[93] Interview, 15 March 2007.

CHALLENGING CHANGE: NONTRADITIONAL SECURITY, DEMOCRACY, AND REGIONALISM

Mely Caballero-Anthony
Nanyang Technological University
Singapore

The Association of Southeast Asian Nations (ASEAN) turned forty in August 2007. To many scholars and other observers who closely followed the evolution of the organization, the celebration came with high expectations. ASEAN watchers especially looked forward to the unveiling of the much-awaited ASEAN Charter, which would set fresh directions for the Association. The Charter was expected to facilitate by 2020 the envisioned establishment of an ASEAN Community with three pillars: an ASEAN Security Community (ASC), an ASEAN Economic Community (AEC), and an ASEAN Socio-Cultural Community. Observers also looked to the Charter to indicate how far ASEAN might be willing and able to move toward a less pragmatic and more normative framework for regionalism in Southeast Asia, including the possible transformation of the organization itself. Would ASEAN widen its traditional focus on interstate affairs to encompass a more people-centered agenda? What policies and actions would such an enlarged horizon imply?

Increasingly in the late 1990s, ASEAN was considered a sunset arrangement because of its perceived failure to avert the multiple repercussions of the Asian financial crisis in 1997.[1] But the subsequent prospects of a Community and a Charter reinvigorated interest in the Association. Since 2001, the grouping has been actively engaged by the major powers—the United States, China, Japan, and India. A number of countries, including the European Union (EU), have also signed or are negotiating free trade agreements (FTAs) with the Association. Prior to the dramatic and, for ASEAN, embarrassing crisis that struck one of its members, Myanmar, in September–October 2007, one could argue that ASEAN's reputation had recovered and was improving, as it sought to refresh and ready itself for the future.

---

[1] See for example, Jürgen Rüland, "ASEAN and the Asian Crisis: Theoretical Implications and Practical Consequences for Southeast Asian Regionalism," *The Pacific Review* 13, no. 3 (August 2000), 421–51; Jeannie Henderson, *Reassessing ASEAN*, Adelphi Paper 323 (London: Oxford University Press for IISS, 1999); and Shaun Narine, *Explaining ASEAN: Regionalism in Southeast Asia* (Boulder, CO: Lynne Rienner Publishers, 2002).

Especially since the events in Myanmar in 2007, it is advisable to tread carefully, avoiding unrealistic expectations that the ASC is bound to succeed, but also not joining the camp of those who dismiss such a venture as wholly beyond ASEAN's ability to realize. Of the three proposed pillars, the ASC drew particular interest, in view of the new mechanisms and initiatives that were included in its blueprint. These measures were supposed to reflect the more proactive stance that ASEAN was being asked to take toward emerging challenges to security in Southeast Asia. Apart from their unconventional nature, these innovations were also significant in that they addressed key issues that had come to characterize the "new regionalism" then—and still—under way elsewhere in the world.

New regionalism is an effort to extend and deepen cooperation on multiple dimensions, including improved multilevel governance and devolution within countries and a strengthened framework of international law between them. These novel patterns and policies of interaction reflect a compelling need felt by regional players to integrate noneconomic issues of justice, security, and culture into existing agendas for trade and investment. These players are also driven by a political ambition to establish or strengthen regional coherence and regional identity.[2] These goals and steps also reflect the states' desire to be able to "mediate the range of economic and social pressures generated by globalisation."[3] Mediation here refers to the capacity of states and other actors to organize themselves, and to craft appropriate measures to mitigate the destabilizing impacts of global forces.[4]

Such ideas form a useful background for discussing the interaction of security, democracy, and regionalism in Southeast Asia and ASEAN's hopes for a new life after forty. Do the vision of an ASEAN Community and the new initiatives introduced to that end—particularly the security pillar, the ASC—reflect a shift in the character of regionalism in Southeast Asia?

Critical to the answer is the broadening of regionalist horizons to include an awareness of nontraditional security threats and a corresponding priority on cultivating nontraditional security (NTS)—"nontraditional" in that it goes beyond the security that states can achieve through diplomacy and deterrence to incorporate "human security" as a goal of regionalism. Has this more ambitious agenda pushed ASEAN's members to reconsider its characteristic informality

---

[2] See Björn Hettne, "Globalisation and the New Regionalism: The Second Great Transformation," in *Globalism and the New Regionalism*, ed. Björn Hettne, András Inotai, and Osvaldo Sunkel (London: Macmillan, 1999), xvi.

[3] See Jean Grugel, "New Regionalism and Modes of Governance—Comparing U.S. and EU Strategies in Latin America," *European Journal of International Relations* 10, no. 40 (2004), 603–26.

[4] Anthony Payne, "Globalisation and Modes of Regionalist Governance," in *Debating Governance: Authority, Steering and Democracy*, ed. J. Pierre (Oxford: Oxford University Press, 2000), 201–18.

and pragmatic lack of institutionalization and to favor a more normative, rules-based framework for interstate relations? NTS as a policy frontier further prompts us to examine how the democratization and political liberalization that have emerged in Southeast Asia, however unevenly, have influenced the changing shape of regionalism.

In this context, this chapter has two objectives. First, it examines the extent to which emerging NTS challenges are moving ASEAN members toward deeper engagements at multiple levels, from states to societies, and how this may be altering the nature of Southeast Asian regionalism. Second, it explores whether democratization is coloring the normative content of ASEAN's agenda and widening its arena to involve new actors, in both public and private sectors, in contesting the longstanding elite norms and consensus associated with "old regionalism" in Southeast Asia. I argue that both causal variables and the interplay between them are indeed shaping the dynamics of regionalism. I do not privilege the influence of NTS over democracy or vice versa. Nor does the influence of one occur at the expense of the other. On the contrary, security and democracy are complementary drivers in the push for change that can be discerned inside ASEAN as it enters its fifth decade.

The ASEAN Charter was signed in November 2007, but in mid-2008 it was still too early to attribute definitive results to the new regional processes brought on by the challenges of NTS and democracy. Nonetheless, changes were not only under way but were also proving conducive to linkages, tensions, and coalitions that differed markedly from the style and structure of regionalism in the past. The resulting patterns of cooperation and contestation will entail social learning by different actors. That common experience could prove beneficial to ASEAN as it seeks support for better ways to address the new security challenges it faces.

The chapter begins with a brief discussion of NTS threats and their effects on ASEAN. I review how these challenges have generated a number of regional initiatives, notably the ASC, that allow for shifts in patterns of inter- and intrastate relations, leading to a possible recalibration of regional norms. I also discuss how democratic processes taking place in some parts of the region are affecting prevailing regional practices. The conclusion draws on this analysis to offer some thoughts on the state of regionalism in Southeast Asia.

The Rise of NTS: From Comprehensive to Human Security

Most of the threats and risks to security in Asia are "nontraditional" in nature.[5] They arise mainly from nonmilitary sources. They are simultaneously transnational and subnational in scope—neither wholly domestic nor purely interstate. They

---

[5] For evidence to this effect, see, e.g., Mely Caballero-Anthony, Ralf Emmers, and Amitav Acharya, eds., *Non-Traditional Security in Asia: Dilemmas in Securitisation* (London: Ashgate, 2006).

develop fast, at short notice, and spread rapidly due to globalization including the revolution in communications. These conditions tend to render national responses inadequate and to require cooperation across regions and beyond. Moreover, in these nontraditional issues the object of security is no longer just the sovereignty or territorial integrity of the state, but can include the well-being, dignity, and even the survival of human beings, as individuals and members of society.[6] Infectious disease, climate change and environmental degradation, transnational crimes such as sea piracy, cyber crime, trafficking in drugs and people, and even poverty are increasingly common topics for discussion in academic and policy circles alike. Officials are more and more likely to treat these NTS threats as dangers not only to social welfare but to the national sovereignty and territorial integrity of states as well.

Nonmilitary threats to the security of states and peoples are on the rise. Reports and images of natural disasters afflicting parts of Southeast Asia have become more frequent. The prospect of future pandemics has galvanized concern. As this and the following sections of this chapter will illustrate, these issues of NTS and their impacts on ASEAN have begun to foster new regionalism in Southeast Asia.

ASEAN's discourse on security has changed. A watershed in this respect was the Asian financial crisis (1997–99). It transformed the conceptualization of security in the region. The financial contagion and the damage it did challenged the previously conventional concept of "comprehensive security." In response to the crisis, the idea of human security crept into the security lexicon used by ASEAN officials.

The first to articulate the idea of "human security" was Dr. Surin Pitsuwan. Speaking as the foreign minister of Thailand at the 31st ASEAN Post-Ministerial Conference (PMC) in July 1998, he recommended establishing an ASEAN PMC Caucus on Human Security. "We are," he said,

> looking into the eye of the future social storm. The social and economic dislocation, poverty, disease, illiteracy, alienation, disorientation among our peoples would surely lead to violence, rebellions, instability and insecurity. All these would impact upon all the achievements that we have made together so far. And these would inevitably threaten the region as a whole. … I am proposing, Mr. Chairman, that we here at the PMC consider setting up an ASEAN-PMC Caucus on Human Security. Those members who are interested and ready should join hands in mapping out steps and strategies

---

[6] See Ralf Emmers, Mely Caballero-Anthony, and Amitav Acharya, eds., *Studying Non-Traditional Security in Asia: Trends and Issues* (Singapore: Marshall Cavendish, 2006); and Caballero-Anthony et al., *Non-Traditional Security in Asia*.

for [a] long-term approach to the cure for and prevention of "human insecurity" in our region.[7]

ASEAN did not follow up on Surin's idea. But he continued to talk about human security, and other regional actors took up the idea. Increasingly in ASEAN discourse, voices were heard urging the Association to rethink its fealty to comprehensive security, and replace it with a concept more focused on the plight of individuals and societies.

Comprehensive security gave paramount importance to the stability of the state, and to economic development as a major means to that end. In this discourse, the state had been reified and enshrined as the primary unit of analysis and the sole legitimate actor entrusted with defining security, providing it, and inducing the economic growth needed to provide it. The notion of comprehensive security had originated in a desire to enlarge the concept of security beyond purely military concerns. Yet it remained every bit as state-centric as the narrower idea it had replaced.[8]

By undercutting economic growth to devastating effect, the financial crisis directly challenged comprehensive security and its developmental method. The crisis, in the World Bank's words, "exacerbated pre-existing social vulnerabilities" and triggered "falling incomes, rising absolute poverty and malnutrition, declining public services, threats to educational and health status, increased pressure on women, and increased crime and violence."[9] In this dire context, it made sense to address the security of society in broad terms, beyond merely assuring state security through material growth.

It looked as though Surin's time had come. Apparently unstoppable forces of globalization were engulfing and damaging many parts of Asia. Suddenly, in the face of such an assault, once-satisfying arguments for nation-building by secure states committed to economic growth looked flimsy. The challenge was to make the concept of security responsive to the needs of vulnerable individuals and societies, apart from the needs and interests of the state.

ASEAN's member governments did not immediately converge in support of human security. The introduction of social safety-net policies in Indonesia, Thailand, Malaysia, and the Philippines did indicate, nevertheless, that these states were under intense pressure to take seriously the increasing salience of

---

[7] Statement by Thai Foreign Minister Surin Pitsuwan, Manila, 23 July 1998, <http://www.aseansec.org/3950.htm>.

[8] For more on comprehensive security, see Muthiah Alagappa, "Comprehensive Security: Interpretation in ASEAN Countries," in Robert Scalapino et al., eds., *Asian Security Issues: Regional and Global* (Berkeley, CA: Institute of East Asian Studies, University of California, 1989); and Muthiah Alagappa, *Asian Security Practices: Material and Ideational Influences* (Stanford, CA: Stanford University Press, 1998).

[9] World Bank, *East Asia: The Road to Recovery* (Washington DC: The World Bank, September 1998), 80.

human security in foreign and domestic discourse, including voices from below.[10] It is not coincidental in this context that in 1998, while the effects of the economic crisis were still being felt, ASEAN launched a Task Force on Social Safety Nets to help the region's peoples recover from that calamity, and adopted a Hanoi Plan of Action for Southeast Asia to become a "socially cohesive" community "with caring societies."[11]

Even before these official initiatives, local civil society organizations had begun to explore alternative approaches to security, often at conferences convened for that purpose.[12] Such a meeting was held, for example, in Bangkok in 1997 by Focus on the Global South, a nongovernmental organization (NGO) attached to the Social Research Institute at Chulalongkorn University in Thailand. The conference theme was "Alternative Security Systems in the Asia-Pacific." The idea was to challenge mainstream security thinking: to move "the understanding of security from a traditional concept to a more comprehensive and pro-active view that addresses the causes of conflict, including socio-economic and gender inequalities, environmental degradation and lack of political participation." The Bangkok meeting eventually became the precursor of several other gatherings in the region held to discuss new approaches to security and development.[13] Notable in this context was a series of conferences organized by the People's Forum, an international network of NGOs, timed to coincide with successive summits of the Asia-Pacific Economic Cooperation (APEC) forum, in Osaka (1995), Manila (1996), Vancouver (1997), and Kuala Lumpur (1998). Attendees at these events expressed opposition to APEC's support for globalization and correspondingly "open" regionalism. Meanwhile, other regional organizations, such as the Alternative ASEAN Network on Burma (AltSEAN), championed the promotion and protection of human rights. AltSEAN was especially vocal in criticizing ASEAN for using its policy of not interfering in the internal affairs of sovereignty member states to justify ignoring the abuse of human rights in Southeast Asia.

The activism of AltSEAN and other NGOs opened up the once exclusive space for security thinking in ASEAN. These groups not only challenged the dominant discourse on security, but also sought to influence policy. They hoped to engender

---

[10] On these policies in relation to human security and ASEAN, see Mely Caballero-Anthony, "Human Security and Comprehensive Security in ASEAN," *Indonesian Quarterly* 28, no. 4 (2000), 412–22.

[11] See ASEAN's *Hanoi Plan of Action*, 1998, <http://www.aseansec.org/old/9812/new_hpoa.htm>.

[12] See Herman Kraft, "The Autonomy Dilemma of Track Two Diplomacy in Southeast Asia," *Security Dialogue* 31, no. 3 (2000), 343–56; and "ASEAN-ISIS and Human Rights Advocacy: The Colloquium on Human Rights (AICHOR)," in *Twenty Years of ASEAN ISIS: Origin, Evolution and Challenges of Track Two Diplomacy*, ed. Hadi Soesastro, Clara Joewono, and Carolina Hernandez (CSIS: Jakarta, 2006).

[13] See Kraft, "Autonomy Dilemma."

"people-centred security systems" to replace the state-centric variety that, in their view, had failed to address the insecurity of persons and societies.[14]

A Wake-up Call: Economic Crisis and Political Change

The NTS agenda that emerged from the Asian economic crisis was not only about individual and social health, safety, and welfare. Equally significant, and even more dramatic, were the political repercussions: popular demands for the liberalization of political life. Events in Indonesia, Malaysia, and Thailand most clearly illustrated this democratic element in NTS.

The economic crisis marked a watershed in Indonesian history. As the national currency plummeted in value, public anger mounted against the country's authoritarian president, Suharto, for his apparent inability to remedy the situation. The government tried to stem the crisis. Acting on the advice of the International Monetary Fund (IMF), the government took various steps to stem the crisis. But the remedies failed to reverse the damage to the banking system and to public confidence in the economy. The prices of basic commodities rose steeply, including a 71 percent increase in gas prices, which led in turn to higher fares for public transportation.

Angry demonstrations broke out in cities across Indonesia. Some of the protests turned violent. A prolonged demonstration at Trisakti University in Jakarta was broken up by state security forces, and four students were killed. Their deaths sparked an even larger wave of anger, so that violent riots raged in several parts of the capital, and mobs looted and burned buildings. Hundreds of deaths were reported. If they could, people fled to safer havens in the countryside. The city came to a standstill.[15] Ethnic and religious conflicts flared in various parts of Indonesia—a considerable shock in a country that had been known for moderation and tolerance. Cries for Suharto to step down proliferated. Finally, in May 1998, he did, ending a presidency that had lasted thirty years.

Media freedom was established. The constitution was amended to include provisions defending human rights. Free and fair nationwide elections were held, and power was decentralized. In 2004, for the first time ever, Indonesians directly elected their president in a peaceful election. In 2007, the American organization Freedom House rated Indonesia the most liberal-democratic country in Southeast Asia.[16]

In Malaysia, the economic crisis opened palpable cleavages between political elites. Amid cries for political reform, Prime Minister Mahathir Mohamad turned

---

[14] For more on these critiques, see Mely Caballero-Anthony, "Re-visioning Human Security in Southeast Asia," *Asian Perspectives* 28, no. 3 (2004), 155–89.

[15] See "Ten Days That Shook Indonesia," from *Indahnesiah.com*, <http://www.indahnesia.com/DB/Story/Item.php>.

[16] See Freedom House Country Report—Indonesia, <http://freedomhouse.org/template.cfm?page=22&year=2007&country=7195>.

on his deputy and heir apparent, Anwar Ibrahim. Anwar became a lightning rod for dissatisfaction with the regime. After being disgraced, arrested, tried, and finally released, he went abroad and spoke vehemently about the need for democracy in Malaysia. By 2007 he was back in Malaysia, still urging political reform.

In Thailand, as the currency plunged and the financial damage spread to the real economy, escalating political conflict obliged the government of Chaovalit Choonhavan to resign.

Beyond the worst-hit countries, the impact of the crisis was felt across the region, challenging ASEAN's leaders and dashing hopes for the region's early recovery. Foreign investors and financial institutions suddenly lost confidence in Southeast Asia's dynamic economies. The ensuing recession jeopardized regional security in the broadest sense, including human security, and gave rise to bilateral frictions among the Association's members.[17]

In these multiple respects, the economic crisis was a wake-up call to the governments in Southeast Asia. Events reaffirmed the close connection between economics and security. The lesson, however, was that no matter how convincing the traditional arguments for state security and economic development, they had proven dismally inadequate to protect the region against a sudden transnational financial storm. Apparently precipitated by currency speculation and a corresponding lack of regulation over capital flows, the crisis had triggered a massive depreciation of Southeast Asian currencies, spilling over into stock market meltdowns and capital flight. The lives of millions were affected. In the face of such a juggernaut, the vulnerability of human security and the limits of state authority were all too clear.

The focus of this book and therefore this chapter does not cover the processes of economic recovery and reform that followed the financial crisis. Rather, it focuses on the consequences of the wake-up call for a broader agenda. An initial monetary crisis had spilled over into the productive economy, prompting political conflicts and calls for political reform and triggering the democratization of Indonesia, the region's largest country. Comparably, the financial damage made ASEAN painfully aware of the need to address a wider range of new and emerging threats to human security, beyond the security of the state. If NTS had once been limited to conceptual discussions for scholars and NGOs, the crisis made it the basis for an actual policy agenda to address a spectrum of dangers to human security.

---

[17] As the recession took its toll on the labor force in Thailand and Malaysia, both governments began to deport hundreds of mainly illegal foreign workers back to Myanmar and Indonesia, respectively. The repatriation of these workers triggered criticism in Indonesia, where the crisis was also affecting the labor situation. See, e.g., Mely Caballero-Anthony, "Challenges to Southeast Asian Security Cooperation," and Rizal Sukma, "Security Implications of the Economic Crisis in Southeast Asia," in *An Asia-Pacific Security Crisis? New Challenges to Regional Stability*, ed. Guy Wilson-Roberts (Wellington, New Zealand: Centre for Strategic Studies, 2001), 39–65.

An Emerging Agenda: Pollution, Migration, Crime, and Disease

Among the many kinds of NTS threats, four have attracted particular attention. I review them briefly here.

The first is pollution, and specifically the periodic haze—smoke from burning forests and brush—that enveloped parts of Southeast Asia in 1997, and most recently in 2006. The haze came mostly from Indonesia and inflicted considerable damage on adjacent Singapore, Malaysia, and Brunei. At the height of the haze crisis in 1997, three ASEAN states suffered most of the environmental impact, including air pollution indices that reached alarming levels, especially in Malaysian Sarawak and in Brunei. Some of those most severely affected were forced to leave their countries until the haze abated. The pollution was estimated to have caused US$ 9 billion in economic losses and to have adversely affected seventy million people.[18] Originating in part from the slash-and-burn practices of farmers in Kalimantan, the haze was borne by winds over state borders, endangering the human security of millions of people in the affected states. For more on this NTS threat, see Simon Tay's chapter in this book.

A second major NTS issue is the illegal or undocumented migration for labor and other purposes. Such movements of people are on the rise in Asia. Southeast Asian countries host an estimated two to three million illegal migrants. Thailand alone has between 500,000 and 700,000.[19] In Malaysia, the 1997 financial crisis left thousands of illegal labor migrants jobless,[20] and sparked the first large-scale repatriation of such persons from Malaysia.[21]

A related source of human insecurity is migration caused by hostility between religious or ethnic groups inside the country the migrants have left behind. A case in point is the unregulated influx of refugees from strife in Myanmar/Burma seeking safe haven inside neighboring Thailand. Reportedly 80 percent of Thailand's migrant workers come from Myanmar, with the remainder from Laos and Cambodia. Of these Burmese, nearly 70 percent belong to minorities inside their homeland, including Karen, Kachin, and

---

[18] ASEAN Secretariat, *Second ASEAN State of the Environment Report 2000*, Public Information Unit, The ASEAN Secretariat, Jakarta, <http://www.rrcap.unep.org/sub-region/aseansoe/Content.pdf>.

[19] *Report on the Workshop on Illegal Migration in Asia*, Centre of Asian Studies, University of Hong Kong, June 2006.

[20] Vijayakumari Kanapathy, "International Migration and Labour Market Developments in Asia: Economic Recovery, the Labour Market and Migrant Workers in Malaysia," paper presented to the 2004 Workshop on International Migration and Labour Markets in Asia, organized by the Japan Institute for Labour Policy and Training, the Organization for Economic Cooperation and Development, and the International Labour Office, Tokyo, Japan, 5–6 February 2004, 407.

[21] Zainal Abidin bin M. Said, "Migration and National Security: A Study of Indonesian Transients in Malaysia," unpublished Master of Arts thesis in Defence Studies, Faculty of Social Sciences and Humanities, Universiti Kebangsaan Malaysia, Bangi (2005), 43.

Shan, who have fled persecution by the Myanmar junta that rules that ASEAN country.[22]

A third NTS threat involves human trafficking for lucrative purposes such as prostitution. This phenomenon has greatly increased in the last decade, as transnational criminal groups have diversified their activities to include laundering money and dealing in drugs and persons. According to the International Organisation for Migration (IOM), between 200,000 and 225,000 women and children are trafficked annually from Southeast Asia—one-third of the global trade in such persons—and 60 percent of this traffic takes place within the region. Moreover, 60 percent of this trafficking occurs within Southeast Asia.[23] Also devastating to human security is the accelerated spread of infectious diseases, such as HIV/AIDS, that such human and drug trafficking can cause.

Closely linked to the problem of migration is another NTS issue: the complex problem of transnational crime. The problem is complex in that it covers a wide range of criminal activities, including illegal arms trading, especially the trafficking of small arms and light weapons (SALW); human smuggling, drug smuggling, and money laundering; illegal fishing and piracy; and more recently, cyber crime and terrorism. Each of these transnational crimes presents a unique threat to the security of persons, societies, and states.

The case of SALW illustrates the complex linkage between the illicit trade in small arms and the smuggling of drugs. In the 1990s in Thailand, for example, the lucrative drug trade enabled producers of narcotics to buy small arms on the black market to support their drug operations. Often drawn from leftover war stockpiles in Cambodia and sold on Thailand's vibrant black market, many of these weapons surfaced in China, just as Chinese-made small arms found their way to Thailand via Vietnam, Laos, and Cambodia.[24]

The web formed by these illegal businesses has also exacerbated the local armed conflicts that have arisen because of easy accesses to SALW. In Indonesia in the 1990s, government operations against SALW yielded large caches of confiscated arms taken from separatist groups such as the Free Papua Organization (*Organisasi Papua Merdeka*), or from warring parties on

---

[22] Kavi Chongkittavorn, "Thailand's Cynical Ploy on Burmese Migrant Workers," *The Nation* [Bangkok], 13 December 2006.

[23] International Organization for Migration, "Part Two: Countering Trafficking in Southeast Asia," in *Combating Trafficking in Southeast Asia: A Review of Policy and Programme Responses*, no. 2 (Geneva: International Organization for Migration Geneva, 2000).

[24] Thithinan Pongsudhirak, "Small Arms Trafficking in Southeast Asia: A Perspective from Thailand," in *Small Is (Not) Beautiful: The Problem of Small Arms in Southeast Asia*, ed. Philips J. Vermonte (Jakarta: Centre for Strategic and International Studies, 2004), 55–69.

the islands of Maluku and Sulawesi.[25] At least 500,000 deaths annually have been attributed to SALW, including 300,000 in armed conflict and 200,000 in incidents involve homicide and suicide.[26]

Infectious diseases pose a fourth and growing danger to human security in Southeast Asia. This is especially true in light of the Asia-wide outbreak of the Severe Acute Respiratory Syndrome (SARS) virus. As the SARS experience showed, in this era of globalization and regionalization, contagious illnesses can quickly damage the security and well-being of all members of a country's society and all aspects of its economy.[27] In the two months following reports of its outbreak in 2003, SARS infected close to 6,000 people and killed 200 in at least twenty-six countries. By the time the World Health Organization (WHO) declared that SARS had peaked, the totals had risen to 8,402 infections and 772 deaths in twenty-nine countries.[28]

SARS significantly damaged the economies of Singapore, Vietnam, Hong Kong, and China. Tourism and travel fell steeply as people avoided these and other virus-hit countries. Declines in consumer confidence and domestic demand pushed many businesses to the brink of collapse. The overall cost of SARS to Asia's economies was estimated to have run between US$ 30 and 50 billion—and up to US$ 150 billion worldwide.[29] The speed and impact of the contagion caught many governments by surprise and added health security to ASEAN's already lengthening prospective NTS agenda.

No sooner had Southeast Asia begun to recover from the SARS crisis than news of the rising incidence of avian influenza cases, reported on a near-daily basis from more and more places, raised alarm that the region might be facing a pandemic of global proportions. By mid-2007, avian flu had already proven deadly in more than half of the 291 reported cases of human infection, most of them in Asia.[30] Vietnam and Indonesia had the highest tolls, accounting for

---

[25] Landry S. Subianto, "Small Arms Problems in Southeast Asia: An Indonesian Case," in *Small Is (Not) Beautiful*, 23–54.

[26] See *Small Arms Survey 2001: Profiling the Problem* (Geneva: Graduate Institute of International Studies, 2001).

[27] For more on SARS and its impacts, see for example, Mely Caballero-Anthony, "SARS in Asia: Crisis, Vulnerabilities, and Regional Responses," *Asian Survey* 45, no. 3 (2005), 475–95; Melissa Curley and Nicholas Thomas, "Human Security and Public Health in Southeast Asia: The SARS Outbreak," *Australian Journal of International Affairs* 58, no. 1 (2004), 17–32; and Elizabeth Prescott, "SARS: A Warning," *Survival* 45, no. 3 (2003), 162–77.

[28] See World Health Organisation (WHO), "Update 73—No New Deaths, But Vigilance Needed for Imported Cases," 4 June 2003, <http://www.who.int/csr/don/2003_06_04/en/index.html>.

[29] See Caballero-Anthony, "SARS in Asia."

[30] See "Cumulative Number of Confirmed Human Cases of Avian Influenza A/(H5N1) Reported to WHO," 11 April 2007, <http://www.who.int/csr/disease/avian_influenza/country/cases_table_2007_04_11/en/index.html>.

105 deaths in all.[31] These totals may seem small, but their modest size obscures the risk that avian flu could still trigger a major contagion. There is nothing minor about the likely future cost of such a catastrophe in East Asia, including Southeast Asia. According to the Asian Development Bank, and even assuming only a moderate level of infection, the economic cost of an avian flu pandemic in East Asia could run anywhere from US$ 99 to 283 billion.[32]

The infrastructure to prevent and control infectious diseases is problematic in many parts of Southeast Asia. Resources allocated to public health are often insufficient to ensure even basic health care.[33] The problem is complicated and exacerbated by the fact that the world's poor people, especially women and children, bear so much of the burden of illness—not only SARS or avian flu, but also other diseases such as HIV/AIDS, malaria, and tuberculosis. In 2002, according to the WHO, 75 percent of all mortalities due to infectious disease occurred in Southeast Asia and sub-Saharan Africa. Of these deaths, 28 percent occurred in Southeast Asia.[34]

Pathogens do not acknowledge national borders, and therefore national solutions alone cannot work against transnationally infectious threats to health. As a virologist at Hong Kong's Queen Mary Hospital once declared: "Viruses do not carry passports."[35] A government can turn away travelers who might be carriers, but no merely national authority can block all routes of transmission.

Pollution, migration, crime, and diseases therefore pose serious, nontraditional, transnational challenges to human security and effective regionalism in Southeast Asia. They warrant inclusion and attention on ASEAN's agenda.

Making the Case for Reform: Toward a More Proactive Regionalism?

Slowly but increasingly, state and nonstate actors have begun to question ASEAN's previous avoidance of NTS issues and to call openly for regional responses to them, even at the risk of appearing to interfere in a member's domestic affairs.

---

[31] "Asia Battles Bird Flu," *The Straits Times* [Singapore], 28 January 2007.

[32] Asian Development Bank, "Avian Flu Pandemic Could Halt Asian Growth, ADB Report Says," 3 November 2005, <http://www.adb.org/Documents/News/2005/nr2005169.asp>.

[33] For a more extensive discussion, see Mely Caballero-Anthony, "Health and Human Security in Asia: Realities and Challenges," paper prepared for the Commission on Human Security and published in Lincoln Chen et al., eds., *Global Health Challenges for Human Security* (Cambridge, MA: Harvard University Press, 2003), 233–55.

[34] Women account for more than 50 percent of new HIV infections and among adults. Pregnant women are the most at risk for malaria. See the HIV page of the Global Health Council, <http://www.globalhealth.org/view_top.php3?id=227>, and the Global Health Council's Infectious Diseases page, <http://www.globalhealth.org/view_top.php3?id=228>.

[35] Interview with Dr. Malik Peiris, CNN International, 7 May 2003.

The first such initiative was taken by former deputy prime minister of Malaysia Anwar Ibrahim. Soon after the 1997 coup d'etat in Cambodia, he floated the idea that ASEAN could and should engage in "constructive intervention" to prevent a member state from succumbing to internal collapse. Such intervention, he argued, could entail several kinds of regional assistance to the affected state: strengthening electoral processes; encouraging legal and administrative reforms; helping develop human capital; and generally bolstering civil society and the rule of law. A year later, another ex-official, former Thai foreign minister Surin Pitsuwan, proposed the comparable idea of "flexible engagement."

At first, most ASEAN leaders flatly rejected these initiatives as unwarranted departures from the "ASEAN Way" of noninterference. Eventually, however, such ideas received more sympathetic attention. The notion that ASEAN, under some conditions, should address domestic circumstances inside a member state and its society soon evolved from Anwar's "constructive intervention" and through Surin's "flexible engagement" to a third phrase, "enhanced interaction," which entered the official vocabulary of the day as an appropriate model for interstate relations in ASEAN. In 1999, plans were announced at that year's ASEAN Ministerial Meeting to hold an annual retreat for regional leaders where they could discuss not only regional problems but domestic ones as well. This announcement was seen as a significant early departure from the standard ASEAN practice of "sweeping issues under the carpet" for the sake of regional unity.

Semantics are one thing, actions another. Some member states resisted incorporating NTS issues into ASEAN's agenda if that meant regional involvement in domestic affairs. Nevertheless, after the financial crisis delivered its wake-up call, ASEAN did wake up. ASEAN did implement measures in support of NTS, although in a manner that was, at best, ad hoc. The most important of these steps are worth listing briefly here:[36]

- In 1997 an ASEAN Troika was innovated to address the domestic crisis then under way in Cambodia. Under this arrangement, three member states could provide emergency security assistance to a member state at the latter's request. The idea was given formal status in 2000.
- Also in 1997, ASEAN adopted a Vision 2020 statement. In 1998 a Hanoi Plan of Action outlined how the new directions specified in the Vision would be implemented in security, economic, and sociocultural terms— terms that would frame the three pillars of the ASEAN Community project announced in 2003.

---

[36] For more on the new modalities that ASEAN adopted after the 1997 financial crises, see Mely Caballero-Anthony, *Regional Security in Southeast Asia: Beyond the ASEAN Way* (Singapore: Institute of Southeast Asian Studies, 2005).

- Still in 1997, ASEAN issued a Regional Haze Action Plan, meant to provide a regional mechanism to fight recurring forest fires and limit the resulting cross-border air pollution.
- In 2001, ASEAN leaders agreed to a set of rules and procedures for the operation of the High Council that the 1976 Treaty of Amity and Cooperation in Southeast Asia had called for as a means of settling disputes between member states—disputes that could involve NTS. As of early 2008 the Council still had not been convened. Nevertheless, by specifying how it would work, ASEAN in 2001 made eventual recourse to the Council more likely, at least in principle.
- In 2002, ASEAN reached an Agreement on Information Exchange and Establishment of Communication Procedures, intended to promote cooperation in combating transnational crimes, including terrorism.
- In 2003, steps were taken to enable ASEAN members jointly to contain infectious diseases. One such measure was the development of an ASEAN Centre for Disease Control (ACDC).

Thus did the acknowledgment of new security challenges—transnational in nature and therefore requiring joint action—give rise to closer regional cooperation. Absent strong institutions for monitoring and enforcement, however, the effectiveness of responses such as those in the preceding list remained in doubt. In particular, to ensure compliance, ASEAN needed a secretariat with a clear mandate, sufficient organizational capacity, and enough financial resources to ensure that regional provisions to counter NTS threats and promote human security would move beyond the realm of paper and actually be carried out on the ground.

It was against this backdrop that Southeast Asian leaders decided to create an ASEAN Security Community (ASC).

Democracy and Human Rights: New Regionalism's Next Frontier?

The idea of forming an ASC originated with Indonesia and was understood broadly as a means of raising security cooperation among ASEAN's member to a higher plane. The Community was intended "to provide a sense of purpose, a practical goal, and a future condition that all [ASEAN] members should strive for."[37] Since the concept was launched in 2003, officials have extensively considered the details of such a community; more recently, nonofficial actors and observers have joined the discussion. In 2004, as laid out in the Vientiane Action Program (VAP), the paths to realizing the ASC and the activities it was supposed to undertake were diverse and comprehensive. They included not merely preventing conflict but also resolving it and rebuilding the peace

---

[37] "Indonesia Proposing ASEAN Security Community Concept," *Jakarta Post*, 16 June 2003.

afterward. The intention was both to shape and share general norms, and to help member states achieve, in particular, political development—including, by implication, democratization.[38]

The blueprint for the Community was significant in two respects. First, the projected roles and goals of the ASC reflected the widening of the "old," or state-focused, notion of security to include the "new," or society-sensitive, discourse associated with NTS. A number of strategies and measures in the VAP embodied the new approach and its priority on human security. Although plans for the ASC included bolstering traditional security, the emphasis on NTS could be seen in specific recommendations for multilateral action by ASEAN: against transnational crime and other cross-border dangers; for closer maritime security cooperation and better law enforcement; and for improved coordination to overcome environmental problems and combat infectious disease.

A second signal feature of the blueprint was its emphasis on building up an institutional capacity to pursue regional ways of dealing with threats to NTS. Ideas in this vein included mechanisms to coordinate joint maritime patrols, for example, on the Strait of Malacca, and to upgrade cooperation against terrorism.[39] Important, too, were proposals to convene an annual ASEAN Defense Ministers Meeting (ADMM) and establish a regional peacekeeping force. The latter idea had not been acted on as of early 2008, but the first ADMM took place in May of the previous year.

As of 2007, some of these initiatives had still not been moved beyond declaration to implementation. But cynicism about ASEAN's inability to "do" anything about regional security, as opposed to talking about it, is unwarranted. ASEAN's security horizons have been enlarged to encourage a wider and deeper kind of regional cooperation—one that could intrude into the domestic affairs of states. In 2007, for example, arrangements to combat terrorism in Southeast Asia were meant to encourage member states to share sensitive intelligence information. Comparably intrusive were the deliberations under way on the idea of a transnational judicial system that would rely on cooperation among members in "collecting evidence, investigating suspects and witnesses ... and extraditing criminals."[40]

---

[38] See *ASEAN Vientiane Action Programme*, 2004, <http://www.aseansec.org./VAP-10thASEANSummit.pdf>.

[39] More on such aspects of the ASC is available, e.g., in Mely Caballero-Anthony, "Regional Structures and Responses to Security Challenges in Southeast Asia," *Indonesian Quarterly* 33, no. 1 (May 2005), 50–60; and Joshua Ho, "Recent Developments and Regional Initiatives in the Straits of Malacca," paper presented at a Workshop on East Asian Energy Efficiency and Maritime Security, organized by the East Asian Institute, Singapore, 18 May 2006.

[40] Xinhua News Agency reports from the China-ASEAN Prosecutors-General Conference, Kunming, China, 8 July 2004, accessed through http://web.lexis-nexis.com.

Especially novel was Indonesia's proposal to organize an ASEAN peacekeeping force. In 2004 a spokesperson for the Indonesian government explained that "ASEAN countries should know one another better than anyone else," implying that member states would be more likely to trust a force recruited from Southeast Asia than one drawn from outside the region.[41] In making this statement, the authorities in Jakarta had in mind the possibility that units organized by ASEAN and drawn from its own member countries could, upon request, take part in peacekeeping and peace-building activities in Southeast Asia.

The notion of a regional force to keep or build peace, even if deployable only upon invitation, was intrusive and therefore controversial. Some member states argued that it was "too early" to consider setting up a force, especially insofar as "each country has its own policy about politics and the military."[42] Yet the idea was not completely rejected. In lieu of an actual multinational force, ASEAN officials in 2008 were considering the possibility of establishing a regional training center for peacekeeping work. Meanwhile, military officials attached to peacekeeping units in Thailand and some other member states have openly advocated setting up a coordinating body to help regional peacekeepers, by organizing joint training exercises and offering relevant courses. Such a center could build on the experience of those ASEAN states (Thailand, Malaysia, the Philippines, and Singapore) that have already conducted peacekeeping operations inside the region (in Cambodia and Timor-Leste). In this context one can be cautiously optimistic, in the medium term, about the possibility that peacekeeping will someday form part of ASEAN's agenda for NTS.

That said, it should be stressed that my outlook here is *cautiously* optimistic. Daunting obstacles remain. Before announcing its new Charter in November 2007, ASEAN lacked the organizational capacity to implement effective responses to NTS threats in a timely manner. Member states could still resist seemingly intrusive measures in the name of sovereignty and noninterference. Nor was it clear in 2007 that the Charter's provisions—discussed in this chapter's penultimate section—would be carried out to enable ASEAN to realize NTS in the region. Subtle shifts were nevertheless under way. Approaches to NTS were under active discussion, including fledgling initiatives to nudge ASEAN beyond standard practice. Indeed, there was a growing impatience with standard practice—a sense that symbolic confidence-building measures, in which the process mattered more than the product, were inadequate to the challenges of the twenty-first century. In the light of such trends, one could realistically anticipate incremental changes without naively expecting the ASEAN to abandon traditional priorities and concerns.

Encouraging, too, is the practical, problem-solving focus of many of these fledging measures for NTS: sharing knowledge to combat transnational

---

[41] "Indonesia Proposes Southeast Asian Peacekeeping Force", 21 February 2004 <http://www.aseansec.org/afp/20p.htm>.

[42] See "ASEAN's Peace," *The Straits Times*, 8 March 2004.

scourges (terrorism, crime, pollution); putting early-warning systems in place to alert the region of sudden threats (contagious diseases, natural disasters); providing postdisaster assistance (relief, reconstruction); and upgrading regional coordination (including even the prospect of harmonizing domestic laws and their enforcement to deny safe havens to international criminals). From ad hoc mechanisms, ASEAN has begun to move into a new phase that might be called "creeping institutionalism," in that it involves working around sensitivities to external interference—and avoiding charges of intrusion by emphasizing the cooperative character of the NTS agenda in which sovereignty is not trumped or superseded, but rather, pooled.

It is in this context that democracy and human rights, however controversial they may be, are becoming Southeast Asian regionalism's next policy frontier, especially in relation to the plan for an ASC to address threats to NTS.

The VAP has committed the ASEAN states, at least on paper, to pay heed to certain issues that were formerly taboo. They had been excluded from ostensibly "comprehensive security" as too sensitive and divisive to consider, let alone resolve. Democracy and human rights were prominent on this list of omissions. Parts of this nonagenda could be subsumed under more euphemistic expressions such as "political development" and "norm-setting," but even those generalities were interpreted and opposed by some as omens of interference in the domestic affairs of member states.

This inauspicious context made all the more striking ASEAN's decision in 2004, in the language of the VAP, to enlist the ASC in building "a democratic, tolerant, participatory and open community in Southeast Asia."[43]

How could this happen? One answer points to the legitimation of NTS discourse following the Asian financial crisis—a development already noted in this chapter. "Nontraditional security" and "human security" were large categories that invited consideration of political affairs. But another answer is even more compelling: The taboo was being eroded by political changes on the ground.

Crucial in this regard was the democratization of Indonesia in the wake of the financial crisis. Important, too, were the political changes and the demands of political change that Malaysia, Thailand, and the Philippines had undergone. In these countries, shifts in the balance between state and society were reflected or projected in calls to democratize the larger region. It was not a coincidence that the proposal for an ASC came from Indonesia, nor that "constructive intervention" and "flexible engagement" as options for ASEAN originated, respectively, in Malaysia and Thailand.

As Alexander Wendt and other scholars have noted, state behavior is not a constant. It is subject to change as the state interacts with other states and with international institutions. Cooperative behavior among states tends to engender a shared sense of identity and collective interest. Comparable interactions

---

[43] See *ASEAN Vientiane Plan of Action*, section 1.2.

between states and institutions can also foster such changes.[44] In a similar vein, Koslowski and Kratochwil have argued that the international system in which states operate can undergo fundamental changes in norms and practices when constituent actors, by altering their own norms and practices, alter the character of intercourse between states, including the rules to which it is meant to conform. By this account, moreover, changes in an international system, such as Southeast Asia under ASEAN's aegis, will depend not only on the changing foreign policies of states but on the nature and direction of identities, beliefs, and practices associated with a range of domestic actors—not just governments, but groups and individuals as well.[45]

The inception of the ASC idea illustrates this broader range of influences. The proposal for such a community originated inside Indonesia and reflected that country's democratization. Rizal Sukma, an Indonesian academic with the Centre for Strategic and International Studies in Jakarta and a contributor to this book, wrote the first concept paper on the ASC and presented it in mid-2003. He was unconstrained by the limitations that he might have faced on Track I, as a sitting official. As a member of a private think tank, on Track III, he could think big, and he did. The ASC he envisioned would equip the Association with a new "sense of purpose, a practical goal, and a future condition that all [of its] members should strive for."[46] If his vision is realized, the ASC will pay major attention to human security, including the promotion and protection of human rights.

But is Sukma's framework realistic? Analysts who are familiar with ASEAN's deliberations have grown accustomed to the tendency for proposals to be watered down as they pass from the creativity of Track III to the practicality of Track I. Such observers were surprised, however, to learn that references to democracy and human rights in the draft blueprint for the ASC had survived the scrutiny and suggestions of the ASEAN Senior Officials Meeting (SOM). Despite considerable redrafting, some such references were also retained at the highest level, in the VAP that ASEAN's leaders adopted in 2004, in which the rationale for the ASC took final official form.

One may still ask, however, how significant those references are, and what they may or may not mean. It will be helpful in that connection briefly to review

---

[44] Alexander Wendt, *Social Theory of International Politics* (Cambridge: Cambridge University Press, 1991). See also Wendt, "Constructing International Politics," *International Security* 20, no. 1 (Summer 1995), 71–81.

[45] Rey Koslowski and Friedrich V. Kratochwil, "Understanding Change in International Politics: The Soviet Empire's Demise and the International System," *International Organization* 48, no. 2 (Spring 1994), 215–47. See particularly 216 and 222–27.

[46] See Rizal Sukma, "The Future of ASEAN: Toward a Security Community," paper presented at a seminar on "ASEAN: Challenges and Prospects in the International Situation," New York, 2 June 2003. See also "Indonesia Proposing ASEAN Security Community Concept," *Jakarta Post*, 16 June 2003.

three topical fields in which the ASC is being located and where analysts will assess its success or failure to encourage political development and cultivate and implement the norms and rules necessary to that end. These fields are democracy, human rights, and popular involvement. A fourth context, the ASEAN Charter, will be taken up in the next section.

The VAP's text on the ASC went beyond recommending the "nurturing of common socio-political values and principles" in general. It specifically placed ASEAN on record as not condoning "unconstitutional and undemocratic changes of government." This avowal was immediately followed and, to an extent, balanced by a reference to sovereignty and noninterference: ASEAN members would also not condone "use of their territory for any actions undermining peace, security and stability of other ASEAN member states."[47]

Yet the support for constitutional and democratic change did amount to a breakthrough. Previously ASEAN had been silent on the subjection of democratization. In contrast, the 2004 VAP endorsed the "value" of democracy in no uncertain terms, including two mentions of the term "democracy" in the document's preamble.

Events in 2004–06, triggered by the violence in southern Thailand and the lack of democratic progress in Myanmar, illustrated this concern. In October 2004 the government of Thai Prime Minister Thaksin Shinawatra clamped down on Thai-Muslim protesters in Tak Bai, a town on the Thai-Malaysian border. Of the demonstrators who were arrested, an estimated eighty-five died in detention. A month later, Thaksin threatened to walk out of the impending ASEAN Summit in Vientiane if, at that event, Malaysia were to bring up the subject of Tak Bai. ASEAN's policy of noninterference, he claimed, should prevent such an "internal" matter from being raised. Replied Malaysia's foreign minister, "There is no such thing as absolute non-interference."[48]

In 2005, at the ASEAN Summit in Kuala Lumpur, some member states privately urged Myanmar not to go through with its assumption of the chairmanship of ASEAN, scheduled by alphabetic rotation to occur in mid-2006. When the junta did decide to forego this honor—and thus save ASEAN from international embarrassment—it seemed that "peer pressure" could be applied and have some effect. Additional evidence of such pressure could be seen in the interest of some ASEAN parliamentarians in pushing for Myanmar's outright "suspension" from the Association, although nonstate actors were waging this campaign. As of this writing, it was still unclear to what extent the ASC could become a significant driver toward more democracy and better governance in the region.

Meanwhile, in the language of the VAP, specific measures were promised to assure and advance human rights, albeit balanced by obligations. A robust

[47] See *ASEAN Vientiane Plan of Action*, Annex on ASC.
[48] "KL Rebuffs Thaksin Over Walkout Vow," *The Nation* [Bangkok], 27 November 2004.

209

agenda was proposed, including taking stock of "existing human rights mechanisms and equivalent bodies, including sectoral bodies that look into the rights of women and children." The text also called for drawing up and adopting a memorandum of understanding "to establish a network of cooperation among existing human rights mechanisms," including developing "an ASEAN instrument on the protection and promotion of the rights of migrant workers, as well as the establishment of an ASEAN commission on the protection and promotion of the rights of women and children." These steps were "to be closely followed by the establishment of programmes to strengthen the rule of law, judiciary systems and legal infrastructure, and good governance," among other reforms.[49]

What do such statements imply? Indonesia's Foreign Minister Hassan Wirajuda has argued that in its plans for the ASC, ASEAN has at last "taken the bull by the horn[s]" by committing itself to build a regional human rights regime.[50] Progress is in fact likely to be more incremental than his metaphor suggests. But however tentatively and incompletely, a consensus of sorts has begun to emerge in ASEAN on behalf of locating human rights at the core of a human security community for Southeast Asia.

Human rights are being mainstreamed into ASEAN's agenda. The advocacy by the informal ASEAN Working Group on Human Rights (AWGHR) back in the early- to mid-1990s is finally bearing fruit.[51] Domestic civil society organizations (CSOs) have played key roles in this process. Since 1996, their efforts have led to the creation of national human rights commissions in four ASEAN states—Indonesia, Malaysia, the Philippines, and Thailand.[52] The work of the AWGHR has been supported and complemented by the initiatives of these and other CSOs. One of these bodies is the network of ASEAN Institutes of Strategic and International Studies (ASEAN-ISIS), which has convened a yearly regional colloquium on human rights and has also organized an annual ASEAN People's Assembly (APA).

---

[49] *Vientiane Action Plan*, Annex 1, par.1.1.4.

[50] Keynote Speech by H. E. Dr. N. Hassan Wirajuda, Minister for Foreign Affairs, Republic of Indonesia, at the Fourth Workshop on the ASEAN Regional Mechanism on Human Rights, Jakarta, 17 June, 2004, <http://www.kbri-canberra.org.au/speeches/2004/040617menlu.htm>.

[51] Since it was formed in 1993, the AWGHR has urged ASEAN to create a human rights mechanism for Southeast Asia. In 2000, ASEAN officials agreed to meet regularly with the Group. For more, see, e.g., Vitit Muntarbhorn, *Roadmap for an ASEAN Human Rights Mechanism*, <http://ww.fnf.org.ph/liberallibrary/roadmap.htm>; and Caballero-Anthony, *Regional Security in Southeast Asia*.

[52] See Caballero-Anthony, "Re-visioning Human Security in Southeast Asia," *Asian Perspectives* 28, no. 3 (2004), 155–89.

APA, first held in 2000, brings together CSOs from the ten member states.[53] One of its projects has been to develop an ASEAN Human Rights Scorecard based on indicators of the state of democracy and human rights in the region. Such a scorecard could then be used to advocate appropriate reforms and protections to better these conditions. APA's work in this arena dovetails well with that of the AWGHR and the national commissions.

Noteworthy, too, is the work of the ASEAN Inter-Parliamentary Organisation (AIPO) since 2004 on behalf of human rights in Myanmar. In early 2005, AIPO formed a regional caucus of legislators in Cambodia, Indonesia, Thailand, and even Singapore, to "monitor and ensure democratisation in Myanmar."[54] The caucus soon began what turned out to be the successful campaign to deny Myanmar its turn to chair ASEAN in 2006–07.

All this being said, on the eve of the unveiling of the ASEAN Charter in November 2007, Southeast Asia still lacked a regional mechanism to encourage and defend respect for human rights. ASEAN's elites had nonetheless come a long way from the strident official opposition to a human rights agenda that marked the "Asian values" debate in the 1990s. Such an agenda has been mainstreamed into the ASC and given priority in this first pillar of the envisaged ASEAN Community—a signal achievement.

In 2007, as ASEAN drafted its Charter, it was indeed possible to look forward to a "new regionalism" in Southeast Asia: a more inclusive and participatory pattern in which diverse nonstate actors could productively engage in the ASEAN's activities at local, national, regional, and extraregional levels.[55]

Challenge and Opportunity: Chartering ASEAN

The hope of a more participatory regionalism had already been strengthened by official statements that the process of drafting the Charter was going to be consultative. The ASEAN Chair in 2005 had promised a "people-oriented Charter" that would help "make ASEAN a people-oriented organisation."[56] Expectations rose accordingly in 2006–07, as did curiosity about how the process would be implemented, and what the content of the Charter would be.

---

[53] See Caballero-Anthony, "Non-State Regional Governance Mechanism for Economic Security: The Case of the ASEAN Peoples' Assembly," *The Pacific Review* 17, no. 4, 2004, 567–85.

[54] Michael Vatikiotis, "Neighbours Lean on Myanmar," *International Herald Tribune*, 2 February 2005.

[55] Björn Hettne, "Globalisation and the New Regionalism: The Second Great Transformation," in *Globalism and the New Regionalism*, ed. Björn Hettne, András Inotia, and Osvaldo Sunkel (London: Macmillan, 1999).

[56] See Chairman's Statement of the 11th ASEAN Summit, July 2005, Kuala Lumpur, Malaysia, <http://www.aseansec.org/18039.htm>.

Anticipation of the Charter focused in particular on two prospects: a requirement to comply and the transformation of norms. Regarding compliance, the Charter was expected to change ASEAN from an informally structured interstate grouping into a more rules-based body equipped with a legal personality. That would require the Association to develop a new culture of adherence to rules. Whatever agreements and arrangements ASEAN had made to address particular threats to NTS—such as the Agreement on Transboundary Haze Pollution, the Convention on Counter Terrorism,[57] or surveillance mechanisms for combating infectious diseases—would become legally binding on member states. Members would have to take their obligations seriously. A system to monitor their compliance would be established. These reforms, it was hoped, would enable the Association more effectively to protect and promote NTS in the region.

Still more significantly, it was hoped that the Charter could bring about, or at any rate encourage, ASEAN's normative transformation. Finally, after forty years, ASEAN would spell out in its Charter just what its institutional norms and values were going to be, and the extent to which these norms and values, backed by new mechanisms for compliance, would commit member states to foster democracy, respect human rights, and serve human security.

The ASEAN Charter took shape in stages. First came the establishment in 2005 of an Eminent Persons Group (EPG) to recommend "bold and visionary" ideas for the Charter's drafters to consider, and to undertake consultations with sectoral groups in the region's societies.[58] A flurry of activities ensued. The quickening of the region's pulse was palpable as a number of CSOs and NGOs responded to the EPG's invitation to get involved in the consultation process.

In this context, a first-ever ASEAN Civil Society Conference (ACSC) was convened in Malaysia on 7–9 December 2005. The event brought together some 120 participants drawn from CSOs around the region.[59] They prepared a "Statement of the ASEAN Civil Society Conference to the 11th ASEAN Summit," and submitted it a few days later to the ASEAN heads of government gathered in Kuala Lumpur. Never before had ASEAN's leaders directly interfaced with civil society groups. The meeting lasted only about a quarter of an hour. But it was nonetheless significant that the heads of government sat and listened as

---

[57] For the agreement and the convention, respectively, see <http://www.aseansec.org/images/agr_haze.pdf> and <http://www.aseansec.org/19250.htm>.

[58] The EPG had ten members, one from each ASEAN member country. It was chaired by former Malaysian Deputy Prime Minister Musa Hitam and included regional luminaries such as former Philippine President Fidel Ramos, former Indonesian Foreign Minister Ali Alatas, and Singapore's Deputy Prime Minister S. Jayakumar.

[59] See "ASEAN Civil Society Speaks Out," *JUST Commentary E-Newsletter* 6, no. 1 (January 2006), <http://www.just-international.org/commentary/E%20News%20Jan%2006.htm#ms1>. The Asian Civil Society Conference brings together a number of civil society groups in the region and is coordinated by the Universiti Institut Teknologi Mara (UiTM), Malaysia.

the ACSC representatives read out in full their prepared statement, entitled "Building a Common Future Together."[60]

The convening of the ACSC lent fresh momentum to efforts by Southeast Asian CSOs to establish a formal and ongoing mechanism for engaging ASEAN, apart from the ASEAN People's Assembly.[61] The result was the birth in February 2006 of an umbrella organization called Solidarity for Asian People's Advocacy (SAPA). SAPA brought together twelve CSOs, including Forum Asia and the Third World Network.[62] In 2006, following the first ASEAN-CSO meeting, in Malaysia in December 2005, four other consultations took place.[63]

The network of think tanks in ASEAN-ISIS was also invited to present its ideas about the Charter. The Track II group did so in a memorandum conveyed to the ASEAN foreign ministers meeting in Bali in April 2006. The scope of the memorandum covered a full range of suggestions for inclusion in the Charter—proposed ASEAN principles, organs, and institutional arrangements; methods of consultation and decision-making; external relations; member rights and obligations; financial matters; and even sanctions.[64] The Institute of Southeast Asian Studies (ISEAS) in Singapore had earlier prepared comparable suggestions, and given them to the EPG and the ASEAN Senior Officials Meeting in time for the 2005 summit in Kuala Lumpur.[65]

Other organizations also offered their thoughts on the Charter, albeit outside the official consultative process. The ASEAN Trade Union Council, for example, drafted an ASEAN Social Charter that it presented to the ASEAN officials in December 2005. The Social Charter was aimed at promoting common labor standards in ASEAN, including employment stability, promotion of health and safety, and fair wages.[66]

After collecting input on the Charter at five meetings, called "Consultations with the People," the EPG finally submitted its recommendations to the ASEAN leaders at their 12th summit, in Cebu in the Philippines in January 2007. The EPG Report attracted a lot of attention for the boldness of its vision and ideas. It was widely circulated and made easily available through the ASEAN Secretariat

---

[60] See "Statement of the ASEAN Civil Society Conference to the 11th ASEAN Summit," 17 December 2005, <http://www.focusweb.org/content/view/774/27>.

[61] APA had been regularly convened since its formation in 2000; see Caballero-Anthony, "Non-State Regional Governance."

[62] "SAPA Core Group Spearheads Coming Strategies in Engaging ASEAN," 11 April 2006, <http://www.forum-asia.org/index.php?option=com_content&task=view&id=64&Itemid=47>.

[63] These occurred in Bangkok (February), Manila (March), Bali (April), and Singapore (June).

[64] See ASEAN-ISIS Memorandum No. 1, The ASEAN Charter, 18 April 2006.

[65] See *Framing the ASEAN Charter: An ISEAS Perspective* (Singapore: Institute of Southeast Asian Studies, 2005).

[66] See "Charter to Protect Workers in ASEAN," *The Star* [Petaling Jaya, Malaysia], 5 December 2005.

website—a significant departure from the past practice of nontransparency. The accessibility of the Report reinforced the perception, at that point in time, that Southeast Asia was indeed on the cusp of an era of "new regionalism."

Focusing that optimism were the two prospects already noted: a requirement to comply and the transformation of norms.

On the first score, the Report recommended a provision for possible sanctions: specifically that ASEAN should be empowered to institute measures "to redress cases of serious breach" of its "objectives [and] major principles," including possible "suspension of any of the rights and privileges of membership."[67] The EPG did not want to completely discard the ASEAN Way. But it did ask that the Way's principles be supplemented by a culture of adherence to legally binding rules—adherence that the Charter should foster, and even require. In this respect the EPG advocated, in effect, nothing less than a sea change in thinking among ASEAN's elites. The Report's references to the obligations of member states, including the prospect of sanctions against noncompliance, reflected the emerging view, both in the EPG and more widely in Southeast Asian civil society, that allowing the lowest common denominator to set standards of state behavior was no longer acceptable in a maturing ASEAN.

As for the norms of democracy and human rights, the EPG recommended that the Charter reaffirm various principles mentioned in previous ASEAN documents. But the Group broke new ground in calling forthrightly for "the active strengthening of democratic values," the promotion of "good governance," and the "rejection of unconstitutional and undemocratic changes of government," as well as respect for "the rule of law, including international humanitarian law, and respect for human rights and fundamental freedoms."[68]

In January 2007, when the EPG presented its report to the ASEAN Summit in Cebu, one could be optimistic that the Charter would indeed reorient the Association in a more progressive direction. But that outlook would be sorely tested by events that unfolded in the months still left before the Charter was due to be completed and signed at the next summit, in November 2007 in Singapore. Notwithstanding ASEAN's formal endorsement of the report, rifts soon opened inside the Association over a number of controversial issues.

Between the Summits in January and November 2007, a High-Level Task Force (HLTF) prepared the actual wording of the Charter. The plan was to submit that draft for approval at the Singapore summit—a crowning achievement to adorn the celebration of ASEAN's fortieth birthday.

ASEAN met this schedule. The Charter was announced on time. In the meantime, however, the mood of the region had dramatically changed. This was in part because the reported differences among ASEAN leaders suggested that the HLTF might water down the EPG's bold vision, and partly because of

---

[67] See "Charter to Protect Workers in ASEAN," 4.

[68] See *Report of the Eminent Persons Group on the ASEAN Charter*, 30 December 2006, <http://www.aseansec.org/19247.pdf> 2.

the unexpected demonstrations that swept Myanmar and were brutally quashed by the regime there in September 2007, mere weeks before the Charter was due to be unveiled.

Led by Buddhist monks, the weeklong demonstrations that erupted in several places in Myanmar were severely repressed by the military junta. The protests and the violence that followed, including what appeared to be the gunning down of a Japanese news reporter, were captured on television and broadcast around the globe, to the shock of Myanmar's neighbors and the international community. The response from ASEAN was noticeably sharp and swift. Not only did ASEAN issue a joint statement expressing its "revulsion" at the atrocities that had just occurred, but it also joined the rest of the international community in urging Myanmar "to exercise utmost restraint," to seek a "political solution," and to "release all political detainees" including the long-detained leader of the opposition, Aung San Suu Kyi.[65]

Despite splendid efforts by the host, Singapore, to ensure that the November 2007 summit ran as smoothly as possible, Myanmar's attendance cast a shadow over the celebration of ASEAN's fortieth anniversary. The mood was further dampened when the finished text of the Charter was "leaked" in Bangkok prior to the summit. Observers read it and saw that its authors had rejected the EPG's bold language on compliance and norms. As if this were not embarrassment enough, the Summit in effect suffered a final coup de grace when Myanmar's junta refused to allow Ibrahim Gambari, a UN envoy who had been trying to intercede there on behalf of moderation, to brief regional leaders on developments inside the country. This refusal came despite the fact that Singapore, as the then chair of ASEAN and host of the Summit, had scheduled and announced the briefing.

Conclusion

At a time when ASEAN was supposed to have reached a zenith by adopting its own Charter, Myanmar's intransigence during the anniversary Summit certainly hurt the Association's credibility. Yet the controversy usefully clarified the significant tensions that were emerging in the region. No one could doubt that ASEAN's governing elites were divided on how far to push the Association toward acquiring the power to ensure compliance and revising its normative framework.

The final text of the Charter did include the following among the purposes of ASEAN: "to strengthen democracy, enhance good governance and the rule of law" and "protect human rights and fundamental freedoms."[70] Presumably in pursuit of the latter goal, the final document also promised that "an ASEAN

---

[69] "Statement by ASEAN Chair, Singapore's Minister for Foreign Affairs George Yeo," New York, 27 September 2007, <http://www.aseansec.org/20976.htm>.

[70] ASEAN Charter, Art.1.7, <http://www.aseansec.org/21069.pdf>.

human rights body" would be established. But the Charter had nothing to say about how this body would function. Absent too was any provision for sanctions or, for that matter, for any punitive mechanism to deal with violations of democratic norms. Further evidence of disagreement among the heads of government surfaced during the summit when Philippine President Gloria Arroyo publicly broke protocol by announcing that her country would be hard pressed to ratify the Charter unless the situation in Myanmar improved.

Noticeable too in December 2007 were the growing tensions between ASEAN leaders and officials on the one hand, and civil society groups and Track II networks on the other. The latter expressed their disgust over the Charter's final text and ASEAN's inaction on Myanmar, despite the tragic events that had transpired there on the very eve of the Summit. A prominent Indonesian figure in ASEAN-ISIS, for example, urged his country's parliament not to ratify the Charter and called on ASEAN to "go back to the drawing board" and come up with a document more in tune with actual Southeast Asian conditions and outlooks.[71] Meanwhile, civil society groups who had taken part in the EPG's consultative process openly criticized the "weak" Charter and declared their intention to prepare their own "people-oriented" version of the document, to be written as they thought it ought to read.

Whatever one thinks of this controversy and its implications, ASEAN's fortieth anniversary was marked by a number of defining moments of tremendous potential consequence for the future of regionalism in Southeast Asia. Human rights, democracy, and the need to cope with challenges to NTS have reached a critical threshold, where elites and civil society groups are pressing for these issues to be addressed and no longer swept under the carpet.

Despite what appeared in December 2007 to be a lost opportunity to equip the Association with a fully credible Charter, one could still argue that demands for reform were already spreading and accelerating in the region. The dangers posed by threats to NTS, the uneven experiences of political transition in the region, the Charter's call for the ASEAN Political-Security Community Council as a means of establishing a security community—these and other aspects of regional realities and regional intentions were increasingly interlinked. The ongoing dynamics of this linkage did not necessarily imply movement in tandem toward greater human security in Southeast Asia, but that scenario could not be ruled out. And one lesson of the anniversary summit was already clear: The nature of regionalism in Southeast Asia was changing.

Change is not new. Crises in the security environment and shifts in policy direction have been common features of regionalism in Southeast Asia since the late 1990s. But these latest developments are unusually distinctive. Whether by force of circumstance related to the crisis in Myanmar, or as a spillover effect of globalization and the spread of democratic norms, the closed black box of

---

[71] Jusuf Wanandi, "ASEAN's Charter: Does a Mediocre Document Really Matter?" *Jakarta Post*, 26 November 2007.

high policymaking inside ASEAN has finally been pried open. In this context of greater transparency and candor, the Indonesian proposal for an ASC that would address issues of democracy, human rights, and human security was not accidental. It reflected the atmosphere of change and stimulated pressure for further change. The ASC and other such initiatives showed just how widely felt the need to respond to NTS challenges had become.

If one works from the premise that structures and practices are dynamically linked, and that actors change the rules and norms that shape their interaction, then the study of regionalism in Southeast Asia must take into account the emerging initiatives and processes that have been the subject of this chapter. These developments could augur significant change—more likely in increments than all of a sudden. In mid-2008, the picture of ASEAN in the future—whether and how it would reach beyond its old modalities, notably its long-standing reliance on member sovereignty—was far from clear. What could be seen were fluid structures that were bound to change, if they were not already changing, the nature of state-to-state and society-to-state interactions in the region.

The fact remains, though, that the process of building an ASEAN Community with a capital C—real, solid, effective—is fraught with difficulties. The developments recounted in this chapter highlight the huge challenges ahead in endowing ASEAN with legal force while reforming its normative framework. Domestic politics inside the member countries will be of particular importance as such visions either fail or are realized. Nevertheless, the stage seems to be set for more engagement with NTS issues, not less. We can expect greater and more frequent contestation in the region by different actors. In that process, the dynamics of regionalism will be enlarged and opened, beyond the traditional confines of diplomacy among state officials behind closed doors.

As ASEAN confronts the lengthening list of NTS challenges in Southeast Asia, these multilevel engagements will in the future become as necessary as they have already become desirable.

BLOWING SMOKE: REGIONAL COOPERATION, INDONESIAN DEMOCRACY, AND THE HAZE

Simon SC Tay[1]

Singapore Insitute of International Affairs

Environmental degradation in Southeast Asia has many facets. Industrial pollution of urban air and waterways, rapid and often illegal deforestation, and damage to marine resources and habitats all come to mind, and all have attracted critical attention. Yet among these nontraditional threats to security, few have been more widely noted than the perennial smoke that still rises from fires in Indonesia and spreads to neighboring countries. As I shall show in this chapter, these fires and the resulting haze have triggered a long series of responses from ASEAN. Yet the flames and smoke have reappeared, to varying extents and intensities, for more than the last fifteen years. Off and on, the haze has threatened health in parts of Malaya, Sarawak, Kalimantan, Sumatra, Brunei Darussalam, and Singapore. The Philippines and Thailand have been affected to a lesser degree. On occasion, local air has been rendered toxic enough to force the closing of schools. Affected areas have lost billions of dollars in health costs and canceled hours. No wonder ASEAN has labeled the haze "the most serious problem in the region."[2]

Originating as it does in one country, while damaging livelihoods in adjacent countries, the haze deserves the attention of anyone interested in regional approaches to environmental security. Of additional interest is how political accountability inside one country—democratic Indonesia—may have hurt or helped its ecological accountability to the larger region.

There are many reasons to criticize the lack of environmental protection in Southeast Asia, from rapid and often illegal deforestation to overfishing and the pollution of urban air and waterways. Yet few examples of environmental concern deserve greater attention from those interested in regionalism than the haze that arises from fires in Indonesia.

---

[1] The author gratefully acknowledges the kind assistance of Ms. Martha Maulidia, who verified a number of the facts and footnotes for this article. The responsibility for any errors remains with the author.

[2] See the report to the WSSD Johannesburg, South Africa, *ASEAN Report to the World Summit on Sustainable Development* [WSSD], 26 August–4 September 2002 (Jakarta: ASEAN Secretariat, 2002), <http://www.aseansec.org/pdf/WSSD.pdf> 35.

The incidence and effects of burning trees, stumps, and brush have been influenced by the climatic conditions known as El Niño, which include drought, wind patterns, and the periodic warming of equatorial waters. But human agency is the main cause. The fires are set by a variety of entities—most notably corporations and individuals acting illegally for short-term economic gain, and officials implementing environmentally unsustainable development policies. The persistence of the haze is evidence that Indonesian laws and governance have failed to solve the problem.

The worst fires on record took place in 1997, the year the Asian financial crisis began. The resulting haze affected an estimated 20 to 70 million people in five countries in the region.[3] Major sectors of the economy were affected, as well as the safety of air and sea travel. Estimates of the economic cost include the Asian Development Bank's figure of US$ 6.3 billion,[4] with the vast majority of these losses suffered by Indonesia itself.[5]

In a series of initiatives dating back to 1995, ASEAN has tried to bring member governments together in efforts to end the haze. In Indonesia, then-president Suharto accepted moral responsibility for the 1997 fires and apologized for the damage done. But the skies did not clear.

Indonesia became a democracy beginning in 1998. An ASEAN Agreement on Transboundary Haze Pollution (the Haze Agreement) came into effect in 2003. Yet the haze in 2006 was worse than it had been since 1997. In 2006, Indonesia's first-ever directly elected president, Susilo Bambang Yudhoyono, apologized again and promised timely action. Yet, as of mid-2008, the Indonesian government had still not ratified the 2003 Haze Agreement, nor taken adequate steps to prevent the problem from flaring up again, off and on, year after year.

Why? What has ASEAN done to date, in the 2003 Haze Agreement and earlier measures, and why have these steps not proved sufficient? Has Indonesia's democratization weakened the ability of the government in Jakarta to remedy the situation? Is the lesson from this experience that ASEAN should stop trying to help Indonesia deal with the problem? Or are there ways in which new regional institutions can combine with Indonesia's new democracy to manage the haze,

---

[3] See K. Phonboon, ed., *Health and Environmental Impacts from the 1997 Asian Haze in Southern Thailand* (Bangkok: Health Systems Research Institute, 1998); World Health Organization (WHO), "Bioregional Workshop on Health Impacts of Haze-related Air Pollution," Kuala Lumpur, 1–4 June, 1998, WHO, Geneva; and A. Heil and J. G. Goldammer, "Smoke-haze Pollution: A Review of the 1997 Episode in Southeast Asia," *Regional Environmental Change* (Freiburg: University of Freiburg, 2001).

[4] Luca Tacconi, *Fires in Indonesia: Causes, Costs and Policy Implication,* CIFOR Occasional Paper No. 38 (Bogor, Indonesia: CIFOR, 2003), <www.cifor.cgiar.org/publications/pdf_files/OccPapers/OP-038.pdf> citing the Asian Development Bank.

[5] Economy and Environment Program for Southeast Asia (EEPSEA) and World Wide Fund for Nature (WWFN), *The Indonesian Fires and Haze of 1997: The Economic Toll,* Research Report (1998), <http://www.idrc.ca/uploads/user-S/10536124150ACF62.pdf>.

and in so doing improve regional cooperation for human security? These are the questions this chapter will address.

Pessimists could doubt that anything will or can be done. One could point to Indonesian nationalism and argue that the country will never agree to be bound by outsiders through the Haze Agreement. One might compare Indonesia's lively democracy with Suharto's authoritarian New Order and conclude that President Yudhoyono is structurally unable to mobilize the consensus needed to mandate firm action. One could also question whether lower-income Indonesia can reasonably be expected to finance a costly effort to stop the fires merely to clear the air above its richer neighbors, Singapore and Malaysia.

In contrast, I make three main arguments in this chapter. First, I argue that ASEAN'S Haze Agreement is an important step forward even if the agreement can neither guarantee Indonesia's compliance nor punish its noncompliance. Second, I contend that, rather than democracy preventing action, shortcomings in Indonesia's present democratic practices are in fact the real obstacles. That is, if Indonesia's democracy can be improved, it will help—not hinder—efforts to prevent the fires. Third, I am optimistic that cooperation will be increasingly possible between Indonesia and other ASEAN member states, with greater burden-sharing among them, which will strengthen the emerging ASEAN Community. That Community can and should include beneficial interaction between domestic political processes and regional interstate collaboration. In this larger context, however intractable the haze problem has been, it has nevertheless helped regional actors to innovate potentially constructive ways of addressing Southeast Asia's new, nontraditional security agenda in tandem with subnational, national, regional, and global actors.

I conclude that although national interests and nationalism predominate, they are amenable to change under the multiple pressures of local and national politics and regional diplomacy and rule-making. The very existence of multilevel efforts to quell the fires and end the haze suggests that ASEAN is moving beyond closed compartmentalization—the fetish of noninterference in any member's affairs—toward open cooperation where more and more issues can be seen by all sides as of common concern.

Visible through the haze, at least in outline, is a future ASEAN that is increasingly willing to create a system of expectations and obligations to address transnational issues—an ASEAN that will help its members to accept responsibility for losses beyond their own borders and take steps necessary to meet those standards.

A Record of Concern: ASEAN's Actions Leading Up to the Agreement

Before exploring the content and implications of the 2003 Haze Agreement, it will be useful to review the history of ASEAN's involvement in this issue.

The seeds of ASEAN's involvement were first sown in 1990 in Kuala Lumpur, Malaysia, at the 4th ASEAN Ministerial Meeting on the Environment

(AMME), which highlighted transboundary pollution in the resulting Accord on the Environment and Development. In 1992, the ASEAN Summit in Singapore identified such pollution as a major environmental concern. The same year, ASEAN's environmental ministers agreed to harmonize policy directions and establish operational and technical cooperation on matters including cross-border air pollution, with specific reference to atmospheric haze caused by forest fires.

In 1994, building on these first efforts, ASEAN went further. At a meeting in Brunei, the environment ministers endorsed an ASEAN Strategic Plan of Action on the Environment. They also met informally in Kuching, Malaysia, and called on ASEAN to help build the capacity of member countries to address the haze and minimize its effects within a Southeast Asian region understood to constitute a single ecosystem. These steps led to a formal ASEAN Meeting on the Management of Trans-boundary Pollution, held in 1995 in Malaysia, which adopted an ASEAN Cooperation Plan on Trans-boundary Pollution, including dirty air.

The Cooperation Plan was a mixed achievement. It was much less formal or binding than comparable documents in other world regions aimed at curbing transboundary harm. But it did set useful precedents. These included two key principles: that national and regional efforts could and should be adjusted to make them complementary, and that a common regional interest in solving the haze problem did not necessarily require the policy responses of regional actors—in effect, their sacrifices—to be equal. These provisions were important insofar as they cooperatively amended the notion of strict equality of treatment across sovereign members, long an axiom of the "ASEAN Way." In effect, at the level of rhetoric, by approving the plan, Indonesia appeared to have accepted disproportionate responsibility for, if not "ownership" of, the haze.

But if the plan's generalities were helpful, it was short on details as to exactly how its intentions would be implemented. The intentions themselves were specific enough. They included setting up early warning systems to prevent fires; establishing regionally uniform fire-risk and air-quality rating scales; banning the burning of biomass during dry periods; circulating information and coordinating responses during haze episodes; and preventing fires caused by economic development projects. But the details of implementation and monitoring were left to a separate body to work out.

That body consisted of the ASEAN Senior Officials on the Environment (ASOEN), made up of officials from all member countries. Despite the principle of differential responsibility and response, Indonesia was treated equally with other ASEAN members.

The senior officials—ASOEN—moved quickly. In September 1995 they created a Haze Technical Task Force (HTTF) and gave it the initial task of putting the Cooperation Plan into operation. But the absence of clear operational directives in the Plan meant that almost nothing was done[6] before the member countries most affected by the haze were again thrown into crisis-management mode with the onset of the most severe and damaging haze on record less than two years later. Instead of working within an agreed system of cooperation, affected governments resorted to emergency discussions and ad hoc bilateral arrangements, especially between Indonesia and Malaysia and between Indonesia and Singapore.[7] What galvanized further action was not the 1995 Plan but the 1997 calamity, generated mainly by large-scale fires on the Indonesian island of Sumatra.

At the 7th AMME, in September 1997, Indonesia's then-president Suharto apologized to neighboring countries for the haze. He did not admit state responsibility. But he did seek the cooperation of other ASEAN countries in coping with the disaster.[8] The HTTF promptly launched a Regional Haze Action Plan (RHAP), which an ASEAN Ministerial Meeting on Haze endorsed in Singapore that December.

The RHAP was mainly intended to monitor, mitigate, and if possible, to prevent land and forest fires, and to strengthen regional capabilities to achieve these ends. Although the language of the RHAP remained fairly broad, its framework for cooperative action had more prescriptive teeth than the 1995 Cooperation Plan. Notably, in agreeing to the RHAP, each ASEAN member state undertook to develop and implement its own National Action Plan, including a range of specific remedial measures.[9]

The 1997 fires concentrated minds and accelerated schedules. The National Plans were supposed to be completed by March 1998, only three months after the RHAP's endorsement by the ministers in Singapore. The HTFF was tasked with holding monthly meetings to review and report progress toward implementing RHAP's provisions. In December 1998, the ASEAN Summit in Vietnam issued a Hanoi Plan of Action that called for full implementation of the RHAP by 2001. In 1999, the ASEAN Environment Ministers updated the

---

[6] The lone exception was Singapore's provision of satellite images of fires and "hot spots" to Indonesia. See S. Tahir Qadri, ed., *Fire, Smoke, and Haze: The ASEAN Response Strategy* (Manila: Asian Development Bank, 2001), <http://www.adb.org/Documents/Reports/Fire_Smoke_Haze/default.asp>.

[7] Simon SC Tay, "ASEAN Cooperation and the Environment," paper presented at the Southeast Asian Roundtable, ISEAS, Singapore, 1–3 November 1999, 13.

[8] Wakana Takahashi, "Environmental Cooperation in Southeast Asia," *Regional/Subregional Environmental Cooperation in Asia and the Pacific* (Shonan, Japan: IGES Environmental Governance Project, 2001), 44.

[9] According to the RHAP, these national plans "should" include: legislation prohibiting open burning; resource mobilization to prevent and curb fires, including the appropriate disposal of flammable agricultural waste; air-quality monitoring and reporting regimes; and the strict enforcement of relevant laws. See Regional Haze Action Plan (1997), <http://www.aseansec.org/9059.htm>.

scheduled implementation of the RHAP by distinguishing short- and medium-term actions to be carried out, respectively, by 2000 and 2003.

The RHAP had enlisted the Asian Development Bank (ADB) as a consultant in support of implementation. A US$ 1 million grant to the ADB yielded a document laying out details as to how the RHAP would be put into effect. That Operational Regional Haze Action Plan (ORHAP) was approved by the ASOEN and the HTTF in July 1999. In the ADB's words,[10] the ORHAP "catalyzed the beginning of ASEAN's reorientation from a passive agency that responds to challenges in an *ex post* manner to a more forward-looking institution that anticipates challenges and responds to them *ex ante*."[11]

Behind the ADB's abstract comment on the consequences of its own consultancy lay an even more significant achievement: the acknowledgment of what everyone knew but had been reluctant to say, namely, that transboundary pollution in Southeast Asia could not be separated from what a single national government—Indonesia's—had or had not done. The ADB also frankly acknowledged that although El Niño among other climatic factors had worsened the haze, the real culprits were human beings bent on material profit.[12]

The fact that ASEAN as a whole, including Indonesia, endorsed the ORHAP indicates that, in 1999, Indonesia was willing indirectly to recognize its responsibility for the problem.

The ORHAP was not a fixed or final plan. It was more of a rolling plan, to be updated and refined annually, than a definitive response to the haze. The ORHAP did include detailed implementation plans (DIPs), with detailed provisions for carrying out the RHAP at regional, subregional, and national levels. The HTTF, among other bodies, was made responsible for managing and monitoring the implementation of ORHAP within ASEAN. An RHAP Coordination and Support Unit (CSU) was to coordinate relevant activities across the action areas of monitoring, prevention, and mitigation.

Unfortunately, for all its details, the ORHAP did not include steps to strengthen the effectiveness of the implementing institutions. In its review, the ADB labeled such a program a "crucial requirement" for success, and singled out the weakness of the CSU in "resources, facilities, and expertise."[13]

In relation to the actual execution of its provisions, notwithstanding ASEAN's effort to operationalize it, the RHAP exemplified a "soft law" approach widely used in the making of international environmental law and

---

[10] Qadri, *Fire, Smoke, and Haze*, chapter 4, 85.

[11] Qadri, *Fire, Smoke, and Haze*, xviii.

[12] Using fires to burn land for palm-oil plantations has been a common case in point. See Qadri, *Fire, Smoke, and Haze*, xviii.

[13] Qadri, *Fire, Smoke, and Haze*, xxiv–xxv. For the ADB, "the weaknesses and rigidities of institutions and institutional instruments" were the "most important impediment" to effective successful fire and haze management.

policy. The RHAP was not and is not a legally binding agreement.[14] Like the ORHAP, its effectiveness depended and depends on the Indonesian government's willingness and capacity to adopt or adapt and then implement needed policies and regulations.

International agencies and extraregional governments—including the ADB, the United Nations Environment Programme (UNEP), the Global Environment Facility, Australia, the United States, Canada, France, Germany, and Japan—have supplied large amounts of relevant funding to ASEAN and its member countries, and especially to Indonesia.[15] Many relevant projects have been undertaken in cooperation with donor agencies and countries and with nongovernmental organizations (NGOs). Nevertheless, *within* ASEAN, since the ADB's consultancy and the publication of its review in 2001, there has been no consistent funding to implement the RHAP.[16]

It is against this acronym-rich background of declaration and documentation that I wish to locate ASEAN's latest response to the periodic blackening of Southeast Asian skies.

More of the Same? The Haze Agreement

The ASEAN Agreement on Transboundary Haze Pollution, or Haze Agreement, came into force on 25 November 2003. It created a legal rather than merely advisory framework for the implementation of previous arrangements, most notably the RHAP.[17] One might have thought that the last thing ASEAN needed was another document. But ASEAN did need a *legally binding* document to strengthen its members' ability to stop the ongoing seasonal cycle of fires and haze.[18] Therein lay the Haze Agreement's uniqueness and value, just as its most important weakness is the failure to date of the Indonesian government to ratify it.

The ASEAN Secretariat developed the Haze Agreement in collaboration with the UNEP, which heralded the accord as "the first regional agreement in the world *binding* a group of states to tackle haze pollution from land and

---

[14] On this point, see Ebinezer R. Florano, *The Case of the ASEAN Regional Haze Action Plan,* paper presented at IDDRI International Environmental Governance, Paris, France, 15–16 March 2004, <http://www.iddri.org/iddri/telecharge/gie/communications/3a_florano1.pdf>.

[15] See Takahashi, *Environmental Cooperation,* 55.

[16] See Takahashi, *Environmental Cooperation,* 42–43.

[17] See Qadri, *Fire, Smoke, and Haze,* 197; Florano, *The Case,* 11 ; and Takahashi, *Environmental Cooperation,* 44.

[18] See Qadri, *Fire, Smoke, and Haze,* 196; and Simon SC Tay, "The Southeast Asian Fires and Haze: A Challenge for International Environmental Law and Development," *Georgetown International Environmental Law Review* 11 (Winter 1999), 298.

forest fires."[19] It was also the first such environmental agreement to come into force under ASEAN's auspices. Formal, binding ASEAN treaties are rare, even in other fields of endeavor such as economic cooperation.

Not everyone has shared the UNEP's enthusiasm. A Singaporean academic, Alan Tan, has argued that it would not matter even if Indonesia did ratify the agreement.[20] Skeptics point to the treaty's lack of sanctions in cases of noncompliance, and the absence of mandatory third-party mechanisms to settle disputes.

Certainly these conditions limit the Haze Agreement, and the facts on the ground are discouraging. Fires and haze recur in Indonesia despite more than a decade of meetings and agreements. ASEAN's "action plans" have proven easier to plan than to enact. But is the Haze Agreement, then, merely another useless piece of paper?

A realistic answer to that question requires two frank acknowledgments. First, ASEAN lacks and will probably always lack the ability to coerce Indonesia, its largest member, into cracking down on those who start the fires and cause the haze. Second, Indonesia's domestic politics have, to an extent, impeded remedial action. But if regional coercion is not an option, neither should ASEAN abandon its long investment in growing a legally *binding* environmental regime in which Indonesia would *voluntarily* accept responsibility for the calamity, and *cooperatively*, with its neighbors, clean regional skies. As for Indonesia's rowdy and sometimes nationalistic politics, I will argue later in this essay that the country's democracy, though part of the problem, can also be part of the solution.

In this light, two questions arise for ASEAN. Is the Haze Agreement, still unratified by Indonesia as of mid-2008, a step toward such a voluntarily binding regime—one that would include Indonesia—or not? Does the Haze Agreement mark a shift for ASEAN away from the principle of strict sovereignty, that is, away from the axiom that whatever goes on inside Indonesia or any other member country is that country's own business?

The Haze Agreement's objective is hardly new: to monitor, mitigate, and prevent the haze through "concerted national efforts and intensified regional and international co-operation" (Article 2).[21] What is novel, however, is the inclusion of principles drawn from international environmental law that allocate particular responsibility to, and qualify the sovereignty of, damage-causing states. Article 3 of the Haze Agreement asserts the sovereign right of states to

---

[19] "UNEP Praises ASEAN Agreement as Model for the World," Haze Online, 28 November 2003, <http://www.edie.net/news/news_story.asp?id=7809>.

[20] Alan Khee-Jin Tan, "The ASEAN Agreement on Transboundary Haze Pollution: Prospect for Compliance and Effectiveness in Post-Suharto Indonesia," *New York University Environmental Law Journal* 13 (2005), 649, 663–64.

[21] *ASEAN Agreement on Transboundary Haze Pollution,* <http://www.disasterdiplomacy.org/aseanhaze.pdf>, 4.

exploit their natural resources, but then limits that right by assigning to every state the responsibility to prevent activities within its jurisdiction from causing damage to other states. No previous ASEAN agreement on the haze has included this qualification, which draws on global environmental law as embodied in the 1992 Rio Declaration on Environment and Development (Principle 2) and the 1972 Stockholm Declaration on Human Environment (Principle 21).[22] For the first time, based on this language, ASEAN has an arguably *legal* basis for rendering Indonesia accountable for the haze—arguable, of course, because Indonesia (as of mid-2008) still had not ratified the agreement. However, Indonesia did sign both the Rio and the Stockholm Declarations.

A second international principle that is, in substance, incorporated into the Haze Agreement is that of "common and differential responsibility" (Art. 3.2).[23] As encapsulated in Principle 7 of the Rio Declaration, this wording draws upon the foundational idea of cooperation among states.[24] But it goes further to legitimate the idea of having various states assume various obligations, with concessions given to developing countries. This differentiated system is intended to create the broadest possible range of states with differing interests that can come together to reach common goals with respect to global environmental issues.

The Haze Agreement also states forthrightly: "Where there are threats of serious or irreversible damage from trans-boundary haze pollution, even without full scientific certainty, precautionary measures shall be taken by Parties concerned" (Art. 3.3). [25] The parties are further required to manage their lands and forests "in an ecologically sound and sustainable manner" (Art. 3.4);[26] and they should, "in addressing trans-boundary haze pollution,"[27] involve "as appropriate, all stakeholders, including local communities, non-governmental organizations, farmers and private enterprises" (Art. 3.5).[28] Having not ratified the Haze Agreement, of course, Indonesia is not a party to it and is not legally bound by its provisions.

The Haze Agreement lays out multiple obligations for each party to follow. These include acting immediately to quell or control fires, strengthening fire-

---

[22] See Report of the United Nations Conference on the Human Environment, Stockholm, 5–16 June 1972 (United Nations publication, Sales No. E.73.II.A.14 and corrigendum), chapter 1, <http://www.unep.org/Documents.multilingual/Default.asp?DocumentID= 97&ArticleID=1503>; and Rio Declaration on Environment and Development (1992), <http://www.un.org/documents/ga/conf151/aconf15126-1annex1.htm>.

[23] See, for example, *ASEAN Agreement on Transboundary Haze Pollution*, 15. Article 20 provides for financial contributions on a voluntary basis, and states that take action against fire can draw on their common resource.

[24] Charter of the United Nations, chapter 6, article 74.

[25] *ASEAN Agreement on Transboundary Haze Pollution*, 4–5.

[26] *ASEAN Agreement on Transboundary Haze Pollution*, 5.

[27] *ASEAN Agreement on Transboundary Haze Pollution*, 5.

[28] *ASEAN Agreement on Transboundary Haze Pollution*, 5.

fighting capabilities, and designating a National Monitoring Center to report on conditions in fire-prone areas. Parties are also committed to implementing "their obligations" under the agreement through legislative and administrative measures (Art. 4.3).

Yet the Haze Agreement lacks benchmarks, standards, or timelines whereby the parties' compliance could be measured and compared. It specifies neither a means to assess compliance nor any penalties for noncompliance. In these respects, although legally binding for its ratifying countries, the agreement's ability to resolve the haze problem is not a proven fact but a future potential. That potential should not, however, be discounted. Studies of other environmental treaties have shown that they can foster compliance by encouragement rather than punishment. Success has been possible in a number of cases because the existence of a treaty prompted the creation of institutional means and "sunshine" methods for monitoring and reporting on the progress (or lack thereof) by obligated states. Together with media publicity and political pressures, some arrangements that lack enforcements have nevertheless been conducive to improvements.[29]

With this potential effectiveness in mind, the institutions that are called for in the Haze Agreement bear special attention. One of these is the ASEAN Coordinating Center for Transboundary Pollution Control. A first for Southeast Asia, this center is charged merely with "facilitating cooperation and coordination"[30] (Art. 5.1)—hardly a bold agenda. A party that declares a fire emergency within its borders can ask the ASEAN Center to help coordinate a response. Such a party can also ask another party to help. But neither the center nor any party can intervene in the sense of forcing the party facing the emergency to accept such help. Nor does the Haze Agreement mandate the center to broker inter-party cooperation in handling such an emergency.

The Haze Agreement does not, however, expressly prevent either the ASEAN Center or its host, the ASEAN Secretariat, from informally suggesting preventive or corrective policies to any of the parties. An instructive example is the peace-brokering "shuttle diplomacy" that the UN secretary-general undertakes on the legally meager basis of his duty to keep the Security Council informed of possible threats to security.

The Haze Agreement also provides for the establishment of three other entities: a conference of the parties, a secretariat within the ASEAN Secretariat, and (as described in Article 20) an ASEAN Transboundary Haze Pollution Control Fund. The Control Fund is an innovation for ASEAN, which typically depends on external sources for its funding, or on the dues that all ten member

---

[29] See Edith Brown Weiss and Harold Jacobson, *Engaging Countries: Strengthening Compliance with International Environmental Accords* (Cambridge, MA: MIT Press, 1998); and Oran R. Young, *The Institutional Dimensions of Environmental Change: Fit, Interplay, and Scale* (Cambridge, MA: MIT Press, 2002).

[30] *ASEAN Agreement on Transboundary Haze Pollution*, 6.

countries, regardless of size or wealth, pay in equal amounts. Contributions to the Control Fund are voluntary, come mainly from ASEAN member states, and reflect what each of these states wants to give.

A skeptic may criticize the Control Fund's voluntary basis. But it does at least open the door to the principle of common but also differential responsibility: the idea that each state can contribute differently to solving a problem, according not only to that state's unique capacity but also to its lesser or greater responsibility for creating the problem in the first place. Already some international pacts differentially obligate industrialized and developing countries that have, respectively, done more and less damage to the global environment. Nor is the Control Fund limited to states as donors. Nonstate actors, already encouraged to help curb the haze (Art. 3.5), can also help fund the fund and thereby gain recognition as legitimate stakeholders in pollution control.[31]

Not all state actors are part of the solution; some are part of the problem. The same could be said of states. The Haze Agreement has disappointed some observers in both respects. It does not identify the main source of the fires—large corporations that burn off land to clear it for plantation use—nor does it identify the main source country, Indonesia.

The agreement is not, however, a useless piece of paper. A detailed, strict, and intrusive treaty is not the only way to grow an effective legal regime, even if such an approach were realistic among the diverse and unequal states of Southeast Asia. The Haze Agreement adheres instead to innovative principles of semisovereign and differentiated responsibility that, although legally binding, are not coercively so. The emphasis is on cooperation to institutionalize monitoring, transparency, and assistance. An attempt to coerce an "errant" state into changing its behavior simply would not work. The agreement seeks instead to encourage and enable the polluting state to entertain co-ownership of the problem and consider new modes of addressing it. Unless and until Indonesia ratifies the treaty, or (with or without outside help) takes adequate measures to end the haze or at least minimize the harm to neighboring states, the approach advocated here cannot be called a success. Yet without such an approach, success would elude the region even more.

For all that ASEAN has done and can do, Indonesia still locates the crux of the problem. As a member of ASEAN, Indonesia was involved in all the negotiations whose results I have discussed. Together with all the other members, Indonesia signed the Haze Agreement. Yet as of mid-2008, among all the ASEAN states, only Indonesia (and the Philippines) had not ratified it.

---

[31] See Euston Quah and Douglas Johnston, "Forest Fires and Environmental Haze in Southeast Asia: Using the Stakeholder Approach to Assign Costs and Responsibilities," *Journal of Environmental Management* 63 (2001), 181–91. See also Euston Quah, "Transboundary Pollution in Southeast Asia: The Indonesian Fires," *World Development* 30, no. 3 (2002), 429–41.

Given that it has been the epicenter of most of the haze-causing fires, I focus on Indonesia in the next section.

A Changing Equation: Democracy and Nationalism in Indonesia

Why has Indonesia, despite mounting outside pressure, still not taken decisive steps to handle the haze? Why has its national legislature not ratified the Haze Agreement? And what, if any, roles do democracy and nationalism play in the answers to these questions?

Vast changes have swept Indonesia's political system since 1997. Their range and complexity lie beyond the scope of this chapter. Political changes relevant to the haze do nevertheless warrant review.

Indonesia has gone from an authoritarian regime under President Suharto to a democracy under the country's first directly elected president, Susilo Bambang Yudhoyono. The legislature, once a quiescent body dominated by the government party, Golkar, now includes many different parties with different interests. Although Golkar remains the largest party, complex coalitions drive different issues. The highly centralized system that Suharto imposed upon a diverse and dispersed archipelago has been radically decentralized. Provincial governors, district heads, and mayors are directly elected, and exercise far more authority than before.

These new conditions have also greatly changed the roles of NGOs, firms, and actors, including the media. They enjoy much more freedom than before, and have proliferated in number. Yet they face many challenges going forward. Questions have arisen as to their unity and purpose. They, too, have had to decentralize as authority has devolved downward from Jakarta. Business interests are strong and have sometimes thwarted or suborned elements of civil society and the media.

These changes have set a new context for efforts to address the fires and haze. Back in 1997, even the most severe critic of Indonesian inaction still had to acknowledge extenuating circumstances: the impact of an extreme El Niño phenomenon, and a financial collapse and economic crisis that stoked enough opposition to President Suharto to bring him down and make democracy possible. The severe haze of 2006 could not, in contrast, be blamed on economic or political shocks, although climatic factors were not wholly absent. Under President Yudhoyono, the country has become basically stable and has returned to the business of growing the economy and attracting foreign investment. The government of such a country should be able to address the fires, especially since Yudhoyono himself has pledged remedial action. In April 2006, he said he felt "ashamed" that his country was exporting such a menace to its neighbors and ordered his officials to take preemptive steps. Said the president, a retired general: "Let us declare a war against haze."[32]

Yet in August 2006, while the fires raged and the smoke accumulated, Indonesian authorities admitted they had made only patchy progress against those responsible for starting the fires and suggested that no solution could be found for a decade. Nor have Indonesian officials always been sympathetic. Forestry Minister M. S. Kaban once actually advised Indonesia's neighbors to be thankful for oxygen on good days, rather than complaining about the bad days. Indonesian politicians have also not shied away from using the haze as a bargaining chip. In 2007, Minister Kaban called on neighboring states to help stem illegal logging in Indonesia if they wanted Indonesia to ratify and implement the Haze Agreement.[33] Some members of the legislature have extended this quid pro quo by advocating, as a precondition for Indonesian cooperation on the treaty, Singaporean and Malaysian assistance against not only illegal logging but also in other arenas, such as anticorruption and extradition.[34] These politicians may not represent majority opinion, but they have expressed their views loudly, and several of them hold positions on parliamentary committees that would oversee any future ratification of the Haze Agreement.

These events defy any expectation that President Yudhoyono's pledge will be carried out or that ratification and implementation will soon occur. Continued inaction may in the meantime jeopardize Indonesia's credibility beyond environmental issues. Questions may arise as to the will and standing of the executive, and therefore the likelihood of the country's future stability. As Indonesia seeks foreign investments in potentially haze-affected areas, including the economic zones on Batam and Bintan—a short ferry ride from Singapore—the costs of inaction could rise.

Dr. Rizal Sukma, an Indonesian expert on international relations and a contributor to this book, has argued that his country faces a serious global image problem. He refers to not only the haze, illegal logging, and the world's fastest rate of deforestation, but also to other blights, including diminished religious tolerance. For him, Indonesian officials who do not act against the haze are engaged in denial: They ignore facts on the ground so long as existing

---

[32] "Save Forests Now, President Yudhoyono Says," *Antara,* April 23, <http://www.antara.co.id/en/arc/2006/4/23/save-forests-now-president-yudhoyono-says>.

[33] M. S. Kaban, "Keynote Speech of Minister of Forestry Republic of Indonesia," Workshop on the ASEAN Agreement on Transboundary Haze Pollution, organized by the Singapore Institute of International Affairs, the World Wildlife Fund–Indonesia, and the Centre for Strategic and International Studies [Indonesia], Jakarta, 11 May 2007, <http://www.siiaonline.org/talks_dialogues2>.

[34] An extradition treaty with Singapore has since been signed. See Alvin Lie [a member of Parliamentary Commission VII from the National Mandate Party], "Diplomasi Asap," *Koran TEMPO,* 21 October 2006, <http://korantempo.com/korantempo/2006/10/21/Opini/krn,20061021,48.id.html>.

regulations or policies address the matter in theory, if not in practice.[35] Some outside Indonesia might go even further to question the country's ethics, or at any rate its neighborliness. When northern Sumatra was struck by a massive tsunami in 2004 and central Java suffered an earthquake two years later, Indonesia accepted help from its neighbors, including Singapore and Malaysia. Yet these friendly neighbors are among the worst affected by the haze and the associated indifference or impotence of Indonesian leaders.

Of course, not all Indonesians are ungrateful or recalcitrant. Many share the neighbors' concern. Their viewpoints were aired in 2007 at a workshop in Jakarta organized by the Singapore Institute of International Affairs, the Centre for Strategic and International Studies in Jakarta, and the Indonesian chapter of the World Wildlife Fund. The participants included Indonesian Forum for Environment (WALHI), the largest pro-green NGO in Indonesia. All wanted to address the haze issue. Local and provincial officials working in the fire-prone regions of Riau and Kalimantan detailed their efforts to prevent or put out the fires.

The Indonesian Ministry for the Environment has also been working to curb the haze, including starting and supporting a process whereby Indonesia could eventually ratify the ASEAN Haze Agreement. Ministry officials at the workshop assured participants that, with or without ratification, they would do their best to deliver on President Yudhoyono's promise to clear the air. These views give at least some cause for optimism, in contrast to some statements from the Forestry Ministry and some politicians.

Differing opinions are normal, especially in a decentralized democracy spanning many diverse islands. But there are additional reasons for domestic contention over the haze. The damage that the fires and haze have wrought on Indonesia's public health and economy has been well documented[36] and runs into billions of dollars, as noted earlier. Indonesians increasingly recognize that the fires and haze hurt their own country the most, and should therefore be tackled for Indonesia's own good and that of its own citizens. The effects on neighboring states are important but secondary from this perspective. Accordingly, environmentalist activists and officials in Jakarta, Sumatra, and

---

[35] Rizal Sukma, "Indonesia Faces Serious Global Image Problem," *The Jakarta Post*, 15 May 2007.

[36] See EEPSEA and WWF, *Indonesian Fires*, and its book-length version edited by David Glover and Timothy Jessup (*Indonesia's Fires and Haze: The Cost of Catastrophe* [ISEAS/IDRC, 1999]), which estimates the fire-related economic loss in terms of timber, agriculture, direct and indirect forest benefits, usable biodiversity, carbon release, and the cost of fighting the fires. Haze-related losses included short-term damages to health, lost industrial production, lost tourism, airline and airport losses, declines in fishing, and the cost of seeding clouds. See also Tacconi, *Fires in Indonesia*, which estimated the economic costs of the 1997–98 fires by comparing the EEPSEA and WWF study with one done in 1999 by the ADB and the Indonesian National Planning Agency (BAPPENAS).

Kalimantan may place a lower priority on ratifying ASEAN's agreement than on mobilizing remedial action inside Indonesia.

NGOs and local officials fighting the fires and haze have been working on projects in flammable areas and assisting people victimized by flame and smoke. The activists and responders see and feel the catastrophe up close. Directly experiencing what it can do, they want to stop it all the more. Compared with those on the ground, a policymaker in an air-conditioned office in far-off Jakarta may know little or nothing of the blight and its impacts. In Jakarta, the issue may be framed as an abstract question: Who should own, and own up to, the problem? Those who have already accepted ownership by impact, given the damage done to their people and interests, do not see eye-to-eye with those who deny ownership by causation—certain agro-industrial firms, ambitious politicians, and venal officials who mutually benefit from cheaply burning off land to plant cash crops.

Is illegal logging a significant culprit behind the fires? If it were, one could understand why Forestry Minister Kaban and some legislators in Jakarta have asked adjacent states for help in ending the practice, in return for Indonesian cooperation against the haze. At the Jakarta workshop, Indonesian NGO representatives recognized that illegal logging was a serious problem in need of solution. But they argued, with evidence, that there is no strong link between this practice and the fires. Kaban's own ministry admits that less than one-quarter of the burning occurs in forest areas.[37] Most of the fires are set on plantation lands, and the hardest to extinguish occur in peatland areas.

The use of fire to clear lands is, in fact, illegal in Indonesia. Some Indonesian officials, and especially spokespeople for the plantation companies, blame small-scale, traditional farmers. The credibility of these sources has been undermined, however, by suspicions and allegations of corruption and collusion between some of the large plantation firms that use fire and the officials who are supposed to control and suppress such illegal acts.[38]

In the dynamics behind Indonesia's failure to ratify the Haze Agreement's terms and its failure to put out the fires, foreign policy and domestic politics are intertwined. Do those dynamics point to democracy as the culprit? Do coalition politics—those who would end the calamity versus those who benefit from it—guarantee deadlock and inaction? Is a democratic government by definition unable to crack down?

No. Democracy per se is not an obstacle to progress on the haze. Indonesia does not need an "effective autocrat" to settle the matter. That argument is

---

[37] According to Kaban, "76 percent of the total fires occurs in land areas and only the remaining 24 percent occurs in forest areas." See Kaban, "Keynote Speech."

[38] See Friends of the Earth, "Paper Tiger, Hidden Dragons 2: April Fools," briefing paper (February 2002); and International Crisis Group, "Indonesia: Natural Resources and Law Enforcement" (December 2001), <http://www.crisisgroup.org/home/index.cfm?id=1453&=1>.

reminiscent of earlier justifications for Suharto's autocracy as an engine of stability and growth. Suharto did apologize for the haze in September 1997, as I have noted, and his stance certainly facilitated the rapid launch of the RHAP and its endorsement by the ASEAN ministers in December of that same haze-ridden year, before the Asian financial crisis and mounting domestic opposition forced his resignation from office the following May.

But this cooperation existed more on paper than on the ground. The Regional Haze Action Plan was always more plan than action. Worth remembering, too, is Suharto's last-minute decision, in March 1998, to appoint as forestry minister his crony Bob Hasan, a timber tycoon long suspected of involvement in illegal logging and fire usage, who was later convicted of corruption and sent to jail. Centralized political power in this instance did not guarantee impartial action to end a calamity on the ground. Quite the contrary: Authoritarian rule was complicit in the ongoing ability of large firms and suborned politicians to violate, directly or indirectly, the law against using fire to clear land.

Would Suharto, were he still in power today, have allowed the fires and haze to go on? It is impossible to know. I would argue merely that democracy as such is not the problem. The problem, instead, is the quality of Indonesian democracy—its shortcomings in practice, not its essence in theory. Democracy is dynamic. Its weaknesses in Indonesia—its association with inaction against a recurring blight—are subject to change. Such changes could indeed raise the likelihood of action, including eventual ratification of the Haze Agreement. But that will depend on how the balance of influence evolves between various groups with diverse interests: activists versus administrators; local leaders in affected areas versus national politicians in Jakarta; officials who deal with foreign policy and ASEAN versus those whose terms of reference are domestic; the environment ministry versus the forestry ministry; and law-abiding versus law-breaking corporations.

A key variable in this political equation is nationalism. Those who oppose ratification of the Haze Agreement tend to argue that it subordinates Indonesian interests to those of neighboring states such as Singapore and Malaysia.[39] Such voices have cited the cost of preventing and fighting fires. Or they have linked ratification to matters that are mainly or wholly unrelated to the haze, such as illegal logging or Singapore's purchases of Indonesian sand from nearby Batam and Bintan. Or these opponents have used ratification as leverage on matters even farther afield, including the now-signed extradition treaty with Singapore or the treatment of undocumented Indonesian workers in Malaysia.[40]

However, if the contents of democracy in Indonesia are changeable over time, so are the meanings and uses of nationalism and "the national interest." President Yudhoyono's shift in public attitude since 2006 illustrates the point.

---

[39] See Lie, "Diplomasi Asap."
[40] See Lie, "Diplomasi Asap."

Levels of Endeavor: Indonesia, ASEAN, and Beyond

A main lesson of this chapter is that Indonesia could do more to end the haze. But even if Indonesia takes ownership of the problem and acts resolutely to solve it, success in doing so will require support from both the Southeast Asian region and the international community beyond.

Since 2003, ASEAN has been working to turn Southeast Asia into an economic, security, and sociocultural community. The Yudhoyono government has been a leading proponent of this strategy, especially the creation of a security community. At the same time, that project carries implications for Indonesia. ASEAN cannot be a genuine security community if its largest member is causing harm to its own people and their neighbors.

It follows from this that Indonesia's ability to lead ASEAN will be affected by what it does or does not do with respect to the fires and haze. For all its faults domestically, Suharto's regime supported ASEAN. Under him, Indonesia's relations with the rest of the region were relatively benign. His foreign policies allowed ASEAN to move forward, and that in turn bestowed on Indonesia an informal recognition of its leadership. When Suharto fell, Indonesia lost that stature. Instead, by and large, the country's domestic challenges challenged the region.

Under President Yudhoyono, Indonesia has shown signs of again wishing to lead Southeast Asia. The full nature, extent, and effects of such leadership are not yet clear. Relations with Malaysia and Singapore on the haze have gone up and down depending on the issue and whether nationalist feelings were involved.

In this uncertain context, ASEAN must not threaten, or be seen as threatening, Indonesia. That will only deal a further setback to efforts to combat the haze. Indonesians will be less willing to act if such action is portrayed as giving in to neighbors who are eager to accuse but are unwilling to help.

Encouraging in this light are the cooperative steps recently taken in two especially fire-prone provinces on Sumatra: Jambi and Riau. In these places local officials have begun, with Jakarta's approval, to work directly with ASEAN member states: Riau with Malaysia, Jambi with Singapore. In Jambi province in 2007, for example, several working sessions among relevant officials were held to draft a master plan to prevent fires in one vulnerable district.

One merit of the plan in Jambi is that it goes beyond officialdom to include community leaders, NGOs, and companies whose stated policy is not to use fire. Innovative, too, is the direct linking of national officials outside Indonesia with provincial and district officials inside. If they are effective, these initiatives could be replicated across other fire-prone localities. If they are both effective and publicized, they will help demonstrate neighborly good will, and could thereby strengthen Indonesia's will to tackle the problem—perhaps even making the Haze Agreement's ratification and implementation at least somewhat more likely.

Whatever solution evolves, it will require funding. Several ASEAN states have agreed to put seed money into the agreement's Haze Pollution Control

Fund. As of mid-2007 Singapore and Malaysia had each pledged only US$ 50,000, a modest amount. Both governments have, however, shouldered more expenses in their district-level projects on Sumatra. If and as Indonesia implements its antihaze plans, more resources will be needed. Indonesia should not be expected to bear the financial burden on its own, but neither should all of the agreement's signatories share the cost equally.

Another innovation I have noted is the involvement of organizations and actors from outside government. In 2007, for example, efforts were under way to initiate a regular consultation on the haze among environmental NGOs and ASEAN-linked think tanks. Beyond addressing the calamity itself, people-to-people activities can also address ASEAN's community-building goals, by fostering a sense of public interests shared across national borders.

This hope is in keeping with a main argument in this chapter. That is, ASEAN, working at a second or intermediate level between Indonesia and the larger world, can and should positively influence Indonesian wherewithal and resolve. This should be done cooperatively, but without merely deferring to the formerly sacrosanct norm of noninterference. A related argument works in reverse, namely from the first (or national) to the second (or regional) level. Regionally assisted endeavors to solve the haze problem on the ground can and should positively influence ASEAN itself, including its community-building agenda for Southeast Asia.

Finally, at a third level beyond the region, if the haze hurts the world's environment, the international community should play a role. The fires and haze do impact biodiversity and, even more, climate change. The fires have threatened important zones of biovariety. National parks and forests in Kalimantan are an example. As for climate change, the release of carbon into the atmosphere has vaulted Indonesia's emissions into third place, behind only the United States and China.[41] No wonder the UNEP dubbed the 1997–98 fires "a global disaster." The fires and haze in 2006 also drew critical global notice.

Despite these implications for the world at large, the international community has not been active in supporting efforts to quell the haze. Yet much could be done at this level. Global organizations and actors could, for example, sponsor projects to retain or replant forests and conserve peatlands. A window of opportunity in this respect was created when Indonesia hosted a key meeting of the parties to the Kyoto Protocol in Bali in December 2007.[42]

---

[41] See Delft Hydraulics and Wetlands International, "PEAT-CO$_2$: Assessment of CO$_2$ Emissions from Drained Peat Lands in Southeast Asia," 12 December 2006, <http://www.wetlands. org/publication.aspx?id=51a80e5f-4479-4200-9be0-66f1aa9f9ca9>; and Pelangi Energi Abadi Citro Enviro (PEACE), *Indonesia and Climate Change: Current Status and Policies,* report commissioned by the World Bank and the Department for International Development, Indonesia (2007), <http://siteresources.worldbank.org/INTINDONESIA/Resources/Environment/ ClimateChange_Full_EN.pdf>.

[42] For a brief summary of the meeting, see <http://unfccc.int/meetings/cop_13/items/4049. php>.

These strategies, whether regional or global, should not be accusatory. That would only fan nationalist recalcitrance inside Indonesia. The international community should instead adopt and reinforce the approach taken in the Haze Agreement. Support should include financial help through the Control Fund, which is already designed to receive contributions from beyond the region. It was, after all, from international agreements on biodiversity and climate change that ASEAN drew one of the agreement's key principles: that states have a common but not identical responsibility for the environment.

Conclusion: ASEAN Seen through the Haze

This chapter has examined a case of interaction between environmental security, Indonesian democracy, and Southeast Asian regionalism. I have used a two-way lens, viewing the regional haze through ASEAN, and ASEAN through the haze. In this concluding section I want to refocus more generally, if briefly, on what this recurring calamity tells us about ASEAN, its nature and future.

First, nationalism still dominates in ASEAN. Much work has been done in recent years to adjust nationalism to regionalism in Southeast Asia. An ASEAN community has been declared and efforts to realize it are under way. As this chapter has shown, many years of discussion and negotiation in many locations have been spent on crafting a regionally supported solution to the haze. Yet despite the transboundary impact of this recurring disaster, a single country—Indonesia—remains the decisive site of remedial action, or inaction.

This conclusion is not limited to the case at hand. In every ASEAN member state, the national level of concern still trumps, arguably, the regional one. Influential actors with narrow interests can, in some situations, wrap themselves in the national flag and thereby use nationalism against the national interest.

This outcome can, however, be avoided. If the self-interested agendas of these actors can be revealed, and if truly national voices and interests can displace them, a cross-border problem can be made more amenable to solution. The potential for such a constructive outcome can be seen in the contrasting views that various Indonesians hold, depending on how the crisis has affected them. In a democracy such as Indonesia, who does and does not speak for the nation and its true interest are, fortunately, contestable questions.

Second, the project of building a regional community can influence national politics. Although the national level is dominant, two-way interaction between national and regional politics does occur. ASEAN's efforts have not put out the fires, but they have succeeded in clarifying the regional—if not global—responsibilities of Indonesia, and motivated some sectors and actors inside Indonesia, including its president, to pledge remedial action. Acknowledging the sway of nationalism therefore does not mean giving up on ASEAN. Regional efforts can and do influence calculations of national interest in member states. Southeast Asian leaders need to speed, not slow, the momentum toward a regional community based on shared concerns.

Third, if they are not to break, the norms of ASEAN must bend. The progression of efforts to respond to the haze has clarified ASEAN's thinking on this matter. That is, ASEAN has moved beyond both its earlier aversion to regional concern with national affairs and its earlier expectation that each member state should pay for solving its own problems or that all members should pay equally to do so. ASEAN has not of course abandoned the principle of member sovereignty, and members still pay equal dues. But the fires and haze have been framed as a common regional concern, thus warranting the Haze Agreement and its Control Fund.

Physically, the haze obscures any view. Politically, however, an evolving ASEAN can be seen in outline through the smoke: a system of expectations but also obligations to address national problems with regional effects, including regional funds to help resolve them. Frustrating though this process has been, it represents, consciously or not, a push toward reinventing ASEAN—adapting it to the conditions and demands of the twenty-first century.

Signs of this may be read in the results of the 13th ASEAN Summit, held in Singapore on 21 November 2007. The Summit celebrated the organization's fortieth anniversary, and marked the occasion by unveiling the Association's new Charter, signed by all ten member countries. The member countries' leaders also made a number of declarations that are relevant to this chapter.

In the Charter, Article 1.9 states that one of ASEAN's purposes is "to promote sustainable development so as to ensure the protection of the region's environment, the sustainability of its natural resources ... and the high quality of life of its peoples."[43] Article 1.8 also calls upon ASEAN "to respond effectively, in accordance with the principle of comprehensive security, to all forms of threats ... and transboundary challenges."

At the Summit, ASEAN also issued a Declaration on Environmental Sustainability.[44] This Declaration includes a pledge: "To implement measures and enhance international and regional cooperation to combat transboundary environmental pollution, including haze pollution, through, among other things, capacity building, enhancing public awareness, strengthening law enforcement, promoting environmentally sustainable practices, as well as combating illegal logging and its associated illegal trade."[45] Further, specifically on the question of forests, the Declaration pledges "to call upon the international community to participate in and contribute to afforestation and reforestation, and to reduce deforestation, forest degradation, and forest fires, including by promoting

---

[43] ASEAN Charter, <http://www.aseansec.org/ASEAN-Charter.pdf>, 4. The Charter is also reprinted in full at the end of this book.

[44] See ASEAN Declaration on Environmental Sustainability, Environmental Protection and Management, Art. 6, <http://www.13thaseansummit.sg/asean/index.php/web/documents/declarations/asean_declaration_on_environmental_sustainability>.

[45] See ASEAN Declaration on Environmental Sustainability, Art. 6.

sustainable forest management and development, and combating illegal logging."[46] These statements signify a growing awareness of environmental protection generally, and of forest fires and haze pollution specifically—the lens through which this chapter looks at ASEAN. Yet these statements have to be implemented.

That said, are clear skies ahead? Indonesia's political promise to address the fires is significant and can be realized. Factors of domestic politics must be considered. A coalition of interests and actors must be gathered to strengthen Indonesian political will and drive remedial action. Democracy is not the problem. Indonesian inaction reflects, instead, an entrenched array of narrow and more or less collusive interests. Those interests can be overcome despite their recourse to nationalism to disguise the benefits they derive from the status quo.

Despite meager progress on the ground to date, efforts to end the haze must be strengthened. New initiatives must be explored and pursued at all three levels—national, regional, and international. This can and must be done, even as those in and near Indonesia who have suffered this seasonal but unnatural disaster steel themselves for the next round of burnt earth and dirty air.

---

[46] See ASEAN Declaration on Environmental Sustainability, Art. 10.

Bypassing Regionalism? Domestic Politics and Nuclear Energy Security

Michael S. Malley
Naval Postgraduate School
United States

Caught between rapidly rising demand for electricity and even faster increases in the price of the fossil fuels needed to generate it, governments across Southeast Asia are turning to nuclear energy. Indonesia and Vietnam are the furthest along. Both expect to have their first nuclear power plants in operation in the late 2010s. But in early 2007, other countries made decisions that may put them on the same path. Thailand's military-led government said it would revive nuclear power plans that had been derailed by the financial crisis of the late 1990s. Thailand expects to bring its first reactor online in 2020. The Philippine government announced it would examine the nuclear option and even consider opening the controversial nuclear plant that was built during the Marcos era but was never used. And Myanmar clinched a deal with Russia to supply its first nuclear research reactor, something it had been seeking for several years. Though too small to generate a supply of electricity, the reactor would mark a major expansion of Myanmar's nuclear capabilities. As of early 2008, Malaysia had no plans to develop nuclear power, but it was conducting a review of energy supplies that included the nuclear option.

Despite their shared interest in nuclear energy and long-standing advocacy of multilateral cooperation, ASEAN members have left the Association almost entirely out of their nuclear plans. This seems particularly surprising in light of nuclear energy's obvious security implications and ASEAN's long-standing commitment to keep regional peace. Moreover, this commitment is embodied, in part, in the treaty that each country signed in 1995 to establish a nuclear-weapons-free zone in Southeast Asia. The Treaty on the Southeast Asia Nuclear-Weapon-Free Zone (or SEANWFZ Treaty) not only banned nuclear weapons from the region, but also established guidelines for the peaceful use of nuclear energy by ASEAN members. Yet, as of early 2008, the Association had done nothing to ensure that its members' policies complied with the treaty's terms.

This seems unlikely to change. Within a national context, ASEAN members treat nuclear energy as a pressing matter that deserves the attention of presidents and prime ministers. Yet in an ASEAN context, their approach has been entirely different: The same national leaders delegated regional nuclear energy policy to their respective energy ministers, who in 2007 passed it farther down the ladder. With little sense of urgency, the ministers asked their subordinates merely to study the possible creation of a nuclear safety network in Southeast Asia and report back at the ministers' next meeting in mid-2008.

How should we account for this lack of interest in cooperation on an issue of such high priority to ASEAN's members and of such potential significance for regional security? The analytical frameworks most commonly used to assess cooperation and conflict in Southeast Asia are clearly insufficient. Over the past decade, the study of Southeast Asian international relations has become increasingly divided between realist and constructivist camps. Realists see state behavior as driven by a competition for survival, but their focus on states' powerful sense of insecurity leads them to exaggerate the obstacles to cooperation. Constructivists tend to overestimate the prospects for cooperation, mainly because of their determination to show that interaction among states can produce shared understandings (e.g., norms) that underpin a less conflict-prone world order than the one realists envision.

Left out of this debate is liberalism, the third major paradigm in international relations theory. In liberal accounts, domestic preferences—not power capabilities or shared norms—determine foreign policy. International cooperation follows from a convergence of national purposes rather than fear of a common external threat or adherence to shared norms. Liberalism anticipates that institutions will play important roles in facilitating cooperation among states that share common goals. Seen from this perspective, the lack of cooperation on nuclear energy among Southeast Asian countries reflects a difference among ASEAN members about *whether* to cooperate, or a preference to pursue cooperation through *non-ASEAN institutions*, or both.

This sort of approach does not rest on an assumption of liberal domestic political systems, only on the view that state preferences reflect the outcome of competition for influence within the domestic political arena. But because liberalism gives analytical priority to the domestic origins of national preferences, it is better equipped than realism or constructivism to address one of the key themes of this book—namely, democracy's relationship to regionalism and security.

My purposes in this chapter are threefold. I intend, in the first place, to show that there is a benefit to supplementing realist and constructivist outlooks on Southeast Asian international relations with an approach drawn from the liberal tradition. Second, I will show that the safety and security of nuclear power are key issues on the horizon for ASEAN. Third, I will argue from an essentially liberal perspective that cooperation among ASEAN members on nuclear issues is likely to be limited, as most members prefer to address nuclear matters outside the ASEAN framework. Although few countries in Southeast Asia are democratic, evidence from Indonesia, the region's most democratic country, suggests that broadening the range of groups involved in nuclear policy will simply intensify the tendency to limit cooperation within ASEAN. Overall, this chapter finds that Southeast Asian governments have marginalized ASEAN, as a venue for policy discussion and decision, from one of the key security issues on the region's horizon. And as long as these national actors prefer to deal with their most pressing issues outside the ASEAN framework, regionalism will not be strengthened.

Domestic Politics and International Cooperation in Southeast Asia

What explains the propensities of countries to cooperate or to come into conflict with one another? In answering this question, realists look to the capabilities of states—especially to defend themselves from attack—relative to those of other states. Since they view cooperation as generally a zero-sum game, they anticipate that it will be rare. And what governments want—their preferences—has little bearing on the prospects for cooperation or conflict: Pressures emanating from the distribution of power in the international system typically override domestic political desires.

Constructivists occasionally refer to domestic political conditions, but not as the main source of change in international politics. Instead, they look to transnational norms and how, through processes of socialization, states redefine what they want and how they interact with one another. In contrast, a liberal account of international relations is more inclined to attribute what happens between countries to the convergence or divergence of their preferences, which themselves are continually shaped and reshaped by political competition within their respective domestic arenas. In order to address this volume's key theme—the relationship between democracy, as a characteristic of domestic politics, and regionalism—the liberal tradition is essential.

Research in this third vein has been diverse. Its best-known variants include democratic peace theory and studies of foreign economic policy.[1] An explicitly liberal theory of international relations makes, nevertheless, several core

---

[1] See, for example, Michael W. Doyle, "Liberalism and World Politics," *American Political Science Review* 80, no. 4 (1986), 1151–69; Michael W. Doyle, "Three Pillars of the Liberal Peace," *American Political Science Review* 99, no. 3 (2005), 463–66; John M. Owen, "How Liberalism Produces Democratic Peace," *International Security* 19, no. 2 (1994), 87–125; Peter J. Katzenstein, ed., *Between Power and Plenty: Foreign Economic Policies of Advanced Industrial States* (Madison, WI: University of Wisconsin Press, 1978), 344; and Beth A. Simmons, *Who Adjusts? Domestic Sources of Foreign Economic Policy during the Interwar Years* (Princeton, NJ: Princeton University Press, 1994), 330.

assumptions.[2] It recognizes that state preferences reflect the interests and values of societal actors who compete with one another to define the goals and policies the state will pursue. Because the state comprises a variety of institutions that are subject to this competition, it is likely that the power to determine policy will be shared and will shift over time.

In the liberal tradition, whether states are inclined to propose cooperation, provoke conflict, or simply coexist depends on how closely their preferences match those of other states, and whether the pursuit of their separate national interests creates benefits, imposes costs, or has no special effect on others. Thus, Southeast Asian countries that seek to develop nuclear power may not cooperate with each other, despite their common interest, simply because there is little benefit to working jointly. They may realize that the resources, technology, expertise, and legitimacy they seek are not available within ASEAN but can be found in various international institutions. Likewise, cooperation to address the safety and security implications of nuclear energy may not take place within the region, despite widespread recognition of such implications. This would occur when countries assign different values to nuclear energy's benefits (e.g., electricity output) and costs (e.g., environmental damage).

Despite liberalism's distinguished pedigree, neither it nor the study of domestic politics more generally has found much of a place in the study of Southeast Asian international relations. Instead, the field has been sharply divided by, or organized around, a debate between realists and constructivists.[3] This debate has enriched the field. But many contributors have been tempted to reduce liberalism to neoliberal institutionalism, which most regard as simply a form of "rationalism" and therefore similar enough to neorealism to be considered alongside it.[4] This is particularly regrettable in the context of

---

[2] See Helen V. Milner, *Interests, Institutions, and Information: Domestic Politics and International Relations* (Princeton, NJ: Princeton University Press, 1997), 309; and Andrew Moravcsik, "Taking Preferences Seriously: A Liberal Theory of International Politics," *International Organization* 51, no. 4 (1997), 513–53.

[3] See Sarah Eaton and Richard Stubbs, "Is ASEAN Powerful? Neo-Realist Versus Constructivist Approaches to Power in Southeast Asia," *Pacific Review* 19, no. 2 (2006), 135–55; and N. Ganesan, "'Mirror, Mirror, on the Wall': Misplaced Polarities in the Study of Southeast Asian Security," *International Relations of the Asia-Pacific* 3 (2003), 221–40.

[4] See Amitav Acharya, "Realism, Institutionalism, and the Asian Economic Crisis," *Contemporary Southeast Asia* 21, no. 1 (1999), 1–29; Donald K. Emmerson, "Security, Community, and Democracy in Southeast Asia: Analyzing ASEAN," *Japanese Journal of Political Science* 6, no. 2 (2005), 165–85; Tsuyoshi Kawasaki, "Neither Skepticism nor Romanticism: The ASEAN Regional Forum as a Solution for the Asia-Pacific Assurance Game," *Pacific Review* 19, no. 2 (2006), 219–37; Hiro Katsumata, "Why Is ASEAN Diplomacy Changing?" *Asian Survey* 44, no. 2 (2004), 237–54; and Jürgen Rüland, "ASEAN and the Asian Crisis: Theoretical Implications and Practical Consequences for Southeast Asian Regionalism," *Pacific Review* 13, no. 3 (2000), 421–51.

nuclear technology, since domestic political factors are widely regarded as key determinants in countries' decisions to transform generic nuclear capacities into weapons-making machines.[5]

One reason why liberalism has received so little attention could be, of course, that scholars have purposely ignored or dismissed it as unfruitful for the study of Southeast Asia. None have done this more bluntly than Donald K. Emmerson, who argued in "an ASEAN context" that "using the people as one's unit of analysis is still misplaced advice. Even in the ostensibly more democratic parts of the region, it is still state elites, in the end, who avoid war or make it."[6]

But this phrasing raises two questions. First, how influential are societal interests before "state elites, in the end" make their decision? And second, isn't the decision to make war—a rare thing in Southeast Asia—an unfairly high standard against which to measure society's influence over the state? If the standard is lowered, and the focus is narrowed to the three most democratic countries in the region during the early 2000s, what becomes clear is that democratization "opened up the foreign policy arena and [gave] access to a larger number of actors." As a result, "public opinion has proved to be a decisive factor pushing executives in these states toward the prominent consideration of business, human rights, and religious issues."[7]

There are two approaches that take seriously the possibility that domestic politics exerts substantial influence on regional outcomes. One has been represented by Etel Solingen. She has doggedly advanced a unique perspective that places domestic politics at the center of the study of Southeast Asian international relations.[8] She has acknowledged the influence of security concerns and ideational

---

[5] See Tanya Ogilvie-White, "Is There a Theory of Nuclear Proliferation? An Analysis of the Contemporary Debate," *Nonproliferation Review* 4, no. 1 (Fall 1996), 43–60; Scott D. Sagan, "Why Do States Build Nuclear Weapons? Three Models in Search of a Bomb," *International Security* 21, no. 3 (Winter 1996–97), 54–86; and Etel Solingen, *Nuclear Logics: Contrasting Paths in East Asia and the Middle East* (Princeton, NJ: Princeton University Press, 2007).

[6] Emmerson, "What Do the Blind-Sided See? Reapproaching Regionalism in Southeast Asia," *The Pacific Review* 18, no. 1 (March 2005), 173.

[7] Jörn Dosch, *The Changing Dynamics of Southeast Asian Politics* (Boulder, CO: Lynne Rienner, 2006), 67.

[8] See Etel Solingen, *Regional Orders at Century's Dawn: Global and Domestic Influences on Grand Strategy* (Princeton, NJ: Princeton University Press, 1998); "ASEAN, Quo Vadis? Domestic Coalitions and Regional Co-Operation," *Contemporary Southeast Asia: A Journal of International & Strategic Affairs* 21, no. 1 (1999), 30–53; "Southeast Asia in a New Era: Domestic Coalitions from Crisis to Recovery," *Asian Survey* 44, no. 2 (2004), 189–212; "ASEAN Cooperation: The Legacy of the Economic Crisis," *International Relations of the Asia Pacific* 5, no. 1 (2005), 1–29; and "Domestic Politics and Regional Cooperation in Southeast Asia and Northeast Asia," in *Regional Cooperation and its Enemies in Northeast Asia: The Impact of Domestic Forces*, ed. Edward Friedman and Sung Chull Kim (London: Routledge, 2006), 17–37.

processes on regionalism and their corresponding centrality in ASEAN studies. But the field's concentration on realist and constructivist approaches neglects, in her view, "an important perspective on what ASEAN is about and what makes it tick."[9]

To supplement these realist and constructivist approaches, Solingen has offered a model that traces "a given regional order to the makeup and grand strategies of domestic coalitions."[10] She has found that relations among countries are more likely to be cooperative when "internationalizing" coalitions are dominant, and conflictual when "backlash" coalitions are in control. Yet this characterization does not predict whether ASEAN countries are more likely to cooperate with one another or with countries outside the region. It may be the case that "internationalizing coalitions" in Southeast Asia prioritize cooperation with wealthier or more powerful countries than with their neighbors. Despite her productivity, the consistency of her findings, her focus on Southeast Asia, and her prominence among students of regionalism generally, Solingen's work has attracted surprisingly little attention from students of ASEAN.

A second approach to domestic politics orients the scholarship of prominent constructivists. Chief among this group is Amitav Acharya, who has devoted more attention than anyone else to the origins of regionalism in Southeast Asia. He has pointed to a "nexus between authoritarianism and the origins of ASEAN." In his view, "a collective retreat from ... liberal democracy was a key factor contributing to ASEAN's formation and consolidation."[11] That retreat was followed by a "return to more 'indigenous' conceptions of authority ... [which] shaped the conduct of foreign policy and regional co-operation, [and] led to the emergence of the 'ASEAN Way'"[12]—the norms of sovereignty, cooperation, and consensus that the Association has endorsed and fostered.

Constructivists also have argued that the more recent rise of democracy has begun to reshape regionalism, and especially its normative content. Acharya has acknowledged that transitions to democracy in Cambodia, Indonesia, the Philippines, and Thailand did not trigger deliberate efforts to undermine "state-centric regionalism."[13] In his view, however, democratization in some ASEAN countries has "altered the political climate of regional interactions," "disrupted the traditional pattern of elite socialization," and "induced ... growing criticism and rejection of the 'ASEAN Way.'"[14] Likewise, Jürgen Haacke has attributed

---

[9] Solingen, "ASEAN Cooperation: The Legacy of the Economic Crisis," 25.

[10] Solingen, "ASEAN Cooperation: The Legacy of the Economic Crisis," 2.

[11] Amitav Acharya, "Democratisation and the Prospects for Participatory Regionalism in Southeast Asia," *Third World Quarterly* 24, no. 2 (2003), 378.

[12] Acharya, "Democratisation and the Prospects for Participatory Regionalism," 379.

[13] Acharya, "Democratisation and the Prospects for Participatory Regionalism," 380.

[14] Acharya, "Democratisation and the Prospects for Participatory Regionalism," 381.

ASEAN members' support for a policy of "enhanced interaction"[15] toward Myanmar (Burma)—a step that implied a weakening of the regional norm against interfering in each other's internal affairs—partly to these members' increasing identification with democratic norms.

Unlike realists, constructivists have willingly accepted the idea that democratization inside some ASEAN member countries has influenced relations among them. But they have acknowledged such influence only to a limited extent, and mainly indirectly, through the growth of a more liberal international ethos or climate of elite opinion. Oddly enough, constructivists have not examined the impact of regime change on foreign policy or other mechanisms through which domestic politics affects regional outcomes. In the following sections, I show how domestic political economy concerns are motivating the nuclear energy policies of major Southeast Asian countries, and how such concerns tend to discourage the same countries from relying on ASEAN institutions to address the safety and security implications of their nuclear plans.

Going Nuclear: Domestic Demand and Regional Concern

Just as rapid increases in the price of oil sparked widespread interest in nuclear energy in the 1970s, the recent and sustained rise in oil prices during the 2000s has encouraged electricity providers throughout the world to look more closely at nuclear power. But the current expansion of civilian nuclear capabilities is occurring amid heightened fear that these trends may contribute to the proliferation of nuclear weapons.[16] Such concern reflects actual experiences, not hypothetical possibilities. In particular, the discoveries since 1990 of Iraq's clandestine nuclear weapons program and A. Q. Khan's black market in nuclear technology have highlighted critical weaknesses in the international nonproliferation regime. This section examines the origins of Southeast Asian countries' growing interest in nuclear energy, and highlights some of the principal security concerns that the development of nuclear industries is likely to present.

Indonesia still exports oil and natural gas. But its reserves are dwindling, and oil production has fallen from a high of 1.4 million barrels per day in 2000 to fewer than 900,000 barrels per day as of mid-2007, the lowest level in thirty-five years. Indeed, since 2003 Indonesia has been a net importer of oil and is unable to fill the quota of 1.45 million barrels per day to which it is entitled as a member—the only Asian member—of the Organization of Petroleum

---

[15] Jürgen Haacke, "'Enhanced Interaction' with Myanmar and the Project of a Security Community: Is ASEAN Refining or Breaking with Its Diplomatic and Security Culture?" *Contemporary Southeast Asia* 27, no. 2 (2005), 210.

[16] See Lee Feinstein and Anne-Marie Slaughter, "A Duty to Prevent," *Foreign Affairs* 83, no. 1 (January/February 2004), 135–50; and Jon B. Wolfsthal, "The Next Nuclear Wave," *Foreign Affairs* 84, no. 1 (January/February 2005), 49–60.

Exporting Countries (OPEC).[17] More importantly, increasing reliance on oil imports means that the government must spend heavily on subsidies to keep domestic prices low. Even after cutting these subsidies enough to double fuel prices in 2005, the government still expected to spend more than US $7 billion annually to cushion consumers from further price rises—an amount equal to twice its projected budget deficit.[18]

The government responded to this challenge by reviving a plan developed in the 1990s to build a nuclear power industry. In 2004, with South Korean assistance, it "began a three-year feasibility study on the future for nuclear power" that envisioned a complex of six reactors, each able to generate 1,000 megawatts.[19]

In 2006 the government intensified its push to develop nuclear power. In January the president signed a decision on national energy policy that called for a mixture of "new energies," including nuclear and biomass, to contribute 5 percent of Indonesian energy consumption by 2025.[20] Later that year, the government released a "grand design" for nuclear power development, calling for "the construction of four nuclear power plants starting in 2007" and scheduled for completion in 2016.[21]

International assistance is essential to these plans. The minister of research and technology said he expected a "foreign country to come to Indonesia with the nuclear technology and needed funds," while Indonesia would "provide the site." He added that countries with the necessary technology and expertise, such as South Korea and Japan, were more likely than Iran to invest in Indonesia's nuclear energy market.[22] In July 2007, Indonesian and South Korean companies signed a preliminary agreement to construct Indonesia's first nuclear power

---

[17] Reuters, "Indonesia to Offer New Oil Exploration Blocks," 15 August 2006. See also Hadi Soesastro and Raymond Atje, "Survey of Recent Developments," *Bulletin of Indonesian Economic Studies* 41, no. 1 (April 2005), 5–34.

[18] Reuters, "Indonesia Says to Up '07 Budget Oil Price to $65/bbl," 15 August 2006; and "Indonesia President Forecasts H2 Pick Up in Economy," 16 August 2006.

[19] See Shawn Donnan, "Indonesia Looks at Stalled Plans for N-Plan," *Financial Times*, 11 February 2004, 2; and Michael Richardson, "If Oil-Crunched Indonesia Goes Nuclear ...," *Straits Times*, 4 June 2004.

[20] The full text of the decision is available, in Indonesian, on the presidential website, <http://www.presidensby.info/DokumenUU.php/81.pdf>.

[21] "RI Exploring Possibility of Cooperating with US to Build Nuclear Power Plant," Antara [Jakarta], 15 July 2006, <http://www.antara.co.id/en/seenws/?id=16372>.

[22] "RI Could Have Nuclear Power Plant in Five Years Time: Minister," Antara, 27 June 2006, <http://www.antara.co.id/en/seenws/?id=15265>.

plant. They expect to complete construction of the 2,000-megawatt facility as early as 2016.[23]

In addition to nurturing these commercial relationships, Indonesia has taken care to fashion policies that are consistent with internationally recognized nuclear norms and practices. By supporting the Treaty on the Non-Proliferation of Nuclear Weapons (NPT) and adopting safeguards recommended by the International Atomic Energy Agency (IAEA), Indonesia has long cultivated a reputation in international circles as a responsible member of the world nuclear community. The significance of its reputation was illustrated in December 2006 when Mohamed ElBaradei, director general of the IAEA, visited Jakarta and praised Indonesia as "a strong and supportive partner of the IAEA." After describing the wide array of technical assistance that the agency had provided to Indonesia, he announced the IAEA's support for Jakarta's "decision to embark on a nuclear power programme."[24]

After Indonesia, Vietnam appears to have the strongest commitment to developing nuclear power. Indeed, until Indonesia accelerated its own plans in 2004, Vietnam was considered the "most likely economy" in the Asia-Pacific region "to become a new member of the community of economies with commercial nuclear power."[25] Although Vietnam exports as much as 40 percent of the energy resources it produces, it expects to become a net energy importer in 2015. The government began to address this concern as early as 1995, when it initiated a range of studies meant to lay the foundation for a nuclear power industry. By 2006 the authorities had identified three sites and approved the construction of two reactors that the country's Atomic Energy Commission expected to begin generating electricity in 2020.[26]

Like Indonesia, Vietnam recognizes that it must rely heavily on foreign support to develop nuclear power. Although it signed bilateral nuclear cooperation agreements with six countries as it accelerated its push for nuclear power between 2004 and 2006, Russia remains its chief partner.[27] The two countries have maintained a close relationship since the Soviet Union supplied Vietnam's first reactor in the 1970s. In addition, there are convincing indications that Vietnam shares Indonesia's strong commitment to international nuclear norms and practices and is seeking to comply with the standard safeguards

---

[23] "Indonesia, South Korea Sign Preliminary Deal to Develop Nuclear Power Plant," Associated Press, 25 July 2007; and "S. Korea Promotes Sale of Indigenous Nuclear Reactor to Indonesia," Yonhap, 25 July 2007.

[24] Mohamed ElBaradei, "Nuclear Power in a Changing World," statement delivered 8 December 2006, <http://www.iaea.org/NewsCenter/Statements/2006/ebsp2006n024.html>.

[25] Asia Pacific Energy Research Centre, *Nuclear Power Generation in the APEC Region* (Tokyo: Asia Pacific Energy Research Centre, Institute of Energy Economics, 2004), 191.

[26] See John Loizou, "Calculating the Costs of Nuclear Energy," *Viet Nam News*, 4 September 2006.

[27] "Seminar on Nuclear Power Held in Capital," *Viet Nam News*, 18 October 2006.

recommended by the IAEA. Indeed, during the same visit to Asia that brought him to Jakarta in late 2006, Mohamed ElBaradei stopped in Hanoi and offered similar praise and support for Vietnam's nuclear plans.[28] Vietnam also has cooperated with the United States and Russia to replace highly enriched, or bomb-grade, uranium in a research reactor with low-enriched uranium, as part of a global effort to keep the more dangerous material out of the hands of terrorists.[29]

Thailand has taken significant steps to revive a nuclear power development program that began in the 1960s but was never implemented because of public opposition in the mid-1970s and the economic crisis in the late 1990s.[30] As in Indonesia and Vietnam, interest in nuclear energy reflects a desire to reduce dependence on increasingly expensive and potentially unstable supplies of other fuels, mainly natural gas and oil. In April 2007, the military-run government in Bangkok approved a long-range power development plan that calls for nuclear energy to generate more than 10 percent of the country's electricity by 2021, and established a panel to supervise plans for the country's first nuclear power plant.[31] Later in 2007, the country's national energy policy council approved a plan that calls for studies to be conducted and legislation to be drafted during 2008–10 in order to create the scientific and legal basis for nuclear power.[32] Like Indonesia and Vietnam, Thailand enjoys the support of the IAEA.[33]

In the Philippines, during the presidency of Ferdinand Marcos in the 1970s and 1980s, a large nuclear power plant was constructed in Bataan but never used. Amid allegations of corruption and concern that the plant was located on geologically unsafe ground, it was mothballed in the late 1980s. Ironically, in mid-2007, just a few months after it finished repaying the debt Marcos had incurred to build the Bataan plant, the Philippine government announced it was considering reviving plans for nuclear power. The energy minister said he would seek the IAEA's assistance to determine whether the never-used plant could be put into operation. Like its Southeast Asian neighbors, the government was motivated by the rapid rise in the prices of other fuels, as well as a fear

---

[28] "IAEA Approves Six Projects for Vietnam as Chief Visits," *Viet Nam News*, 12 December 2006.

[29] Ralph Vartabedian, "A Race with the Terrorists," *Los Angeles Times*, 27 September 2007.

[30] Asia Pacific Energy Research Centre, *Nuclear Power Generation in the APEC Region*, 191.

[31] See Anchalee Kongrut, "Is Thailand Serious about Nuclear Energy?" *Bangkok Post*, 14 April 2007; and Yuthana Praiwan, "New Panel to Pave Way for Nuclear-Energy Acceptance," *Bangkok Post*, 23 April 2007.

[32] "Nuclear Power Scheme Backed," *The Nation* [Bangkok], 19 October 2007.

[33] Mohamed ElBaradei, "Nuclear Power: An Engine for Development," statement delivered in Bangkok, 16 July 2007, <http://www.iaea.org/NewsCenter/Statements/2007/ebsp2007n010.html>.

that power shortages would deter foreign investors and detract from economic growth.[34]

Malaysia has no plans to acquire its own nuclear power plant, but is taking steps that will strengthen its nuclear capabilities and may lead to the adoption of a nuclear power policy after 2010. As part of its 2006–10 economic development plan, Malaysia is conducting a review of energy sources that includes nuclear power.[35] Since it is able to rely on natural gas from its own fields, Malaysia feels less pressure than its neighbors to explore the nuclear alternative. However, it announced a plan in mid-2007 to establish a facility to monitor nuclear programs throughout Southeast Asia. According to Malaysia's foreign minister, the potentially significant increase in nuclear plants around the region created a need for such a facility. "I think people are worried," he said, because "even if you have nuclear energy for peaceful purposes it doesn't mean that your trouble is over," since nuclear problems have "transnational possibilities if anything goes wrong."[36]

One of the chief countries on the minister's mind may have been Myanmar. Its government is planning to develop a nuclear capacity, but on a much smaller scale than other ASEAN members and for reasons that are harder to discern. Since the mid-1990s, the Burmese junta has sought to create a program for nuclear energy research, even asking the IAEA for assistance in 1999. But since at least 2001, there have been persistent reports that the regime may be seeking nuclear technology for purposes that are not entirely peaceful, and that it may be doing so outside normal channels. Indeed, in 2001 the *Far Eastern Economic Review* reported that two Pakistani nuclear scientists, Suleiman Asad and Muhammed Ali Mukhtar, traveled to Myanmar after the United States sought to question them about their links to Osama bin Laden.[37] Two years later, the *Review* reported on an expanding military relationship between Myanmar and North Korea, noting that "North Korean technicians have been spotted by intelligence operatives unloading large crates and heavy construction

---

[34] Agence France-Presse, "Nuclear Power Plant Loan Finally Paid," 13 June 2007; "Energy Chief Eyes Nuclear Plant," *Manila Standard*, 24 September 2007; and Michael Lim Ubac, "Arroyo Orders Study on Use of Nuclear Energy for Power," *The Inquirer*, 20 August 2007, <http://newsinfo.inquirer.net/breakingnews/nation/view_article.php?article_id=83681>.

[35] Mark Hibbs, "Malaysian Agencies Probing Potential for Nuclear Plants," *Nucleonics Week* 47, no. 38 (21 September 2006), 4.

[35] Roslina Mohamad, "ASEAN's 1st Nuclear Lab to Be Located in Rompin," *The Star* [Malaysia], 14 July 2007; and Bernama [Malaysian national news agency], "IAEA Happy with Malaysia's Proposed Nuke Plant," 18 July 2007.

[37] Bertil Lintner, "Burma Joins the Nuclear Club," *Far Eastern Economic Review*, 27 December 2001, 26.

equipment" at the railway station closest to the town where the government planned to build a nuclear research reactor.[38]

Ties between Myanmar and North Korea continue to warm, but observers are divided over the extent to which the Pyongyang regime is providing nuclear weapons assistance. An Australian press report in July 2006 bluntly claimed that "Burma's military junta has attempted to buy nuclear weapons technology from North Korea's rogue regime," and asserted that the United States "issued a heavy-handed warning to Burmese military dictator Than Shwe to cease and desist all such activities after discovering Rangoon's bid" for such technology in late 2005.[39] Other seasoned observers of Myanmar's military believe, however, that the two countries "are apparently only pursuing conventional arms sales and technology transfers."[40] In any event, in April 2007 the two countries agreed to restore diplomatic relations, which had been cut off in 1983 following the assassination, in Rangoon, of South Korean leaders by North Korean assailants.[41]

Despite Myanmar's warming ties with North Korea, Russia seems to be the preferred supplier of nuclear assistance to Rangoon. In May 2007 Russia's atomic energy agency, Rosatom, announced an agreement to build a nuclear research reactor in Myanmar.[42] This marked the culmination of a protracted and contentious series of negotiations, under way since 2000. The Burmese government first signed a contract with a Russian company in 2001 to supply the reactor, but the deal fell through in late 2003 because of Myanmar's inability to pay for it.[43] Since then, Myanmar's ability to pay for the reactor has grown in light of the discovery of natural gas reserves that may be among the largest

---

[38] Bertil Lintner and Shawn W. Crispin, "Dangerous Bedfellows," *Far Eastern Economic Review*, 20 November 2003, 22.

[39] The quotations are from Greg Sheridan, "Burma Seeks Nuclear Weapons Alliance with N Korea," *The Australian*, 5 July 2006, <http://www.theaustralian.news.com.au/story/0,20867,19689419-601,00.html>. See also Greg Sheridan, "Asia's Evil Empires," *The Australian*, 8 July 2006, <http://www.theaustralian.news.com.au/story/0,20867,19722214-601,00.html>.

[40] Bertil Lintner, "Myanmar and North Korea Share a Tunnel Vision," *Asia Times*, 19 July 2006, <http://www.atimes.com/atimes/Southeast_Asia/HG19Ae01.html>.

[41] Clifford McCoy, "Rogues of the World Unite," *Asia Times*, 28 April 2007, <http://www.atimes.com/atimes/Southeast_Asia/ID28Ae01.html>.

[42] Aung Hla Tun, "Is Myanmar Really After Nuclear Power?" Reuters, 16 May 2007.

[43] See William Ashton, "Burma's Nuclear Program: Dream or Nightmare?" *The Irrawaddy*, 1 May 2004, <http://www.irrawaddy.org/article.php?art_id=968>; and Andrew Selth, "Pariah Partners in Arms," *The Irrawaddy*, 1 March 2004, <http://www.irrawaddy.org/article.php?art_id=933>.

in Asia and could enable "the Burmese junta to earn as much as $3 billion annually."[44]

In sum, the largest countries in Southeast Asia have adopted policies to promote the development of nuclear energy. With the exception of Myanmar, their principal interest is to meet increasing domestic demand for electricity. Yet no country in the region can achieve its objectives without international cooperation. Even Indonesia, which has the most advanced nuclear research capacity in Southeast Asia, must rely on foreign partners and international institutions to attain its goals.

For the most part, as in so many other aspects of their economic development, these states stand to gain far more by cooperating with wealthier countries outside the region than through intra-ASEAN collaboration, and by working with existing, global institutions rather than creating their own regional ones. Apart from Myanmar, Southeast Asian nations are working closely with the IAEA. Unlike any ASEAN institution, the IAEA can provide technical assistance and regulatory standards. And compliance with those standards makes it possible for Southeast Asian countries to access the heavily regulated global nuclear markets essential to the success of their own nuclear plans. These advantages of extra-ASEAN cooperation need not weaken regionalism in Southeast Asia, but they are hardly likely to strengthen it either.

Nuclear Energy and Regional Cooperation

Despite their frequently professed goal of creating regional economic and security communities, Southeast Asian countries have shown little interest in working together either to develop nuclear energy or to guard against its potentially harmful consequences. To be sure, nuclear energy presents few opportunities for economic cooperation within ASEAN, since no member possesses the capital or expertise needed to construct and manage a nuclear power reactor. In this regard, each must rely on the support of more developed countries. But in the realm of safety and security, it is far from obvious that regional cooperation is either unwarranted or unattainable. As a former ASEAN secretary general emphasized in mid-2007, the mutual assurances that all members have offered one another in the past "become all the more important" as some members pursue their nuclear energy plans.[45]

The real puzzle is why Southeast Asian countries appear so reluctant to use the mechanisms they created a decade ago to assure one another that they will use nuclear energy safely. In the mid-1990s, ASEAN members negotiated

---

[44] Sunil Jagtiani, "India Looks to Burma to Slake Growing Thirst for Gas," *Christian Science Monitor*, 26 April 2006, 4.

[45] Rodolfo Severino, "Look Past the Headlines to What Matters," *The Straits Times* [Singapore], 23 July 2007.

the Treaty on the Southeast Asia Nuclear-Weapon-Free Zone (SEANWFZ).[46] Every member of the Association signed it, and in 1997 it came into force. In addition to the purpose stated in its title, the treaty includes several articles that are clearly relevant to developments described in the preceding section. Perhaps most important is Article 4, which governs the use of nuclear energy for peaceful purposes. Besides guaranteeing the right of the parties to the treaty to use nuclear energy for "economic development and social progress," it establishes two requirements: (1) that each member subject its nuclear program to a "rigorous nuclear safety assessment" in accordance with standards recommended by the IAEA *before* embarking on the program; and (2) that each party make that assessment available to the other parties.

Additional articles provide for a "control system" that requires adhering states to report "any significant event"—though this term is undefined—to an executive committee charged with overseeing the implementation of the treaty's provisions. The document also gives each party the right to seek clarification about "any situation which may be considered ambiguous or which may give rise to doubts" about any other participating state's compliance with the treaty's terms.

There is no indication that any ASEAN member on its own, or the executive committee established by the SEANWFZ Treaty, has ever invoked the agreement's provisions. Nor is there any public record that any ASEAN member has notified the executive committee of any "significant event," or taken any other steps to reassure fellow members that its own nuclear energy plans, already known to exist, are in accord with the treaty.

This is remarkable for several reasons. In the first place, it seems reasonable to expect that countries would take their treaty obligations seriously, particularly those that are consonant with the association's long-standing purpose of enhancing regional security and its more recent commitment to building a so-called ASEAN Community. When Russia announced in 2007 that it would provide Myanmar with a research reactor, the head of the IAEA told reporters that he had seen only press reports, not official plans.[47] Even if the SEANWFZ Treaty does not define "significant event," the decision to acquire a nuclear reactor surely qualified as one. And since the head of the IAEA himself was unaware of the plans, the event certainly called into question Myanmar's compliance with the treaty. Yet there was no indication that ASEAN or any of its members sought any clarification or exercised any other pertinent rights under the agreement.

Second, the sharply higher level of interest in nuclear power in 2007 coincided with an official review of the treaty's first decade. This review was mandated by the text itself, but resulted in only a brief statement by the countries' foreign ministers in July 2007, which made no reference at all to the widespread

---

[46] The text of the SEANWFZ Treaty is available at <http://www.aseansec.org/2082.htm>.
[47] Agence France-Presse, "IAEA Chief Unaware of Myanmar Plan," 18 July 2007.

and rapidly growing interest in nuclear energy among signatory states. Instead, the review noted simply that members had "abided by their responsibilities and obligations" and reiterated ASEAN's commitment to achieving the main purposes of SEANWFZ.[48] Equally notable is that the Association chose not to amend the treaty. Left aside, for instance, was any effort to clarify just what sort of "significant event" must be reported to the executive committee.

Third, ASEAN's only formal response to recent developments occurred at the Association's annual ministerial meeting a month after the release of the treaty review. The response came at the initiative of Singapore, a party with no nuclear plans of its own but substantial concerns about the safety and security of prospective nuclear plants in the region.[49] At their annual meeting in late August 2007, ASEAN's energy ministers agreed to Singapore's proposal to set up a Nuclear Energy Safety Subsector Network. However, this agreement was only "in-principle": the network would be just one of seven in ASEAN's energy bureaucracy, and the network would be asked only to "explore nuclear safety issues."[50] The energy ministers postponed final approval until their next annual meeting, when they expected a report from their senior officials on the proposed terms of reference and composition of the network. Remarkably, the ministers' statement made no reference at all to the SEANWFZ Treaty in general or to its provisions for nuclear safety in particular.

The reasons for such a limited and highly qualified agreement only emerged in the wake of the energy ministers' meeting. Speaking off the record to an industry newsletter on the sidelines of an IAEA meeting in Vienna, Southeast Asian diplomats described a sharp split within ASEAN.[51] Indonesia and Malaysia preferred to rely solely on a global nuclear regulatory framework under IAEA leadership, while Singapore and the Philippines sought to supplement that with a regional arrangement. But their differences involved more than a principled choice between globalism and regionalism. Singapore had discussed the possibility of gaining "leverage" over its neighbors' nuclear safety policies by integrating its electricity grid with theirs. And its neighbors were reluctant to permit ASEAN a role in nuclear regulation precisely because it would create an opportunity for Singapore to achieve such influence.

---

[48] The text of the "Joint Statement on the Commission for the Treaty on the Southeast Asia Nuclear-Weapon-Free Zone, Manila, 30 July 2007" is available at <http://www.aseansec.org/20775.htm>.

[49] See Matthew Phan, "ASEAN Needs Nuclear Safety Commission," *Business Times* [Singapore], 7 September 2007; and Kyodo News Agency, "ASEAN Energy Ministers Agree to Form Nuclear Safety Caucus," 23 August 2007.

[50] "Energising ASEAN to Power a Dynamic Asia," Joint Ministerial Statement of the 25th ASEAN Ministers on Energy Meeting, Singapore, 23 August 2007, <http://www.aseansec.org/20843.htm>.

[51] Mark Hibbs, "ASEAN Incursion into Nuclear Safety, Nonproliferation May Be Modest," *Nucleonics Week* 48, no. 40 (4 October 2007), 16.

This instance of ASEAN members' neglect of their own association contrasts sharply with their regard for global institutions, especially the IAEA. These states tend to favor more international cooperation than realists would predict, but not within Southeast Asia, contrary to what constructivist accounts of the strength of ASEAN norms would lead us to expect.

The evidence presented in this section and the preceding one demonstrates three points. First, only Singapore and the Philippines have shown a substantial interest in developing ASEAN institutions capable of addressing nuclear safety and security. Second, the more determined countries are to develop nuclear energy, the more they prefer to work through the IAEA. This is in line with a liberal view of international relations in the sense that countries with similar preferences tend to adopt similar positions. Third, the lack of cooperation among Southeast Asian countries reflects a difference in outlook between those that are seeking nuclear energy in the near term and those that are merely considering it, as well as a sense that a state hoping to generate nuclear power can gain more from working with a global institution such as the IAEA than from cooperating with regional neighbors to that end. ASEAN has little to offer members that want to acquire and operate nuclear power reactors. The IAEA has much. As in most liberal accounts, institutions facilitate cooperation. But in this case, the most important institutions are not to be found in Southeast Asia.

Even if some ASEAN members prefer, as a matter of principle, to rely on global rather than regional regulatory frameworks, they have a spotty record of actually ratifying key nuclear security agreements.[52] The most important of these is the "additional protocol" introduced by the IAEA in the late 1990s to close a loophole in the NPT that Iraq and North Korea had exploited in order secretly to develop nuclear weapons. This protocol permits more intrusive monitoring of the nuclear programs of NPT signatories and makes it less likely that civilian programs can be diverted for military purposes. Yet in Southeast Asia as of early 2008, such a protocol was in force only in Indonesia, even though most countries had signed one. Similarly, the IAEA's Convention on Nuclear Safety was in force only in Indonesia and Singapore. And although by then all Southeast Asian states had signed the Comprehensive Test Ban Treaty, it still had not been ratified by Myanmar, Indonesia, or Thailand.[53]

---

[52] See Tanya Ogilvie-White, "Non-proliferation and Counterterrorism Cooperation in Southeast Asia: Meeting Global Obligations through Regional Security Architectures?" *Contemporary Southeast Asia* 28, no. 1 (April 2006), 1–26.

[53] See "Status of Additional Protocols," <http://www.iaea.org/OurWork/SV/Safeguards/sg_protocol.html> (data current as of 22 January 2008); "Convention on Nuclear Safety," <http://www-ns.iaea.org/conventions/nuclear-safety.htm> (data as of 15 November 2007); and the "Status of Signature and Ratification," <http://www.ctbto.org/> (data as of 29 February 2008).

Democracy's Impact on Nuclear Energy and Regional Cooperation

By international standards, Indonesia and the Philippines were the only democracies in Southeast Asia during 2007. But if more Southeast Asian governments became democratic, would they expand ASEAN's role in regulating the safety and security of nuclear energy? Frankly, this seems unlikely. After all, democratic Indonesia is the strongest advocate of handling nuclear matters at the global level, while illiberal Singapore is the main proponent of creating regional institutions to manage them.

Another possibility is that the widespread emergence of democracy across the region would foster regional integration among nationally organized civil society associations. But this assumes that such organizations would view regional mobilization as more effective than either strengthening national networks or forging links with international partners. The record is not promising. For a brief time during the late 1990s and early 2000s, when democracy still appeared to be strengthening in Southeast Asia, the potential for domestic political change to transform relations among Southeast Asian states did stimulate interest in the possible development of "participatory regionalism," as suggested by the formation of an ASEAN People's Assembly (APA) to complement the Association's elite-dominated institutions.[54] Little has become of the APA, however, and it certainly has not influenced the debate on nuclear energy.

In order for democracy to encourage Southeast Asian countries to promote regional solutions to nuclear problems, the people empowered by democracy would have to urge such a policy on their governments. But as of 2007 there was little sign that the public in any ASEAN member country was advocating such an approach. And unless democracy were to become widespread and such demands were to represent a Southeast Asian consensus, regionalism could be weakened, or at least not strengthened. After all, when Indonesia, Thailand, and the Philippines were democratic in the late 1990s and early 2000s, their efforts to inject concern for liberal notions of human rights into ASEAN created friction with other members. That experience may not have undermined regionalism, but it did not enhance it, let alone transform it along democratic lines.

The lack of democracy in Southeast Asia makes it difficult to identify precisely its impact on either nuclear policy or regionalism. However, Indonesia affords a rich illustration of the two-way dynamics between domestic politics and foreign relations that can develop around these issues. In particular, Indonesia's experience demonstrates democracy's potential to disrupt well-established notions of the national interest and to reorient foreign policy toward parts of the world far beyond Southeast Asia. In this case, although both legislative and executive leaders were inclined to support nuclear energy, they favored

---

[54] Mely Caballero-Anthony. "Non-State Regional Governance Mechanism for Economic Security: The Case of the ASEAN Peoples' Assembly," *Pacific Review* 17, no. 4 (2004), 567–85; and Acharya, "Democratisation and the Prospects for Participatory Regionalism in Southeast Asia," 375–90.

conflicting foreign policy positions—a conflict with implications not only for the success or failure of the nuclear energy initiative itself, but also for the nature and effectiveness of Southeast Asian regionalism.

Indonesia was the only country in Southeast Asia rated by Freedom House in 2007 as "Free."[55] Policymakers in Jakarta had to contend with a wide array of opponents. Not surprisingly, some of the country's most important nongovernmental organizations (NGOs) were campaigning against the development of nuclear energy. The largest environmental group, the Indonesian Forum for Environment (WALHI), was mobilizing to oppose the construction of a nuclear power plant. The largest religious group, Nahdlatul Ulama (NU), with tens of millions of members including many living near the proposed plant's location, asked the government to reconsider its plan.[56] WALHI's leader even denounced the project as potential "genocide."[57] These groups were concerned not only about the risks of nuclear energy, but also about the country's general inability to manage public infrastructure safely, as well as the threat posed by frequent earthquakes and volcanic eruptions.

Such fears are well grounded. In 2007, hundreds died in ferry accidents, and two fatal air crashes prompted the European Union and the United States to ban all Indonesian airlines from their skies. In addition to the well-known tsunami that killed more than 160,000 Indonesians in late 2004, serious earthquakes have struck Java, the densely populated island on which the government plans to construct its first nuclear power plant. In 2006, one of those quakes killed more than five thousand people, and the other damaged an oil refinery seriously enough that it had to be shut down temporarily.

Anti-nuclear groups in Indonesia are finding sympathy among highly placed politicians. In 2007 a former president, who also led NU, suggested that the Java plant project be abandoned. And leading politicians from each of the major political parties turned up for an independence day celebration-cum-antinuclear protest in the village most likely to be the site of the plant.[58]

---

[55] See Freedom House, "Freedom in the World Country Rankings, 1972–2006, <http://www.freedomhouse.org/uploads/fiw/FIWAllScores.xls>.

[56] Information about WALHI's campaign can be viewed at <http://www.walhi.or.id/kampanye/energi/pltn/>. On NU's opposition, see "NU Minta Pemerintah Kaji Ulang PLTN Muria," *Suara Merdeka*, 14 July 2007, <http://www.suaramerdeka.com/harian/0707/14/mur06.htm>.

[57] "PLTN di Muria Musnahkan Etnik," Jawa Pos, 5 April 2007, <http://www.jawapos.co.id/index.php?act=detail_c&id=279238>; and Ian MacKinnon, "Javans Fired Up over Reactor Next to Volcano," *The Guardian*, 5 April 2007, <http://www.guardian.co.uk/world/2007/apr/05/indonesia.international>.

[58] "Gus Dur: If Still Full of Doubt, No Need to Build a Nuclear Power Plant," Antara, 13 July 2007, <http://www.antara.co.id/en/arc/2007/7/13/gus-dur-if-still-full-of-doubt-no-need-to-build-a-nuclear-power-plant>; and "Upacara Bendera Masyarakat Balong Tolak PLTN," *Tempointeraktif*, 17 August 2007, <http://www.tempointeraktif.com/hg/nusa/jawamadura/2007/08/17/brk,20070817-105785,id.html>.

However, as of 2007, these groups had not forged alliances with similar groups in other Southeast Asian countries.

Democratization has also encouraged civil society groups and elected officials to shape the discussion of issues directly concerned with nuclear weapons proliferation. Traditionally, such issues were under the tight control of the foreign ministry and rarely a subject of public discussion. But since 2005 Indonesian politicians have been drawn into a sharp debate over the nature of the nuclear program being pursued by the government of Iran.

Although this debate has only rarely been linked to Indonesia's own efforts to develop a nuclear power industry, it raises questions about how that industry might be managed in the future. In particular, it suggests that domestic political coalitions exist that do not share Indonesia's long-standing commitments to international nuclear norms and practices. While they explicitly oppose nuclear proliferation, they are sympathetic to Iran, which they perceive as being treated unfairly by stronger, mainly Western states.

In 2004, as international pressure mounted regarding its nuclear intentions, Tehran began a diplomatic offensive meant to secure Indonesian support at the IAEA, where Indonesia held a seat on the board of governors. Indonesia's government was reluctant to side with Iran in the latter's dispute with the IAEA. On the one hand, Jakarta's plan to create its own nuclear power industry inclined it to defend vigorously all countries' right to put nuclear energy to peaceful use. On the other hand, its long-standing support for international nuclear norms and practices and its immediate need for international support to advance its national plans for nuclear energy discouraged Indonesia from taking steps that appeared to align it with Iran.

Indonesian officials enunciated this position frequently, clearly, and publicly. Most notable, however, was a speech delivered by a high-ranking foreign ministry official at a public seminar held by the Indonesian Academy of Sciences in April 2005 to discuss the topic of "Indonesia and Iran's Nuclear Issue." The key speakers were, in addition to the Iranian and Russian ambassadors to Indonesia, the secretary general of Indonesia's Department of Foreign Affairs, who also happened to have chaired one of the three "main committees" at the 2005 NPT review conference. In his speech, the Indonesian representative repeated his own country's long-held positions in favor of the peaceful use of nuclear energy and against nuclear proliferation, reviewed the history of Iran's commitments to the IAEA and its failure to meet them, and said that signing the additional protocol and cooperating with the IAEA constituted "the only way" for Iran to "address the doubt" that its actions "may have created."[59]

In response to the resistance it met in Indonesia's executive branch, Iran sought support from Indonesian legislators and civil society leaders. Its first step was an aggressive one: It invited the speaker of Indonesia's House of

---

[59] Sudjanan Parnohadiningrat, "Indonesia and Iran's Nuclear Issue," in *Indonesia and Iran's Nuclear Issue*, ed. Indriana Kartini (Jakarta: LIPI Press, 2005), 6.

Representatives and other legislative leaders to visit their counterparts in Tehran on dates that coincided with the February 2006 meeting of the IAEA board of governors, which would vote to refer Iran to the UN Security Council (UNSC). During that visit, legislators from across Indonesia's political spectrum toured nuclear facilities in Isfahan. Afterward, according to Indonesia's official news agency, Antara, they "concluded that the Iranian nuclear power programme was for peaceful purposes. There was no possibility for Iran to develop the facility into a nuclear weapon programme."[60] Moreover, upon returning to Jakarta they criticized the Indonesian foreign minister's decision to abstain from voting in the IAEA board on the resolution to refer Iran to the UNSC rather than side with the small minority of three countries that had opposed the resolution.[61]

Subsequently, senior Indonesian legislative and civil society leaders continued to take positions that favored Iran and opposed the policy of their own government. During a summit meeting of developing countries that Indonesia hosted in May 2006, Iranian President Mahmoud Ahmadinejad failed to win support from his hosts. As if to emphasize that Jakarta did not accept Tehran's assertion that its program was devoted entirely to peaceful purposes, Indonesia's foreign minister commented that his government wanted Iran "to be more transparent in its programme."[62] In contrast, the speaker of Indonesia's House of Representatives was considerably less cautious. He and his legislative colleagues offered Ahmedinejad a reception far warmer than the one extended by Indonesia's president and foreign minister. And in August, while hosting an Iranian legislative delegation, the House speaker endorsed cooperation with Iran on nuclear enrichment—precisely the issue that had been at stake in the IAEA vote in February 2006.[63]

In early 2007, legislative-executive tensions again worsened over the question of whether to support or oppose sanctions against Iran. This time the international consensus was stronger, but divisions within Indonesia were deeper and the impact on its domestic politics more serious. At the start of the year, Indonesia assumed a nonpermanent seat on the UNSC and almost immediately was confronted with the need to take a stand on Iran's nuclear

[60] Antara, "Indonesian Legislators Observe Iranian Nuclear Power Plant," 9 February 2006.

[61] Antara, "MPs Regret Indonesia's Abstain [sic] on Iranian Nuclear Issue," 15 February 2006.

[62] See "Officials Set Agenda for Weekend D-8 Summit on Bali," *The Jakarta Post*, 10 May 2006; and Tomi Soetjipto and Muklis Ali, "Iran President Says West Nuclear Concern a 'Big Lie,'" Reuters, 10 May 2006. The foreign minister is quoted in Shawn Donnan and Gareth Smyth, "Tehran Searches for Allies in Muslim World," *Financial Times*, 10 May 2006.

[63] "RI Should Cooperate with Iran on Nuclear Projects: House Speaker," *Jakarta Post*, 28 August 2006; and "Indonesia Bisa Bekerja Sama dengan Iran," *Kompas*, 28 August 2006.

program. Dissatisfied with Tehran's response to a resolution (1737) that the Council had adopted in late 2006, several countries sought a new one that would widen sanctions. Ironically, this resolution was the result of the process that Indonesia had tried to sidestep a year earlier by abstaining from the vote at the IAEA meeting. This time, Jakarta joined a unanimous vote in favor of the resolution, after securing modest changes to mollify its domestic opponents, some of whom had hosted Iranian delegations over the preceding weeks.[64]

Back in Indonesia, leading political, academic, and religious figures denounced their government's vote as a sign of its weakness and willingness to align with the United States and Israel.[65] Within weeks, a majority of legislators, drawn from all parties except that of the president, had signed a petition to employ a rarely used constitutional right to compel the executive branch to submit to formal questioning. For several months the two sides vigorously debated each branch's constitutional rights and the country's foreign policy priorities. They agreed that the government should oppose nuclear proliferation and support nuclear disarmament. But legislators were more inclined to take positions they expected to be popular with voters. And since vastly more Indonesians held favorable views of Iran than of the United States, the legislators were willing to discount both the risks that Iran's nuclear activity posed and the value of upholding international nuclear norms.

This controversy demonstrates two key points about the potential impact of democratization on regionalism and nuclear energy policy in Southeast Asia. The first is that, contrary to many predictions in the late 1990s, democratization at the national level need not move regionalism in a more participatory direction. The policy priorities of democratically elected national leaders may differ markedly from those of ASEAN. If the discrepancy is great, democracy could have a highly disruptive impact on regionalism generally, and on ASEAN's nuclear policy in particular.

The second point is that Indonesia's foreign affairs bureaucracy has been highly durable, and able thus far to sustain the country's main foreign policy commitments. Throughout Southeast Asia, foreign policy has been more insulated from social pressure than from other issues, such as agriculture or education. In most other ASEAN capitals, the agencies responsible for foreign affairs tend to be just as well institutionalized as they are in Jakarta. Hence, as in Indonesia, their national policies on nuclear energy are likely to endure, resisting public pressure without being impervious to it.

---

[64] Abdul Khalik, "Muhammadiyah Backs Iran's Nuclear Program," *Jakarta Post*, 9 February 2007; and Abdillah Toha, "No Real Evidence of Iran's Launch of Nuclear Weapons Development," *Jakarta Post*, 6 March 2007.

[65] "Sikap RI atas Iran Menuai Kecaman," *Pikiran Rakyat*, 27 March 2007; and "Hassan Wirajuda Dicecar DPR," *Koran Tempo*, 30 March 2007.

Conclusion

During the first four decades of the Association, ASEAN members *agreed* to cooperate more often than they actually cooperated. Some say that they implemented only about 30 percent of their commitments.[66] In the realm of nuclear energy and nuclear weapons, the percentage appears even lower. The states that have nuclear weapons, especially the United States, do not adhere to the SEANWFZ Treaty, and ASEAN members have made no public efforts to indicate that their peaceful use of nuclear energy complies with its terms.

In the past, the absence of cooperation in these areas did not reflect a core weakness in ASEAN institutions, since members' nuclear capabilities were very low and the great powers' nuclear weapons were not aimed at Southeast Asia. Yet as countries intensify their efforts to develop nuclear power industries, their lack of cooperation with each other will acquire more significance for the future of regionalism. That lack suggests that the Association is peripheral to one of the most important sets of issues on the region's horizon.

The reasons for this have little to do either with the weakness of ASEAN norms or the insecurity of members vis-à-vis each other, although such norms are weak and mutual suspicions are common. Instead, I have argued, members find non-ASEAN institutions to be a more effective means through which to achieve their own, domestically motivated goals. And democracy seems unlikely to reverse this course.

The absence or weakness of cooperation does not imply a corresponding rise in conflict. Members may choose simply to coexist. But coexistence is not a recipe for sustaining regionalism, let alone strengthening it. That can be done only by cooperating in the more conventional sense of formulating, pursuing, and implementing common policies to address significant shared challenges. ASEAN has not risen to the nuclear occasion.

---

[66] Tommy Koh, Walter Woon, Andrew Tan, and Chan Sze-Wei, "The ASEAN Charter," *PacNet*, no. 33A (6 September 2007).

ARGUMENTS

TOWARD RELATIVE DECENCY:
THE CASE FOR PRUDENCE

David Martin Jones
University of Queensland
Australia

In Europe in the eighteenth century, proponents of the Enlightenment argued that external and internal security were ineluctably linked to rational progress toward a universal condition of democratic pluralism. That linkage of security and democracy was both the fondest dream and a notable legacy of the Enlightenment project. In Southeast Asia in the twenty-first century, that project has resurfaced in the effort by the Association of Southeast Asian Nations (ASEAN) to acquire a legal persona by basing itself, for the first time, on a Charter.

This democracy-security nexus dates from Immanuel Kant's eschatological hope for universal and perpetual peace, founded on a *foedus pacificum*, or league of peace—a confederation of constitutional regimes.[1] Central to this understanding is a teleology that assumes a progressive global movement toward a reasonable, rule-governed, international order founded on universally agreed norms, rather than on the dictates of state interest, culture, power, or self.

This hope informs Francis Fukuyama's influential post-Cold War treatise on "the end of history."[2] It also represents the methodological premise of journals devoted to the study of democracy and democratization, and illustrates contemporary normative and constructivist views of the evolving character of international society. In its most philosophically coherent post-Cold War formulation, John Rawls maintained, in *The Law of Peoples*, that any hope we have of reaching this benign historical terminus—what he called a realistic utopia—rests "on there being reasonable liberal and constitutional (and decent) regimes sufficiently established and effective to yield a viable Society of Peoples."[3] Those living in such a society would, in this conception, "follow the ideals and principles of the Law of Peoples in their mutual relations."[4]

---

[1] Immanuel Kant, "Perpetual Peace," *Political Writings* (Cambridge: Cambridge University Press, 1976 [1795]).

[2] Francis Fukuyama, *The End of History and the Last Man* (New York: Free Press, 1992).

[3] John Rawls, *The Law of Peoples* (London: Harvard University Press, 2002), 30.

[4] Rawls, *Law*, 3.

In Rawls' scheme, the prospect for both global and, in the Southeast Asian context featured here, regional peace and progress requires the projection of a "Law of Peoples," or more precisely a norm of justice as fairness, into the international order. This norm should shape both the conduct of states and regions as the latter have evolved as postnational constellations in the years since Europe's Treaty of Rome in 1957.

Rawls maintained that a just Society of Peoples would include not only constitutionally democratic regimes, but also what he termed "decent" hierarchical regimes of a nonliberal character. Such a political formula, linking democracy, security, economic development, and justice, would seem, superficially, to suit the ASEAN case. Significantly, Rawls distinguished decent regimes from outlaw states that routinely violate human rights—"burdened societies" suffering from either inadequate resources or political culture—and benevolent absolutisms. Decent regimes, Rawls argued, would tolerate a reasonable, associationist form of political life where people "are viewed in public life as members of different groups, and each group is represented in the legal system by a body in a decent consultation hierarchy."[5] Such a form of association, although possessing a comprehensive and nonnegotiable religious or political doctrine, would nonetheless respect the social and political order of different societies. It would have no aggressive aims, and its system of law would secure for all of its members "what have come to be known as human rights."[6]

In order to explore further the conditions of this nonliberal but just regime, Rawls hypothesized a model Muslim state, which he called "Kazanistan." Legitimate authority in Kazanistan brooks no separation of church and state, and only Muslims can hold the reins of political authority and influence. This evidently nonliberal arrangement, nevertheless, tolerates and encourages other religions and cultures, and includes a mechanism to consult all groups in the Islamic polity. In Rawls' formulation, such a regime would, like its liberal constitutional counterpart, accept a reasonable pluralism in its foreign relations and endorse a principle of reciprocity that would tolerate different domestic political and religious practices.

From this perspective, endorsing reasonable pluralism is the sine qua non for a universal and achievable Law of Peoples. Such a law would support and promulgate eight principles, among them the following: Peoples are free and independent and their independence must be respected. Peoples are equals and have a duty to observe nonintervention. Peoples have a right to self-defense, but also have a duty "to assist other people living under unfavorable conditions" and "must 'honor human rights.'"[7]

---

[5] Rawls, *Law*, 64.

[6] Rawls, *Law*, 65.

[7] The full list also specifies that peoples are to observe treaties and undertakings, as well as certain specified restrictions on the conduct of war. See Rawls, *Law*, 35–38.

In Rawls' view, constitutional democracies secure democratic peace and go to war only "with unsatisfied societies or outlaw states."[8] Rawls' realistic utopia does not necessarily require the triumph of a liberal-democratic end of history. Viewed through the Law of Peoples, stability is achieved by decent as well as democratic societies and "for the right reasons."

The "right reasons" informing a just Society of Peoples, moreover, contrast dramatically with a realist understanding of sovereignty and the primacy of state interest. The instrumental reason of the state, including its concern for its own power and national interest, is discounted by those who portray postnational constellations as a form of postmodern inclusivity.[9] For Rawls, recalibrating the international or regional order means "we must formulate the powers of sovereignty in light of a reasonable Law of Peoples and deny to states the traditional rights to . . . unrestricted autonomy."[10]

This perspective "accords with a recent dramatic shift in how many would like international law to be understood. Since World War II, international law has become stricter. It tends to limit a state's right to wage war to instances of self-defense . . . and it also tends restrict a state's right to internal sovereignty. The role of human rights connects most obviously with the latter change as part of the effort to provide a suitable definition and limit on a government's internal sovereignty."[11] The seductive promise that Rawls offers is that, if people are taken as they are and laws as they might be, a just, cosmopolitan, and peaceful world order can become a realistic eschatological hope. Nor is this hope confined geographically to Western democracies. It embraces decent associationist, nonliberal societies as well. Indeed, it could plausibly apply to an arrangement, such as ASEAN, that possesses both a "decent consultation hierarchy" and respects "the social and political order of different societies."

Rawls also insists, however, that a just international law promotes a society of peoples, not states. Liberal or decent peoples limit their interests according to principles that are reasonable and reciprocal. In this they differ in "character" from states that pursue their own interests, however prudently or rationally[12] Rawls' disdain for state sovereignty sits uneasily with ASEAN's origin and development. It ignores the central issue that political realists from Aristotle

---

[8] Rawls, *Law*, 48.

[9] Those who advocate some redistributive or postnational condition would include Jürgen Habermas, "What Holds Europeans Together," in Habermas and Jacques Derrida, *Old Europe, New Europe, Core Europe* (London: Verso, 2005); Thomas Pogge, *Global Institutions and Responsibilities Achieving Global Justice* (Malden, MA: Blackwell, 2006); David Held, *Global Covenant: The Social Democratic Alternative to the Washington Consensus* (Cambridge: Polity 2004); and Charles Beitz, *Political Theory and International Relations* (Princeton, NJ: Princeton University Press, 1999).

[10] Rawls, *Law*, 27.

[11] Rawls, *Law*, 27.

[12] Rawls, *Law*, 27–29.

through Machiavelli to Leo Strauss have raised, namely that statecraft actually demands a prudential awareness not only of what is the most just regime but also of what might only be the best regime achievable in the circumstances. It is precisely this prudential, pragmatic approach to institutional design that has informed the evolution of ASEAN.

In light of what a just, pluralist, and stable order in Southeast Asia entails, one must evaluate recent attempts to reform ASEAN along the lines of an integrated, and increasingly democratic, economic, security, and cultural community. We turn first to this issue, and subsequently consider why public reasoning about a realistic utopia—one that would put democracy promotion before the prudent pursuit of deeper economic integration—might damage rather than enhance ASEAN's development.

ASEAN à la Rawls: A Risky Wish?

In the wake of fallout from the Asian financial crisis (AFC), ASEAN launched a number of initiatives to enhance the region's security and growth and to project best managerial practice and norms of good international citizenship on a wider scale. A case in point was the ASEAN Plus Three mechanism, meant to involve China, Japan, and South Korea in a wider East Asian Community. A series of visions and roadmaps announced at ASEAN meetings were central to this process. After 1997, ASEAN summits agreed to a plethora of plans and protocols designed both to increase Southeast Asian integration and establish a wider regional leadership role for the organization.[13] The resulting documents ranged from relatively technical, sectoral protocols to declarations that developed and refined the Association's character, most notably the Declaration of ASEAN Concord II (or Bali Concord II), which established a framework to achieve an integrated ASEAN Community built on the pillars of economic, security, and sociocultural cooperation and integration. Other framework agreements, such as those that established an ASEAN Investment Area (1998) and an ASEAN Development Fund (2005), were meant to give financial substance to the Association's Vision 2020, which was announced at the informal Kuala Lumpur Summit in 1997.[14] A subsequent Hanoi Plan of Action and Vientiane Action Program were launched to strengthen macroeconomic and financial cooperation, enhance economic integration, and promote the development of science and technology in Southeast Asia. Since 1997, the ASEAN process has also established a structure governing ASEAN's external trade through framework agreements

---

[13] The *Table of ASEAN Treaties/Agreements and Ratifications* as of July 2005 reveals that, of the 138 agreements, declarations, memorandums of understanding, protocols, and treaties governing inter-ASEAN conduct or made between the organization and states external to it, 99 have been codified, ratified, or declared since 1997. See <http://www.aseansec.org/Ratification/pdf>.

[14] The Vision sought "to enhance economic cooperation through economic development strategies." See <http://www.aseansec.org/1814.htm>.

for economic partnerships with Japan (2003) and India (2003), and a Strategic Partnership for Peace and Prosperity with China (2004).

Even more ambitiously, at ASEAN's 2005 summit in Kuala Lumpur, Southeast Asian leaders declared their intention to create a Charter for the Association—a "crowning achievement" to be completed by the group's fortieth birthday, in 2007.[15] On schedule in Singapore in November 2007, the heads of the member governments signed the ASEAN Charter. Once all ten ASEAN states have ratified the Charter, it will come into effect. For the first time, under the Charter's terms, ASEAN will acquire a legal personality of its own—an organizational identity separable from the identities of its individual member states.

On the one hand, if ratified, the Charter would simply recast in legal form what ASEAN has already become. The Charter restates principles, goals, and ideals already contained in previous ASEAN agreements, including the foundational ASEAN Declaration (1967) and the Treaty of Amity and Cooperation (1976), and revalidates these and all of ASEAN's other prior commitments.

Yet the Charter is more than a reassertion. In addition to reendorsing regional cooperation, member consensus, national sovereignty, and other mainstays of ASEAN rhetoric, the Charter lists a novel goal among the organization's purposes: "to strengthen democracy, enhance good governance and the rule of law, and to promote and protect human rights and fundamental freedoms...."[16]

Although an earlier Cebu Declaration on the Blueprint of an ASEAN Charter (2006) used even more adventurous language, the Charter did call, in effect, for regional transformation. The Charter describes itself as the "legal and institutional framework" for the "promotion and protection of human rights and fundamental freedoms," and commits the Association to establishing a "human rights body."[17] According to such language, and the bold agenda it implies, the Charter echoes the more detailed recommendations promulgated in *The Report of the Eminent Persons Group* [EPG] *on the ASEAN Charter*, published in December 2006. The EPG Report underlined the fact that ASEAN's traditional principles and objectives had to be adapted to "the new realities confronting ASEAN."[18] Along Rawlsian lines, the EPG Report explicitly linked ASEAN's continuing peace and stability to "the active strengthening of democratic values, good governance, [and the] rejection of unconstitutional and undemocratic changes of government."[19] It therefore recommended that the new

---

[15] See <http://www.aseansec.org/18030.htm>.

[16] ASEAN Charter, Art. 1.7, <http://www.aseansec.org/21069.pdf>.

[17] Charter, Preamble and Articles 14.1, 14.2.

[18] *The Report of the Eminent Persons Group on the ASEAN Charter,* <http://www.aseansec.org/19247.pdf> p. 3.

[19] *Report of the Eminent Persons Group,* 3.

Charter include among ASEAN's principles and objectives "the strengthening of democratic values, ensuring good governance, upholding the rule of law, [and] respect for human rights and international humanitarian law."[20]

To facilitate ASEAN's transformation into a community of caring democratic societies that would meet the criteria of a just Society of Peoples, the EPG additionally proposed to modify ASEAN's procedural norm of nonbinding consensus. The EPG Report acknowledged that ASEAN's consensual style of decision-making had been helpful in reassuring member states that their sovereignty and national interests would not be compromised. But the EPG went on to argue that, although consensus should be tried first, failure to achieve it should not be allowed to block decisions and thereby "create an impasse in ASEAN cooperation." Consensus should "aid, but not impede, ASEAN's cohesion and effectiveness."[21]

Reiterating the point more forcefully in their conclusion, the EPG contended that "ASEAN must establish a culture of honouring and implementing its decisions and agreements, and carrying them out in time." Indeed, in the EPG's view, "ASEAN's problem is not one of lack of vision, ideas, and action plans. The real problem is one of ensuring compliance and effective implementation of decisions."[22] To address this long-standing weakness in ASEAN practice, the Charter announced, if somewhat uncertainly, an "enhanced dispute settlement mechanism" and "a formula for flexible participation" in the building of an ASEAN Economic Community.[23]

The Charter not only enhances ASEAN's institutional capacity. It also seeks to transvalue the norms that have long informed the Association's diplomatic practices, and thus to facilitate the eventual transformation of Southeast Asia's sovereign and heterogeneous states into a community governed by common rules. On behalf of such a transformation, the EPG recommended that ASEAN be given the power "to take measures to redress cases of serious breach" of these new norms and rules.[24] And the Charter does state, though again somewhat more cautiously than the EPG Report, that "a serious breach of," or even mere "non-compliance" with, the Charter "shall be referred to the ASEAN Summit for decision."[25]

Democratizing Southeast Asian security will require an elite-led transformation of ASEAN's rules and conduct, and *a fortiori* those of its member states. A successful outcome will offer the prospect of a secure, just,

---

[20] *Report of the Eminent Persons Group*, par. 27.

[21] *Report of the Eminent Persons Group*, par. 30.

[22] *Report of the Eminent Persons Group*, par. 44.

[23] The Charter's Article 21.2 allows for the implementation of economic commitments by some member states—"ASEAN Minus X"—where there is a consensus to do so. See also Art. 24.3.

[24] *Report of the Eminent Persons Group*, par. 6.

[25] See Charter, Art. 20.4.

and integrated ASEAN community whose General Will (to use Rousseau's term), more than the mere sum of the wishes of its constituent governments, will shape the lives of its peoples.

The transformative politics intimated in the Cebu Declaration, elaborated in the EPG Report and codified in the Charter, point toward a normative community of ASEAN peoples very different from the conditional and limited association that ASEAN's founding fathers envisaged in 1967. But the question arises: Is such a transformation feasible? States and organizations, like peoples and individuals, are well advised to exercise caution when making wishes.

Kant, Can't, or Cant: Does Democracy Promote Security?

Central to the idea that democracy promotes security and that its norms can influence both regions and states is the assumption that different but desirable political, economic, and social goods are not only compatible but also causally related. This universal value-prioritizing perspective relegates state sovereignty to a second-order concern. The promotion of human rights, democracy, and decency ultimately trumps the autonomous authority of the state. Consonant with this perspective is the Charter's modest but evident support for elite-level moves toward a more democratic, transparent, tolerant, and reasonably pluralist regional order. The Charter plausibly lays the basis for a "reasonably just" regional "Society of Peoples."[26]

The project is unlikely to succeed, however, if it rests on a faulty theory of international relations and ignores the specific economic and political problems that Southeast Asian states confront.

Ultimately, a normative rather than an empirical understanding of human development pervades the belief that security and democracy are always and everywhere compatible. It is unreasonable to assume that the world is evolving toward toward conditions of freedom, equality, and justice, and that the spread of international law, the globalization of communications, and the increasing attractiveness of state practices that are liberal, or at least decent, all work toward this progressive end.

In fact, such conditions do not currently prevail outside a few developed states that house a minority of the world's population—and are present nowhere in Southeast Asia. One could indeed argue that the emergence of an abstract rationalism that anticipates and promotes a universal condition of natural and now human right has had, since the nineteenth century, a damaging effect. It has unsettled the traditional practices of monarchies, empires, and republics. It has also laid the ground for ideological wars, more total and more frequent than the limited violence that prevailed in the era preceding the tyranny of single truths.

---

[26] Rawls, *Law*, 128.

There is, of course, some evidence to support the view that liberal democracies do not go to war with one another, preferring to resolve their disagreements by rational negotiation.[27] Yet relations between liberal democracies and nondemocracies—whether the latter are totalitarian, monarchical, absolutist, or authoritarian in character—have rarely been easy. As a result, trends in world affairs since the nineteenth century have favored anarchy and war, not pluralism and peace.[28] This reality contrasts sharply with the teleological premise that undemocratic states are outmoded, and must therefore either reform themselves or be reformed, whether by domestic or foreign actors and events.

Analysts should not confuse fact with value, nor—in their eagerness to picture what ought to be—fail to see what is. It may be helpful therefore, in Southeast Asia, to consider from a realist or state-focused perspective the security dilemmas that confront ASEAN policymakers, the foreign policy traditions that shape their responses, and how ASEAN might deal with what Alain Minc terms the "durable disorder" of the post-Cold War era, including the relative merits of sweeping political democratization compared with the more piecemeal and mundane economic project of market integration.[29]

In order to assess these matters prudentially rather than idealistically, however, we must first say something about the world order as it is and the place of Southeast Asian states within it.

Post-Cold War Trends: Neomedievalism, Millenial Capital, and the Market State

Philip Cerny has characterized the emerging post-Cold War politico-economic structure as "neomedieval"—a set of overlapping jurisdictions and cross-cutting allegiances in which the transnational character of global exchanges undermines the territoriality and allegiances of the nation state.[30] New and more rapid modes

---

[27] See Michael Doyle, *Ways of War and Peace: Realism, Liberalism, and Socialism* (New York: W. W. Norton, 1997). See also Doyle, "Kant, Liberal Legacies, and Foreign Affairs," *Philosophy and Public Affairs* 12, no. 3 (Summer 1983), 213; and John R. Oneal and Bruce M. Russett, "The Classic Liberals Were Right: Democracy, Interdependence, and Conflict, 1950–1985," *International Studies Quarterly* 41 (June 1997), 267–94.

[28] This is so in the sense that war is a condition in which no certain process or sovereign rule-making and enforcing authority exists. See Thomas Hobbes, *The Leviathan*, book 1, chapter 13, "Of the Natural Condition of Mankind Concerning their Felicity or Misery."

[29] See Alain Minc, *Ce Monde Qui Vient* (Paris: Grasset, 2004).

[30] See Philip G. Cerny, "Plurality, Pluralism, and Power: Elements of Pluralist Analysis in an Age of Globalization," in *Pluralism: Developments in the Theory and Practice of Democracy*, ed. Rainer Eisfeld (Opladen, Germany and Farmington Hills, MI: Barbara Budrich Publishers on behalf of the International Political Science Association, 2006), 81–111.

of physical and virtual communication, most notably the Internet, have altered the character of civil political association and political space.

At the same time, what Walter Russell Mead calls "millennial capital," driven by the development since 1990 of wide, deep, and global financial markets, has undermined both state- and region-based capitalism. The Fordist contract with the post-World War II democratic nation-state, an arrangement based on the assumption that workers and managers remained within the same locality, no longer holds. These changes have upset a key support for the presumed harmonic convergence between capitalism and the social democratic order, both nationally and internationally, and are recasting local and global socioeconomic relations in an unprecedented manner. The new mobility of workers and capital cannot sustain a state-based welfare blanket stretching from the cradle to the grave.

In this context, millennial capital, crudely depicted as unleashed by globalization and deregulation, is actually about regulation to protect the existence and efficiency of markets and permit wider access to their benefits. As Mead explains,

> [N]ational regulation may be decreasing, but the rise of millennial capitalism is creating new forms of international regulation that simply did not exist in the past. Free trade agreements (notably bilateral rather than multilateral or regional) ... create new transnational forms of regulation and justice.[31]

Millennial capitalism is also affected by the demographic changes that are redefining the social and political character of citizenship in our neomedieval, post-Fordist era. The globalized division of labor and the death of the blue-collar working class have significantly affected modern states and the regions they inhabit. As population growth slows and reverses in many of Europe and East Asia's developed democratic or decent states, the social arrangements that once bolstered the legitimacy of democracy are becoming unsustainable.

The neomedieval framework of millennial capital has revolutionized the international political economy and alienated both elite and mass constituencies around the world. It has created an interconnected but by no means integrated world, a condition best captured by Alain Minc's concept of "durable disorder." This fluid condition of multiple and cross-cutting allegiances has not, however, undermined the state as a form of political organization. Indeed, durable disorder has been driven by a particular variant of the nation-state model, namely the increasingly privatized, networked market state that has been called the "Anglo-Saxon model."

Dating from the days of Margaret Thatcher in the United Kingdom and Ronald Reagan in the United States, durable disorder continued in a more emollient form when Tony Blair and Bill Clinton were in office. In a manner

---

[31] Walter Russell Mead, *Power, Terror Peace, and War: America's Grand Strategy in a World at Risk* (New York: Alfred A. Knopf, 2004), 74.

reminiscent of Blair's vision of a "third way," the market-state model integrates global trade, transcending regional arrangements such as the European Union (EU), ASEAN, or the proposed East Asian community. The market state, having brought about durable disorder, is both reinforced by economic growth and resulting wealth on the one hand, yet threatened on the other by the porosity of borders and the corresponding flows of migration around the world.

The implications of durable disorder for regional membership and regional security only began to come into focus in the aftermaths of the 1997 AFC and the 9/11 and 7/7 terrorist attacks in the United States and the United Kingdom, respectively, in 2001 and 2005. One such consequence is a heightened investment in the infrastructure of security, locally and globally, including rising levels of surveillance. Resulting pressures on national budgets, combined with the globalization of the labor market, encourage the privatization of social services such as education, welfare, health care, and the provision of pensions. Inexorably, these changes erode the faith of teleological democrats in an inclusive political community based on shared participation for the common good. In this context, the market state's authority is legitimated not by the equality of its citizens understood as a community, but by its capacity to offer and enhance competitive opportunities for particular individuals.[32]

When the market state networks with other states to maximize values such as trade, wealth, and security, the resulting agreements are most often bilateral, or possibly trilateral, in nature. This trend further undermines regional and multilateral arrangements. Since the AFC and the spread of transnational low-intensity violence, multilateral frameworks such as the United Nations, the North Atlantic Treaty Organization (NATO), the International Monetary Fund (IMF), the World Trade Organization (WTO), the Asia Pacific Economic Cooperation (APEC) forum, and ASEAN have seen their influence diminish. All need radical reform if they are to retain relevance in the emerging transnational political economy of our twenty-first-century world.

As the post-Cold War era morphed from a *zeit* without a *geist* into durable disorder that offers scant promise for normative political or economic convergence, a significant, nonliberal alternative to the market state has arisen and adapted to these new conditions. A number of Southeast Asian states offer sustainable versions of this new model—a nonliberal polity that is friendly to millennial capital. The most consolidated and enduring illustration of the model in Southeast Asia is Singapore. Here a techno-mandarinate organizes all aspects of social and political life and distributes the economic product via an administrative apparatus of state-licensed, hierarchically ordered, ethnoreligious community groups, without having to tolerate a politics based on autonomous

---

[32] See Philip Bobbit, "Everything We Think about the War on Terror Is Wrong," *The Spectator* (20 May 2006), 14. As Bobbit puts it: "What you do with it—that's up to you. We will not assure you of equality, and we will not insure your steadily improving security, but the total wealth of society will be maximized."

civil actors freely articulating their interests in public forums. Instead, the administrative state enterprisingly defines identities and entitlements, and distributes them according to a consensually agreed managerial formula. The model simultaneously orients the economy toward global markets and curtails liberal space for civil society and political pluralism.

Undoubtedly, the Singapore model (or its Malaysian variant, or the one to which Thaksin Shinawatra's *Thai Rak Thai* party in Thailand aspired before the September 2006 coup) appeals to a managerial technocratic mindset generally, and provides an ideal type to which the People's Republic of China might aspire. Such arrangements, moreover, can build infrastructure and achieve internal security and managerial efficiency more effectively than a relatively open society. In Rawlsian terms, such regimes could arguably aspire to a form of "decent" hierarchy, although with benevolently absolutist characteristics that Rawls would deny.

Durable disorder, then, is congenial both to liberal market states and to administratively decent ones. It remains vulnerable, however, to those who consider the evolving global market economy "hideously schizophrenic," to use the Islamist ideologist Sayyid Qutb's prescient phrase.[33] Put more precisely, modernity—secular, modular, market-oriented—is being dialectically challenged by those who seek simultaneously to exploit, for irrational and nihilistic ends, the structures of a networked fast world that are conducive to increased wealth and increased vulnerability.

Given the evolving character of millennial capital, what are the prospects for putative supranational communities like ASEAN, which have struggled to adjust to its implications—a struggle that, in different words, the EPG Report acknowledged?

ASEAN Norms: Durable Disorder and the Craft of the Politically Possible

Durable disorder has had an ambiguous effect on ASEAN's growth prospects and *amour propre*. Initially, roughly from 1985 to 1996, millennial capital bequeathed its blessings upon the emerging tiger economies of Southeast Asia. Only with the advent of the AFC did millennial capital show how capricious it could be. A decade later, in 2007, the AFC's damage to regional economic confidence and levels of foreign direct investment (FDI) was still being felt, notwithstanding ASEAN's rhetoric about regional community.

Durable disorder has also weakened and in some cases badly disrupted the development pact between political elites and masses within states that restricted political freedom in exchange for a share of the profits from state-managed, export-driven growth. Among durable disorder's more evident post-AFC

---

[33] See Sayyid Qutb, *Milestones on the Road* (Kuwait: International Islamic Federation of Student Organizations, 1971).

political repercussions in Southeast Asia are regime change in Indonesia and Thailand, political uncertainty in Malaysia and the Philippines, and a retreat to the jungle city of Naypyidaw by the patronocracy that rules Myanmar.

Less obviously, economic and political uncertainties have lent plausibility to those who offer a radical, millenarian, Islamist alternative to market-friendly rule. In Southeast Asia this challenge takes the shape of al Qaeda's Southeast Asian franchise, *Jemaah Islamiyah*, which is dedicated to erecting a *Darul Islam Nusantara*—an Islamic state in Southeast Asia. Elsewhere this alternative is manifest in reinvigorated separatist movements in Thailand and the Philippines, and in opportunistic political Islam. In the latter instance, Islamist organizations use the democratic process to advance programs meant to clean up the corrupt legacy of a Mahathir or a Suharto, respectively Malaysia's prime minister (1981–2003) and Indonesia's president (1968–98). At the same time, these organizations propagate a new and relatively intolerant political morality. In Southeast Asia, the prospect of a benign end of history where justice and democracy, peace and reason, economic growth and market integration come together in a "realistic utopian" project seems indefinitely postponed.

The question remains: In this world of cultural particularities, criss-crossing commitments, and market-driven turbulence, would greater democracy enhance ASEAN's security? Or would it instead threaten the achievements of the region's administrative states?

In contrast with the idealist "oughtism" that colors rationalist accounts of historical development, realist "prudentialism" has always emphasized dealing with the world as it is. The former outlook is less useful than the latter in the actual world. For modern democratic realists, political pluralism is not a cause of security but its consequence. To this contingent, the art of politics requires an awareness of the possible, not the pursuit of an abstract norm. Central to this awareness is the cultivation of practical wisdom or prudence—what the Greek city-state world held to be "the highest form of political wisdom."[34] As Leo Strauss explained, this is the only morally intelligible framework in which "the right handling of situations" can occur.[35] Prudence is inseparable from moral virtue, and also from the art of government or, more precisely, the habit of choosing wisely.

Such an understanding translates intelligibly into a modern Southeast Asian context. In Asian political theory, regional statesmanship historically promotes prudence, and the art of the politically possible, not abstract doctrines of right. According to the theory's more elitist and traditional versions, the wealth and harmony of the people reflected the skill of the ruler. Relations between the ruled and the ruler were hierarchical rather than democratic, yet each had

---

[34] Leo Strauss, *The City and Man* (Chicago, IL: University of Chicago Press, 1964), 24.

[35] Strauss, *City and Man*, 28.

obligations toward the other.[36] In ASEAN discourse, this understanding is termed *pragmatism*. In particular, pragmatism means a readiness to acknowledge both the limits upon and the integrity of ASEAN-member states—conditions that will subsequently determine the pace of regional integration.

ASEAN's durability reflects the craft of its statesmen. The limited, conservative project that its founders instantiated in 1967 reflected what was possible at that time, in the postcolonial context of the Cold War. ASEAN was not the product of a normative preoccupation with human rights or democracy. Its first generation of leaders was pragmatic. They recognized the limitations of regional cooperation. It was, they understood, a state-based process that required postcolonial elites to accept colonial borders. Those boundaries might have been arbitrarily drawn and were often contested, but the leaders knew that they were, for all intents and purposes, fixed.

ASEAN's central objective was, and remains, pragmatic: to sustain regional order. As its first declaration in Bangkok in 1967 avowed, the Association was forming not a movement of peoples but an *association* of states. Although it has become fashionable to interpret ASEAN in antirealist terms of norms and communities, it remains an essentially intergovernmental project. Viewed from a realist perspective, recent declarations of an inclusive and normatively transforming community,[37] and the regional scholarship that echoes these statements, have made it easier to forget and harder to understand ASEAN's limited associative purpose.

The founders' pragmatism in 1967 reflected the failure of earlier experiments in Southeast Asian regionalism—the South East Asia Treaty Organization (SEATO), the Association of South East Asia (ASA), and Maphilindo.[38] Chief among the goals of that year's Bangkok Declaration by ASEAN's founding

---

[36] Precolonial understandings of the Sultanate in Southeast Asia upheld this view, but it is probably best summarized in the Confucian formula that "the ruler should first concern himself with his own virtue. Possessing virtue he will win the people. Possessing the People he will win the Realm." See J. R. Legge, ed. and trans., *The Great Learning*, vol. 1, in *The Chinese Classics*, 7 vols. (Oxford: Oxford University Press, 1893), 131.

[37] For example, the *Declaration of ASEAN Concord 11 (Bali Concord 11)* in Bali, Indonesia, in October 2003 envisaged "a dynamic, cohesive, resilient and integrated ASEAN community" (see <http://www.aseansec.org/15159.htm>). The *ASEAN Vision 2020* (Hanoi, December 1997) also envisaged a Southeast Asia "bound by a common regional identity." See <http://www.aseansec.org/1814.htm>.

[38] See Yoshiyuki Hagiwasa, "Formation and Development of the Association of Southeast Asian Nations," *The Developing Economies* 11, no. 4 (December 1973), 443–65. SEATO, which lasted from 1995 to 1997, involved only two Southeast Asian states—the Philippines and Thailand. ASA (1961–66) was a failed attempt at cooperation among the Philippines, Thailand, and Malaya. Maphilindo was meant to join Malaysia, the Philippines, and Indonesia in a greater Malay confederation, but it never got off the ground. Its aspirations dissolved in Indonesia's confrontation (*Konfrontasi*) of Malaysia, which ended in 1966.

members—Indonesia, Malaysia, the Philippines, Singapore, and Thailand—were the promotion of peace, stability, and economic growth in Southeast Asia.[39] ASEAN's formation marked the end of earlier conflicts over the postcolonial regional order and Indonesia's acknowledgment that the recently decolonized states of Malaysia and Singapore were entitled to places in that order.

From its inception, the Association emphasized its intergovernmental nature and its disinclination to become a supranational organization. The preeminent scholar writing on ASEAN in the twentieth century, Michael Leifer, noted that the Association did not even intend to become an alliance. By the end of the Cold War, ASEAN had developed, he wrote, at best a "collegial identity."[40] This identity emerged in response to the Indochina crisis occasioned by Vietnam's invasion of Cambodia in 1978—an evident breach of the ASEAN principle of accepting and respecting the interstate boundaries left behind by the departing colonial powers. Vietnam's actions contravened the Association's landmark Treaty of Amity and Cooperation (1976), which upheld the principle of noninterference in the internal affairs of member states as the sovereignty-reinforcing, unilateral-action-denying sine qua non of regional order.

At the end of the Cold War, ASEAN stood revealed as a diplomatic community of weak states. Its collegial style represented the "institutional fruit" of subregional conflict resolution between 1976 and 1991. Leifer did argue that it could also be viewed as an "embryonic security community" practicing cooperative (rather than deterrent) security.[41] But what Leifer meant by "security community" was a basically realist undertaking that reconciled previously conflicting states through dialogue, conflict avoidance, and the limited management of disputes. In this, ASEAN's practice contained "an evident dimension of balance of power" within "an institutional framework of multilateral constraint."[42] For Leifer, to see the Association as engendering collective security or as forming an integrated security, economic, and sociocultural community embracing democracy in a sovereignty-transcending

---

[39] See the ASEAN Declaration (Bangkok Declaration), Bangkok, 8 August 1967, <http://www.aseansec.org/1212htm>.

[40] Michael Leifer, *ASEAN and the Security of Southeast Asia* (London: Routledge, 1989), 153. See also Leifer, "ASEAN's Search for Regional Order," in *Michael Leifer: Selected Works on Southeast Asia*, ed. Chin Kin Wah and Leo Suryadinata (Singapore: ISEAS, 2005), 104; and Leifer, "The Indochina Problem," in *Asian-Pacific Security After the Cold War*, ed. T. B. Millar and James Walter (St. Leonards, NSW, Australia: Allen and Unwin, 1993), 68. For an earlier, skeptical view of relations between Southeast Asian states, see Peter Lyon, *War and Peace in Southeast Asia* (London: Oxford University Press, 1969).

[41] Michael Leifer, *ASEAN's Search for Regional Order* (Singapore: Faculty of Arts and Social Sciences, National University of Singapore, 1987), 4. See also Leifer, *ASEAN and the Security of Southeast Asia*, 139, 157.

[42] Leifer, "Truth about the Balance of Power," in Chin and Suryadinata, *Michael Leifer*, 153.

sense was to commit "a category mistake."[43] To mislabel ASEAN in this way was to misunderstand the Association's essentially pragmatic, limited, and state-based character.

ASEAN's international and regional diplomatic stature improved dramatically in the 1990s. The original ASEAN states maintained regional peace and sustained impressive economic growth from 1985 to 1997.[44] By 1998 the Association had expanded to encompass Myanmar (or Burma) and the Indochinese states (Laos, Cambodia, and Vietnam) that it had been aligned against from 1978 to 1991. For decades, these governments had contested the regional order that ASEAN represented. Their inclusion in the Association was a seminal achievement of the organization's realism—prudential, state-driven, and sovereignty-reinforcing. As Mahathir Mohamad observed in 2001, because of their "political pragmatism and economic dynamism," the ASEAN countries "collectively and individually" had bolstered "the peace and stability of the region."[45]

To paraphrase the language of the 2006 Cebu Declaration on the Blueprint of an ASEAN Charter, ASEAN functions mainly as a *concert* of regional states whose leaders recognize the importance of regional order and stability for the independent and interdependent development of Southeast Asia. This limited and sustainable goal has enabled the states that comprise the grouping to exploit the benefits of regional security for their respective developmental purposes. The lesson of this experience would appear to be that democratization was a road wisely not taken. Arguably, had ASEAN decided to promote democracy and human rights at the expense of the autonomy of its members to determine their own forms of rule, the grouping would today be less integrated, less developed, less secure—and less of a regional community.

The ASEAN Charter is ambiguous in this context, an ambiguity that reflects the diversity and ambivalence of its authors. On the one hand, the Charter repeats and thus reinforces the principles of noninterference and state sovereignty that ASEAN's earlier "milestone treaties" upheld. On the other hand, the text also supports democracy, transparency, and human rights—ideas whose intrusive pursuit would abrogate those same principles. Also in the Charter are provisions that could, if further specified and implemented, enable the Association to become more proactive, to the possible further discomfort of its less democratic members.

In trying to have it both ways, the Charter risks incoherence. Actually implementing liberal rules could unravel the Association's proven practical

---

[43] Leifer, "The ASEAN Peace Process: A Category Mistake," *Pacific Review* 12, no. 1 (1999), 32.

[44] The Philippines proved the exception in this respect. In that case, neither an authoritarian nor a democratic style of government succeeded in engineering significant economic growth.

[45] Mahathir Mohamad, *Reflections on ASEAN: Selected Speeches of Dr. Mahathir Mohamad* (Subang, Malaysia: Pelanduk, 2004), 251.

utility as a group of independent states whose prudence has helped keep peace and security in the region. Southeast Asia's nonliberal political culture is flexible, but it remains essentially conservative. It is likely to resist abstract rationalism in the service of one-size-fits-all liberal norms. And even if that did not happen, the external promotion of democratic norms would exacerbate the turbulence already associated with millennial capital, and thus rapidly destabilize rather than reinforce regional order.

Dilemmas of Democracy: Indonesia, the Philippines, and Thailand

Liberal democracy, including its institutional fruit—pluralism, multipartism, an independent judiciary, press freedom, individual rights—is not a plant indigenous to Southeast Asia. Not so very long ago, a Singapore School made much of "Asian values." Of essentially nonliberal provenance, these values were portrayed as responsible for the remarkable political cohesion and economic development of East Asia. The cultural distinctiveness of East Asia was somewhat exaggerated for ideological effect in the context of an eagerly anticipated Pacific Century. It remains evident, however, that the development process in Southeast Asia was driven not by liberal-democratic values but by prudent single parties and spirited men of prowess, whether monarchs, aristocrats, or major-generals.

In the uncertain circumstances of the Cold War, single or dominant parties drew upon nonliberal, traditional understandings to sustain elite guidance of heterogeneous populations and their linkage to the requirements of export-oriented growth within the territorial unit of the developmental state. Examples include the United Malays National Organization (UMNO) in Malaysia, the People's Action Party (PAP) in Singapore, benevolently absolutist sultans in Brunei, monarchies with military and religious backing like the reinvented Chakri dynasty in Thailand, and during Suharto's New Order in Indonesia, corporatism informed by Javanese practices of discussion and consensus (*musyawarah mufakat*) and deference to superiors (*bapakisme*), including most notably Suharto himself.

These reinvented cultural understandings varied from state to state. But they shared a political understanding that emphasized hierarchy and duty, not abstract right. According to this conception, releasing the autonomous individual self from its bureaucratically determined and constraining web of relationships would invite not liberty but license. In this context, regular elections serve to reinforce rule by an elite technocracy, rather than functioning as a certain method of delivering uncertain outcomes.

The downside of this model was the corruption, cronyism, and nepotism that marked relations between government and business in Southeast Asia, and which the AFC exposed. Corruption and unaccountability did negatively affect the ASEAN states, tarnishing their luster for foreign investors. The financial crisis delegitimated the New Order regime in Indonesia and occasioned yet another round of constitution-writing in Thailand. Yet in these two countries, and in the Philippines, subsequent democratization has generated no obvious elite or mass enthusiasm for liberal democracy, political pluralism, or the unpredictable results of contested elections.

A brief examination of these three ASEAN cases illustrates why. Indonesia, the Philippines, and Thailand share a history of domination by strong men rather than single parties. Accordingly, the military has at various times assumed a crucial role in political development. More recently, as national economies developed and an urbanized middle class pressed for democratic change and greater transparency, the political, business, and military elites of these states, however reluctantly, opened up the possibility of multiparty politics.

This pressure grew especially acute in Indonesia in the wake of the AFC. Indonesian democratization has proceeded somewhat unevenly since the country's first post-New Order elections in 1999. Business, military, political, religious, and regional elites did, nevertheless, conditionally accept the idea of holding elections without knowing in advance who the winners would be. The country's first direct presidential balloting in 2004 gave that office to a former general, Susilo Bambang Yudhoyono (often know as SBY), to occupy until 2009. His running mate, Jusuf Kalla, became vice president. Yudhoyono's Democrat Party was small, but in parliamentary elections held earlier in 2004, Kalla's Golkar party, representing the old bureaucratic and business elites, won the largest number of seats.

This transition has not been without its political achievements. The new government negotiated an apparently stable peace with a rebel movement in the province of Aceh; an autonomy-granting Law on the Governance of Aceh passed parliament in July 2006. In 2007, although Papuan separatism remained a problem, the government seemed to have managed the difficult balance between accommodating demands for regional autonomy without unduly compromising its own central authority.

Yet the economy has struggled to attract FDI since the financial meltdown of 1997. FDI fell 44 percent year-on-year between January and September 2006.[46] In 2007, inflation and unemployment were high and domestic consumption and confidence low. Corruption, already a serious problem across the archipelago at both central and regional government levels, has been exacerbated by the devolution of authority brought about by democratization. In its 2006, in a ranking of 159 countries from least to most corrupt, Transparency International placed Indonesia in 137th place, next to Liberia.[47]

Significantly, Yudhoyono's government has also been criticized for its failure to move more decisively against the country's slow and venal bureaucracy. Meanwhile, a heady mixture of corruption, inflation, and poverty, exposed to public view in a climate of media freedom, has fed the appeal of political Islam as reflected in the rise of the Prosperous Justice Party. Related to this party's

---

[46] "Investors Need Incentives," *Asia Monitor* 17 (12 December 2006), 2.

[47] Rebecca Weisser, "SBY Passes First Tests," *The Australian* (31 July 2006).

stands against corruption and pornography and for a more stringent application of Muslim morality has been the introduction of elements of Islamic law in some 30 of the country's 440 districts. At the same time, as of 2007, the more apocalyptically inclined Islamism practiced by *Jemaah Islamiyah* and its affiliates remained a worrying presence in democratizing Indonesia and continued to unsettle relations between Christian and Muslim communities. In Indonesia, the process of democratization, coupled with economic uncertainty, has had the unintended effect of stoking the transnational ambitions of a radical Islamism that challenges the state-based national and regional order. This side effect of the promotion of democracy is more likely, in turn, to promote insecurity in Southeast Asia.

As with the former Yugoslavia and post-Saddam Iraq, instituting democracy in Southeast Asia may reinforce communalist attachments rather than reasonable pluralism and tolerance. A more prudent first generation of regional statesmen were aware of this risk, having experienced its quotidian manifestation in ethnic riots and interreligious tensions in the period of decolonization.

The Philippines offers a telling example of how tension between Christian and Muslim communities has disrupted internal security since decolonization. Whatever the democratizing consequences of post-Marcos "people power" may or may not have been, it has intensified communal divisions, as the Catholic majority continues to struggle with the separatist-communalist demands of Muslims in Mindanao.

Separatism is not the only challenge to the fragile democracy that has struggled to establish itself in the Philippines over the past twenty years. The government of President Gloria Macapagal-Arroyo has lived with the threat of coup or impeachment ever since her contested victory in the presidential elections of 2004. Allegations of electoral fraud remain unanswered, to the detriment of her legitimacy. In a country where, periodically since 1986, "people power" has overthrown unpopular rulers, Arroyo's authority has come to rest increasingly on the support of the military elite, itself preoccupied with managing discontent in the army's ranks. Such dependence will remain a concern so long as the coup represents the preferred unofficial mechanism for ousting civilian rulers and changing constitutions in democratizing Southeast Asia. Significantly, two coup attempts by middle-ranking officers in the Philippines were exposed in February and May 2006.

Thailand is another case in point. The military coup in Bangkok on 19 September 2006, staged by General Sonthi Boonyaratglin ostensibly to restore democratic rule and constitutional propriety, revealed yet again the gap between abstract democratic values and actual political development in one of the more economically dynamic states in Southeast Asia.

Political tension escalated after 2001, as Prime Minister Thaksin Shinawatra extended an oligarchic hold over the Thai political process, despite a constitution designed after 1997 to secure the rule of law and authorize independent commissions to check corruption and the arbitrary use of power. Under this "democratic charter," Thaksin, Thailand's biggest businessman in media and communications, turned his Thai Rak Thai party into a powerful engine of corporatist control. He consolidated power through three election victories between 2001 and 2006. As of 2007, in a characteristically Southeast Asian combination of money politics, paternalism, and largesse (the latter directed especially toward the poor northeastern part of the country), Thailand was developing along the technocratically guided lines of single-party rule favored by its economically successful and politically stable ASEAN neighbors, Malaysia and Singapore.

General Sonthi's "friendly" coup in 2006 was the product of a short-lived alliance between prodemocracy groups, Bangkok elites, and circles around the king and his privy council who exercised patrimonial influence over the Bangkok masses. Later that same year the National Security Council decided to appoint an interim prime minister, who would govern for a year under an interim constitution, and to nominate a 242-member legislative assembly, composed largely of former military members, bureaucrats, and academics. But these steps only increased tension between the Council, Bangkok, and the regions, and students and civil society groups stuck between the rock that was Thaksin and the hard place of reinvented elite guidance.

The fall and exile of Thaksin leaves purportedly democratizing Thailand with a political dilemma. The middle classes want a swift return to constitutional rule. Yet new elections will only reveal the continuing appeal of Thaksin and his party to the rural poor. In 2007 the king, in his sixtieth year of rule, and his privy council were trying to restore stability. Ultimately, the Thai elites will need to craft a prudent, pragmatic solution to this dilemma, not merely for Thailand's sake, but for the further development, political stability, and investment appeal of Southeast Asia.

These three cases show that enlisting ASEAN in the promotion of democracy in its region would not necessarily contribute to security in, or enhance the developmental prospects of Indonesia, the Philippines, or Thailand. But what of the later-developing states, ASEAN's northern tier? They are all of authoritarian hue. They joined ASEAN only recently. And they did so in no small measure because ASEAN assured them of noninterference in their internal affairs. We now turn to these cases.

Democratic Development? Singapore and the Northern Tier

ASEAN's Charter notwithstanding, the most successful model in Southeast Asia continues to be that of a nonliberal, development-oriented, one-party state, along the lines suggested by Singapore's PAP and Malaysia's UMNO. In Singapore in particular, the evidence of sustained growth, political stability, and the capacity to absorb financial and economic shock falsifies the idea that liberalism is a universally necessary condition of such achievements. The ongoing ability of Singapore's administrative state to offer the most efficient location for business and services in Southeast Asia belies prognostications of inevitable atrophy. The city-state's successful mix of social and political control with a degree of transparency and economic accountability is not an anomaly. It represents a stable long-term developmental ideal type that most Asians would consider not only materially acceptable but also politically decent.

Therefore, inducing a more accountable, pluralist model in ASEAN's less democratic and more impoverished northern tier—Laos, Cambodia, Myanmar, and Vietnam—would not necessarily improve these states' economic prospects. As for stabilizing the region, if ASEAN were to exert real pressure on these regimes to conform to a universal standard of liberal democracy, they would resign from the Association rather than risk their own disintegration.

Myanmar, Cambodia, and Laos compete with several African countries for the dubious honor of having the lowest per capita gross domestic product (GDP) on the planet. In Rawlsian terms they are "burdened" states. They and Vietnam are groping their way out of the economic and political night that their versions of communism or socialism visited upon them. Yet as of 2007 there was little in their behavior to suggest a burgeoning popular or elite interest in the reasonable pluralism afforded by liberal institutions.

Consider, first, Cambodia, with a scant gross national income of US$ 380.[48] Prime Minister Hun Sen's growing control over parliament, business, and the press has effectively muzzled Cambodia's nascent civil society. When, in August 2006, the legislature passed an antidefamation law that overrides parliamentary immunity, the U.S. ambassador called it an act of "collective self-castration."[49] All this notwithstanding, the stability of evolving dominant-party rule has facilitated an accommodation between the Cambodian government and its perennial critic, Sam Rainsy, whom King Norodom Sihamoni pardoned in February 2006. The government has moved, somewhat glacially, toward a joint UN-Cambodian tribunal to try the aging remnants of the genocidal Khmer Rouge regime that was responsible for the deaths of as many as two million Cambodians between 1975 and 1979.

Stability has also enabled the economy to expand at a rapid pace. In 2007, the Asian Development Bank (ADB) predicted a growth rate of around 9 percent over the ensuing two years.[50] If economic dynamism and political stability continue, they will be associated not with a liberal democracy but with an opaque regime in which power has been increasingly concentrated in Hun Sen's hands.

---

[48] See <http://newsvote.bbc.co.uk//mapps/pagetools/print/news.bbc.co.uk/2/hi/asia-pacific/countr>.

[49] "Investors Need Incentives," 2.

[50] "ADB Forecasts 9 Pct Growth Rate for Cambodian Economy in Next 2 Years," *People's Daily Online*, 27 March 2007, <http://english.peopledaily.com.cn/200703/27/eng20070327_361436.html>.

Laotian politics are no more transparent. As in Cambodia, a Marxist-Leninist-Maoist-inspired party seized power in 1975. The resulting Lao People's Democratic Republic was ruled by the highly secretive Lao People's Revolutionary Party (LPRP). After 1986—unlike Cambodia but like Vietnam—the LPRP adopted market-friendly reforms. These reforms did not prevent the LPRP from exercising strict control over the developmental process. Former president Khamtay Siphandone opened Laos to foreign aid. But he maintained the party's authoritarian grip. In 1994 he declared criticism of the party "contrary to historical reality and the national interest."[51] Again, aggregate economic success has accompanied a less than liberal-democratic strategy. Emerging from an admittedly very low base, growth has averaged more than 7 percent annually since 2004. Industrial production has superseded that of agriculture. The flow of FDI into mining and hydropower has been forecast to reach US$ 327 million by 2007.[52]

Since joining ASEAN in 1995, Laos has deepened economic ties with its fellow members Thailand and Vietnam, and with China. Ninety percent of Laotian trade is covered by ASEAN's Common Effective Preferential Tariff Scheme, and Laos stands to benefit greatly from the ASEAN Free Trade Area (AFTA). Two-way trade between Laos and Vietnam has grown exponentially, totaling US$ 688 million from 2001 to 2005. China and Thailand remain, nevertheless, Vientiane's key economic partners. Thailand in particular is enmeshed in projects to develop infrastructure and boost hydroelectric power.[53]

Elections in April 2006 to the 115-member National Assembly enabled the LPRP, as the country's only legal party, to retain absolute dominance over the institutional landscape. In the eyes of one analyst, the outlook is for "continuing tight party control, resistance to any kind of political reform or transparency, [and] encouragement of foreign investment."[54] According to another observer, "the regime is very confident their system is working."[55]

---

[51] "Lao Communist Party Chief Steps Down But Reforms Unlikely," Agence France-Presse (21 March 2006).

[52] The Director General of the Department of Geology and Mines estimated the value of mineral-export revenues at more than US$ 200 million by the second quarter of 2006 (*Asia Monitor*, no. 17 [6 August 2006], 2).

[53] In 2006, Chinese premier Wen Jiabao pledged to new Laos President Choummaly Sayasone that China would facilitate Laotian commodity exports, as reported in "Laos Risk Summary," *Asia Monitor* no. 17, 6 August 2006, 2. In that same year the Export-Import Bank of Thailand agreed to manage and back the issue of a ten-to-twelve-year Laotian government bond worth US$ 78 million.

[54] Quoted in Denis D. Gray, "Communist Party to Continue Tight Control over Laos," Associated Press (22 March 2006).

[55] "Lao Communist Party Chief Steps Down but Reforms Unlikely," Agence France-Presse (21 March 2006).

A similar strategy of Leninist-party guidance being adapted to the demands of the market has marked the political and economic evolution of Vietnam, which embarked on a policy of economic renovation, or *doi moi*, in the mid-1980s. Vietnam entered ASEAN in 1995 and proceeded rapidly to integrate itself into the global economy. Since 2002, the country has registered the fastest growth of any economy in Southeast Asia, averaging over 8 percent per year. Vietnam hosted the annual APEC leaders' meeting in November 2006, a framework it had only joined in 1998. The economy's growth, like that of its more developed co-members in ASEAN, is geared to exports and FDI.

Ironically in light of their previous history, the United States has become Vietnam's major trading partner. The permanent normalizing of its trade relations with the United States facilitated Vietnam's entry into the WTO in late 2006, and enhanced both its economy's attractiveness to foreign investors and its prospects for further growth.[56]

The Communist Party of Vietnam (CPV) has successfully stage-managed development. At its congress in April 2006, the CPV appointed a new guard of younger leaders committed to quickening the country's economic growth while maintaining the party's vanguard status. (A comparable change in leadership occurred in Laos.) As Pham The Duyet, chairman of the Vietnam Fatherland Front explained, "There cannot be any multiparty system[;] it is a matter of principle."[57]

The congress and the naming of new leaders coincided with revelations of a major corruption scandal that permeated the upper echelons of the party.[58] In part because the CPV and the politburo are unaccountable, structural corruption is a continuing drag on the economy's growth. Nevertheless, bureaucratically led development remains central to Vietnam's political stability and investment appeal.

In Myanmar, the nonliberal pattern of development that the State Peace and Development Council (SPDC) has pursued has not lessened the burden that the poor suffer in that burdened society, to use Rawls' label. As for human rights, the SPDC's record on that score has made Myanmar a Rawlsian outlaw state.

---

[56] "U.S., Vietnam Hail Vote to Normalize Trade Relations," *Financial Times* (12 December 2006).

[57] Nga Pham, "Vietnam Congress Mixes Old with New," BBC News (25 April 2006), <http://news.bbc.co.uk/2/hi/asia-pacific/4941792.stm>.

[58] The scandal, revealed in the normally docile, state-controlled press, centered on the transport ministry project management bureau, known as PMU-18, which manages over US$ 2 billion worth of infrastructure contracts. Rather than build roads, senior members of the ministry gambled over US$ 7 million on European soccer matches.

ASEAN's policy of constructively engaging Myanmar since the junta became a member in 1997 has failed to modify the junta's arbitrary exercise of power.[59] ASEAN's collegial style has had little impact upon the reclusive leadership of a state in which "child and forced labor is common[,] aid workers are treated with suspicion, foreign journalists are blacklisted, local media is censored and giving information to outsiders is a jailable offence."[60]

Transparency International lists Myanmar as one of the world's most corrupt states. Spurred by paranoia mixed with astrology, the SPDC has moved the capital from Yangon to a heavily fortified site near Pyinmana, 400 kilometers inland. This retreat into a fortress city illustrates the government's siege mentality, as the country faces economic meltdown and popular unrest.

Would the promotion of a more robust ASEAN Charter transform the politics of this outlaw regime? The only pressure that ASEAN could exert would be to threaten Myanmar with expulsion for failing to implement democracy and protect human rights, insofar as the Charter refers to them. But that would imply a strenuous reading of those few references. And expulsion, were it even possible, would merely fragment regional order without necessarily undermining the SPDC. Significantly, the SPDC declined the chairmanship of ASEAN in 2006 rather than relinquish any aspect of its authoritarian grip.

The People's Republic of China (PRC) covertly supports the junta's intransigence. This is noteworthy, given China's growing importance to the political economy of the ASEAN states. In January 2006 the SPDC concluded a contract to supply natural gas from the Bay of Bengal to southern China. Unlike teleological democrats and liberal interpreters of the Charter, China, the rising regional hegemon, has little problem with the Myanmar regime. Even if it did, it would not interfere in the internal affairs of a neighboring state.

The international community is pressuring ASEAN to adopt a more intrusively democratizing approach to issues of governance and human rights in the burdened societies and outlaw states that belong to the Association. But such an approach would not only contravene the established regional norm of noninterference that has over time secured and extended the basis of regional stability, demonstrably the sine qua non of Southeast Asia's development. It would also run against China's evolving policy of regional good neighborliness based on respect for national sovereignty. Like the late-developing, postcommunist, and burdened states in ASEAN, China has adapted, after some tergiversation, to ASEAN's collegial and nonbinding consensual style. In that process, China has developed a new security outlook on the region. The institutional fruits of this new attitude include the ASEAN Declaration on the Conduct of the Parties in South China Sea (2002); China's trade agreement with ASEAN (2002), which

---

[59] The military junta took power after canceling the 1990 election that resulted in a landslide victory for the opposition National League for Democracy.

[60] Connie Levett, "A Land Where Freedom Is a Dirty Word," *Sydney Morning Herald* (20 May 2006).

facilitated a rapid increase in Sino-ASEAN trade; and Chinese participation in the ASEAN Plus Three framework and East Asian Summit.

China has endorsed, and is comfortable with, the ASEAN Treaty of Amity and Cooperation. That comfort level is reflected in China's increasingly cooperative relationship with Southeast Asia. The treaty's content neatly matches the five principles of peaceful coexistence that Zhou Enlai outlined in 1955, including respect for sovereignty. Retreating from the sovereignty principle, the adoption of which has contributed to regional stability and warmer relations with Beijing, would jeopardize these achievements. In addition, were ASEAN actively to promote democracy, transparency, and abstract rights inside its member states, the consequences for Southeast Asia would be profound.

Policy Choices: Democracy Promotion or Market Integration?

The AFC illustrated how markedly the new era of millennial capital differed from its nation-state–centered precursor.[61] In many circles, the crisis was taken as evidence that the East and Southeast Asian development model needed radical economic and political restructuring. Acceptance of this conclusion was both the condition and the substance of IMF prescriptions for healing the crippled economies of Thailand and Indonesia after 1997.

In the wake of the AFC, Southeast Asia's ruling elites were obliged to adjust to a new world of durable disorder, in which footloose and relatively inexpensive money circulated at high speeds through markets that were increasingly connected but by no means integrated. Durable disorder rendered developing and developed Southeast Asia more dependent upon, and more exposed to, the vagaries of the fast world of stock exchanges that never sleep and capital inflows that are all too reversible. Regimes that adapt most successfully to this new global political economy must not only remain open to the market. They must also possess political stability, a degree of sufficient transparency, and the techno-managerial capacity to adjust flexibly to the threats to, and the opportunities for, economic growth that increased connectivity offers.[62]

Southeast Asian regimes are extremely diverse: an outlaw autocratic military junta in Myanmar; politically burdened postcommunist regimes in Cambodia, Laos, and Vietnam; reasonably pluralist, presidential constitutional systems with multiparty assemblies in the Philippines and Indonesia; hierarchical and relatively decent consolidated one-party–dominant parliamentary systems in Malaysia and Singapore; and two variations on relatively benevolent absolutism—a royalist and coup-initiated but ostensibly democracy-restoring security council in Thailand, and an old-fashioned sultanate in Brunei. Despite their variety, in adjusting to the vagaries of millennial capital, these countries

---

[61] Mead, *Power, Terror, Peace and War*, 73–77.

[62] The threats posed include transnational terror, crime, and increased environmental and biological risk.

have shown, on balance, a cultural preference for an administrative rather than a liberal-democratic state as the basis for managing the challenge. This nonliberal model cannot be entirely autocratic, secretive, and unaccountable, as Myanmar's economic and political failure and the more nuanced but still notable shortcomings of development in Cambodia, and even Vietnam, attest. Yet multiparty systems with constitutional safeguards have also fallen short when it comes to securing stability, as the turbulence in the Philippines, Thailand, and Indonesia since 1997 clearly show. The most successful approach remains a technocratic-administrative model that features flexible, pragmatic leadership by a dominant party subject to regular elections, coupled with a degree of economic transparency.

The city-state of Singapore is the classic example of this preferred Southeast Asian model. Its main elements are visible in Malaysia, Thailand, Indonesia, the Philippines, and Vietnam: controlled (or responsible) media, regular elections, market accountability, and technocratic guidance over time to achieve developmental goals. Underlying the model is a felt need to maintain cohesion in the face of global and regional uncertainty. The strategy relies on an elite pact that links ethnic, religious, economic, and military interests in a coalition whose purpose is not democracy but development.

Rather than promote public reason and abstract norms, ASEAN wants and needs to build a common Southeast Asian market. Only an integrated market can bring down to earth and put into effect the Association's vision of a "stable, prosperous and highly competitive ASEAN region in which there is a free flow of goods, services [and] investment."[63] In reality, the region is a fragmented market characterized by "high transaction costs" and "an unpredictable policy environment."[64] As the authors of the 2006 EPG Report lamented, "ASEAN's problem is not one of lack of vision, ideas or action plans. The problem is one of ensuring compliance."[65] ASEAN's commitment to national sovereignty and nonbinding consensus hinders the realization of an integrated market and ignores the member states' dependence on transnational commerce and FDI.

Would liberal-democratic values improve ASEAN's ability to meet its economic goals? As the second editor of *The Economist*, Walter Bagehot, observed back in 1850, the fig seller needs order before he can sell his figs.

Conclusion: Prudent Cooperation Trumps Abstract Reason

The pragmatic decisions of statesmen in the changing circumstances of the Cold War established the conditions for regional growth and stability. The

---

[63] *Declaration of ASEAN Concord 11 (Bali Concord 11)*, B1.

[64] ASEAN commissioned the McKinsey report in 2002. Its findings were cited in and endorsed by the *Report of the Eminent Persons Group on the ASEAN Charter*, December 2006, <http://www.aseansec.org/19247pdf>, 12.

[65] *Report of the Eminent Persons Group*, 3.

eventual stabilization of Southeast Asia was a signal achievement. This order, and the sovereignty of each state within it, allowed the ASEAN states to pursue export-focused growth and political development, each in its own distinct manner. Regional stability was a product of pragmatism, not ideology. In the light of this practical experience, it is not obvious that Southeast Asia's security would necessarily benefit from the application of abstract norms of democratic accountability and human rights under international law at the behest of any supranational agency. On the contrary, regional peace as a pragmatic understanding among autonomous states could be jeopardized.

Trying to oblige ASEAN's members to conform to such an abstract ideal would trigger feelings of uncertainty among them. The most successfully developed members of ASEAN have been organized along nonliberal lines. Liberal democracy has done little to deliver stability, development, or even justice in those states that have toyed with it. There is no reason why its promotion from above, that is, from ASEAN, would improve its appeal.

Democracy promotion might instead promote the disintegration of the Association by undermining its precondition, namely, the sovereignty of the states that compose it. An ASEAN-led effort to instill respect for human rights and international law could encourage communalist sentiments and movements to reject liberal democracy, possibly to the point of unraveling the regional order, or to accept and use democratic means, but only to achieve undemocratic ends.

ASEAN needs to devote its attention to what maximizes general utility in Southeast Asia. ASEAN does need reform. But the purpose of reform should be to improve upon what the Association has already achieved, and in the light of historical experience. In this context, enhancing mechanisms to promote integration toward a single market—as opposed to a rationalist assault on the sovereign authority of member states—is more in keeping with the prudential task of building regional cooperation.

The ASEAN case demonstrates the need for political theorists to take account of regional particularity before promoting a universal Law of Peoples. Respectively compared with democracy and universalist ideology, decency and cultural particularity held greater appeal than Rawls realized. He overestimated the motivation of a city-state like Singapore to move beyond relative decency toward liberal democracy. The difficulty with a Rawlsian perspective is that it requires some notion of pragmatism or prudence to make it real. His schematic taxonomy lacks historical and cultural nuance. In the ASEAN context, this means putting economic growth ahead of democratic values, rather than the other way around.

The Rawlsian project is a realistic utopia. But a real dystopia could result from ASEAN's instigating constitutional change before market integration in Southeast Asia, where millennial capital is fickle and normative niceties do not determine foreign investment decisions. In Southeast Asia, a piecemeal approach to reform fits regional practice better than a transformative agenda for democratization.

Among the states that constitute the region, and on any measure of health, education, and welfare, the relative decency of Singapore, or the absolutist benevolence of Brunei, offer greater human security than do the more democratic regimes of the Philippines and Indonesia. It is this route toward relative decency that burdened societies such as Vietnam, Laos, and Cambodia are following, albeit with limited success. Myanmar remains an outlaw. From a Rawlsian perspective, prudentially modified, ASEAN's various states need to achieve a condition of reasonable decency, not reasonable pluralism.

"The question of whether a certain matter is or is not solely within the jurisdiction of a state is an essentially relative question."
—Permanent Court of International Justice, 1923[1]

"With the heightened international interest in universalizing a regime of human rights, there is a marked and most welcome shift in public attitudes. To try to resist it would be politically as unwise as it is morally indefensible."
—Javier Perez de Cuellar
Former Secretary-General of the United Nations[2]

"Where anything that is happening within the borders of a sovereign nation is perceived to have any negative effect on the collective interest of the community ... then it would be—it seems to be the consensus now—it would be, and should be, made a concern of this community."
—Musa Hitam
Former Malaysian Deputy Prime Minister and member of the ASEAN Eminent Persons Group[3]

---

[1] Cited in Bruce Cronin, "Multilateral Intervention and the International Community," in *International Intervention: Sovereignty versus Responsibility*, ed. Michael Keren and Donald A. Sylvan (London: Frank Cass, 2002), 147.

[2] Cited in Francis M. Deng, Sadikiel Kimaro, Terrence Lyons, Donald Rothchild, and I. William Zartman, *Sovereignty as Responsibility: Conflict Management in Africa* (Washington DC: Brookings Institution, 1996), 14.

[3] Kyodo News International, "ASEAN to Review 'Cherished' Non-interference Policy," 13 December 2005.

Toward Responsible Sovereignty: The Case for Intervention

Erik Martinez Kuhonta
McGill University
Canada

The central questions that persistently nag at the Association of Southeast Asian Nations (ASEAN) involve its relevance. How relevant is the Association in dealing with contemporary problems in its region? Can ASEAN address the global trend toward democracy? Can its members cooperate to solve emerging transnational problems, ranging from environmental pollution to financial crises? Is the "ASEAN Way" conducive to specific policies that significantly improve the lives of Southeast Asians? These questions—articulated at conferences, in policy papers, and in the popular media—continue to swirl around ASEAN.

At one level the question of relevance is unfair. Since its founding in 1967, ASEAN has proven its value by creating a stable and peaceful region. Since 1967, no two member states have waged war against each other. This is not a feat to be scoffed at. In the late 1960s, ethnic, Communist, and interstate tensions abounded in Southeast Asia, as they did in other parts of the developing world, such as the Middle East and Africa. ASEAN has made huge strides in establishing a zone of peace—or a security community—in its region.

At another level, the question of relevance will simply not go away. There are too many issues that ASEAN has simply failed to address. These include transnational problems and questions of human rights and democracy. Most vexing of all is the dilemma over what, if anything, to do about the dictatorship in Myanmar (or Burma), an ASEAN member. The Association has been unable to respond adequately to this issue, swaying back and forth between upholding the principle of noninterference and intermittently seeking some form of change through private dialogue. Until this problem is solved, ASEAN will be unable to shed the perception that it is an ineffective organization.

Two related norms that define ASEAN hold the Association back in dealing productively with contemporary Southeast Asian problems: first, the principle of sovereignty and noninterference, and second, the ASEAN Way of group consensus, discreet dialogue, and informal procedure. The principle of sovereignty, including its corollary norm, noninterference, prevents ASEAN from criticizing despotic behavior by one of its members. Although this very principle, by proscribing violence across borders, undergirded the formation

293

of a security community, ASEAN's resulting deference to member sovereignty has stunted its ability to advance democratic values.[4] ASEAN's member states have defended noninterference precisely because most of them are illiberal regimes.

The ASEAN Way has been instrumental in fostering a community by defining distinct norms of interaction. These norms of interaction are based on the cultural values of Southeast Asian societies, thereby strengthening a sense of "we"-ness. This in turn has solidified the region's sense of security. But the ASEAN Way reduces ASEAN policy to its least common denominator. Instead of being proactive, ASEAN defers to a consensual view, ensuring that no member is unhappy with its decision. The ASEAN Way therefore makes regional cooperation and policy implementation a singularly slow affair.

Noninterference and the ASEAN Way are linked in reinforcing ASEAN's tendency to act slowly or not at all. The norm of noninterference prevents ASEAN from tackling its members' internal problems, while the ASEAN Way dilutes policy through informal procedures and consensual decision-making. In this light, it is not surprising that ASEAN is often seen as an organization devoid of dynamism.

If ASEAN is to shed its image as an obsolescent entity, it must radically shift gears. I will argue in this chapter that the real test for ASEAN lies in its ability to rethink its cardinal principle of sovereignty and noninterference. I will focus mainly on noninterference, rather than on the ASEAN Way, because the norm of noninterference represents the more serious obstacle to ASEAN's ability to address contemporary problems. Decisiveness is crucial, and for that the ASEAN Way must be reconceived. But ultimately the real issue is less a matter of internal procedure than whether the Association will or will not actually intervene to address a problem, whether it has to do with democracy or something else.

Even Ali Alatas, formerly a foreign minister of Indonesia and a strong proponent of sovereignty, has commented that noninterference has to be relaxed if ASEAN is to remain relevant: "Respect for sovereignty will remain a basic principle for ASEAN, but increasingly we realize that we have to be flexible, that we have to be non-doctrinaire in some of these things. We realize that we have to reinvent ourselves in order to remain relevant, in order to remain effective."[5]

This chapter begins by reviewing the origins of ASEAN and the importance of the norm of noninterference in shaping the Association. The second and third sections focus on the debate over noninterference in the case of Myanmar,

---

[4] Hence the adjective in ASEAN's "illiberal peace." Noninterference has ensured the peace, but also the persistence of illiberal rule. This idea is developed in Erik Martinez Kuhonta, "Walking a Tightrope: Democracy versus Sovereignty in ASEAN's Illiberal Peace," *Pacific Review* 19, no. 3 (2006), 337–58.

[5] Agence France-Presse, "ASEAN Must Reinvent Itself, Loosen Non-Interference Policy: Alatas," 7 January 2004.

including the saga of its accession to ASEAN and the Association's failure to effect political reform in its new member. In a broader context, the chapter then examines how the relationship between sovereignty and interference has been reconceptualized in global politics. This fourth section shows that the balance in the post–Cold War period has gradually shifted toward a more qualified form of sovereignty, in which there is greater room for some degree of interference. In the conclusion, I make the case for finally dropping the principle of noninterference from ASEAN's modus operandi.

The Origins of ASEAN

Sovereignty acted as the center of gravity in postcolonial Southeast Asia because the region had just emerged from centuries of foreign domination. Its states were still trying to establish their legitimacy in the international arena. One of their fundamental concerns was the need to secure their borders among unfriendly neighbors. Given this, sovereignty most clearly guided these states' behavior, especially in international relations; without sovereignty, development would have been in constant jeopardy. As Nikolas Busse has written, "The normative ideal of sovereignty became the standard prescription for almost every political disease in the region and the cornerstone of ASEAN's attempts at creating a regional order."[6]

Since the 1967 Bangkok Declaration that launched the Association, ASEAN's key treaties have all emphasized the importance of sovereignty and noninterference. The Bangkok Declaration affirmed that "the countries of Southeast Asia ... are determined to ensure their stability and security from external interference in any form or manifestation." The 1971 Zone of Peace, Freedom and Neutrality (ZOPFAN) Declaration acknowledged the right of every country "to lead its national existence free from outside interference in its internal affairs as this interference will adversely affect its freedom, independence, and integrity." The first three clauses of Article 2 of the Treaty of Amity and Cooperation (1976) are all concerned with sovereignty and noninterference.[7] In theory and in practice, ASEAN has relentlessly underscored the belief that stability and progress in the region can be built only upon the legitimacy of state boundaries.

The noninterference policy was also crucial to ASEAN from the beginning. Although the norm of noninterference was not fully adhered to, it set some broad guidelines for patterns of interaction within the organization. The norm has had three important goals: preventing criticism of the domestic politics of one's neighbors, and the type of regime such politics might imply; denying support or sanctuary to opposition or rebel groups seeking to overthrow an incumbent

---

[6] Nikolas Busse, "Constructivism and Southeast Asian Security," *Pacific Review* 12, no. 1 (1999), 47.

[7] These documents are available at <http://www.aseansec.org/145.htm>.

government; and providing support to member states in their struggles against destabilizing forces.[8]

Southeast Asia in the early-to-mid 1960s was in dire need of an overarching mechanism that could stabilize the region. Tensions were high. Indonesia was in the midst of waging its *Konfrontasi* campaign against the formation of a Malaysia Federation incorporating Sabah and Sarawak on the north coast of the mainly Indonesian island of Borneo. The Philippines and Malaysia were in a long-running dispute over control of Sabah. Thailand and Malaysia had boundary problems related to ethnic and communist insurgencies, while Singapore had just been expelled from Malaysia and remained deeply insecure in a sea of Malay countries. All of these tensions could have led to war, and small-scale skirmishes did occur in the name of *Konfrontasi*.

Malaysian Foreign Minister Ghazali Shafie would later describe ASEAN as "a development out of the pains of *Konfrontasi*."[9] ASEAN's immediate task was to solidify the reconciliation process between Malaysia and Indonesia. After the 1965 coup in Jakarta that brought Suharto to power, *Konfrontasi* was ended. In order to institutionalize the peace process, Suharto initiated confidence-building gestures by organizing joint controls and liaison teams for communications in Borneo. The Malaysian and Indonesian governments worked together to root out Communist networks and weaken indigenous groups that might seek to resist the Malaysian Federation. The Indonesian government then recognized the first local elections in Borneo, thereby confirming its acceptance of Malaysian sovereignty over Sabah and Sarawak. When Malaysia later faced the worst moment in its history—the riots of 13 May 1969—Indonesia refrained from any criticism of its neighboring government's actions. Normal relations were fully restored not long after, when President Suharto visited Malaysia in March 1970.[10]

The dispute between Malaysia and the Philippines over control of Sabah was another major irritant that led to significant conflict in the region. Under President Ferdinand Marcos, the Philippines continued to bring up the country's right of sovereignty over Sabah. Tensions between the two countries rose to a fever pitch when news spread in March 1968 that the Philippines was training military contingents on Corregidor Island for an assault on Sabah.

Although the first mechanism for resolving the Corregidor affair arose through the United Nations, eventually a cooling-off period was initiated in August 1968 at the 2nd ASEAN Ministerial Meeting (AMM), in Jakarta—the annual gathering of ASEAN foreign ministers. Despite persisting tensions, eventually the two countries were able to moderate their relations. President

---

[8] Amitav Acharya, *Constructing a Security Community in Southeast Asia: ASEAN and the Problem of Regional Order* (London: Routledge, 2001), 58.

[9] Quoted in Michael Leifer, *ASEAN and the Security of South-East Asia* (London: Routledge, 1989), 2.

[10] See Michael Antolik, *ASEAN and the Diplomacy of Accommodation* (Armonk, NY: M.E. Sharpe, 1990).

Marcos was never willing to fully renounce his country's claim to Sabah, but by joining ASEAN and accepting its norms of sovereignty and noninterference, Malaysia and the Philippines had become part of a structure that could indirectly address, if not solve, the claim over Sabah.

Thailand and Malaysia had similarly tense relations. The Malayan Communist Party sought refuge in southern Thailand, while the Thai government had to deal with an ethnic insurgency that threatened its control over the same area. Each side needed the other's cooperation to address their respective problems. Although accusations were rife—the two countries accused each other of supporting the other's nemesis, or not doing enough to weaken the insurgents—Malaysia and Thailand agreed to joint border patrols and intelligence-sharing.

Singapore's expulsion from Malaysia in 1965 was a traumatic experience that underscored the mainly ethnic-Chinese city-state's isolation deep in the heart of the Malay archipelago. Tensions flared in March 1968 when Singapore sought to assert its sovereignty by announcing that it would repatriate 45,000 Malaysian workers who had been left unemployed due to the closure of British military bases. Malaysian authorities responded by threatening to expel 60,000 Singaporeans from Malaysia. A few months later, in October, Singapore enraged Jakarta by executing Indonesian marines who had been captured during *Konfrontasi*. Each of these incidents could have spiraled into interstate violence. Instead, ultimately, each side restrained itself.

In 1986, a visit to Singapore by Israeli President Chaim Herzog once again sparked hostility between the city-state and majority-Muslim Malaysia. Significantly, however, on this occasion Malaysia's then-prime minister Mahathir bin Mohamad did not publicly challenge Singapore, and went so far as to restrain public protest after three thousand people joined an anti-Singapore rally in Johor Bahru, a Malaysian city adjacent to Singapore. Clearly, since the 1960s, ASEAN had matured and learned how to deal with heated intramural disputes. "The lesson learned was not that Singapore must compromise its sovereignty to placate Muslim sensitivities," wrote one analyst, "but that Singapore, for its own well-being, must not ignore the effects of its policies on neighboring societies."[11]

The central point to infer from these conflicts is that ASEAN has made significant progress in dealing with interstate relations. How has this occurred?

In Southeast Asia, prior to ASEAN's establishment, there were neither guiding principles nor means of solving such disputes. ASEAN provided the framework for easing tensions through its style of diplomacy—informal, discreet, and nonconfrontational. This approach is firmly grounded in respect for each member's sovereignty. Sukarno showed no respect for Malaysia's borders during *Konfrontasi*. Marcos also challenged Malaysia's territorial integrity. But in both instances—the most severe of their kind in ASEAN's history—the likely aggressors eventually moderated their position and accepted their neighbor's

---

[11] Antolik, *ASEAN and the Diplomacy of Accommodation*, 43.

sovereign rights. Years later a foreign minister of Singapore looked back on that period and concluded that "non-interference in the affairs of another country was ... the key factor as to why no military conflict had broken out between any two member states since 1967."[12]

As I have noted, since *Konfrontasi* no war has been waged among members of the Association. This is a remarkable achievement given the region's turbulent history. War is no longer seen as a means of solving disputes in the region, to the point that some analysts have conceptualized ASEAN as a "nascent security community."[13] Yet despite such progress, a question still bedevils ASEAN: Beyond resolving interstate conflicts in a peaceful manner, what else has it accomplished? Has its past success in solving regional disputes through the norms of sovereignty and noninterference prevented it from making progress in other areas? Will the fostering of peace in Southeast Asia remain its sole achievement?

Between Democracy and Sovereignty: The Case of Myanmar[14]

Some thirty years after ASEAN was founded, the region was mired in a number of crises that called the organization's continuing relevance into question. Myanmar posed the most profound problem.[15] At the 30th AMM, in Kuala Lumpur in July 1997, ASEAN welcomed Myanmar as a member despite a flurry of criticism from human rights voices and international actors. ASEAN argued that its policy of constructive engagement stood a better chance of inducing political reform inside Myanmar than could be expected from publicly haranguing the junta.

Myanmar's entry into ASEAN thus became a real test of the Association's noninterference rule. At a time when democracy had swept through the globe, could ASEAN prove to a skeptical international public that its own normative order could stimulate political change? And if it could not, would it cease to be relevant in the eyes of the world?

The process leading up to Myanmar's accession to ASEAN was fraught with intense diplomatic sparring. The United States and the European Union (EU) were adamant that Myanmar should not be granted any form of international legitimacy after its violent annulment of the 1990 elections. At the 9th ASEAN-EU Ministerial Meeting, in Luxembourg in 1991, the EU for the first time

---

[12] Statement by S. Jayakumar in *The Straits Times* [Singapore], 25 July 1997, quoted in Acharya, *Constructing a Security Community in Southeast Asia*, 57.

[13] Acharya, *Constructing a Security Community in Southeast Asia*.

[14] The discussion of Myanmar in this section draws on Kuhonta, "Walking a Tightrope."

[15] For a study of the problem of noninterference in Cambodia, see Kim Hourn Kao and Jeffrey A. Kaplan, eds., *Principles under Pressure: Cambodia and ASEAN's Non-Interference Policy* (Phnom Penh: Cambodian Institute for Cooperation and Peace, 1999).

strongly criticized ASEAN's policy toward Myanmar.[16] Since then, the EU has firmly opposed any form of ASEAN rapprochement with the junta.[17]

At the time of Myanmar's accession, Prime Minister Mahathir in particular was adamant that ASEAN should ignore outside pressure and bring Myanmar into the fold. Only with the country inside the organization could one envisage internal reform. Constructive engagement—collegially, behind closed doors, urging the junta to change its ways—remained ASEAN's policy for years following Myanmar's affiliation [18]

Civil society groups in the region, however, vocally objected to Myanmar's admission. A number of policy analysts in the ASEAN Institutes of Strategic and International Studies (ASEAN-ISIS), a network of think tanks, dissented from the positions taken by their governments and argued that conditions in Myanmar were egregious enough to warrant breaching the norm of noninterference. Jusuf Wanandi, chair of the Center for Strategic and International Studies in Jakarta, argued that ASEAN should look beyond its noninterference policy and refuse to admit Myanmar.[19]

In July 1998, at its 31st AMM in Manila, ASEAN conceded that no progress had been made in Myanmar on democracy or human rights. Criticism of ASEAN's policy of constructive engagement was fierce. Debbie Stothard, coordinator for the Alternative ASEAN Network on Myanmar, cited increased assaults on the democratic movement, attacks on ethnic minorities, repression of civil freedoms, continued closures of universities, and increased drug production.[20] Philippine Senator Aquilino Pimentel raised the possibility of expelling Myanmar from ASEAN: "Perhaps it is now time," he suggested, "to seek a review and revision of our country's support of Myanmar into ASEAN and probably even move for the expulsion of Myanmar from ASEAN."[21]

---

[16] Kavi Chongkittavorn, personal communication, 5 April 2005.

[17] Prior to the debacle inside Myanmar in September 2007 (mentioned in the ensuing sections of this chapter and also discussed in the chapter on Myanmar in this book), the EU was involved in a debate over its antagonistic position toward Myanmar. For example, Robert Taylor and Morton Pedersen ("Supporting Myanmar/Myanmar's National Reconciliation Process: Challenges and Opportunities," January 2005, <http://www.ibiblio.org/obl/docs3/Independant_Report-Burma_Day.htm>) prepared a report for the European Commission that called for closer relations between the EU and the Myanmar government. These would have included making regular high-level visits to the country, revising the use of sanctions, and lifting political constraints on aid.

[18] See Acharya, *Constructing a Security Community in Southeast Asia,* 109–10, on the origins of constructive engagement.

[19] Jusuf Wanandi, "Partners Should Nudge Burma," *International Herald Tribune,* 5 June 1997.

[20] Deutsche Presse-Agentur, "ASEAN: Myanmar Makes No Progress on Road to Democracy," 25 July 1998.

[21] Deutsche Presse-Agentur, "Top Philippine Legislator Calls for Myanmar's Expulsion from ASEAN," 3 August 1998.

At the 1998 AMM, in Manila, Thailand's Foreign Minister Surin Pitsuwan took a bold step. In an effort to move beyond ASEAN's principle of noninterference, he circulated a policy paper advocating "flexible engagement" as a new policy framework through which the Association's members could relate to one another.[22] This idea, in effect, would have ended the noninterference policy. But only Domingo Siazon, then foreign minister of the Philippines, supported the Thai proposal. ASEAN as a whole accepted a more minimally interventionist stance on issues of economics and the environment, but drew a sharp line between that and being proactive on democracy or human rights.[23]

Indonesian Foreign Minister Ali Alatas offered the term "enhanced interaction" as a compromise to Surin's proposal and the status quo. Alatas made clear how far ASEAN was willing to go: "If the proposition is [that], within ASEAN, we should be more frank in discussing views that may originate in one country but have an impact on the other ASEAN countries, then let's do it ... [But] using fancy names like flexible engagement and constructive intervention—that we cannot accept."[24]

In 1999 at the 32nd AMM, in Singapore, the foreign ministers actually discussed human rights, governance, and civil society.[25] Nevertheless, two full years after Myanmar had gained membership in ASEAN, reforming the junta was still a distant goal. One of Thailand's major English-language newspapers editorialized that constructive engagement had "failed—totally and spectacularly." Since Myanmar's accession to ASEAN, the "only important changes in Burma" had been "for the worse." Two years earlier, "Burma's senior dictator," Khin Nyunt, had at least been willing to talk with the country's "only independent democratic force," Aung San Suu Kyi's National League for

---

[22] See Ministry of Foreign Affairs of the Government of Thailand, "Thailand's Non-Paper on the Flexible Engagement Approach," 27 July 1998, <http://www.thaiembdc.org/pressctr/pr/pr743.htm>.

[23] As one delegate from Myanmar said: "Talking about economics is okay, but not human rights." See Deutsche Presse-Agentur, "ASEAN Moves Closer to Limited Intervention," 24 July 1998.

[24] "In the Bunker," *Far Eastern Economic Review*, 6 August 1998. Malaysia's Foreign Minister Abdullah Badawi had this to say in response to arguments that ASEAN was too meek in criticizing its members:

> We know that this cannot be further from the truth. We have not only commented and criticized, we have even expressed reservations when necessary. But we do all of this quietly, befitting a community of friends bonded in cooperation and ever mindful of the fact that fractious relations undermine the capacity of ASEAN to work together on issues critical to our collective being. We do it in this quiet way because criticizing loudly, posturing adversarially and grandstanding ... does more harm than good. (Robin Ramcharan, "ASEAN and Non-Interference: A Principle Maintained," *Contemporary Southeast Asia* 22, no. 1 [2000], 80.)

[25] "Sharper Image," *Far Eastern Economic Review*, 5 August 1999.

Democracy (NLD). "Today, the regime will not talk to any democrat." In the junta's pronouncements, earlier promises to investigate accusations of forced labor had been replaced by the fatuous claim that the Burmese people actually loved to "volunteer their labor for the glory of the Tatmadaw"—Myanmar's army.[26]

By the end of 2000, however, there were indications that some change was creeping in. In December, the EU finally held high-level talks with ASEAN that had been suspended since 1997 in protest over Myanmar's presence. Held in the Laotian capital, Vientiane, the talks did yield a concrete result: The junta agreed to receive an EU "troika" mission in January 2001.[27] More importantly, news began to filter out that Aung San Suu Kyi had been engaged in secret dialogues with the military junta since the previous October.

In April 2000, Kofi Annan appointed Razali Ismail as the UN Special Envoy to Myanmar. A retired career diplomat from Malaysia with close ties to Mahathir, Razali quickly emerged as a pivotal player in reaching out to both the junta and the NLD and gaining their confidence.[28] After five visits to Myanmar, he was able to produce a fundamental breakthrough. On 6 May 2002, Aung San Suu Kyi was released unconditionally from house arrest as the international community hailed a "new dawn" in Myanmar.[29]

The "new dawn" turned out to be a false start. Once Suu Kyi was released, she resumed her popular trips across Myanmar. The acclaim she received greatly perturbed the junta, especially its top leader, Senior General Than Shwe. As it had done before when she traveled the country, the military begin to harass her convoy. The intimidation climaxed in a violent outburst in northern Myanmar on the night of 30 May 2003. Pro-junta thugs attacked her convoy with sharpened bamboo poles and killed an estimated seventy to eighty people, including both locals and members of the NLD. Survivors of the ambush reported that drug-emboldened goons charged at the convoy mercilessly and that Suu Kyi survived only because her followers piled on top of her to protect her. Following the attack, the authorities seized her and placed her in solitary confinement before transferring her back into house arrest in the capital, Yangon, at the end of September.

In the light of these developments, one must ask: Has the junta actually benefited from having joined ASEAN?

---

[26] "ASEAN Fails to Engage Rangoon," *Bangkok Post*, 11 July 1999.

[27] Agence France-Presse, "EU Ministers Hail Progress on Myanmar as They End ASEAN Boycott," 12 December 2000.

[28] Myanmar Deputy Foreign Minister Khin Maung Win commented that "because Mr. Razali is from Asia I believe he has a better understanding of the issues involved," and that "he appreciates the complexities and sensitivities." See Agence France-Presse, "UN Envoy to Myanmar Carries Hope for Junta-Opposition Dialogue," 4 January 2001.

[29] "Burma's Symbol of Hope Steps into the Sunlight," *Financial Times*, 7 May 2002.

Yes, it has, in two ways. First, Myanmar's membership has helped to legitimate the junta by association with an important regional institution. Obviously its affiliation did not raise the junta's standing among Western governments. But the Burmese generals did gain prestige from the interactions with other Southeast Asian leaders that membership enabled them to have. Taking part in the numerous meetings that ASEAN holds has conferred legitimacy on the regime and furnished it with extensive regional contacts for it to use in furthering its economic and political interests.

Second, participation in ASEAN has strengthened the military's hold on power. Since Myanmar entered the Association in 1997, human rights abuses by the regime have increased, dialogue between the junta and the NLD has stalled, and the repression of Suu Kyi has reached an unprecedented level. As a full-fledged member of ASEAN, the junta has been able to protect itself by invoking the mantra of noninterference. The generals have little political incentive to reform their behavior now that they are inside ASEAN. As one veteran expert on the country wrote back in 1988, "There seems little question that in the near term, entry into ASEAN will strengthen Myanmar internationally and prompt little in the way of significant political or economic changes in the Myanmar system."[30]

To be sure, accession to ASEAN has not been the paramount factor helping the junta stay in power. Many factors have facilitated the consolidation of authoritarian military rule. It is worth emphasizing, however, that with ASEAN's stamp of legitimacy, it became easier for the junta to brush aside criticism from the West and remain unfazed by threats of diplomatic and economic sanctions. Still more importantly, with ASEAN's support, Myanmar enjoys access to regional markets that can be used to serve the junta's interests.

If they have strengthened the junta, ASEAN's actions may have been even more consequential in weakening and isolating the democratic opposition. ASEAN's noninterference principle has always been intended to protect existing regimes, whether they be democratic or authoritarian. In any member country, those opposing the incumbent government naturally fall out of favor in ASEAN's normative framework. In this context, as Amitav Acharya has pointed out, constructive engagement may actually imply "a particular kind of interference *in support of the regime*."[31]

The Shifting Sands of Noninterference

In the 1990s, leaders across the region grew less reticent about criticizing their neighbors for acts against domestic opposition. In 1998, for example, Indonesia and the Philippines were highly critical of Mahathir's vindictive effort to impugn

---

[30] David Steinberg, "Myanmar: Regional Relationships and Internal Concerns," *Southeast Asian Affairs 1988* (Singapore: Institute of Southeast Asian Studies, 1988), 183.

[31] Acharya, *Constructing a Security Community in Southeast Asia,* 114. Italics added.

and ruin his political-heir-turned-rival, Anwar Ibrahim. Since then, the idea that states can command absolute sovereignty has been forcefully challenged. The emergence of democratic regimes in Southeast Asia has added heft to supporters of human rights and liberal values. Under such pressure, ASEAN's strict adherence to the noninterference policy has begun to waver.

The attack on Suu Kyi's convoy in May 2003 brought forth the strongest condemnation of the Myanmar junta. At the foreign ministers' meeting in Phnom Penh in June, ASEAN issued a statement calling for Suu Kyi's release. Several foreign ministers denied that this was interference, since Myanmar accepted ASEAN's statement at the meeting, but clearly ASEAN had broken from its habit of responding soporifically to political crises in the region.[32]

In July, Mahathir warned that Myanmar could be expelled from ASEAN if it did not change its behavior. This was a stunning reversal for the man who had been the strongest advocate of Myanmar's entry into ASEAN in 1997. In September 2003, Indonesia sent the former foreign minister Ali Alatas as a special envoy to Myanmar.[33] The day after he left, Thai Foreign Minister Surakiart Sathirathai arrived to call on the junta. With the Bali Summit upcoming in October 2003, ASEAN had hoped to dim the spotlight on the crisis in Myanmar. All of these remonstrations led nowhere, however, as the junta refused to release Suu Kyi.

A few years later, ASEAN surprised the international community by openly challenging Myanmar's right to chair the body in 2006. Parliamentarians from Malaysia, Singapore, Thailand, Indonesia, and the Philippines voiced severe displeasure at the prospect of Myanmar holding court for ASEAN. In Indonesia, the parliament's Commission on Defense and Foreign Affairs called on the government to boycott ASEAN if Myanmar took the chairmanship.[34] The Philippine Senate passed a motion calling on ASEAN to deny Myanmar the chairmanship, and in Thailand seventy-seven senators signed a petition urging their government to toughen their policy on Myanmar.[35]

In Malaysia, a group of parliamentarians from the governing coalition filed a motion calling on their government to deny Myanmar the chairmanship of ASEAN if it did not release Suu Kyi and thousands of political prisoners. One of the sponsors of the bill, Nazri Abdul Aziz, a minister in the prime minister's department and the leader of government business in the Malaysian parliament, commented, "There must be a time for constructive engagement[;]

---

[32] "Spotlight on Burma at ASEAN Meeting," *The Nation* [Bangkok], 18 June 2003.

[33] It is worth pointing out that Alatas had been one of the strongest opponents of Surin's idea of "flexible engagement.'

[34] Lim Kit Siang, "Singapore Parliamentary Caucus on Burma," 6 March 2005, <http://www.dapmalaysia.org/english/2005/may05/lks/lks3492.htm>.

[35] "Senate Turns Up Heat on Government over Burma," *The Nation* [Bangkok], 10 May 2005.

it cannot go on and on forever."[36] The bill was eventually shelved, although the commotion over the bill allowed Malaysian parliamentarians to vent openly their dissatisfaction with the lack of political change in Myanmar.[37] The vehemence of Malaysian rhetoric against the junta was noteworthy since the Malaysian government had earlier been the chief backer of the junta. And the fact that Nazri Abdul Aziz worked in the prime minister's department was thought to indicate that the harder line he advocated had come from the prime minister himself.

At the AMM in Vientiane in July 2005, Myanmar decided to postpone its chairmanship of ASEAN. This came as a great relief to Southeast Asian leaders who feared that ASEAN would sustain serious damage by allowing itself to be led by such an odious regime. U.S. Secretary of State Condoleezza Rice's decision not to attend the ASEAN Regional Forum (ARF) was seen as a taste of things to come, had Myanmar occupied the chair. When Myanmar declined to do so, ASEAN appeared to have weathered the storm and appeased Western critics, who had made very clear that they would not attend ASEAN's meetings with Myanmar presiding.

In 1997 ASEAN had stressed that its policy of constructive engagement, rather than isolation and sanctions, was more likely to bring about political reform in Myanmar. But reform did not occur. The policy of constructive engagement appeared to have virtually no effect on the junta. The arrest and sentencing of the only general, Khin Nyunt, who had been willing at least to meet and talk with Suu Kyi, struck an especially ominous note in this context.[38] He was purged in 2004, and since then the junta has stamped out any potential niches of dissent within the military.

ASEAN members may increasingly breach the doctrine of noninterference, but this does not mean that ASEAN is about to give priority to democracy and human rights.[39] On both of the occasions when ASEAN decided to take a more critical stand toward Myanmar, significant pressure from the West was crucial. The real issue that troubles ASEAN is the fear of losing face and becoming irrelevant on the world stage. ASEAN Secretary General Ong Keng Yong put it

---

[36] Reuters, "Southeast Asia's Club of Nations Turns Up Heat on Myanmar," 24 March 2005.

[37] "Burma Motion in Parliament Put Off," *Malaysiakini*, 26 April 2005.

[38] An International Crisis Group (ICG) Report noted that Khin Nyunt's standing within the military hierarchy was "an important indication of the prospects for political progress." See ICG, "Myanmar: Solutions, Engagement or Another Way Forward," ICG Asia Report no. 78, Brussels, 26 April 2004.

[39] In 2005 the former secretary-general of ASEAN, Filipino Rodolfo Severino, defended noninterference in the process of rotating the ASEAN chair from state to state in English-alphabetic order. Does intervention mean, he asked, whether "when you don't like what another member is doing, you skip the rotation process?" This would be, in his view, "a rather dangerous move." Quoted in *Bangkok Post*, "KL Ups the Ante on Rangoon," 27 March 2005.

this way in 2003: "There is a negative image and rather adverse kind of remarks passed about ASEAN [because of the situation in Myanmar] ... We want to minimize the adverse impact on our organization as a whole."[40]

As discussed in detail in Kyaw Yin Hlaing's chapter on Myanmar in this book, that negative image and those critical remarks were dramatically intensified in September 2007 by the violent and dispiriting repression of the "saffron revolution" in Myanmar, and by ASEAN's unwillingness to do more than allow Singapore's Foreign Minister George Yeo, as the ASEAN chair, to express "revulsion" over reports of the junta's crackdown.[41] But this was not the end of the story. Having expressed its disgust in the strongest language that ASEAN had ever addressed to its pariah member, the Association could hardly proceed to say and do nothing in the hope that the issue would go away. The Myanmar problem was not about to disappear. Changing global norms would not allow it to, as the next section will show. Nor would those norms permit the Association to stand idly by, ignoring the mounting damage to its reputation.

The Changing Nature of Sovereignty and Intervention

ASEAN's disgust over the junta's behavior in 2007, following the earlier, more gradual steps taken by the organization toward breaching the norm of noninterference, are part of a global trend that challenges the absolute value of sovereignty. It will be useful now to place the debate over noninterference in this broader perspective. What could be said of the controversy over sovereignty versus interference, as of 2007? Democracies had come to predominate in the post–Cold War world, and state failure had become a major international concern. Had these developments led to a reappraisal of the importance of sovereignty?

The tension between sovereignty and democracy / human rights can be traced in its contemporary form to the charter of the United Nations (UN). Article 1.3 of the charter states that the UN's goal is to "encourag[e] respect for human rights and for fundamental freedoms for all." According to article 2.1, however, the "organization is based on the principle of the sovereign equality of all its members," while Article 2.7 says that "nothing contained in the present charter shall authorize the United Nations to intervene in matters which are essentially within the domestic jurisdiction." Furthermore, the UN General Assembly's Declaration on Intervention (1965) asserts that no state has a right to intervene, directly or indirectly, in the internal or external affairs of another

---

[40] "Suu Kyi Arrest Threatens ASEAN Credibility," *Financial Times*, 6 October 2003.
[41] Reuters, "ASEAN Condemns Myanmar Violence," 27 September 2007.

state. Thus, from its very birth, the UN sought to uphold both the values of human rights and state sovereignty. [42]

In an important article in *World Politics*, Robert Jackson and Carl Rosberg clearly articulated the tension between sovereignty and democracy. They argued that international law had enshrined sovereignty as the central norm in the international system, thereby sustaining weak states and allowing them to rule as they wished within their boundaries.[43] This form of sovereignty could be best understood as "negative sovereignty," that is, freedom from outside interference.[44] The long-term result of the consolidation of negative sovereignty was to create states that were juridical but not empirical—states that were recognized but that lacked actual capacity.

The consequences of this disjuncture between empirical and juridical statehood are profound. When it comes to political development, states are under no necessary pressure to improve their capacities to provide public goods. Whether they can rule effectively or not, their rule is guaranteed, at least externally. In terms of human rights, the consolidation of the norm of sovereignty in effect strengthens the position of elites vis-à-vis civil society. Sovereignty ratifies the rulership of elites irrespective of how they perform or how they treat their citizens. As long as the international system remains stable, violence and repression can persist within national boundaries.[45] As Jackson put it, "The same institution [sovereignty] which provided international recognition, dignity, and independence to all colonized populations could be exploited to deny domestic civility, liberty, and welfare to some."[46]

By the 1990s, however, the idea that sovereignty was absolute began to be rethought. This shift in thinking arose in a post–Cold War context as conflicts between states began to abate, while conflicts within states grew more prevalent. With intrastate conflicts becoming more salient and the problem of state failure or collapse more severe, it became difficult simply to stand by while societies were torn apart by violence. Although the post–Cold war period was marked

---

[42] See S. Neil McFarlane, *Intervention in Contemporary World Politics*, Adelphi Paper 350 (Oxford: Oxford University Press, 2002).

[43] Robert Jackson and Carl G. Rosberg, "Why Africa's Weak States Persist: The Empirical and the Juridical in Statehood," *World Politics* 35, no. 1 (1982), 1–24.

[44] In contrast, "positive sovereignty" is a substantive rather than a formal condition. It, too, refers to the right of noninterference. More importantly, however, positive sovereignty denotes the ability of a state to provide public goods. See Robert Jackson, *Quasi-States: Sovereignty, International Relations and the Third World* (Cambridge: Cambridge University Press, 1990), 27–29.

[45] Reversing Waltz's famous thesis that anarchy characterizes the international system while relative order prevails within states, observing the principle of negative sovereignty ensures that order reigns externally while internally, inside states, violence and instability can reign. See Kenneth N. Waltz, *Theory of International Politics* (New York: McGraw-Hill, 1978).

[46] Jackson, *Quasi-States*, 202.

by a rise in democratic states, the move to reconceptualize sovereignty was less a positive reflection of liberal gains than a response to civil wars and acts of violence, including genocide, that shocked the conscience of humankind.[47]

In 1991, UN Secretary-General Javier Perez de Cuellar commented: "We are clearly witnessing what is probably an irresistible shift in public attitudes towards the belief that the defense of the oppressed in the name of morality should prevail over frontiers and legal documents." He went on to ask whether this shift in outlook called into question "one of the cardinal principles of international law," a principle "diametrically opposed to" the defense of the oppressed, "namely, the obligation of non-interference in the internal affairs of states."[48] A year later, de Cuellar's successor at the UN, Boutros Boutros-Ghali, answered his predecessor's question: "Respect for a [state's] fundamental sovereignty and integrity is crucial to any common international progress ... [but] the time of absolute and exclusive sovereignty ... has passed."[49]

With Kofi Annan at the helm of the UN, the debate over sovereignty and interference gathered momentum. In an article in *The Economist*, Annan argued that two concepts of sovereignty stood side by side: one centered on the state and one centered on the individual.[50] Sovereignty centered on the individual was a new and distinct concept. Individual-centered sovereignty referred to the fundamental freedom of every person. It underlined the notion that the purpose of sovereignty was to ensure individual freedom—as understood in its broadest sense—and not to allow states to hide behind inviolable borders. Such thinking was solidly in line with Annan's vision of freedom and democracy as underpinning progress and development.[51]

The idea that sovereignty should be focused on individual well-being achieved its fullest fruition in 2001 in *The Responsibility to Protect*, a report by a high-powered International Commission on Intervention and State Sovereignty,

---

[47] As Jack Donnelly, an expert on human rights, has written: "The threshold of coercive intervention is likely to be crossed only when the case stops being seen as a human rights issue and becomes a conventional international conflict (Iraq) or involves the breakdown of the authority of the state (Somalia)." See Donnelly, "State Sovereignty and International Intervention: The Case of Human Rights," in *Beyond Westphalia? State Sovereignty and International Intervention*, ed. Gene M. Lyons and Michael Mastanduno (Baltimore: Johns Hopkins University Press, 1995), 115–46.

[48] Cited in Lyons and Mastanduno, *Beyond Westphalia?*, 2.

[49] See Boutros Boutros-Ghali, "An Agenda for Peace," Report of the Secretary-General Pursuant to the Statement Adopted by the Summit Meeting of the Security Council, 1992.

[50] Kofi A. Annan, "Two Concepts of Sovereignty," *The Economist*, 18 September, 1999.

[51] See, for example, Annan's May 2005 speech at the University of Pennsylvania Commencement, in *Almanac* 51, no. 33 (24 May 2005), 4.

which Annan convened.[52] The Commission boldly asserted that sovereignty was ultimately about a state's responsibility to protect its citizens. While the report acknowledged that sovereignty still implied an external referent—namely, noninterference—it stressed the importance of state responsibility. Sovereignty, in other words, now had to be earned—precisely the notion that Jackson and Rosberg had argued was deeply missing in the international system.[53]

The significance of sovereignty as responsibility is threefold. First, it places the burden on states to ensure the protection of their citizens. Second, it implies that elites are responsible, both internally to their citizens and externally to the international community. Third, it means that state elites will be held responsible for their actions.[54]

The Commission underscored, above all, that intervention should be based not on the right to intervene but on the responsibility to protect. The spotlight of concern should not be on the actors who intervene but on those who need support. Responsibility for protection allows the international community to bridge sovereignty and intervention, since the failure to act responsibly provides the basis for intervention. The right to sovereignty comes at a price: responsibility toward citizens and the international community. Absent that responsibility, the international community can trump the sovereignty of an abusive state.

Given this shift in thinking about sovereignty, there is now a greater basis for legitimating some form of intervention. But what does intervention mean? According to one useful definition, "the essence of intervention is the attempt to compel." Regardless of whether intervention employs physical or economic pressure, what matters is the compulsion or constraint to achieve some change in the actor upon whom pressure is being exerted.[55] Another definition states that interventionist behavior occurs "whenever the form of the behavior constitutes a sharp break with then-existing forms *and* whenever it is directed at changing or preserving the structure of political authority in the target society."[56] Interventions, by this definition, must be clearly differentiated from any foreign policy decisions. Interventions must be "convention-breaking" and "authority-

---

[52] International Commission on Intervention and State Sovereignty (ICISS), *The Responsibility to Protect* (Ottawa: International Development Research Center, December 1991).

[53] To use Krasner's terms, this meant that sovereignty had to encompass domestic sovereignty, international legal sovereignty, and Westphalian sovereignty. See Stephen D. Krasner, "Problematic Sovereignty," in *Problematic Sovereignty: Contested Rules and Political Possibilities*, ed. Stephen D. Krasner (New York: Columbia University Press, 2001), 1–23.

[54] ICISS, *The Responsibility to Protect*, 13.

[55] Ann Van Wynen Thomas and A. J. Thomas, Jr., *Non-Intervention: The Law and Its Import in the Americas* (Dallas, TX: Southern Methodist University Press, 1956), 72.

[56] James N. Rosenau, "Intervention as a Scientific Concept," *Journal of Conflict Resolution* 13, no. 2 (1969), 161.

oriented." Combining these two sound definitions, intervention or interference can be thought of as behavior that is convention-breaking, authority-oriented, and compelling in nature.

Defining intervention in this way gives us a conceptual handle on the term. But because the range of interventions can be very wide, it is important to identify in a given instance the extent of intervention being exerted. For this purpose it helps to disaggregate interference on a continuum from the highest degree of intervention, the use of military force, to the lowest degree, verging on noninterference, as shown in Figure 10.1.[57]

At the high end of the scale lies military coercion, in which force is used to restore order and where a national border is trespassed. Humanitarian intervention, which may or may not be accompanied by military intervention, also involves the physical crossing of borders. Next in line is the application of sanctions to correct a regime's behavior or to bring a regime down. Next to sanctions, at the lower end of the spectrum, is suasion through diplomacy, whether public or private.

Figure 10.1 Continuum of Degree of Unsolicited or Solicited Interference

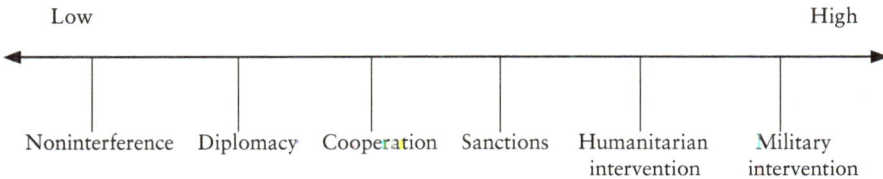

Low High

Noninterference Diplomacy Cooperation Sanctions Humanitarian intervention Military intervention

Each level of interference may correspond to a particular issue. State failure or acts of genocide may necessitate military intervention. A famine may spur humanitarian intervention. Violations of human rights, the annulment of elections, systematic repression against a democratic opposition, or institutionalized discrimination against a racial group may incur punishment through diplomatic rebuke or, more forcefully, punitive sanctions. Resolving or managing transnational problems—environmental pollution, drug trafficking, or an influx of refugees—may call for diplomatic dialogue.

Acknowledging gradations of interference is important. Doing so makes it easier to see how ASEAN, notwithstanding its frustration over Myanmar, could, through small steps, become less allergic to intervention. As the global climate has shifted, so could ASEAN incrementally revise its commitment to its member states' sovereignty.

---

[57] Lyons and Mastanduno offer a similar and simpler scale for conceptualizing intervention. See *Beyond Westphalia?*, 10. See also Donnelly's typology of four types of intervention: (1) authorized coercive interference, (2) prohibited coercive interference, (3) authorized noncoercive interference, and (4) unregulated noncoercive interference ("State Sovereignty and International Intervention," 119–20).

In Southeast Asia it is not necessary for sovereignty to be entirely trumped by international law and global norms—by what Jack Donnelly calls the internationalist model. Most of the cases of domestic irresponsibility by ASEAN's member states are not so egregious that they invite outright military intervention. They require some weakening of sovereignty—especially in the case of Myanmar—but not its abandonment.

In the aftermath of the junta's repression of September 2007, conditions in Myanmar would most likely require an intermediate degree of interference—something more than persuasion but less than invasion. Sanctions of some form exemplify this middle level of intervention. Sanctions against Myanmar would not sacrifice respect for its sovereignty, but they would, by their more coercive nature, emphatically convey ASEAN's desire for significant reform inside its most errant member.

Conclusion

Where, then, does this discussion of sovereignty and interference leave us, both globally and concerning Myanmar?

Two circumstances should be stressed. First, global trends point to a conditional form of sovereignty in which states have to earn their right to govern without intervention from the international community. Second, it should be clear that ASEAN's default position, based on constructive engagement, has failed miserably. If that policy was meant to nudge the Myanmar junta toward some degree of reform, it may be fairly called a complete disaster. Recent moves toward some loosening of the noninterference norm by Singapore and Malaysia, including Singapore's expression of ASEAN's "revulsion" over the junta's crackdown in September 2007, indicate that even some of ASEAN's greatest stalwarts have begun to lose patience with the policy of constructive engagement.

Given the trend toward conditional sovereignty and the failure of constructive engagement, what should ASEAN do? The evidence I have presented in this chapter points to a different path that ASEAN should take if it is to be a catalyst for reform in Myanmar.

There are two ways to recommend a different path. One relies on a normative argument; the other emphasizes practical concerns. At a normative level, ASEAN could consider a more forceful push for human rights and democracy in Myanmar based on the idea of "moral interdependence"—the sense of satisfaction or revulsion that the people of one state derive from observing the internal behavior of another state.[58] An initiative of this kind would match the global shift toward the idea of sovereignty as responsibility. If ASEAN wants to maintain its political relevance by following this global shift, it should move away from the policy of noninterference.

---

[58] Donnelly, "State Sovereignty and International Intervention."

Second, as a matter of practice, ASEAN must directly address the failure of constructive engagement. Some degree of more active interference is warranted, simply because of that failure. Simon Tay has noted correctly that while there has been some intervention in ASEAN, it has not "developed consistently and comprehensively into a full political dialogue."[59] Even more than a full political dialogue is required. In recent years, ASEAN leaders, including Mahathir, have articulated sharper criticisms of the Myanmar junta. But this, too, seems insufficient. Interference should now entail going beyond strong diplomatic language to fashion a more forceful institutional response. Returning to Figure 10.1, ASEAN may have to take action that reaches the mid-level of the interference continuum, perhaps by initiating punitive sanctions against the junta. Whether this will succeed in fostering reform is an open question, but what is patently clear is that constructive engagement has failed.

Zeroing in on the specific details of how one might move away from the noninterference norm, Carolina Hernandez has proposed four useful suggestions for a more productive debate over whether to intervene. Participants in the debate should (1) specify the conditions under which the relevant aspects of the ASEAN Way might be relaxed; (2) identify the particular sorts of problems where "flexible engagement" (Surin's proposal) would make sense and might be allowed; (3) specify who would be authorized to get involved; and (4) indicate whether and to what extent the outcome of external involvement would be binding on the state being subjected to it.[60]

Addressing the first two points, but especially the specific circumstances in which flexible engagement might be allowed, it is helpful to consider a number of behaviors that, according to ASEAN's former secretary-general Rodolfo Severino, all member states might agree are unacceptable: genocide, the use of rape as a weapon of war, the worst forms of child labor, the deployment of child soldiers, trafficking in illicit drugs, and the curtailment of freedom to practice one's religion.[61] A few of these would clearly fall under "acts of conscience that shock humankind." Given their severity, these issues could and should necessitate some relaxation of the noninterference norm. One might go further and argue that the annulment of elections and the systematic repression of a democratic opposition also merit some degree of interference.

---

[59] Simon SC Tay, "Institutions and Processes: Dilemmas and Possibilities," in *A New ASEAN in a New Millennium*, ed. Simon SC Tay, Jesus Estanislao, and Hadi Soesastro (Jakarta: Centre for Strategic and International Studies / Singapore: Singapore Institute of International Affairs, 2000), 165.

[60] Carolina G. Hernandez, "Challenges for Society and Politics," in *A New ASEAN in a New Millennium*, 105–122.

[61] See Rodolfo C. Severino, *Southeast Asia in Search of an ASEAN Community: Insights from the Former ASEAN Secretary-General* (Singapore: Institute of Southeast Asian Studies, 2006), 155. Note, however, that Severino is strongly against interference.

As to who could get involved, several ASEAN-ISIS analysts have called for a coalition of the willing as a means of initiating more proactive responses.[62] Steps to form such a coalition would diverge from the ASEAN tendency to seek consensus and thereby delay or prevent collective action. Severino's guidelines offer a useful way of handling the question of noninterference. The details will require more thought. But the main point now is that ASEAN needs to thoroughly rethink its institutional behavior.

Two important counterarguments can be made against my thesis here. Some may argue that jettisoning the noninterference norm would open up a Pandora's box and lead to conflict across the region, now that sovereignty is no longer so highly prized. This argument assumes, however, that ASEAN's zone of peace is inherently ephemeral and that four decades of interaction and accommodation can easily dissipate. To advocate the maintenance of the noninterference norm out of concern that ASEAN may not hold together does not give adequate credit to a history in which political and economic interdependence have sustained a regional institution and cemented regional security.

The second objection involves sanctions. Would they succeed? Those who are skeptical of the internationalist model in general and the utility of sanctions in particular may argue that sanctions are not likely to work in Southeast Asia, especially if a key country such as China is not on board. Sanctioning an ASEAN state could hurt it less than other ASEAN states are hurt if, for example, the business the other members did before sanctions is simply redirected to economies outside the region, including China. More importantly, inside the targeted country, sanctions may weigh most heavily on ordinary citizens who will lose their jobs when investments are withdrawn.[63] Such skeptics may be right. Unless regional actors and global powers coordinate punitive sanctions, such steps are unlikely to succeed in generating political reform.[64]

Ultimately, however, the main reason why interference becomes necessary in light of the failure of constructive engagement brings us back to the question of relevance, with which this chapter began.

Can ASEAN expect to remain relevant if it does not address the deplorable conditions prevailing in Myanmar and the outrageous behavior of its rulers? The answer is a resounding no. This is so because expectations inside and outside

---

[62] See Tay et al., *A New ASEAN in a New Millennium*, and Hernandez, "Challenges for Society and Politics."

[63] Pedersen estimates that 30,000 to 50,000 workers may have been laid off in Myanmar following the U.S. imposition of sanctions in July 2003. See Morton B. Pedersen, "The Challenge of Transition in Myanmar," in *Myanmar: Beyond Politics to Social Imperatives*, ed. Kyaw Yin Hlaing, Robert H. Taylor, and Tin Maung Maung Than (Singapore: Institute of Southeast Asian Studies, 2005).

[64] On the merits of sanctions in Myanmar, see ICG, "Myanmar: Solutions, Engagement or Another Way Forward."

Southeast Asia are that ASEAN, as the nearest and most appropriate institution, ought to do something to assuage these grievous conditions.

This is not just about defending or promoting democracy and human rights. It is about rescuing ASEAN's prestige. ASEAN is clearly at a loss when ASEAN-EU dialogues are canceled, or when the U.S. Secretary of State snubs an ARF meeting. Whether ASEAN likes it or not, its inability to adequately engage Myanmar will continue to haunt the Association's image and performance. To quote Hernandez again: "The imperative for ASEAN to reinvent or re-engineer itself appears to be the logical path to take, if it wishes to remain relevant to its members and continue to enjoy the respect of its partners as a credible and dependable regional and global actor."[65] If ASEAN's vision of its region as a truly "caring society"[66] is to seem anything but hypocritical, its leaders must venture beyond current practice and try more forcefully and creatively to moderate and reform the flagrantly offending state in their own back yard.

---

[65] Hernandez, "Challenges for Society and Politics," 122.
[66] ASEAN Vision 2020, <http://www.aseansec.org/1814.htm>.

The text of the ASEAN Charter is reproduced here with the permission of the ASEAN Secretariat, Jakarta, Indonesia.

In addition to the main text, the Charter includes four indexes. Annex 1 is reproduced here in its entirety because it shows the span of bodies under each of the three pillars in the ASEAN Community—pillars to which various authors in ths book refer. The remaining three annexes are not reproduced, but are instead summarized at the end of the reprinted Charter text.

The ASEAN Charter, together with its four Annexes, may be viewed and online and downloaded in PDF format, from the ASEAN website at <http://www.aseansec.org/21069.pdf>.

PREAMBLE

WE, THE PEOPLES of the Member States of the Association of Southeast Asian Nations (ASEAN), as represented by the Heads of State or Government of Brunei Darussalam, the Kingdom of Cambodia, the Republic of Indonesia, the Lao People's Democratic Republic, Malaysia, the Union of Myanmar, the Republic of the Philippines, the Republic of Singapore, the Kingdom of Thailand and the Socialist Republic of Viet Nam:

NOTING with satisfaction the significant achievements and expansion of ASEAN since its establishment in Bangkok through the promulgation of The ASEAN Declaration;

RECALLING the decisions to establish an ASEAN Charter in the Vientiane Action Programme, the Kuala Lumpur Declaration on the Establishment of the ASEAN Charter and the Cebu Declaration on the Blueprint of the ASEAN Charter;

MINDFUL of the existence of mutual interests and interdependence among the peoples and Member States of ASEAN which are bound by geography, common objectives and shared destiny;

INSPIRED by and united under One Vision, One Identity and One Caring and Sharing Community;

UNITED by a common desire and collective will to live in a region of lasting peace, security and stability, sustained economic growth, shared prosperity and social progress, and to promote our vital interests, ideals and aspirations;

RESPECTING the fundamental importance of amity and cooperation, and the principles of sovereignty, equality, territorial integrity, non-interference, consensus and unity in diversity;

ADHERING to the principles of democracy, the rule of law and good governance, respect for and protection of human rights and fundamental freedoms;

RESOLVED to ensure sustainable development for the benefit of present and future generations and to place the well-being, livelihood and welfare of the peoples at the centre of the ASEAN community building process;

CONVINCED of the need to strengthen existing bonds of regional solidarity to realise an ASEAN Community that is politically cohesive, economically integrated and socially responsible in order to effectively respond to current and future challenges and opportunities;

COMMITTED to intensifying community building through enhanced regional cooperation and integration, in particular by establishing an ASEAN Community comprising the ASEAN Security Community, the ASEAN Economic Community and the ASEAN Socio-Cultural Community, as provided for in the Bali Declaration of ASEAN Concord II;

HEREBY DECIDE to establish, through this Charter, the legal and institutional framework for ASEAN,

AND TO THIS END, the Heads of State or Government of the Member States of ASEAN, assembled in Singapore on the historic occasion of the 40th anniversary of the founding of ASEAN, have agreed to this Charter.

CHAPTER I: PURPOSES AND PRINCIPLES

ARTICLE 1: PURPOSES

The Purposes of ASEAN are:

1. To maintain and enhance peace, security and stability and further strengthen peace-oriented values in the region;

2. To enhance regional resilience by promoting greater political, security, economic and socio-cultural cooperation;

3. To preserve Southeast Asia as a Nuclear Weapon-Free Zone and free of all other weapons of mass destruction;

4. To ensure that the peoples and Member States of ASEAN live in peace with the world at large in a just, democratic and harmonious environment;

5. To create a single market and production base which is stable, prosperous, highly competitive and economically integrated with effective facilitation for trade and investment in which there is free flow of goods, services and investment; facilitated movement of business persons, professionals, talents and labour; and freer flow of capital;

6. To alleviate poverty and narrow the development gap within ASEAN through mutual assistance and cooperation;

7. To strengthen democracy, enhance good governance and the rule of law, and to promote and protect human rights and fundamental freedoms, with due regard to the rights and responsibilities of the Member States of ASEAN;

8. To respond effectively, in accordance with the principle of comprehensive security, to all forms of threats, transnational crimes and transboundary challenges;

9. To promote sustainable development so as to ensure the protection of the region's environment, the sustainability of its natural resources, the preservation of its cultural heritage and the high quality of life of its peoples;

10. To develop human resources through closer cooperation in education and life-long learning, and in science and technology, for the empowerment of the peoples of ASEAN and for the strengthening of the ASEAN Community;

11. To enhance the well-being and livelihood of the peoples of ASEAN by providing them with equitable access to opportunities for human development, social welfare and justice;

12. To strengthen cooperation in building a safe, secure and drug-free environment for the peoples of ASEAN;

13. To promote a people-oriented ASEAN in which all sectors of society are encouraged to participate in, and benefit from, the process of ASEAN integration and community building;

14. To promote an ASEAN identity through the fostering of greater awareness of the diverse culture and heritage of the region; and

15. To maintain the centrality and proactive role of ASEAN as the primary driving force in its relations and cooperation with its external partners in a regional architecture that is open, transparent and inclusive.

ARTICLE 2: PRINCIPLES

1. In pursuit of the Purposes stated in Article 1, ASEAN and its Member States reaffirm and adhere to the fundamental principles contained in the declarations, agreements, conventions, concords, treaties and other instruments of ASEAN.

2. ASEAN and its Member States shall act in accordance with the following Principles:

(a) respect for the independence, sovereignty, equality, territorial integrity and national identity of all ASEAN Member States;

(b) shared commitment and collective responsibility in enhancing regional peace, security and prosperity;

(c) renunciation of aggression and of the threat or use of force or other actions in any manner inconsistent with international law;

(d) reliance on peaceful settlement of disputes;

(e) non-interference in the internal affairs of ASEAN Member States;

(f) respect for the right of every Member State to lead its national existence free from external interference, subversion and coercion;

(g) enhanced consultations on matters seriously affecting the common interest of ASEAN;

(h) adherence to the rule of law, good governance, the principles of democracy and constitutional government;

(i) respect for fundamental freedoms, the promotion and protection of human rights, and the promotion of social justice;

(j) upholding the United Nations Charter and international law, including international humanitarian law, subscribed to by ASEAN Member States;

(k) abstention from participation in any policy or activity, including the use of its territory, pursued by any ASEAN Member State or non-ASEAN State or any non-State actor, which threatens the sovereignty, territorial integrity or political and economic stability of ASEAN Member States;

(l) respect for the different cultures, languages and religions of the peoples of ASEAN, while emphasising their common values in the spirit of unity in diversity;

(m) the centrality of ASEAN in external political, economic, social and cultural relations while remaining actively engaged, outward-looking, inclusive and non-discriminatory; and

(n) adherence to multilateral trade rules and ASEAN's rules-based regimes for effective implementation of economic commitments and progressive reduction towards elimination of all barriers to regional economic integration, in a market-driven economy.

CHAPTER II: LEGAL PERSONALITY

ARTICLE 3: LEGAL PERSONALITY OF ASEAN

ASEAN, as an inter-governmental organisation, is hereby conferred legal personality.

CHAPTER III: MEMBERSHIP

ARTICLE 4: MEMBER STATES

The Member States of ASEAN are Brunei Darussalam, the Kingdom of Cambodia, the Republic of Indonesia, the Lao People's Democratic Republic, Malaysia, the Union of Myanmar, the Republic of the Philippines, the Republic of Singapore, the Kingdom of Thailand and the Socialist Republic of Viet Nam.

ARTICLE 5: RIGHTS AND OBLIGATIONS

1. Member States shall have equal rights and obligations under this Charter.

2. Member States shall take all necessary measures, including the enactment of appropriate domestic legislation, to effectively implement the provisions of this Charter and to comply with all obligations of membership.

3. In the case of a serious breach of the Charter or non-compliance, the matter shall be referred to Article 20.

ARTICLE 6: ADMISSION OF NEW MEMBERS

1. The procedure for application and admission to ASEAN shall be prescribed by the ASEAN Coordinating Council.

2. Admission shall be based on the following criteria:

(a) location in the recognised geographical region of Southeast Asia;

(b) recognition by all ASEAN Member States;

(c) agreement to be bound and to abide by the Charter; and

(d) ability and willingness to carry out the obligations of Membership.

3. Admission shall be decided by consensus by the ASEAN Summit, upon the recommendation of the ASEAN Coordinating Council.

4. An applicant State shall be admitted to ASEAN upon signing an Instrument of Accession to the Charter.

CHAPTER IV: ORGANS

ARTICLE 7: ASEAN SUMMIT

1. The ASEAN Summit shall comprise the Heads of State or Government of the Member States.

2. The ASEAN Summit shall:

(a) be the supreme policy-making body of ASEAN;

(b) deliberate, provide policy guidance and take decisions on key issues pertaining to the realisation of the objectives of ASEAN, important matters of interest to Member States and all issues referred to it by the ASEAN Coordinating Council, the ASEAN Community Councils and ASEAN Sectoral Ministerial Bodies;

(c) instruct the relevant Ministers in each of the Councils concerned to hold ad hoc inter-Ministerial meetings, and address important issues concerning ASEAN that cut across the Community Councils. Rules of procedure for such meetings shall be adopted by the ASEAN Coordinating Council;

(d) address emergency situations affecting ASEAN by taking appropriate actions;

(e) decide on matters referred to it under Chapters VII and VIII;

(f) authorise the establishment and the dissolution of Sectoral Ministerial Bodies and other ASEAN institutions; and

(g) appoint the Secretary-General of ASEAN, with the rank and status of Minister, who will serve with the confidence and at the pleasure of the Heads of State or Government upon the recommendation of the ASEAN Foreign Ministers Meeting.

3. ASEAN Summit Meetings shall be:

(a) held twice annually, and be hosted by the Member State holding the ASEAN Chairmanship; and

(b) convened, whenever necessary, as special or ad hoc meetings to be chaired by the Member State holding the ASEAN Chairmanship, at venues to be agreed upon by ASEAN Member States.

ARTICLE 8: ASEAN COORDINATING COUNCIL

1. The ASEAN Coordinating Council shall comprise the ASEAN Foreign Ministers and meet at least twice a year.

2. The ASEAN Coordinating Council shall:

(a) prepare the meetings of the ASEAN Summit;

(b) coordinate the implementation of agreements and decisions of the ASEAN Summit;

(c) coordinate with the ASEAN Community Councils to enhance policy coherence, efficiency and cooperation among them;

(d) coordinate the reports of the ASEAN Community Councils to the ASEAN Summit;

(e) consider the annual report of the Secretary-General on the work of ASEAN;

(f) consider the report of the Secretary-General on the functions and operations of the ASEAN Secretariat and other relevant bodies;

(g) approve the appointment and termination of the Deputy Secretaries-General upon the recommendation of the Secretary-General; and

(h) undertake other tasks provided for in this Charter or such other functions as may be assigned by the ASEAN Summit.

3. The ASEAN Coordinating Council shall be supported by the relevant senior officials.

ARTICLE 9: ASEAN COMMUNITY COUNCILS

1. The ASEAN Community Councils shall comprise the ASEAN Political-Security Community Council, ASEAN Economic Community Council, and ASEAN Socio-Cultural Community Council.

2. Each ASEAN Community Council shall have under its purview the relevant ASEAN Sectoral Ministerial Bodies.

3. Each Member State shall designate its national representation for each ASEAN Community Council meeting.

4. In order to realise the objectives of each of the three pillars of the ASEAN Community, each ASEAN Community Council shall:

(a) ensure the implementation of the relevant decisions of the ASEAN Summit;

(b) coordinate the work of the different sectors under its purview, and on issues which cut across the other Community Councils; and

(c) submit reports and recommendations to the ASEAN Summit on matters under its purview.

5. Each ASEAN Community Council shall meet at least twice a year and shall be chaired by the appropriate Minister from the Member State holding the ASEAN Chairmanship.

6. Each ASEAN Community Council shall be supported by the relevant senior officials.

ARTICLE 10: ASEAN SECTORAL MINISTERIAL BODIES

1. ASEAN Sectoral Ministerial Bodies shall:

(a) function in accordance with their respective established mandates;

(b) implement the agreements and decisions of the ASEAN Summit under their respective purview;

(c) strengthen cooperation in their respective fields in support of ASEAN integration and community building; and

(d) submit reports and recommendations to their respective Community Councils.

2. Each ASEAN Sectoral Ministerial Body may have under its purview the relevant senior officials and subsidiary bodies to undertake its functions as contained in Annex 1. The Annex may be updated by the Secretary-General of ASEAN upon the recommendation of the Committee of Permanent Representatives without recourse to the provision on Amendments under this Charter.

ARTICLE 11: SECRETARY-GENERAL OF ASEAN AND ASEAN SECRETARIAT

1. The Secretary-General of ASEAN shall be appointed by the ASEAN Summit for a non-renewable term of office of five years, selected from among nationals of the ASEAN Member States based on alphabetical rotation, with due consideration to integrity, capability and professional experience, and gender equality.

2. The Secretary-General shall:

   (a) carry out the duties and responsibilities of this high office in accordance with the provisions of this Charter and relevant ASEAN instruments, protocols and established practices;

   (b) facilitate and monitor progress in the implementation of ASEAN agreements and decisions, and submit an annual report on the work of ASEAN to the ASEAN Summit;

   (c) participate in meetings of the ASEAN Summit, the ASEAN Community Councils, the ASEAN Coordinating Council, and ASEAN Sectoral Ministerial Bodies and other relevant ASEAN meetings;

   (d) present the views of ASEAN and participate in meetings with external parties in accordance with approved policy guidelines and mandate given to the Secretary-General; and

   (e) recommend the appointment and termination of the Deputy Secretaries-General to the ASEAN Coordinating Council for approval.

3. The Secretary-General shall also be the Chief Administrative Officer of ASEAN.

4. The Secretary-General shall be assisted by four Deputy Secretaries-General with the rank and status of Deputy Ministers. The Deputy Secretaries-General shall be accountable to the Secretary-General in carrying out their functions.

5. The four Deputy Secretaries-General shall be of different nationalities from the Secretary-General and shall come from four different ASEAN Member States.

6. The four Deputy Secretaries-General shall comprise:

   (a) two Deputy Secretaries-General who will serve a non-renewable term of three years, selected from among nationals of the ASEAN Member States based on alphabetical rotation, with due consideration to integrity, qualifications, competence, experience and gender equality; and

(b) two Deputy Secretaries-General who will serve a term of three years, which may be renewed for another three years. These two Deputy Secretaries-General shall be openly recruited based on merit.

7. The ASEAN Secretariat shall comprise the Secretary-General and such staff as may be required.

8. The Secretary-General and the staff shall:

(a) uphold the highest standards of integrity, efficiency, and competence in the performance of their duties;

(b) not seek or receive instructions from any government or external party outside of ASEAN; and

(c) refrain from any action which might reflect on their position as ASEAN Secretariat officials responsible only to ASEAN.

9. Each ASEAN Member State undertakes to respect the exclusively ASEAN character of the responsibilities of the Secretary-General and the staff, and not to seek to influence them in the discharge of their responsibilities.

ARTICLE 12: COMMITTEE OF PERMANENT REPRESENTATIVES TO ASEAN

1. Each ASEAN Member State shall appoint a Permanent Representative to ASEAN with the rank of Ambassador based in Jakarta.

2. The Permanent Representatives collectively constitute a Committee of Permanent Representatives, which shall:

(a) support the work of the ASEAN Community Councils and ASEAN Sectoral Ministerial Bodies;

(b) coordinate with ASEAN National Secretariats and other ASEAN Sectoral Ministerial Bodies;

(c) liaise with the Secretary-General of ASEAN and the ASEAN Secretariat on all subjects relevant to its work;

(d) facilitate ASEAN cooperation with external partners; and

(e) perform such other functions as may be determined by the ASEAN Coordinating Council.

ARTICLE 13: ASEAN NATIONAL SECRETARIATS

Each ASEAN Member State shall establish an ASEAN National Secretariat which shall:

(a) serve as the national focal point;

(b) be the repository of information on all ASEAN matters at the national level;

(c) coordinate the implementation of ASEAN decisions at the national level;

(d) coordinate and support the national preparations of ASEAN meetings;

(e) promote ASEAN identity and awareness at the national level; and

(f) contribute to ASEAN community building.

ARTICLE 14: ASEAN HUMAN RIGHTS BODY

1. In conformity with the purposes and principles of the ASEAN Charter relating to the promotion and protection of human rights and fundamental freedoms, ASEAN shall establish an ASEAN human rights body.

2. This ASEAN human rights body shall operate in accordance with the terms of reference to be determined by the ASEAN Foreign Ministers Meeting.

ARTICLE 15: ASEAN FOUNDATION

1. The ASEAN Foundation shall support the Secretary-General of ASEAN and collaborate with the relevant ASEAN bodies to support ASEAN community building by promoting greater awareness of the ASEAN identity, people-to-people interaction, and close collaboration among the business sector, civil society, academia and other stakeholders in ASEAN.

2. The ASEAN Foundation shall be accountable to the Secretary-General of ASEAN, who shall submit its report to the ASEAN Summit through the ASEAN Coordinating Council.

CHAPTER V: ENTITIES ASSOCIATED WITH ASEAN

ARTICLE 16: ENTITIES ASSOCIATED WITH ASEAN

1. ASEAN may engage with entities which support the ASEAN Charter, in particular its purposes and principles. These associated entities are listed in Annex 2.

2. Rules of procedure and criteria for engagement shall be prescribed by the Committee of Permanent Representatives upon the recommendation of the Secretary-General of ASEAN.

3. Annex 2 may be updated by the Secretary-General of ASEAN upon the recommendation of the Committee of Permanent Representatives without recourse to the provision on Amendments under this Charter.

CHAPTER VI: IMMUNITIES AND PRIVILEGES

ARTICLE 17: IMMUNITIES AND PRIVILEGES OF ASEAN

1. ASEAN shall enjoy in the territories of the Member States such immunities and privileges as are necessary for the fulfilment of its purposes.

2. The immunities and privileges shall be laid down in separate agreements between ASEAN and the host Member State.

ARTICLE 18: IMMUNITIES AND PRIVILEGES OF THE SECRETARY-GENERAL OF ASEAN AND STAFF OF THE ASEAN SECRETARIAT

1. The Secretary-General of ASEAN and staff of the ASEAN Secretariat participating in official ASEAN activities or representing ASEAN in the Member States shall enjoy such immunities and privileges as are necessary for the independent exercise of their functions.

2. The immunities and privileges under this Article shall be laid down in a separate ASEAN agreement.

ARTICLE 19: IMMUNITIES AND PRIVILEGES OF THE PERMANENT REPRESENTATIVES AND OFFICIALS ON ASEAN DUTIES

1. The Permanent Representatives of the Member States to ASEAN and officials of the Member States participating in official ASEAN activities or representing ASEAN in the Member States shall enjoy such immunities and privileges as are necessary for the exercise of their functions.

2. The immunities and privileges of the Permanent Representatives and officials on ASEAN duties shall be governed by the 1961 Vienna Convention on Diplomatic Relations or in accordance with the national law of the ASEAN Member State concerned.

CHAPTER VII: DECISION-MAKING

ARTICLE 20: CONSULTATION AND CONSENSUS

1. As a basic principle, decision-making in ASEAN shall be based on consultation and consensus.

2. Where consensus cannot be achieved, the ASEAN Summit may decide how a specific decision can be made.

3. Nothing in paragraphs 1 and 2 of this Article shall affect the modes of decision-making as contained in the relevant ASEAN legal instruments.

4. In the case of a serious breach of the Charter or non-compliance, the matter shall be referred to the ASEAN Summit for decision.

ARTICLE 21: IMPLEMENTATION AND PROCEDURE

1. Each ASEAN Community Council shall prescribe its own rules of procedure.

2. In the implementation of economic commitments, a formula for flexible participation, including the ASEAN Minus X formula, may be applied where there is a consensus to do so.

CHAPTER VIII: SETTLEMENT OF DISPUTES

ARTICLE 22: GENERAL PRINCIPLES

1. Member States shall endeavour to resolve peacefully all disputes in a timely manner through dialogue, consultation and negotiation.

2. ASEAN shall maintain and establish dispute settlement mechanisms in all fields of ASEAN cooperation.

ARTICLE 23: GOOD OFFICES, CONCILIATION AND MEDIATION

1. Member States which are parties to a dispute may at any time agree to resort to good offices, conciliation or mediation in order to resolve the dispute within an agreed time limit.

2. Parties to the dispute may request the Chairman of ASEAN or the Secretary-General of ASEAN, acting in an ex-officio capacity, to provide good offices, conciliation or mediation.

ARTICLE 24: DISPUTE SETTLEMENT MECHANISMS IN SPECIFIC INSTRUMENTS

1. Disputes relating to specific ASEAN instruments shall be settled through the mechanisms and procedures provided for in such instruments.

2. Disputes which do not concern the interpretation or application of any ASEAN instrument shall be resolved peacefully in accordance with the Treaty of Amity and Cooperation in Southeast Asia and its rules of procedure.

3. Where not otherwise specifically provided, disputes which concern the interpretation or application of ASEAN economic agreements shall be settled in accordance with the ASEAN Protocol on Enhanced Dispute Settlement Mechanism.

ARTICLE 25: ESTABLISHMENT OF DISPUTE SETTLEMENT MECHANISMS

Where not otherwise specifically provided, appropriate dispute settlement mechanisms, including arbitration, shall be established for disputes which concern the interpretation or application of this Charter and other ASEAN instruments.

ARTICLE 26: UNRESOLVED DISPUTES

When a dispute remains unresolved, after the application of the preceding provisions of this Chapter, this dispute shall be referred to the ASEAN Summit, for its decision.

ARTICLE 27: COMPLIANCE

1. The Secretary-General of ASEAN, assisted by the ASEAN Secretariat or any other designated ASEAN body, shall monitor the compliance with the findings, recommendations or decisions resulting from an ASEAN dispute settlement mechanism, and submit a report to the ASEAN Summit.

2. Any Member State affected by non-compliance with the findings, recommendations or decisions resulting from an ASEAN dispute settlement mechanism, may refer the matter to the ASEAN Summit for a decision.

ARTICLE 28: UNITED NATIONS CHARTER PROVISIONS AND OTHER RELEVANT INTERNATIONAL PROCEDURES

Unless otherwise provided for in this Charter, Member States have the right of recourse to the modes of peaceful settlement contained in Article 33(1) of the Charter of the United Nations or any other international legal instruments to which the disputing Member States are parties.

CHAPTER IX: BUDGET AND FINANCE

ARTICLE 29: GENERAL PRINCIPLES

1. ASEAN shall establish financial rules and procedures in accordance with international standards.

2. ASEAN shall observe sound financial management policies and practices and budgetary discipline.

3. Financial accounts shall be subject to internal and external audits.

ARTICLE 30: OPERATIONAL BUDGET AND FINANCES OF THE ASEAN SECRETARIAT

1. The ASEAN Secretariat shall be provided with the necessary financial resources to perform its functions effectively.

2. The operational budget of the ASEAN Secretariat shall be met by ASEAN Member States through equal annual contributions which shall be remitted in a timely manner.

3. The Secretary-General shall prepare the annual operational budget of the ASEAN Secretariat for approval by the ASEAN Coordinating Council upon the recommendation of the Committee of Permanent Representatives.

4. The ASEAN Secretariat shall operate in accordance with the financial rules and procedures determined by the ASEAN Coordinating Council upon the recommendation of the Committee of Permanent Representatives.

CHAPTER X: ADMINISTRATION AND PROCEDURE

Article 31: Chairman of ASEAN

1. The Chairmanship of ASEAN shall rotate annually, based on the alphabetical order of the English names of Member States.

2. ASEAN shall have, in a calendar year, a single Chairmanship by which the Member State assuming the Chairmanship shall chair:

    (a) the ASEAN Summit and related summits;

    (b) the ASEAN Coordinating Council;

    (c) the three ASEAN Community Councils;

(d) where appropriate, the relevant ASEAN Sectoral Ministerial Bodies and senior officials; and

(e) the Committee of Permanent Representatives.

ARTICLE 32: ROLE OF THE CHAIRMAN OF ASEAN

The Member State holding the Chairmanship of ASEAN shall:

(a) actively promote and enhance the interests and well-being of ASEAN, including efforts to build an ASEAN Community through policy initiatives, coordination, consensus and cooperation;

(b) ensure the centrality of ASEAN;

(c) ensure an effective and timely response to urgent issues or crisis situations affecting ASEAN, including providing its good offices and such other arrangements to immediately address these concerns;

(d) represent ASEAN in strengthening and promoting closer relations with external partners; and

(e) carry out such other tasks and functions as may be mandated.

ARTICLE 33: DIPLOMATIC PROTOCOL AND PRACTICES

ASEAN and its Member States shall adhere to existing diplomatic protocol and practices in the conduct of all activities relating to ASEAN. Any changes shall be approved by the ASEAN Coordinating Council upon the recommendation of the Committee of Permanent Representatives.

ARTICLE 34: WORKING LANGUAGE OF ASEAN

The working language of ASEAN shall be English.

CHAPTER XI: IDENTITY AND SYMBOLS

ARTICLE 35: ASEAN IDENTITY

ASEAN shall promote its common ASEAN identity and a sense of belonging among its peoples in order to achieve its shared destiny, goals and values.

ARTICLE 36: ASEAN MOTTO

The ASEAN motto shall be: "*One Vision, One Identity, One Community.*"

ARTICLE 37: ASEAN FLAG

The ASEAN flag shall be as shown in Annex 3 [not reproduced in these pages, but available online from the ASEAN website at <http://www.aseansec.org/21069.pdf>].

ARTICLE 38: ASEAN EMBLEM

The ASEAN emblem shall be as shown in Annex 4 [not reproduced in these pages, but available online from the ASEAN website at <http://www.aseansec.org/21069.pdf>].

ARTICLE 39: ASEAN DAY

The eighth of August shall be observed as ASEAN Day.

ARTICLE 40: ASEAN ANTHEM

ASEAN shall have an anthem.

CHAPTER XII: EXTERNAL RELATIONS

ARTICLE 41: CONDUCT OF EXTERNAL RELATIONS

1. ASEAN shall develop friendly relations and mutually beneficial dialogue, cooperation and partnerships with countries and sub-regional, regional and international organisations and institutions.

2. The external relations of ASEAN shall adhere to the purposes and principles set forth in this Charter.

3. ASEAN shall be the primary driving force in regional arrangements that it initiates and maintain its centrality in regional cooperation and community building.

4. In the conduct of external relations of ASEAN, Member States shall, on the basis of unity and solidarity, coordinate and endeavour to develop common positions and pursue joint actions.

5. The strategic policy directions of ASEAN's external relations shall be set by the ASEAN Summit upon the recommendation of the ASEAN Foreign Ministers Meeting.

6. The ASEAN Foreign Ministers Meeting shall ensure consistency and coherence in the conduct of ASEAN's external relations.

7. ASEAN may conclude agreements with countries or sub-regional, regional and international organisations and institutions. The procedures for concluding such

agreements shall be prescribed by the ASEAN Coordinating Council in consultation with the ASEAN Community Councils.

ARTICLE 42: DIALOGUE COORDINATOR

1. Member States, acting as Country Coordinators, shall take turns to take overall responsibility in coordinating and promoting the interests of ASEAN in its relations with the relevant Dialogue Partners, regional and international organisations and institutions.

2. In relations with the external partners, the Country Coordinators shall, inter alia:

(a) represent ASEAN and enhance relations on the basis of mutual respect and equality, in conformity with ASEAN's principles;

(b) co-chair relevant meetings between ASEAN and external partners; and

(c) be supported by the relevant ASEAN Committees in Third Countries and International Organisations.

ARTICLE 43: ASEAN COMMITTEES IN THIRD COUNTRIES AND INTERNATIONAL ORGANISATIONS

1. ASEAN Committees in Third Countries may be established in non-ASEAN countries comprising heads of diplomatic missions of ASEAN Member States. Similar Committees may be established relating to international organisations. Such Committees shall promote ASEAN's interests and identity in the host countries and international organisations.

2. The ASEAN Foreign Ministers Meeting shall determine the rules of procedure of such Committees.

ARTICLE 44: STATUS OF EXTERNAL PARTIES

1. In conducting ASEAN's external relations, the ASEAN Foreign Ministers Meeting may confer on an external party the formal status of Dialogue Partner, Sectoral Dialogue Partner, Development Partner, Special Observer, Guest, or other status that may be established henceforth.

2. External parties may be invited to ASEAN meetings or cooperative activities without being conferred any formal status, in accordance with the rules of procedure.

ARTICLE 45: RELATIONS WITH THE UNITED NATIONS SYSTEM AND OTHER INTERNATIONAL ORGANISATIONS AND INSTITUTIONS

1. ASEAN may seek an appropriate status with the United Nations system as well as with other sub-regional, regional, international organisations and institutions.

2. The ASEAN Coordinating Council shall decide on the participation of ASEAN in other sub-regional, regional, international organisations and institutions.

ARTICLE 46: ACCREDITATION OF NON-ASEAN MEMBER STATES TO ASEAN

Non-ASEAN Member States and relevant inter-governmental organisations may appoint and accredit Ambassadors to ASEAN. The ASEAN Foreign Ministers Meeting shall decide on such accreditation.

CHAPTER XIII: GENERAL AND FINAL PROVISIONS

ARTICLE 47: SIGNATURE, RATIFICATION, DEPOSITORY AND ENTRY INTO FORCE

1. This Charter shall be signed by all ASEAN Member States.

2. This Charter shall be subject to ratification by all ASEAN Member States in accordance with their respective internal procedures.

3. Instruments of ratification shall be deposited with the Secretary-General of ASEAN who shall promptly notify all Member States of each deposit.

4. This Charter shall enter into force on the thirtieth day following the date of deposit of the tenth instrument of ratification with the Secretary-General of ASEAN.

ARTICLE 48: AMENDMENTS

1. Any Member State may propose amendments to the Charter.

2. Proposed amendments to the Charter shall be submitted by the ASEAN Coordinating Council by consensus to the ASEAN Summit for its decision.

3. Amendments to the Charter agreed to by consensus by the ASEAN Summit shall be ratified by all Member States in accordance with Article 47.

4. An amendment shall enter into force on the thirtieth day following the date of deposit of the last instrument of ratification with the Secretary-General of ASEAN.

ARTICLE 49: TERMS OF REFERENCE AND RULES OF PROCEDURE

Unless otherwise provided for in this Charter, the ASEAN Coordinating Council shall determine the terms of reference and rules of procedure and shall ensure their consistency.

ARTICLE 50 : REVIEW

This Charter may be reviewed five years after its entry into force or as otherwise determined by the ASEAN Summit.

ARTICLE 51: INTERPRETATION OF THE CHARTER

1. Upon the request of any Member State, the interpretation of the Charter shall be undertaken by the ASEAN Secretariat in accordance with the rules of procedure determined by the ASEAN Coordinating Council.

2. Any dispute arising from the interpretation of the Charter shall be settled in accordance with the relevant provisions in Chapter VIII.

3. Headings and titles used throughout the Charter shall only be for the purpose of reference.

ARTICLE 52: LEGAL CONTINUITY

1. All treaties, conventions, agreements, concords, declarations, protocols and other ASEAN instruments which have been in effect before the entry into force of this Charter shall continue to be valid.

2. In case of inconsistency between the rights and obligations of ASEAN Member States under such instruments and this Charter, the Charter shall prevail.

ARTICLE 53: ORIGINAL TEXT

The signed original text of this Charter in English shall be deposited with the Secretary-General of ASEAN, who shall provide a certified copy to each Member State.

ARTICLE 54: REGISTRATION OF THE ASEAN CHARTER

This Charter shall be registered by the Secretary-General of ASEAN with the Secretariat of the United Nations, pursuant to Article 102, paragraph 1 of the Charter of the United Nations.

ARTICLE 55: ASEAN ASSETS

The assets and funds of the Organisation shall be vested in the name of ASEAN.

Done in Singapore on the Twentieth Day of November in the Year Two Thousand and Seven, in a single original in the English language.

[handwritten signatures not reproduced here]

For Brunei Darussalam:
HAJI HASSANAL BOLKIAH
Sultan of Brunei Darussalam

For the Kingdom of Cambodia:
SAMDECH HUN SEN
Prime Minister

For the Republic of Indonesia:
DR. SUSILO BAMBANG YUDHOYONO
President

For the Lao People's Democratic Republic:
BOUASONE BOUPHAVANH
Prime Minister

For Malaysia:
DATO' SERI ABDULLAH AHMAD BADAWI
Prime Minister

For the Union of Myanmar:
GENERAL THEIN SEIN
Prime Minister

For the Republic of the Philippines:
GLORIA MACAPAGAL-ARROYO
President

For the Republic of Singapore:
LEE HSIEN LOONG
Prime Minister

For the Kingdom of Thailand:
GENERAL SURAYUD CHULANONT (RET.)
Prime Minister

For the Socialist Republic of Viet Nam:
NGUYEN TAN DUNG
Prime Minister

ANNEX 1: ASEAN SECTORAL MINISTERIAL BODIES

I. ASEAN POLITICAL-SECURITY COMMUNITY

1. ASEAN Foreign Ministers Meeting (AMM)
- ASEAN Senior Officials Meeting (ASEAN SOM)
- ASEAN Standing Committee (ASC)
- Senior Officials Meeting on Development Planning (SOMDP)

2. Commission on the Southeast Asia Nuclear Weapon-Free Zone (SEANWFZ Commission)
- Executive Committee of the SEANWFZ Commission

3. ASEAN Defence Ministers Meeting (ADMM)
- ASEAN Defence Senior Officials Meeting (ADSOM)

4. ASEAN Law Ministers Meeting (ALAWMM)
- ASEAN Senior Law Officials Meeting (ASLOM)

5. ASEAN Ministerial Meeting on Transnational Crime (AMMTC)
- Senior Officials Meeting on Transnational Crime (SOMTC)
- ASEAN Senior Officials on Drugs Matters (ASOD)
- Directors-General of Immigration Departments and Heads of Consular Affairs Divisions of Ministries of Foreign Affairs Meeting (DGICM)

6. ASEAN Regional Forum (ARF)
- ASEAN Regional Forum Senior Officials Meeting (ARF SOM)

II. ASEAN ECONOMIC COMMUNITY

1. ASEAN Economic Ministers Meeting (AEM)
- High Level Task Force on ASEAN Economic Integration (HLTF-EI)
- Senior Economic Officials Meeting (SEOM)

2. ASEAN Free Trade Area (AFTA) Council

3. ASEAN Investment Area (AIA) Council

4. ASEAN Finance Ministers Meeting (AFMM)
- ASEAN Finance and Central Bank Deputies Meeting (AFDM)
- ASEAN Director-General of Customs Meeting (Customs DG)

5. ASEAN Ministers Meeting on Agriculture and Forestry (AMAF)
- Senior Officials Meeting of the ASEAN Ministers on Agriculture and Forestry (SOM-AMAF)
- ASEAN Senior Officials on Forestry (ASOF)

6. ASEAN Ministers on Energy Meeting (AMEM)
- Senior Officials Meeting on Energy (SOME)

7. ASEAN Ministerial Meeting on Minerals (AMMin)
- ASEAN Senior Officials Meeting on Minerals (ASOMM)

8. ASEAN Ministerial Meeting on Science and Technology (AMMST)
- Committee on Science and Technology (COST)

9. ASEAN Telecommunications and Information Technology Ministers Meeting (TELMIN)
- Telecommunications and Information Technology Senior Officials Meeting (TELSOM)
- ASEAN Telecommunication Regulators' Council (ATRC)

10. ASEAN Transport Ministers Meeting (ATM)
- Senior Transport Officials Meeting (STOM)

11. Meeting of the ASEAN Tourism Ministers (M-ATM)
- Meeting of the ASEAN National Tourism Organisations (ASEAN NTOs)

12. ASEAN Mekong Basin Development Cooperation (AMBDC)
- ASEAN Mekong Basin Development Cooperation Steering Committee (AMBDC SC)
- High Level Finance Committee (HLFC)

13. ASEAN Centre for Energy

14. ASEAN-Japan Centre in Tokyo

III. ASEAN SOCIO-CULTURAL COMMUNITY

1. ASEAN Ministers Responsible for Information (AMRI)
- Senior Officials Meeting Responsible for Information (SOMRI)

2. ASEAN Ministers Responsible for Culture and Arts (AMCA)
- Senior Officials Meeting for Culture and Arts (SOMCA)

3. ASEAN Education Ministers Meeting (ASED)
- Senior Officials Meeting on Education (SOM-ED)

4. ASEAN Ministerial Meeting on Disaster Management (AMMDM)
- ASEAN Committee on Disaster Management (ACDM)

5. ASEAN Ministerial Meeting on the Environment (AMME)
- ASEAN Senior Officials on the Environment (ASOEN)

6. Conference of the Parties to the ASEAN Agreement on Transboundary Haze Pollution (COP)
- Committee (COM) under the COP to the ASEAN Agreement on Transboundary Haze Pollution

7. ASEAN Health Ministers Meeting (AHMM)
- Senior Officials Meeting on Health Development (SOMHD)

8. ASEAN Labour Ministers Meeting (ALMM)
- Senior Labour Officials Meeting (SLOM)
- ASEAN Committee on the Implementation of the ASEAN Declaration on the Protection and Promotion of the Rights of Migrant Workers

9. ASEAN Ministers on Rural Development and Poverty Eradication (AMRDPE)
- Senior Officials Meeting on Rural Development and Poverty Eradication (SOMRDPE)

10. ASEAN Ministerial Meeting on Social Welfare and Development (AMMSWD)
- Senior Officials Meeting on Social Welfare and Development (SOMSWD)

11. ASEAN Ministerial Meeting on Youth (AMMY)
- Senior Officials Meeting on Youth (SOMY)

12. ASEAN Conference on Civil Service Matters (ACCSM)

13. ASEAN Biodiversity Centre

14. ASEAN Coordinating Centre for Humanitarian Assistance in Disaster Management (AHA Centre)

15. ASEAN Earthquakes Information Centre

16. ASEAN Specialised Meteorological Centre

17. ASEAN University Network (AUN)

ANNEX 2: ENTITIES ASSOCIATED WITH ASEAN

[Listed in this annex are 76 regional entities: "accredited civil society organisations" (51); "business organisations" (19); "other stakeholders in ASEAN" (4); "parliamentarians" (1, the ASEAN Inter-Parliamentary Assembly); and "think tanks and academic institutions" (1, the ASEAN-ISIS Network). Several aspects of the list are noteworthy in relation to the themes discussed in this book. No trade unions or nonprofessional labor organizations are listed, at least none identifiable as such from their names. Environmentalist organizations are also unrepresented. The CSOs listed are professional, specialized, and (except for AIPA) not obviously political in character. Only one of the listed entities describes itself as focused on human rights or democracy, i.e., the Working Group for an ASEAN Human Rights Mechanism (an "other stakeholder"); only one is devoted to public policy research (ASEAN-ISIS); and none is engaged in classroom education.

[Presumably only regional entities can qualify for association with ASEAN, although the Charter itself does not say so. Article 16.1 of the Charter does say that such associated entities must "support the Charter" and especially "its purposes and principles." An existing organization could have been omitted from the list in Annex 2 because it did not support the Charter, or did not wish to be associated with ASEAN, or for both reasons. ASEAN itself may have had a different reason for not listing the organization. Such considerations could also explain the absence on the list of certain types of organization. Relevant too is the difficulty of developing and maintaining a presence in so many different ASEAN member states. –Ed.]

ANNEX 3 (ASEAN FLAG) and ANNEX 4 (ASEAN EMBLEM)

[On both the flag and the emblem, a sheaf of ten stalks of padi tied together inside a circle represents "all the countries in Southeast Asia bound together in friendship and solidarity" inside the Association. The flag's and the emblem's colors—blue, red, white, and yellow—stand for the main colors of the flags and crests of the member states, and respectively for "peace and stability" (blue), "courage and dynamism" (red), "purity" (white), and "prosperity" (yellow). –Ed.]

BIBLIOGRAPHY

Key ASEAN Documents Available Online

ASEAN Agreement on Transboundary Haze Pollution, 2002
http://www.aseansec.org/images/agr_haze.pdf

ASEAN Basic Documents
http://www.aseansec.org/145.htm

ASEAN Charter Process
http://www.aseansec.org/AC.htm

ASEAN Convention on Counter Terrorism, 2007
http://www.aseansec.org/19250.htm

ASEAN Declaration (Bangkok Declaration), 1967
http://www.aseansec.org/1212.htm

ASEAN Declaration on Joint Action to Counter Terrorism, 2001
http://www.aseansec.org/5620.htm

ASEAN Report to the World Summit on Sustainable Development, 2002
http://www.aseansec.org/pdf/WSSD.pdf

ASEAN Security Community Plan of Action
http://www.aseansec.org/16826.htm

ASEAN Security Community Plan of Action Annex
http://www.aseansec.org/16829.htm

ASEAN Vientiane Action Programme, 2004
http://www.aseansec.org/Publ-VAP. pdf

ASEAN Vision 2020
http://www.aseansec.org/1814.htm

Charter of the Association of Southeast Asian Nations, 2007
http://www.aseansec.org/21069.pdf

Declaration of ASEAN Concord II (Bali Concord II), 2003
http://www.aseansec.org/15159.htm

Joint Statement on the Commission for the Treaty on the Southeast Asia Nuclear
    Weapon-Free Zone, Manila, 2007
http://www.aseansec.org/20775.htm>

Kuala Lumpur Declaration on the Establishment of the ASEAN Charter, 2005
http://www.aseansec.org/18030.htm

Regional Haze Action Plan, 1997
http://www.aseansec.org/9059.htm

Report of the Eminent Persons' Group on the ASEAN Charter, 2006
http://www.aseansec.org/19247.pdf

Table of ASEAN Treaties/Agreements and Ratification (1971–)
http://www.aseansec.org/Ratification.pdf

Treaty on the Southeast Asian Nuclear-Weapon-Free Zone (SEANWFZ), 1995
http://www.aseansec.org/2082.htm

* * *

The 2008 World Factbook. Washington, DC: Central Intelligence Agency,
    2008 <https://www.cia.gov/library/publications/the-world-factbook/
    rankorder/2004rank.html>.
Acharya, Amitav. "Realism, Institutionalism, and the Asian Economic Crisis."
    Contemporary Southeast Asia 21, no. 1 (1999), 1–29.
———. *Constructing a Security Community in Southeast Asia: ASEAN and
    the Problem of Regional Order*. London: Routledge, 2001.
———. "Human Security: East versus West." *International Journal* 3 (2001).
———. "Democratisation and the Prospects for Participatory Regionalism in
    Southeast Asia." *Third World Quarterly* 24, no. 2 (April 2003), 375–90.
Agence France-Presse. "EU Ministers Hail Progress on Myanmar as They End
    ASEAN Boycott." 12 December 2000.
———. "UN Envoy to Myanmar Carries Hope for Junta-Opposition Dialogue."
    4 January 2001.
———. "ASEAN Must Reinvent Itself, Loosen Non-Interference Policy: Alatas."
    7 January, 2004.
———. "Lao Communist Party Chief Steps Down but Reforms Unlikely." 21
    March 2006.
———. "Nuclear Power Plant Loan Finally Paid." 13 June 2007.
———. "IAEA Chief Unaware of Myanmar Plan." 18 July 2007.
———. "EU Sees No Quick-Fix after Irish Reject Treaty." 16 June 2008.

Agencies. "Massacre of the Monks in Burma." *Herald Sun* [Australia], 2 October 2007 <http://www.news.com.au/heraldsun/story/0,21985,22515138-661,00.html>.

Alagappa, Muthiah. "Comprehensive Security: Interpretation in ASEAN Countries." In *Asian Security Issues Regional and Global*, edited by Robert Scalapino et al. Berkeley, CA: Institute of East Asian Studies, University of California, 1989.

———. *Asian Security Practices: Material and Ideational Influences.* Stanford, CA: Stanford University Press, 1998.

Alatas, Ali. "The ASEAN Charter." Keynote address, conference on "Shaping ASEAN's Future: The Road Ahead." 4th ASEAN Leadership Forum, Jakarta, 17 April 2007.

Amnesty International. "Myanmar: The Kayin (Karen) State: Militarization and Human Rights." 1 June 1999 <http://www.amnesty.org/en/library/info/ASA16/012/1999/en>.

Annan, Kofi A. "Two Concepts of Sovereignty." *The Economist*, 18 September, 1999.

———. Commencement Address at the University of Pennsylvania, *Almanac* 51, no. 33 (24 May 2005).

Antara [Jakarta]. "Save Forests Now, President Yudhoyono Says," 23 April 2006 <http://www.antara.co.id/en/arc/2006/4/23/save-forests-now-president-yudhoyono-says>.

———. "RI Could Have Nuclear Power Plant in Five Years Time: Minister." 27 June 2006 <http://www.antara.co.id/en/seenws/?id=15265>.

———. "Gus Dur: If Still Full of Doubt, No Need to Build a Nuclear Power Plant," 13 July 2007 <http://www.antara.co.id/en/arc/2007/7/13/gus-dur-if-still-full-of-doubt-no-need-to-build-a-nuclear-power-plant>.

———. "RI Exploring Possibility of Cooperating with US to Build Nuclear Power Plant," 15 July 2006 <http://www.antara.co.id/en/seenws/?id=16372>.

Antolik, Michael. *ASEAN and the Diplomacy of Accommodation.* Armonk, NY: M.E. Sharpe, 1990.

Anwar, Dewi Fortuna. "Human Security: An Intractable Problem in Asia." In *Asian Security Order: Instrumental and Normative Features*, edited by Muthiah Alagappa. Stanford, CA: Stanford University Press, 2003.

Aradau, Claudia. "Limits of Security, Limits of Politics? A Response." *Journal of International Relations and Development* 9 (2006).

ASEAN Civil Society Conference. "Statement of the ASEAN Civil Society Conference to the 11th ASEAN Summit." 17 December 2005 <http://www.focusweb.org/content/view/774/27>.

ASEAN Institutes of Strategic and International Studies (ASEAN-ISIS). "The ASEAN Charter. Memorandum 1/2006." Bali, Indonesia, 18 April 2006, unpublished.

————. The ASEAN Charter, Memorandum No. 1/2006. 18 April 2006 (revised) <http://www.siiaonline.org/uploads/693/AI-Memo-18April-ASEAN_Charter.doc>.

ASEAN Secretariat. ASEAN Declaration on the South China Sea. Manila, Philippines, 22 July 1992.

————. *Hanoi Plan of Action*, 1998 <http://www.aseansec.org/old/9812/new_hpoa.htm>.

————. ASEAN Declaration on Joint Action to Counter Terrorism. Bandar Seri Begawan, 5 November 2001 <http://www.aseansec.org/5620.htm>.

————. Declaration of ASEAN Concord II (Bali Concord II). Bali, Indonesia, 7 October 2003 <http://www.aseansec.org/15159.htm>.

————. "Indonesia Proposes Southeast Asian Peacekeeping Force." Press release, 21 February 2004 <http://www.aseansec.org/afp/20p. htm>.

————. Chairman's Statement of the 11ᵗʰ ASEAN Summit. Kuala Lumpur, Malaysia, July 2005 <http://www.aseansec.org/18039.htm>.

————. *ASEAN Statistical Yearbook 2006.*

————. "Energising ASEAN to Power a Dynamic Asia," Joint Ministerial Statement of the 25th ASEAN Ministers on Energy Meeting, Singapore, 23 August 2007 <http://www.aseansec.org/20843.htm>.

————. "Statement by ASEAN Chair, Singapore's Minister for Foreign Affairs George Yeo." New York, 27 September 2007 <http://www.aseansec.org/20976.htm>.

————. "ASEAN Members Urged to Support International Emergency Relief for Cyclone Victims in Myanmar." Press release, 5 May 2008 <http://www.aseansec.org/21505.htm>.

————. "ASEAN Stands Ready to Help the Affected Population in Myanmar in Response to Cyclone Nargis." Press release, 9 May 2008 <http://www.aseansec.org/21527.htm>.

————. "ASEAN Emergency Rapid Assessment Team Mission Report, 9–18 May 2008: Cyclone Nargis, Myanmar." <http://www.aseansec.org/21558.pdf>.

————. "Special ASEAN Foreign Ministers Meeting Chairman's Statement." Singapore, 19 May 2008 <http://www.aseansec.org/21557.htm>.

————. "Post Nargis Joint Assessment Teams Complete Assessment of Cyclone Nargis-Affected Areas." Press release, 1 June 2008 <http://www.aseansec.org/21679.htm>.

————. "Tripartite Core Group Witnessing the Unloading of Relief Supplies for the Cyclone Nargis-affected Areas." Press release, 7 June 2008 <http://www.aseansec.org/21623.htm>.

————. "Myanmar Deputy Foreign Minister Sent Off 250-Person Post Nargis Joint Assessment Teams." Press release, 9 June 2008 <http://www.aseansec.org/21630.htm>.

————. "SG Surin Assured of Smooth Aid Operations." Press release, 14 June 2008 <http://www.aseansec.org/21648.htm>.

———. "Guidelines on the ASEAN Cooperation Fund for Disaster Assistance." N.d. <http://www.aseansec.org/21532.htm>.

ASEAN Secretariat, Public Information Unit. *Second ASEAN State of the Environment Report 2000* <http://www.rrcap. unep. org/sub-region/aseansoe/Content.pdf>.

Ashton, William. "Burma's Nuclear Program: Dream or Nightmare?" *The Irrawaddy*, 1 May 2004 <http://www.irrawaddy.org/article.php?art_id=968>.

Asia Monitor. "Laos Risk Summary." No. 17 (6 August 2006).

———. "Investors Need Incentives." No. 17 (12 December 2006).

Asia Pacific Energy Research Centre. *Nuclear Power Generation in the APEC Region.* Tokyo: Asia Pacific Energy Research Centre, Institute of Energy Economics, 2004.

Asian Defence and Diplomacy. "Armies Against Terror." *Asian Defence and Diplomacy* 10, no. 10 (October 2003), 47–49.

Asian Development Bank. "Avian Flu Pandemic Could Halt Asian Growth, ADB Report Says." 3 November 2005 <http://www.adb.org/Documents/News/2005/nr2005169.asp>.

Asian Forum for Human Rights and Development (Forum-Asia)."SAPA Core Group Spearheads Coming Strategies in Engaging ASEAN." 11 April 2006 <http://www.forum-asia.org/index.php?option=com_content&task=view&id=64&Itemid=47>.

Asian Human Rights Commission. "Asian Human Rights Commission: Burma: Dramatic Price Rises, Protests, and Arrests Oblige International Response." BurmaNet News, 22 August 2007 <http://www.burmanet.org/news/2007/08/22/asian-human-rights-commission-burma-dramatic-price-rises-protests-and-arrests-oblige-international-response>.

Associated Press."Indonesia, South Korea Sign Preliminary Deal to Develop Nuclear Power Plant." 25 July 2007.

———. "Thailand's New PM Defends Myanmar." MercuryNews.com, 16 March 2008 <http://www.mercurynews.com/breakingnews/ci_8592938>.

———. "Aung San Suu Kyi's Statement." 8 November 2007 <http://ap. google.com/article/ALeqM5gyhLpt3U4pZY688FfNh8cTpuNBdgD8SPNP3G3>.

Associated Press Worldstream. "Indonesia Proposes ASEAN Peace-keeping Force, Extradition Treaty to Bolster Regional Security." 22 February 2004.

Aziz, Gamar Abdul. "ASEAN Cannot Remain Silent over Myanmar Unrest: PM Lee." Channelnewsasia.com [Singapore], 28 September 2007 <http://www.channelnewsasia.com/stories/singaporelocalnews/view/302532/1/.html>.

Bangkok Post. "KL Ups the Ante on Rangoon." 27 March 2005.

———. "ASEAN Fails to Engage Rangoon." 11 July 1999.

Barr, Michael D. "The Little Red Dot Speaks." *Asian Analysis* [Canberra, Australia], January 2001 <http://www.aseanfocus.com/asiananalysis/article.cfm?articleID=345>.

BBC. "Pilger on Daw Suu s Standoff." 28 July 1998 <http://www.burmalibrary.org/reg.burma/archives/199807/msg00709.html>.

BBCBurmese.com. "Double Veto for Burma Resolution," 14 January 2007 <http://www.bbc.co.uk/burmese/highlights/story/2007/01/070114_doubleveto_burma_unsc.shtml>.

BBC Monitoring International Reports. "ASEAN Regional Forum in Malaysia Talks of Shared Intelligence to Fight Terror." 23 March 2003.

BBCNews.com. "ASEM 2: Guide to the Issues," 4 April 1998 <http://news.bbc.co.uk/2/hi/special_report/1998/03/98/asem_2/71528.stm>.

―――. "Q&A: Protests in Burma." 2 October 2007 <http://news.bbc.co.uk/2/hi/asia-pacific/7010202.stm>.

―――. "Burma Marks Independence Day." 4 January 2008 <http://news.bbc.co.uk/2/hi/asia-pacific/7171008.stm>.

―――."Burma 'Approves New Constitution.'" 15 May 2008 <http://news.bbc.co.uk/2/hi/asia-pacific/7402105.stm>.

―――. "Vietnam Congress Mixes Old with New." N.d. <http://newsvote.bbc.uk/mpapps/pagetools/print/news.bbc.uk/2/hi/asia-pacific/49417>.

Beitz, Charles. *Political Theory and International Relations*. Princeton, NJ: Princeton University Press, 1999.

Berger, Sebastien. "Aung San Suu Kyi: Leader Offered Meeting." 10 October 2007 <http://www.telegraph.co.uk/news/main.jhtml?xml=/news/2007/10/05/wburma105.xml>.

Bernama [Malaysia]. "Kuala Lumpur Declaration on the Establishment of the ASEAN Charter." 12 December 2005 <http://webevents.bernama.com/events/aseansummit/speech.php?id=378>.

―――. "IAEA Happy with Malaysia's Proposed Nuke Plant." 18 July 2007.

Bobbit, Philip. "Everything We Think about the War on Terror Is Wrong." *The Spectator*, 20 May 2006.

Boston Globe. "A Snub for Syria." 29 March 2008 <http://www.boston.com/bostonglobe/editorial_opinion/editorials/articles/2008/03/29/a_snub_for_syria>.

Boutros-Ghali, Boutros. "An Agenda for Peace." Report of the Secretary-General Pursuant to the Statement Adopted by the Summit Meeting of the [United Nations] Security Council, 1992.

Boyle, Joe. "Burma's Bittersweet Independence." BBC News, 4 January 2008 <http://news.bbc.co.uk/2/hi/asia-pacific/7171361.stm>.

Burke, Anthony. "Caught Between National and Human Security: Knowledge and Power in Post-Crisis Asia." *Pacifica Review* 13, no. 3 (2001).

Busse, Nikolas. "Constructivism and Southeast Asian Security." *Pacific Review* 12, no. 1 (1999).

Buzan, Barry. *People, States, and Fear. An Agenda for International Security Studies*, 2nd ed. Boulder, CO: Lynne Rienner Publishers. 1991.

Buzan, Barry, Ole Wæver, and Jaap de Wilde. *Security: A New Framework for Analysis*. Boulder, CO: Lynne Rienner, 1998.

Caballero-Anthony, Mely. "Human Security and Comprehensive Security in ASEAN," *Indonesian Quarterly* 28, no. 4 (2000), 412–22.

———. "Health and Human Security in Asia: Realities and Challenges." In *Global Health Challenges for Human Security*, edited by Lincoln Chen, et al. Cambridge, MA: Harvard University Press, 2003.

———. "Non-State Regional Governance Mechanism for Economic Security: The Case of the ASEAN Peoples' Assembly." *Pacific Review* 17, no. 4 (2004), 567–85.

———. "Re-visioning Human Security in Southeast Asia." *Asian Perspectives* 28, no. 3 (2004), 155–89.

———. *Regional Security in Southeast Asia: Beyond the ASEAN Way.* Singapore: Institute of Southeast Asian Studies, 2005.

———. "Regional Structures and Responses to Security Challenges in Southeast Asia." *Indonesian Quarterly* 33, no. 1 (May 2005), 50–60.

———. "SARS in Asia: Crisis, Vulnerabilities, and Regional Responses." *Asian Survey* 45, no. 3, (2005), 475–95.

Caballero-Anthony, Mely, Ralf Emmers, and Amitav Acharya, eds. *Non-Traditional Security in Asia: Dilemmas in Securitisation.* London: Ashgate 2006.

Cerny, Philip G. "Plurality, Pluralism, and Power: Elements of Pluralist Analysis in an Age of Globalization." In *Pluralism: Developments in the Theory and Practice of Democracy*, edited by Rainer Eisfeld. Opladen, Germany, and Farmington Hills, MI: Barbara Budrich Publishers, on behalf of the International Political Science Association, 2006.

Chandra, Alexander C. *Southeast Asian Civil Society and the ASEAN Charter: The Way Forward.* Solidarity for Asian People's Advocacy [SAPA], 1 October 2006 <http://www.asiasapa.org/index.php?option=com_content&task=view&id=41&Itemid=50>.

Chen, Lincoln, et al., eds. *Global Health Challenges for Human Security.* Cambridge, MA: Harvard University Press, 2003.

Chia, Siow Yue. "Whither East Asian Regionalism? An ASEAN Perspective." *Asian Economic Papers* 6, no. 3 (October 1997) <http://www.mitpressjournals.org/doi/pdfplus/10.1162/asep. 2007.6.3.1>.

Chin, Kin Wah, and Leo Suryadinata, eds. *Michael Leifer: Selected Works on Southeast Asia.* Singapore: Institute of Southeast Asian Studies, 2005.

Chongkittavorn, Kavi. "Thailand's Cynical Ploy on Burmese Migrant Workers." *The Nation* [Bangkok], 13 December 2006.

———. "Limited Time to Salvage the ASEAN Charter." *The Nation* [Bangkok], 11 June 2007.

Collier, David, and Steven Levitsky. "Democracy with Adjectives: Conceptual Innovation in Comparative Research." *World Politics* 49, no. 3 (1997), 429–30.

Commission for Holding the Referendum of the Union of Myanmar. "Announcement No. 12/2008," Ministry of Foreign Affairs, Naypyidaw,

26 May 2008 <http://www.mofa.gov.mm/news/Announcements/26may08. html>.

Council on Foreign Relations. "A Conversation with Surin Pitsuwan." 14 May 2008 <http://www.cfr.org/publication/16284/conversation_with_surin_ pitsuwan_rush_transcript_federal_news_service.htm>.

Cronin, Bruce. "Multilateral Intervention and the International Community." In *International Intervention: Sovereignty versus Responsibility*, edited by Michael Keren and Donald A. Sylvan. London: Frank Cass, 2002.

Curley, Melissa, and Nicholas Thomas. "Human Security and Public Health in Southeast Asia: The SARS Outbreak." *Australian Journal of International Affairs* 58, no. 1 (2004), 17–32.

Delft Hydraulics and Wetlands International. "PEAT-CO$_2$: Assessment of CO$_2$ Emissions from Drained Peat Lands in Southeast Asia." 12 December 2006 <http://www.wetlands.org/publication.aspx?id=51a80e5f-4479-4200-9be0-66f1aa9f9ca9>.

Democratic Voice of Burma. "Burmese Democracy Party View Exclusion from National Convention." 3 February 2005 <http://www.burmanet.org/news/2005/02/03/democratic-voice-of-burma-burmese-democracy-party-views-exclusion-from-national-convention>.

Deng, Francis M., Sadikiel Kimaro, Terrence Lyons, Donald Rothchild, and I. William Zartman. *Sovereignty as Responsibility: Conflict Management in Africa*. Washington, DC: Brookings Institution, 1996.

Dent, Christopher M. "The Asia-Pacific's New Economic Bilateralism and Regional Political Economy." Pp. 72–94 in *Asia-Pacific Economic and Security Cooperation: New Regional Agendas*, edited by Christopher M. Dent. Hampshire, UK: Palgrave Macmillan, 2003.

———, ed. *Asia-Pacific Economic and Security Cooperation: New Regional Agendas*. Hampshire, UK: Palgrave Macmillan, 2003.

Deutsch, Karl W., Sidney A. Burrell, and Robert A. Kann. *Political Community and the North Atlantic Area: International Organization in the Light of Historical Experience*. Princeton, NJ: Princeton University Press, 1957.

Deutsche Presse-Agentur. "ASEAN Moves Closer to Limited Intervention." 24 July 1998.

———. "ASEAN: Myanmar Makes No Progress on Road to Democracy." 25 July 1998.

———. "Top Philippine Legislator Calls for Myanmar's Expulsion from ASEAN," 3 August 1998.

Diamond, Larry. "Can the Whole World Become Democratic? Democracy, Development, and International Policies." University of California-Irvine Center for the Study of Democracy, 2003 <http://repositories.cdlib.org/csd/03-05>.

———. "The Democratic Rollback: The Resurgence of the Predatory State." *Foreign Affairs* 87, no. 2 (March–April 2008).

———. *The Spirit of Democracy: The Struggle to Build Free Societies throughout the World*. New York: Times Books, 2008.

Donnan, Shawn. "Indonesia Looks at Stalled Plans for N-Plan." *Financial Times*, 11 February 2004.

Donnan, Shawn, and Gareth Smyth. "Tehran Searches for Allies in Muslim World." *Financial Times*, 10 May 2006.

Donnelly, Jack. "State Sovereignty and International Intervention: The Case of Human Rights." Pp. 115–46 in *Beyond Westphalia? State Sovereignty and International Intervention*, edited by Gene M. Lyons and Michael Mastanduno. Baltimore, MD: Johns Hopkins University Press, 1995.

Dosch, Jörn. "The Post-Cold War Development of Regionalism in East Asia." In *Regionalism in East Asia. Paradigm Shifting?* edited by Fu-Kuo Liu and Philippe Regnier. London: RoutledgeCurzon, 2003.

———. "Vietnam's ASEAN Membership Revisited: Golden Opportunity or Golden Cage?" *Contemporary Southeast Asia* 28, no. 2 (2006), 234–58.

———. *The Changing Dynamics of Southeast Asian Politics*. Boulder, CO and London: Lynne Rienner Publishers, 2007.

Dosch, Jörn, and Ta Minh Tuan. "Recent Changes in Vietnam's Foreign Policy: Implications for Vietnam-ASEAN Relations." Pp. 197–213 in *Rethinking Vietnam*, ed. Duncan McCargo. London: RoutledgeCurzon, 2004.

Doyle, Michael W. "Kant, Liberal Legacies, and Foreign Affairs, Part I" *Philosophy and Public Affairs* 12, no. 3 (Summer 1983).

———. "Liberalism and World Politics." *American Political Science Review* 80, no. 4 (1986), 1151–69.

———. *Ways of War and Peace: Realism, Liberalism, and Socialism*. New York: W. W. Norton, 1997.

———. "Three Pillars of the Liberal Peace." *American Political Science Review* 99, no. 3 (2005).

Eaton, Sarah, and Richard Stubbs. "Is ASEAN Powerful? Neo-Realist Versus Constructivist Approaches to Power in Southeast Asia." *Pacific Review* 19, no. 2 (2006), 135–55.

Economy and Environment Program for Southeast Asia [EEPSEA] and World Wide Fund for Nature [WWFN]. *The Indonesian Fires and Haze of 1997: The Economic Toll*, Research Report, 1998 <http://www.idrc.ca/uploads/user-S/10536124150ACF62.pdf>.

ElBaradei, Mohamed. "Nuclear Power in a Changing World." 8 December 2006 <http://www.iaea.org/NewsCenter/Statements/2006/ebsp2006n024.html>.

———. "Nuclear Power: An Engine for Development." 16 July 2007 <http://www.iaea.org/NewsCenter/Statements/2007/ebsp2007n010.html>.

Eisfeld, Rainer, ed. *Pluralism: Developments in the Theory and Practice of Democracy*. Opladen, Germany, and Farmington Hills, MI: Barbara Budrich Publishers on behalf of the International Political Science Association, 2006.

Ellis, Eric. "Singapore, a Friend Indeed to Burma." *Sydney Morning Herald*, 1 October 2007 <http://www.smh.com.au/news/business/singapore-a-friend-indeed-to-burma/2007/09/30/1191090945019.html>.

Eminent Persons Group [EPG]. *Report of the Eminent Persons Group (EPG) on the ASEAN Charter* <http://www.aseansec.org/19247.pdf>.

Emmers, Ralf, Mely Caballero-Anthony, and Amitav Acharya, eds., *Studying Non-Traditional Security in Asia: Trends and Issues*. Singapore: Marshall Cavendish, 2006.

Emmerson, Donald K. "Region and Recalcitrance: Rethinking Democracy through Southeast Asia." *The Pacific Review* 8, no. 2 (1995).

———. "Goldilocks's Problem: Rethinking Security and Sovereignty in Asia." Pp. 89–111 in *The Many Faces of Asian Security: Beyond 2000*, edited by Sheldon W. Simon. Lanham, MD: Rowman and Littlefield, 2001.

———. "Security, Community, and Democracy in Southeast Asia: Analyzing ASEAN." *Japanese Journal of Political Science* 6, no. 2 (2005), 165–85.

———. "What Do the Blind-sided See? Reapproaching Regionalism in Southeaast Asia." *The Pacific Review* 18, no. 1 (March 1995).

———. "Challenging ASEAN: A 'Topological' View." *Contemporary Southeast Asia* 29, no. 3 (2007), 424–46.

———. "ASEAN's 'Black Swans,'" *Journal of Democracy* 19, no. 3 (July 2008).

England, Vaudine."Singapore Greets Wahid Outburst with Silence." *South China Morning Post*, 28 November 2000 <http://www.singapore-window.org/sw00/001128sc.htm>.

Environmental Data Interactive Exchange [EDIE]. "UNEP Praises ASEAN Agreement as Model for the World." 28 November 2003 <http://www.edie.net/news/news_story.asp?id=7809>.

Erlanger, Steven. "France Urges UN to Force Cyclone Aid on Myanmar." *International Herald Tribune*, 7 May 2008 <http://www.iht.com/articles/2008/05/07/europe/cyclone.php>.

Evans, Gareth. "Human Security and Society." *The Asia-Australia Papers*, no. 2 (September 1999).

———."Facing Up to Our Responsibilities." *The Guardian* [London], 12 May 2008.

Far Eastern Economic Review. "In the Bunker." 6 August 1998.

———. "Sharper Image." 5 August 1999.

Feinstein, Lee, and Anne-Marie Slaughter. "A Duty to Prevent." *Foreign Affairs* 83, no. 1 (January/February 2004), 136–50.

Fence between True Opinions and Lies. Opinion papers about power struggles within the military regime written by Burmese political activists and analysts, various dates <http://laphilosophe.wordpress.com/category/burma/>.

Ferguson, James R. "New Forms of Southeast Asian Governance: From 'Codes of Conduct' to 'Greater East Asia.'" In *Non-Traditional Security Issues in Southeast Asia*, edited by Mely Caballero-Anthony, Ralf Emmers, and Amitav Acharya. London: Ashgate 2006.

Financial Times. "Burma's Symbol of Hope Steps into the Sunlight." 7 May 2002.

———."Suu Kyi Arrest Threatens ASEAN Credibility." 6 October 2003.

———. "U.S., Vietnam Hail Vote to Normalize Trade Relations." 12 December 2006.

Florano, Ebinezer R. *The Case of the ASEAN Regional Haze Action Plan.* Paper presented at IDDRI International Environmental Governance, Paris, France, 15–16 March 2004 <http://www.iddri.org/iddri/telecharge/gie/communications/3a_florano1.pdf>.

Foreign Policy. "The Failed States Index 2007 [for 2006]." July–August 2007 <http://www.foreignpolicy.com/story/cms.php?story_id=3865&print=1>.

Forum2000. "Referendum Farce in Burma." N.d. <http://www.forum2000. cz/en/about-us/news-archive/detail/referendum-farce-in-burma-1/>.

Freedom House. "Freedom in the World Country Rankings, 1972–2006 <http:// www.freedomhouse.org/uploads/fiw/FIWAllScores.xls>

———. Freedom House Country Report—Indonesia 2007 <http://freedomhouse. org/template.cfm?page=22&year=2007&country=7195>.

———. *Freedom in the World 2008* [for 2007]. <http://www.freedomhouse.org/ uploads/fiw08launch/FIW08Tables.pdf>.

———. "Methodology." *Freedom in the World 2007* [for 2006] <http://www. freedomhouse.org/template.cfm?page=351&ana_page=333&year=2007>.

———. "Historical Country Ratings." *Freedom in the World 2008* [for 2007 and earlier] <http://www.freedomhouse.org/uploads/fiw08launch/FIW08Tables. pdf>.

———."Table of Independent Countries." *Freedom in the World 2008* and *Freedom in the World 2007.*

Friedman, Edward. "On Alien Western Democracy." In *Globalization and Democratization in Asia: The Construction of Identity*, edited by Catarina Kinnvall and Kristina Jönsson. London: Routledge, 2002.

Friedman, Edward, and Sung Chull Kim, eds. *Regional Cooperation and its Enemies in Northeast Asia: The Impact of Domestic Forces.* London: Routledge, 2006.

Friends of the Earth. *International Crisis Group, Indonesia: Natural Resources and Law Enforcement.* December 2001 <http://www.crisisgroup. org/home/ index.cfm?id=1453&=1>.

———. *Paper Tiger, Hidden Dragons 2: April Fools.* Briefing paper, February 2002.

Fukuyama, Francis.*The End of History and the Last Man.* New York: Free Press, 1992.

Fuller, Thomas. "At Least 15 Died in Crackdown, Myanmar Tells Envoy." *New York Times*, 17 November 2007 <http://www.nytimes.com/2007/11/17/ world/asia/17myanmar.html>.

Fund for Peace. "Failed States Index 2007 [for 2006]." <http://www.fundforpeace. org/web/index.php>.

Gainsborough, Martin. "Party Control: Electoral Campaigning in Vietnam in the Run-up to the May 2002 National Assembly Elections." *Pacific Affairs* 78, no. 1 (2005), 57–75.

Ganesan, N. "'Mirror, Mirror, on the Wall': Misplaced Polarities in the Study of Southeast Asian Security." *International Relations of the Asia-Pacific* 3 (2003), 221–40.

George, Cherian. "Calibrated Coercion and the Maintenance of Hegemony in Singapore." Working Paper Series No. 48, Asia Research Institute, National University of Singapore, September 2005 <http://www.ari.nus.edu.sg/docs/wps/wps05_048.pdf>.

Gilson, Julie. "Complex Regional Multilateralism: 'Strategising' Japan's Responses to Southeast Asia." *Pacific Review* 17, no. 1 (2004), 71–94.

Global Health Council, HIV page, n.d. <http://www.globalhealth.org/view_top.php3?id=227>.

———. Infectious diseases page, n.d. <http://www.globalhealth.org/view_top.php3?id=228>.

Glover, David, and Timothy Jessup. *Indonesia's Fires and Haze: The Cost of Catastrophe*. Ottawa: Institute of Southeast Asian Studies/International Development Research Center [IDRC], 1999.

GMANews.TV.com. "Arroyo Urges Congress to Ratify Asean Charter." 13 June 2008 <http://www.gmanews.tv/story/101019/Arroyo-urges-Congress-to-ratify-Asean-Charter>.

Goddard, Cliff. *The Languages of East and Southeast Asia: An Introduction*. Oxford: Oxford University Press, 2005.

———. "Languages of Indonesia (Papua)." In Raymond Gordon, Jr., *Ethnologue: Languages of the World*. 15th ed. Dallas, TX: SIL International, 2005 <http://www.ethnologue.com/show_country.asp?name=IDP>.

Gordon, Raymond, Jr. *Ethnologue: Languages of the World*. 15th ed. Dallas, TX: SIL International, 2005.

Graduate Institute of International Studies. *Small Arms Survey 2001: Profiling the Problem*. Geneva: Graduate Institute of International Studies, 2001.

Gray, Denis D. "Communist Party to Continue Tight Control over Laos." Associated Press, 22 March 2006.

Greste, Peter. "Fresh Dilemmas over Zimbabwe." BBCNews, 22 June 2008 <http://news.bbc.co.uk/2/hi/africa/7468399.stm>.

Grugel, Jean. "New Regionalism and Modes of Governance—Comparing U.S. and EU Strategies in Latin America." *European Journal of International Relations* 10, no. 40 (2004), 603–26.

Haacke, Jürgen. "'Enhanced Interaction' with Myanmar and the Project of a Security Community: Is ASEAN Refining or Breaking with its Diplomatic and Security Culture?" *Contemporary Southeast Asia* 27, no. 2 (August 2005).

Habermas, Jürgen. "What Holds Europeans Together." In Jurgen Habermas and Jacques Derrida. *Old Europe New Europe and Core Europe*. London: Verso, 2005.

Habermas, Jürgen, and Jacques Derrida. *Old Europe, New Europe, Core Europe*. London: Verso, 2005.

Hagiwara, Yoshiyuki. "Formation and Development of the Association of Southeast Asian Nations." *The Developing Economies* 11, no. 4 (December 1973), 443–65.

Heil A., and J. G. Goldammer. "Smoke-haze Pollution: A Review of the 1997 Episode in Southeast Asia." *Regional Environmental Change*. Freiburg: University of Freiburg, 2001.

Held, David. *Global Covenant: The Social Democratic Alternative to the Washington Consensus*. Cambridge: Polity Press, 2004.

Henderson, Jeannie. *Reassessing ASEAN*, Adelphi Paper 323. London: Oxford University Press for IISS, 1999.

Hernandez, Carolina G. "Challenges for Society and Politics." Pp. 105–22 in *A New ASEAN in a New Millennium* by Simon SC Tay, Jesus Estanislao, and Hadi Soesastro. Jakarta: Center for Strategic and International Studies and Singapore, Singapore Institute of International Affairs, 2000.

Hettne, Björn. "Globalisation and the New Regionalism: The Second Great Transformation." In *Globalism and the New Regionalism*, edited by Björn Hettne, András Inotai, and Osvaldo Sunkel. London: Macmillan, 1999.

Hettne, Björn, András Inotia, and Osvaldo Sunkel, eds. *Globalism and the New Regionalism*. London: Macmillan, 1999.

Hew, Denis. *Brick by Brick: The Building of an ASEAN Economic Community*. Singapore: Institute of Southeast Asian Studies/Canberra: Asia Pacific Press, 2007.

Hibbs, Mark. "Malaysian Agencies Probing Potential for Nuclear Plants." *Nucleonics Week* 47, no. 38 (21 September 2006).

———. "ASEAN Incursion into Nuclear Safety, Nonproliferation May Be Modest." *Nucleonics* Week 48, no. 40 (4 October 2007).

Higgott, Richard. "U.S. Foreign Policy and the 'Securitization' of Economic Globalization," *International Politics* 41, no. 2 (2004), 147–75.

Ho, Joshua. "Recent Developments and Regional Initiatives in the Straits of Malacca." Paper presented at Workshop on East Asian Energy Efficiency and Maritime Security, East Asian Institute, Singapore, 18 May 2006.

Hong, Carolyn. "ASEAN Reaffirms Security Community," *The Straits Times* [Singapore], 10 May 2006.

Hoshino, Shinyasu. "How Can Human Security Be Placed on the Regional Collaborative Agenda?" *Asia-Australia Papers* no. 2 (September 1999).

Human Development Report Office, *Human Development Report 2007/2008*. New York: United Nations Development Programme, 2007.

Huntington, Samuel P. *The Third Wave: Democratization in the Late Twentieth Century*. Norman, OK: University of Oklahoma Press, 1991.

Huysmans, Jeff. "Defining Social Constructivism in Security Studies: The Normative Dilemma of Writing Security." *Alternatives: Global, Local, Political* 27 (2002).

————. "Language and the Mobilization of Security Expectations: The Normative Dilemma of Speaking and Writing Security." Paper presented at the ECPR Joint Sessions, Mannheim, 26–31 March, 2006.

Indahnesiah.com. "Ten Days that Shook Indonesia." N.d. <http://www.indahnesia.com/DB/Story/Item.php>.

Indonesian Department of Foreign Affairs. "Towards an ASEAN Security Community: Indonesia's Non-Paper." June 2003.

Institute of Southeast Asian Studies [ISEAS]. *Framing the ASEAN Charter: An ISEAS Perspective.* Singapore: Institute of Southeast Asian Studies, 2005.

International Atomic Energy Agency [IAEA]. Comprehensive Test Ban Treaty, "Convention on Nuclear Safety." <http://www-ns.iaea.org/conventions/nuclear-safety.htm> (data as of 15 November 2007).

————. Comprehensive Test Ban Treaty, "Status of Additional Protocols." <http://www.iaea.org/OurWork/SV/Safeguards/sg_protocol.html> (data as of 22 January 2008).

————. Comprehensive Test Ban Treaty, "Status of Signature and Ratification." <http://www.ctbto.org/> (data as of 29 February 2008).

International Commission on Intervention and State Sovereignty [ICISS]. *The Responsibility to Protect.* Ottawa: International Development Research Center (IDRC), December 1991.

International Crisis Group [ICG]. "Myanmar: Solutions, Engagement or Another Way Forward." ICG Asia Report no. 78, Brussels, 26 April 2004.

International Enterprise Singapore. "About [the] ASEAN Free Trade Area [AFTA]." N.d. <http://www.iesingapore.gov.sg/wps/portal/!ut/p/kcxml/04_Sj9SPykssy0xPLMnMz0vM0Y_QjzKLN4g3CwkFSYGY5oFmpFoYo4YImah3lCxUF-4WEgYQszXIz83VT9I31s_QL8gNzQ0NKLcEQAenL7-/delta/base64xml/L3dJdyEvd0ZNQUFzQUMvNElVRS82XzBfNlRW>.

International Organization for Migration. "Part Two: Countering Trafficking in Southeast Asia." In *Combating Trafficking in Southeast Asia: A Review of Policy and Programme Responses,* no. 2. Geneva: International Organization for Migration Geneva, 2000.

The Irrawaddy [Burma]. "Burmese Monks Demand Government Apology." BurmaNet News, 10 September 2007 <http://www.burmanet.org/news/2007/09/10/irrawaddy-burmese-monks-demand-government-apology-yeni>.

Islamic Republic News Agency. "Junta Wants 'Discipline-Flourishing Democracy' in Myanmar." 5 January 2007 <http://www2.irna.ir/en/news/view/menu-239/0701058175140530.htm>.

Jackson, Robert. *Quasi-States: Sovereignty, International Relations and the Third World* (Cambridge: Cambridge University Press, 1990).

Jackson, Robert, and Carl G. Rosberg. "Why Africa's Weak States Persist: The Empirical and the Juridical in Statehood." *World Politics* 35, no. 1 (1982), 1–24.

Jagtiani, Sunil. "India Looks to Burma to Slake Growing Thirst for Gas." *Christian Science Monitor*, 26 April 2006.

Jakarta Post. "Indonesia Proposing ASEAN Security Community Concept." 16 June 2003.

———. "Officials Set Agenda for Weekend D-8 Summit on Bali." 10 May 2006.

———. "RI Should Cooperate with Iran on Nuclear Projects: House Speaker." 28 August 2006.

———. "Indonesia Holds Ground on ASEAN Charter." 15 June 2007.

Jawa Pos [Jakarta]."PLTN di Muria Musnahkan Etnik." 5 April 2007 <http://www.jawapos.co.id/index.php?act=detail_c&id=279238>.

JUST Commentary E-Newsletter. "ASEAN Civil Society Speaks Out." *JUST Commentary E-Newsletter* 6, no. 1 (January 2006) <http://www.just-international.org/commentary/E%20News%20Jan%2006.htm#ms1>.

Kaban, M. S. "Keynote Speech of Minister of Forestry Republic of Indonesia." Workshop on the ASEAN Agreement on Transboundary Haze, organized by the Singapore Institute of International Affairs, the World Wildlife Fund-Indonesia, and the Centre for Strategic and International Studies (Indonesia). Jakarta, 11 May 2007 <http://www.siiaonline.org/talks_dialogues2>.

Kanapathy, Vijayakumari. "International Migration and Labour Market Developments in Asia: Economic Recovery, the Labour Market and Migrant Workers in Malaysia," Paper presented to the 2004 Workshop on International Migration and Labour Markets in Asia, organized by the Japan Institute for Labour Policy and Training, the Organization for Economic Cooperation and Development, and the International Labour Office, Tokyo, Japan, 5–6 February 2004.

Kant, Immanuel. "Perpetual Peace." *Political Writings* (Cambridge: Cambridge University Press, 1976 [1795]).

Kao, Kim Hourn, and Jeffrey A. Kaplan, eds. *Principles under Pressure: Cambodia and ASEAN's Non-Interference Policy*. Phnom Penh: Cambodian Institute for Cooperation and Peace, 1999.

Kartini, Indriana, ed. *Indonesia and Iran's Nuclear Issue*. Jakarta: LIPI Press, 2005.

Katsumata, Hiro. "Why is ASEAN Diplomacy Changing?" *Asian Survey* 44, no. 2 (2004), 237–54.

Katzenstein, Peter J. ed. *Between Power and Plenty: Foreign Economic Policies of Advanced Industrial States*. Madison, WI: University of Wisconsin Press, 1978.

Kawasaki, Tsuyoshi. "Neither Skepticism nor Romanticism: The ASEAN Regional Forum as a Solution for the Asia-Pacific Assurance Game." *Pacific Review* 19, no. 2 (2006), 219–37.

Kean, Leslie, and Dennis Bernstein. "The Burma-Singapore Axis: Globalizing the Heroin Trade." *Covert Action Quarterly*, Spring 1998 <http://www. thirdworldtraveler.com/Global_Secrets_Lies/BurmaSingapore_Drugs. html>.

Keren, Michael, and Donald A. Sylvan. *International Intervention: Sovereignty versus Responsibility*. London: Frank Cass, 2002.

Khalik, Abdul. "Muhammadiyah Backs Iran's Nuclear Program." *Jakarta Post*, 9 February 2007.

Kinnvall, Catarina, and Kristina Jönsson, eds. *Globalization and Democratization in Asia: The Construction of Identity*. London: Routledge, 2002.

Koh, Tommy, Walter Woon, Andrew Tan, and Chan Sze-Wei. "The ASEAN Charter." *PacNet* no. 33A (6 September 2007).

Kolås, Ashild, and Stein Tonnesson. "Burma and Its Neighbors: The Geopolitics of Gas." *Austral Policy Forum* , 7 September 2006 <http://www.nautilus. org/fora/security/0674KolasTonnesson.html> 10.

Kompas [Indonesia]. "Indonesia Bisa Bekerja Sama dengan Iran." 28 August 2006.

Kongrut, Anchalee. "Is Thailand Serious about Nuclear Energy?" *Bangkok Post*, 14 April 2007.

Koran Tempo [Indonesia]. "Hassan Wirajuda Dicecar DPR." 30 March 2007.

Koslowski, Rey, and Friedrich V. Kratochwil. "Understanding Change in International Politics: The Soviet Empire's Demise and the International System." *International Organization* 48, no. 2 (Spring 1994), 215–47.

Kraft, Herman. "The Autonomy Dilemma of Track Two Diplomacy in Southeast Asia." *Security Dialogue* 31, no. 3 (2000), 343–56.

————. "ASEAN-ISIS and Human Rights Advocacy: The Colloquium on Human Rights (AICHOR)." In *Twenty Years of ASEAN ISIS: Origin, Evolution and Challenges of Track Two Diplomacy*, edited by Hadi Soesastro, Clara Joewono, and Carolina Hernandez. Jakarta: CSIS, 2006.

Krasner, Stephen D. "Problematic Sovereignty." Pp. 1–13 in *Problematic Sovereignty: Contested Rules and Political Possibilities*, edited by Stephen D. Krasner. New York: Columbia University Press, 2001.

————, ed. *Problematic Sovereignty: Contested Rules and Political Possibilities*. New York: Columbia University Press, 2001.

Krauze, Enrique. *Por una Democracia sin Adjetivos*. Mexico City: Joaquin Mortiz/Planeta, 1986.

Kuhonta, Eric Martinez. "Walking a Tightrope: Democracy versus Sovereignty in ASEAN's Illiberal Peace." *The Pacific Review* 19, no. 3 (2006), 337–58.

Kyaw, Htet Aung. "Road Map to Division." *Irrawaddy Online Edition*, 17 September 2003 <http://irrawaddy.org/opinion_story.php?art_id=400>.

Kyaw Yin Hlaing. "Myanmar in 2003: Frustration and Despair?" *Asian Survey* 44, no. 1 (January/February 2004), 87–92.

————. "Myanmar in 2004: Why Military Rule Continues." *Southeast Asian Affairs* (2005).

———. "Aung San Suu Kyi of Myanmar: A Review of the Lady's Biographies." *Contemporary Southeast Asia* 29, no. 2 (August 2007).

———. "Factional and Power Struggle in Post-Independence Burma." *Journal of Southeast Asian Studies* 39, no.1 (2008).

Kyaw Yin Hlaing, Robert H. Taylor, and Tin Maung Maung Than, eds. *Myanmar: Beyond Politics to Social Imperatives*. Singapore: Institute of Southeast Asian Studies, 2005.

Kyodo News Agency. "ASEAN to Review 'Cherished' Non-interference Policy." 13 December 2005.

———. "ASEAN Energy Ministers Agree to Form Nuclear Safety Caucus." 23 August 2007.

Legge, J. R., ed. and trans. *The Great Learning*, vol. 1, in *The Chinese Classics*, 7 vols. Oxford: Oxford University Press 1893.

Leifer, Michael. *Indonesia's Foreign Policy*. London: Allen & Unwin, 1983.

———. *ASEAN's Search for Regional Order*. Singapore: Faculty of Arts and Social Sciences, National University of Singapore, 1987.

———. *ASEAN and the Security of Southeast Asia*. London: Routledge, 1989.

———. "The Indochina Problem." In *Asian-Pacific Security After the Cold War*, edited by T. B. Millar and James Walter (St Leonards, NSW, Australia: Allen and Unwin, 1993.

———. "The ASEAN Peace Process: A Category Mistake." *Pacific Review* 12, no. 1 (1999).

———. *Singapore's Foreign Policy: Coping with Vulnerability*. London and New York: Routledge, 2000.

———. "ASEAN's Search for Regional Order." In *Michael Leifer: Selected Works on Southeast Asia*, edited by Kin Wah Chin and Leo Suryadinata. Singapore: Institute of Southeast Asian Studies, 2005.

———. "Truth about the Balance of Power." In *Michael Leifer: Selected Works on Southeast Asia*, edited by Kin Wah Chin and Leo Suryadinata. Singapore: Institute of Southeast Asian Studies, 2005.

Levett, Connie. "A Land Where Freedom is a Dirty Word." *Sydney Morning Herald,* 20 May 2006.

Lie, Alvin. "Diplomasi Asap." *Koran Tempo,* 21 October 2006 <http://korantempo. com/korantempo/2006/10/21/Opini/krn,20061021,48.id.html>.

Lintner, Bertil. "Signs of a Power Struggle within the Ruling Junta." *Far Eastern Economic Review*, 20 March 1997 <http://www.burmalibrary.org/reg. burma/archives/199703/msg00292.html>.

———. "Burma Joins the Nuclear Club," *Far Eastern Economic Review*, 27 December 2001.

———. "Myanmar and North Korea Share a Tunnel Vision." *Asia Times*, 19 July 2006 <http://www.atimes.com/atimes/Southeast_Asia/HG19Ae01.html>.

Lintner, Bertil, and Shawn W. Crispin. "Dangerous Bedfellows." *Far Eastern Economic Review*, 20 November 2003.

Liu, Fu-Ku, and Philippe Regnier, eds. *Regionalism in East Asia. Paradigm Shifting?* London: RoutledgeCurzon, 2003.

Loizou, John. "Calculating the Costs of Nuclear Energy." *Viet Nam News*, 4 September 2006.

Lwin, Nyi Nyi. *Economic and Military Cooperation between China and Burma.* September 2006 <http://www.narinjara.com/Reports/BReport.ASP>.

Lyon, Peter. *War and Peace in Southeast Asia.* London: Oxford University Press, 1969.

Lyons, Gene M., and Michael Mastanduno, eds. *Beyond Westphalia? State Sovereignty and International Intervention.* Baltimore, MD: Johns Hopkins University Press, 1995.

MacKinnon, Ian. "Javans Fired Up over Reactor Next to Volcano." *The Guardian*, 5 April 2007 <http://www.guardian.co.uk/indonesia/Story/0,,2050170,00. html>.

Malaysiakini.com. "Burma Motion in Parliament Put Off." 26 April 2005.

Manila Standard. "Energy Chief Eyes Nuclear Plant." 24 September 2007.

Manila Times. Democrat Banned from Myanmar Elections." 21 February 2008 <http://www.manilatimes.net/national/2008/feb/21/yehey/world/ 20080221wor1.html>.

McCargo, Duncan. ed. *Rethinking Vietnam.* London: RoutledgeCurzon, 2004.

McCoy, Clifford. "Rogues of the World Unite." *Asia Times*, 28 April 2007 <http://www.atimes.com/atimes/Southeast_Asia/ID28Ae01.html>.

McFarlane, S. Neil. *Intervention in Contemporary World Politics.* Adelphi Paper 350. Oxford: Oxford University Press, 2002.

Mead, Walter Russell. *Power, Terror, Peace, and War: America's Grand Strategy in a World at Risk.* New York: Alfred A. Knopf, 2004.

Meldrum, Andrew. "African Leaders Break Silence over Mugabe's Human Rights Abuses." *The Guardian*, 4 January 2006 <http://www.guardian. co.uk/world/2006/jan/04/zimbabwe.andrewmeldrum>.

Millar, T. B., and James Walter, eds. *Asian-Pacific Security After the Cold War.* St Leonards, NSW, Australia: Allen and Unwin, 1993.

Milner, Helen V. *Interests, Institutions, and Information: Domestic Politics and International Relations.* Princeton, NJ: Princeton University Press, 1997.

Minc, Alain. *Ce Monde Qui Vient.* Paris: Grasset, 2004.

Ministry of Foreign Affairs of the Government of Thailand. "Thailand's Non-Paper on the Flexible Engagement Approach." 27 July 1998 <http://www. thaiembdc.org/pressctr/pr/pr743.htm>.

Mizzima News Group. "Democracy Supporters Call for Tripartite Dialogue in Burma." 20 March 2001 <http://burmalibrary.org/reg.burma/ archives/200103/msg00054.html>.

Moe, Wai. "ASEAN Countries Vote against UN Resolution on Burma." 21 November 2007 <http://www.irrawaddy.org/article.php?art_id=9386>.

Mohamad, Mahathir. *Reflections on ASEAN: Selected Speeches of Dr. Mahathir Mohamad*. Subang, Malaysia: Pelanduk, 2004.

Mohamad, Roslina. "ASEAN's 1st Nuclear Lab to Be Located in Rompin." *The Star* [Malaysia], 14 July 2007.

Montesano, Michael J. "Vietnam in 2004: 'A Country Hanging in the Balance.'" *Southeast Asian Affairs*. Singapore: Institute of Southeast Asian Studies, 2005.

Moravcsik, Andrew. "Taking Preferences Seriously: A Liberal Theory of International Politics." *International Organization* 51, no. 4 (1997), 513–53.

Muntarbhorn, Vitit. *Roadmap for an ASEAN Human Rights Mechanism*. <http://www.fnf.org.ph/liberallibrary/roadmap. htm>.

Myoe, Maung Aung. *Regionalism in Myanmar's Foreign Policy: Past, Present and Future*. Working Paper. Asia Research Institute, Singapore, 2006.

Narine, Shaun. *Explaining ASEAN: Regionalism in Southeast Asia*. Boulder, CO: Lynne Rienner Publishers, Inc., 2002.

The Nation [Bangkok]. "Spotlight on Burma at ASEAN Meeting." 18 June 2003.

———. "KL Rebuffs Thaksin Over Walkout Vow." 27 November 2004.

———. "Senate Turns Up Heat on Government over Burma." 10 May 2005.

———. "Nuclear Power Scheme Backed." 19 October 2007.

National League for Democracy. "Statement for National Convention." 14 May 2004 <http://www.dassk.com/contents.php?id=757>.

Nelson, Chris. *The Nelson Report*, 12 May 2008 <http://www.samuelsinternational. com/NelRpt.html>.

Netto, Anil. "Charter for ASEAN Bloc Bypasses Civil Society." InterPress Service, 2 November, 2006.

The New Light of Myanmar. "Announcement on Results of the Referendum Held in the Whole Country." 27 May 2008 <http://www.myanmar-embassy-tokyo.net/news/may/2008-05-27-NLME.pdf> .

The New Straits Times [Malaysia]. "Water: The Singapore-Malaysia Dispute—The Facts." 21 July 2003 <http://www.singapore-window.org/sw03/030721ns. htm>.

The New York Times. "Burmese Enduring in Spite of Junta, Aid Workers Say." 18 June 2008.

Nguyen, Xuan Thang, ed. *Development Gap and Economic Security in ASEAN*. Hanoi: Social Science Publishing House, 2006.

Nguyen, Xuan Thang. "Development Gaps and Economic Security in ASEAN Economies." Unpublished draft final report, "Non-traditional Security: Development Gaps and Economic Security in ASEAN Economies" research project. Hanoi: Institute of World Economics and Politics, September 2005.

Nyo, Soe Win. "SLORC Power Struggle Intensifies." *DAB Newsletter*, January 1995 <http://www.burmalibrary.org/reg.burma/archives/199605/msg00027. html>.

Ogilvie-White, Tanya. "Is There a Theory of Nuclear Proliferation? An Analysis of the Contemporary Debate," *Nonproliferation Review* 4, no. 1 (Fall 1996), 43–60.

———. "Non-proliferation and Counterterrorism Cooperation in Southeast Asia: Meeting Global Obligations through Regional Security Architectures?" *Contemporary Southeast Asia* 28, no. 1 (April 2006), 1–26.

O'Neal, John, and Bruce Russett. "The Classic Liberals Were Right: Democracy, Independence, and Conflict." *International Studies Quarterly* 31 (June 1997), 423–38.

Ong Keng Yong. Address to an Asia Society luncheon, Hong Kong, 1 November 2005. Quoted in "ASEAN Sees Close Cooperation on Bird Flu, Disaster Relief, Crime." *Voice of America,* 1 November 2005.

Oo, Maung Maung. "Fall from Fortune." *The Irrawaddy* 9, no. 1, January 2001 <http://www.irrawaddy.org/article.php?art_id=2107>.

Owen, John M. "How Liberalism Produces Democratic Peace." *International Security* 19, no. 2 (1994), 87–125.

Park, Tong Whan, Dae-Won Ko, and Kyu-Ryoon Kim. "Democratization and Foreign Policy Change in the East Asian NICs." In *Foreign Policy Restructuring: How Governments Respond to Global Change*, edited by Jerel A. Rosati et al. Columbia, SC: University of South Carolina Press, 1994.

Parnohadiningrat, Sudjanan. "Indonesia and Iran's Nuclear Issue." In *Indonesia and Iran's Nuclear Issue*, edited by Indriana Kartini. Jakarta: LIPI Press, 2005.

Paung, Shah. "Monks Take Officials Hostage for Hours in Upper Burma Standoff." *The Irrawaddy*, 16 June 2008 <http://www.irrawaddy.org/article.php?art_id=8524>.

Payne, Anthony. "Globalisation and Modes of Regionalist Governance." Pp. 201–18 in *Debating Governance: Authority, Steering and Democracy*, edited by J. Pierre. Oxford: Oxford University Press, 2000.

Pedersen, Morton B. "The Challenge of Transition in Myanmar." In *Myanmar: Beyond Politics to Social Imperatives*, edited by Kyaw Yin Hlaing, Robert H. Taylor, and Tin Maung Maung Than. Singapore: Institute of Southeast Asian Studies, 2005.

Pelangi Energi Abadi Citro Enviro (PEACE). *Indonesia and Climate Change: Current Status and Policies.* Report commissioned by the World Bank and the Department for International Development, Indonesia, 2007 <http://siteresources.worldbank.org/INTINDONESIA/Resources/Environment/ClimateChange_Full_EN.pdf>.

People's Daily Online. "ADB Forecasts 9 Pct Growth Rate for Cambodian Economy in Next 2 Years." 27 March 2007 <http://english.peopledaily.com.cn/200703/27/eng20070327_361436.html>.

Pevehouse, Jon C. *Democracy from Above? Regional Organizations and Democratization.* New York: Cambridge University Press, 2005.

Phan, Matthew. "ASEAN Needs Nuclear Safety Commission." *Business Times* [Singapore], 7 September 2007.

Pham, Nga. "Vietnam Congress Mixes Old with New." BBC News, 25 April 2006 <http://news.bbc.co.uk/2/hi/asia-pacific/4941792.stm>.

Phonboon, K.. ed. *Health and Environmental Impacts from the 1997 Asian Haze in Southern Thailand*. Bangkok: Health Systems Research Institute, 1998.

Pierre, J., ed. *Debating Governance: Authority, Steering and Democracy*. Oxford: Oxford University Press, 2000.

Pikiran Rakyat [Bandung, Indonesia]."Sikap RI atas Iran Menuai Kecaman." 27 March 2007.

Pogge, Thomas. *Global Institutions and Responsibilities: Achieving Global Justice*. Malden, MA: Blackwell, 2006.

Pongsudhirak, Thithinan. "Small Arms Trafficking in Southeast Asia: A Perspective from Thailand." Pp. 55–69 in *Small is (Not) Beautiful: The Problem of Small Arms in Southeast Asia*, edited by Philips J Vermonte. Jakarta: Centre for Strategic and International Studies, 2004.

Porter, Gareth. *Vietnam: The Politics of Bureaucratic Socialism*. Ithaca, NY: Cornell University Press, 1993.

Praiwan, Yuthana. "New Panel to Pave Way for Nuclear-Energy Acceptance." *Bangkok Post*, 23 April 2007.

Prescott, Elizabeth. "SARS: A Warning." *Survival* 45, no. 3, (2003), 162–77.

Qadri, S. Tahir, ed. *Fire, Smoke, and Haze: The ASEAN Response Strategy*. Manila: Asian Development Bank, 2001 <http://www.adb.org/Documents/Reports/Fire_Smoke_Haze/default.asp>.

Quah, Euston. "Transboundary Pollution in Southeast Asia: The Indonesian Fires," *World Development* 30, no. 3 (2002), 429–41.

Quah, Euston, and Douglas Johnston. "Forest Fires and Environmental Haze in Southeast Asia: Using the Stakeholder Approach to Assign Costs and Responsibilities." *Journal of Environmental Management* 63 (2001).

Qutb, Sayyid. *Milestones on the Road*. Kuwait: International Islamic Federation of Student Organizations, 1971.

Radio Free Asia [Burmese language program]. "Burma's Fuel Protest." 19 September 2007 <http://www.rfa.org/english/news/social/2007/09/19/burma_fuelprotest>.

Rajan, Ramkishen S., et al. *Singapore and Free Trade Agreements: Economic Relations with Japan and the United States*. Singapore: Institute of Southeast Asian Studies, 2001.

Ramachandran, Sudha. "India Presses Burma over Insurgents." *Asia Times*, 20 September 2006 <http://www.yuyu.net/burmanet2-l/archive/1238.html>.

Rawls, John. *The Law of Peoples*. London: Harvard University Press, 2002.

Report on the Workshop on Illegal Migration in Asia. Centre of Asian Studies, University of Hong Kong, June 2006.

The Responsibility to Protect: Report of the International Commission on Intervention and State Sovereignty. Ottawa: International Development and Research Centre, 2001) <http://www.iciss.ca/report-en.asp>.

Reuters. "Southeast Asia's Club of Nations Turns up Heat on Myanmar." 24 March 2005.

———."Indonesia to Offer New Oil Exploration Blocks." 15 August 2006.

———. "Indonesia Says to Up '07 Budget Oil Price to $65/bbl." 15 August 2006.

———. "Indonesia President Forecasts H2 Pick Up in Economy." 16 August 2006.

———. "ASEAN Condemns Myanmar Violence," 27 September 2007.

Richardson, Michael. "Voting for Burma, ASEAN Aims at Unity in Its Region." *International Herald Tribune*, 2 July 1997 <http://www.iht.com/articles/1997/06/02/asean.t.php>.

———. "If Oil-Crunched Indonesia Goes Nuclear . . . " *The Straits Times*, June 4, 2004.

Robison, Richard, and Vedi R. Hadiz. *Reorganising Power in Indonesia: The Politics of Oligarchy in the Age of Markets*. London: RoutledgeCurzon, 2004.

Rosati, Jerel A., et al. *Foreign Policy Restructuring: How Governments Respond to Global Change*. Columbia, SC: University of South Carolina Press, 1994.

Rosecrance, Richard. *The Rise of the Trading State: Commerce and Conquest in the Modern World*. New York: Basic Books, 1986.

Rosenau, James N. "Intervention as a Scientific Concept." *Journal of Conflict Resolution* 13, no. 2 (1969).

Rowen, Henry S. "The Short March: China's Road to Democracy." *The National Interest* 45 (Fall 1996).

———. "When Will the Chinese People Be Free?" *Journal of Democracy* 18, no. 3 (July 2007).

Rüland, Jürgen. "ASEAN and the Asian Crisis: Theoretical Implications and Practical Consequences for Southeast Asian Regionalism." *Pacific Review* 13, no. 3 (August 2000), 421–51.

Rules of Procedure of the High Council of the Treaty of Amity and Cooperation in Southeast Asia, adopted in Hanoi, 23 July 2001.

Russett, Bruce M. *Grasping the Democratic Peace: Principles for a Post-Cold War World*. Rev. edn. Princeton, NJ: Princeton University Press, 1995 [1993].

Sagan, Scott D. "Why Do States Build Nuclear Weapons? Three Models in Search of a Bomb." *International Security* 21, no. 3 (Winter 1996–97), 54–86.

Sandhu, K. S., et al. *The ASEAN Reader*. Singapore: Institute of Southeast Asian Studies, 1992.

Scalapino, Robert, et al., eds. *Asian Security Issues: Regional and Global*. Berkeley, CA: Institute of East Asian Studies, University of California, 1989.

Seith, Andrew. *Burma's Secret Military Partners*. Canberra Papers on Strategy and Defence, no. 136. Canberra: Australian National University Strategic and Defence Studies Centre, 2000.

———."Pariah Partners in Arms." *The Irrawaddy*, 1 March 2004 <http://www.irrawaddy.org/article.php?art_id=933>.

Severino, Rodolfo C., compiler. *Framing the ASEAN Charter. AN ISEAS Perspective*. Singapore: Institute of Southeast Asian Studies, 2005.

———. *Southeast Asia in Search of an ASEAN Community: Insights from the Former ASEAN Secretary-General*. Singapore: Institute of Southeast Asian Studies, 2006.

———."Look Past the Headlines to What Matters." *The Straits Times* [Singapore], 23 July 2007.

Sheng, Lijun. *China-ASEAN Free Trade Area: Origins, Developments and Strategic Motivations*. ISEAS Working Paper: International Politics and Security Issues Series, no. 1. Singapore: Institute of Southeast Asian Studies, 2003.

Sheridan, Greg. "Burma Seeks Nuclear Weapons Alliance with N Korea." *The Australian*, 5 July 2006 <http://www.theaustralian.news.com.au/story/0,20867,19689419-601,00.html>.

———. "Asia's Evil Empires." *The Australian*, 8 July 2006 <http://www.theaustralian.news.com.au/story/0,20867,19722214-601,00.html>.

Shin, Gi-Wook, and Daniel C. Sneider, eds. *Cross Currents: Regionalism and Nationalism in Northeast Asia*. Stanford, CA: Walter H. Shorenstein Asia-Pacific Research Center, 2007.

Siang, Lim Kit. "Singapore Parliamentary Caucus on Burma." 6 March 2005 <http://www.dapmalaysia.org/english/2005/may05/lks/lks3492.htm>.

Simmons, Beth A. *Who Adjusts? Domestic Sources of Foreign Economic Policy during the Interwar Years*. Princeton, NJ: Princeton University Press, 1994.

Simon, Sheldon W., ed. *The Many Faces of Asian Security*. Lanham, MD: Rowman & Littlefield, 2001.

Soesastro, Hadi, and Raymond Atje. "Survey of Recent Developments." *Bulletin of Indonesian Economic Studies* 41, no. 1 (April 2005), 5–34.

Soesastro, Hadi, Clara Joewono, and Carolina Hernandez, eds. *Twenty-Years of ASEAN ISIS: Origin, Evolution and Challenges of Track Two Diplomacy*. Jakarta: CSIS, 2006.

Soetjipto, Tomi, and Muklis Ali. "Iran President Says West Nuclear Concern a 'Big Lie.'" *Reuters*, 10 May 2006.

Solidarity for Asian People's Advocacy [SAPA]. *Submission on Political and Human Security to the ASEAN EPG on the ASEAN Charter*. 17 April 2006, Ubud, Bali <http://seaca.net/viewArticle.php?aID=945>.

———. "SAPA Letter to the EPG on the ASEAN Charter Reiterating the Key Points of Its Submission." 24 November 2006 <http://www.asiasapa.org/index.php?option=com_content&task=view&id=34&Itemid=50>.

———. "Bloody Hands on the Charter: Shame!" 20 November 2007 <http://www.asiasapa.org/index.php?option=com_content&task=view&id=72&Itemid=43>.

———. "Civil Society Organisations Come Together to Criticise Failings of the ASEAN Charter." 23 November 2007 <http://www.asiasapa.org/index.php?option=com_content&task=view&id=74&Itemid=42>.

Solidarity for Asian People's Advocacies Working Group on ASEAN. "Analysis of the ASEAN Charter." 2007 <http://www.focusweb.org/analysis-of-the-asean-charter.html?Itemid=145>.

Solingen, Etel. *Regional Orders at Century's Dawn: Global and Domestic Influences on Grand Strategy.* Princeton, NJ: Princeton University Press, 1998.

———. "ASEAN, Quo Vadis? Domestic Coalitions and Regional Co-Operation." *Contemporary Southeast Asia: A Journal of International & Strategic Affairs* 21, no. 1 (1999), 30–53.

———. "Southeast Asia in a New Era: Domestic Coalitions from Crisis to Recovery." *Asian Survey* 44, no. 2 (2004), 189–212.

———. "ASEAN Cooperation: The Legacy of the Economic Crisis." *International Relations of the Asia Pacific* 5, no. 1 (2005), 1–29.

———. "Domestic Politics and Regional Cooperation in Southeast and Northeast Asia." Pp. 17–37 in *Regional Cooperation and its Enemies in Northeast Asia: The Impact of Domestic Forces,* edited by Edward Friedman and Sung Chull Kim. London: Routledge, 2006.

——— *Nuclear Logics: Contrasting Paths in East Asia and the Middle East.* Princeton, NJ: Princeton University Press, 2007.

The Star [Malaysia]."Charter to Protect Workers in ASEAN." 5 December 2005.

Steinberg, David I. "Myanmar: Regional Relationships and Internal Concerns." *Southeast Asian Affairs 1988.* Singapore: Institute of Southeast Asian Studies, 1988.

———. "Burma: Feel-Good US Sanctions Wrongheaded." *YaleGlobal,* 19 May 2004.

Steinberg, David I., Tsumori Shigeru, Andrew Selth, Pavin Chachavalpongpun, Peter Christian Hauswedell, and Kyaw Yin Hlaing. "Panel Discussion: Alliances and the Problems of Burma/Myanmar Policy: The United States, Japan, Thailand, Australia, and the European Union." Washington, DC, Sasakawa Peace Foundation, 2006).

The Straits Times [Singapore]."ASEAN Views on a Regional Military." 14 August 2000.

———."ASEAN's Peace." 8 March 2004.

———."Asia Battles Bird Flu." 28 January 2007.

Strauss, Leo. *The City and Man.* Chicago, IL: University of Chicago Press, 1964.

Suara Merdeka [Indonesia]. "NU Minta Pemerintah Kaji Ulang PLTN Muria." 14 July 2007 <http://www.suaramerdeka.com/harian/0707/14/mur06.htm>.

———. "Security Implications of the Economic Crisis in Southeast Asia." Pp. 39–65 in *An Asia-Pacific Security Crisis? New Challenges to Regional*

Stability, edited by Guy Wilson-Roberts. Wellington, New Zealand: Centre for Strategic Studies, 2001.

————. "The Future of ASEAN: Toward a Security Community."Paper presented to "ASEAN: Challenges and Prospects in the International Situation" seminar. New York, 2 June 2003.

————. "Southeast Asian Security: An Overview." Unpublished paper, 9th Asian Security Conference, Institute for Defense and Security Analysis, New Delhi, 9–10 February 2007.

————. "Indonesia Faces Serious Global Image Problem." *Jakarta Post*, 15 May 2007.

Subianto, Landry S. "Small Arms Problems in Southeast Asia: An Indonesian Case," Pp. 23–54 in *Small is (Not) Beautiful: The Problem of Small Arms in Southeast Asia*, edited by Philips J Vermonte. Jakarta: Centre for Strategic and International Studies, 2004.

Sudarsono, Juwono. *Surviving Globalization: Indonesia and the World*. Jakarta: Jakarta Post Books, 1996.

Suryodiningrat, Meidyatama. "Looking for Common Values, A Community Driven ASEAN." *Jakarta Post*, 9 August 2004 <http://yaleglobal.yale. edu/display.article?id=4353>.

Swanström, Niklas, and Emma Björnehed. "Conflict Resolution of Terrorist Conflicts in Southeast Asia." *Terrorism and Political Violence* 16, no. 2 (2004).

Tacconi, Luca. *Fires in Indonesia: Causes, Costs and Policy Implication*. CIFOR Occasional Paper no. 38. Bogor, Indonesia: CIFOR, 2003 <www.cifor.cgiar. org/publications/pdf_files/OccPapers/OP-038.pdf>.

Takahashi, Wakana. "Environmental Cooperation in Southeast Asia." In *Regional/Subregional Environmental Cooperation in Asia and the Pacific*. Shonan, Japan: IGES Environmental Governance Project, 2001.

Tan, Alan Khee-Jin. "The ASEAN Agreement on Transboundary Haze Pollution: Prospects for Compliance and Effectiveness in Post-Suharto Indonesia." *New York University Environmental Law Journal* 13 (2005).

Tan, Andrew T. H., and J. D. Kenneth Boutin. "Introduction." In *Non-Traditional Security Issues in Southeast Asia*, edited by Andrew T. H. Tan and J. D. Kenneth Boutin. Singapore: Select Publishing, 2001.

Tan, Andrew T. H., and J. D. Kenneth Boutin, eds. *Non-Traditional Security Issues in Southeast Asia*. Singapore: Select Publishing, 2001.

Taureck, Rita. "Securitization Theory and Securitization Studies." *Journal of International Relations and Development* 9, no. 1 (March 2006).

Tay, Simon SC. "Institutions and Processes: Dilemmas and Possibilities." In *A New ASEAN in a New Millennium*, edited by Simon SC Tay, Jesus Estanislao, and Hadi Soesastro. Jakarta: Centre for Strategic and International Studies/ Singapore: Singapore Institute of International Affairs, 2000.

————. "ASEAN Cooperation and the Environment." Paper presented at the Southeast Asian Roundtable, Institute of Southeast Asian Studies, Singapore, 1–3 November 1999.

————. "The Southeast Asian Fires and Haze: A Challenge for International Environmental Law and Development." *Georgetown International Environmental Law Review* 11 (Winter 1999).

Tay, Simon SC, Jesus Estanislao, and Hadi Soesastro, eds. *A New ASEAN in a New Millennium*. Jakarta: Centre for Strategic and International Studies/ Singapore: Singapore Institute of International Affairs, 2000.

————, eds. *Reinventing ASEAN*. Singapore: Institute of Southeast Asian Studies, 2001.

Taylor, Robert, and Morton Pedersen. "Supporting Myanmar/Myanmar's National Reconciliation Process: Challenges and Opportunities." January 2005 <http:// www.ibiblio.org/obl/docs3/Independant_Report-Burma_Day.htm>.

Tempointeraktif [Indonesia]. "Upacara Bendera Masyarakat Balong Tolak PLTN." 17 August 2007 <http://www.tempointeraktif.com/hg/nusa/ jawamadura/2007/08/17/brk,20070817-105785,id.html>.

Thai Press Reports. "ASEAN Air Force Chiefs Meet in Indonesia." 23 November 2006.

Than, Mya. *Myanmar in ASEAN: Regional Cooperation Experience*. Singapore: Institute of Southeast Asian Studies, 2005.

Thomas, Ann Van Wynen, and A.J. Thomas, Jr. *Non-Intervention: The Law and its Import in the Americas*. Dallas, TX: Southern Methodist University Press, 1956.

Toha, Abdillah. "No Real Evidence of Iran's Launch of Nuclear Weapons Development." *Jakarta Post*, 6 March 2007.

Treaty of Lisbon Amending the Treaty on European Union and the Treaty Establishing the European Community, Final Provisions, Article 6.1 <http:// europa.eu/lisbon_treaty/index_en.htm>.

Tun, Aung Hla. "Is Myanmar Really After Nuclear Power?" *Reuters*, 16 May 2007.

Ubac, Michael Lim. "Arroyo Orders Study on Use of Nuclear Energy for Power" *The Inquirer*, 20 August 2007 <http://newsinfo.inquirer.net/breakingnews/ nation/view_article.php?article_id=83681>.

Union of International Organizations, ed. *Yearbook of International Organizations: Guide to Global and Civil Society Networks*. Munich: K. G. Saur Verlag, 2007.

United Nations. Report of the United Nations Conference on the Human Environment, Stockholm, 5–16 June 1972 (United Nations publication, Sales No. E.73.II.A.14 and corrigendum) <http://www.unep. org/Documents. multilingual/Default.asp?DocumentID=97&ArticleID=1503>.

————. Rio Declaration on Environment and Development, 1992 <http://www. un.org/documents/ga/conf151/aconf15126-1annex1.htm>.

United Nations Development Programme. *Human Development Report 1994.* New York: Oxford University Press, 1994.

United Nations General Assembly. "World Summit Outcome." 15 September 2005 <http://www.responsibilitytoprotect.org/index.php/united_nations/398?theme=alt1>.

United Nations Security Council. Resolution No. 1674, 28 April 2006 <http://domino.un.org/UNISPAl.NSF/361eea1cc08301c485256cf600606959/e52 9762befa456f88525716100-45ebef!OpenDocument>.

U.S.-ASEAN Joint Declaration on Combating Terrorism. Washington, DC, 1 August 2002 <http://www.state.gov/p/eap/rls/ot/12428.htm.

Vartabedian, Ralph. "A Race with the Terrorists." *Los Angeles Times,* 27 September 2007.

Vatikiotis, Michael. "Neighbours Lean on Myanmar." *International Herald Tribune,* 2 February 2005.

Vermonte, Philips J., ed. *Small is (Not) Beautiful: The Problem of Small Arms in Southeast Asia.* Jakarta: Centre for Strategic and International Studies, 2004.

Viet Nam News. "Seminar on Nuclear Power Held in Capital," 18 October 2006.

———. "IAEA Approves Six Projects for Vietnam as Chief Visits," 12 December 2006.

Waltz, Kenneth N. *Theory of International Politics.* New York: McGraw-Hill, 1978.

Wanandi, Jusuf. "Partners Should Nudge Burma." *International Herald Tribune,* 5 June 1997.

———. "ASEAN's Charter: Does a Mediocre Document Really Matter?" *Jakarta Post,* 26 November 2007.

Weatherbee, Donald E. *International Relations in Southeast Asia: The Struggle for Autonomy.* Lanham, MD: Rowman & Littlefield, 2005.

Weiss, Edith Brown, and Harold Jacobson. *Engaging Countries: Strengthening Compliance with International Environmental Accords.* Cambridge, MA: MIT Press, 1998.

Weisser, Rebecca. "SBY Passes First Tests." *The Australian,* 31 July 2006.

Wendt, Alexander. *Social Theory of International Politics.* Cambridge: Cambridge University Press, 1991.

———. "Constructing International Politics." *International Security* 20, no. 1 (Summer 1995), 71–81.

Wilson-Roberts, Guy, ed. *An Asia-Pacific Security Crisis? New Challenges to Regional Stability.* Wellington, New Zealand: Centre for Strategic Studies, 2001.

Wirajuda, H. E. Dr. N. Hassan. Keynote Speech." Fourth Workshop on the ASEAN Regional Mechanism on Human Rights, Jakarta, 17 June, 2004 <http://www.kbri-canberra.org.au/speeches/2004/040617menlu.htm>.

Wolfsthal, Jon B. "The Next Nuclear Wave." *Foreign Affairs* 84, no. 1 (January/February 2005), 49–60.

World Bank. *East Asia: The Road to Recovery.* Washington, DC: The World Bank, September 1998.

World Health Organisation [WHO]. "Bioregional Workshop on Health Impacts of Haze-related Air Pollution." Kuala Lumpur, 1–4 June 1998.

———. *Update 73—No New Deaths, but Vigilance Needed for Imported Cases.* 4 June 2003 <http://www.who.int/csr/don/2003_06_04/en/index.html>.

———. Cumulative Number of Confirmed Human Cases of Avian Influenza A/(H5N1) Reported to WHO, 11 April 2007 <http://www.who.int/csr/disease/avian_influenza/country/cases_table_2007_04_11/en/index.html>.

Yeo, George. "Statement by ASEAN Chair, Singapore's Minister for Foreign Affairs George Yeo in New York, 27 September 2007." <http://app. mfa. gov.sg/2006/press/view_press.asp?post_id=3125>.

Yonhap News Agency [South Korea]. "S. Korea Promotes Sale of Indigenous Nuclear Reactor to Indonesia." 25 July 2007.

Young, Oran R. *The Institutional Dimensions of Environmental Change: Fit, Interplay, and Scale.* Cambridge, MA: MIT Press, 2002.

Zainal Abidin bin M. Said. "Migration and National Security: A Study of Indonesian Transients in Malaysia." Unpublished thesis, Faculty of Social Sciences and Humanities, Universiti Kebangsaan Malaysia, Bangi, 2005.

Zaw, Aung. "Aung San Suu Kyi: Between SLORC and a Hardline." *The Irrawaddy*, 13 June 1995 <http://burmalibrary.org/reg.burma/archives/199506/msg00059.html>.

Zoellick, Robert. "Countering Terror with Trade." *Washington Post,* 20 September 2001.

INDEX

Note: A list of acronyms can be found on pp. xv–xviii.

A

accountability, responsibility
  national sovereignty and, 69–70, 308–10
  noninterference *vs.*, 121–26
  for nontraditional security, debates about, 72
  See also cooperation, inter-state; national sovereignty
Aceh province, Indonesia, 282
Acharya, Amitav, 51*n*79, 64, 246, 302
administrative states, 289
African Union (AU), 18–19
Ahmadinejad, Mahmoud, 260
air pollution
  ASEAN policy initiatives, 220–25
  efforts to address within Indonesia, 232–33
  inter-state cooperation on, 220, 227, 229, 235–37
  sources, 199, 219–20
  See also ASEAN Agreement on Transboundary Haze Pollution; cooperation, inter-state
Alagappa, Muthiah, 8–9
Alatas, Ali, 102*n*13, 294, 300, 303.
All Burma Federation of Students Unions, 167
Alliance of All Burma Buddhist Monks, 169–70
al Qaeda, 276
Alternative ASEAN Network on Burma (AltSEAN), 196, 299
Annan, Kofi, 301, 307
Anwar Ibrahim, 202–3, 303
Arab League, 18
Arab Maghreb Union, 19
Aradau, Claudia, 66

Arroyo, Gloria *See* Macapagal-Arroyo, Gloria.
Asad, Suleiman, 251
ASEAN, 154
  chairmanship: provisions in Charter, 329–30; role and responsibilities, 31–32, 327, 329–30; rotation of, debates about, 32–33, 209, 211, 303–4
  challenges facing: capacity for reform, 53–56; conflicting goals and mandates, 31, 279–80; 40th anniversary, 24–25; organizational reform, 92–93, 120–21; overview, 4, 19–20; trans-boundary air pollution, 238–39
  dispute-resolution function, 104, 124–26, 295–98, 327
  effectiveness/relevance of: achievements, xvi, 60–61, 91, 220–21; debates about, 3–4, 115–16, 293–94, 300–305; interrelations between security, democracy and regionalism, 51–53; limits to, relations to limited financial resources, 121; national sovereignty/ noninterference principles and, 8, 40–50, 304; organizational issues, 30–32, 312–13; response to Cyclone Nargis, xv, xvi, 32, 51–52;
  financial and institutional constraints, 121–22, 129–31
  founding and goals, xv, 13*n*25, 24–25, 59, 91–97, 106–7, 154, 246, 277–79
  identity: legal identity/authority, 31, 101–2, 118, 225–26, 269, 319; symbols of, 116, 330–31
  membership in: criteria for, 110, 185–86; expansion, 91, 279–

ABOUT THE CONTRIBUTORS

Mely Caballero-Anthony is an associate professor at the S. Rajaratnam School of International Studies (RSIS), Nanyang Technological University, Singapore. She also holds the concurrent positions of head of the school's Centre for Non-Traditional Security Studies, and secretary-general of the newly established Consortium of Non-Traditional Security Studies in Asia (NTS-Asia). Among her research interests are regionalism and regional security in the Asia-Pacific, multilateral security cooperation, Southeast Asian politics and international relations, and conflict prevention and management, as well as human security.

Her recent publications include *Studying Non-Traditional Security in Asia* (2006), *Understanding Non-Traditional Security in Asia* (2006), *Regional Security in Southeast Asia* (2005), and UN *Peace Operations and Asian Security* (2005). She has also written extensively on ASEAN, the ASEAN Regional Forum, and Asia-Pacific security in journals such as *Asia Pacific Security Outlook*, *Asian Perspective*, *Asian Survey*, *Contemporary Southeast Asia*, *Indonesian Quarterly*, *International Peacekeeping*, *Journal of International Affairs*, *Pacific Review*, and *Southeast Asian Affairs*. She has also published many chapters in books on her topics of concern.

Caballero-Anthony has been active in Track II work through her association with the Council for Security Cooperation in the Asia Pacific and the ASEAN Institutes of Strategic and International Studies. She has held position as senior analyst at the Institute of Strategic and International Studies, Malaysia; visiting research fellow at the Japan Institute of International Affairs; research officer at the Centre of Asian Studies, University of Hong Kong; and research fellow at the Institute of Southeast Asian Studies, Singapore.

Jörn Dosch is a professor of Asia-Pacific studies in the department of East Asian studies, University of Leeds, UK. He specializes in the politics and international relations of Southeast Asia. His recent research interests have included ASEAN and the institutional aspects of regionalism, nontraditional security in Southeast Asia, subregional cooperation in the Mekong Valley, and the impact of democratization on how foreign policy is made in Indonesia, the Philippines, and Thailand.

Dosch is the author of *The Changing Dynamics of Southeast Asia Politics* (2007) and coauthor of *The New Global Politics of the Asia-Pacific* (2004), among some sixty other books and papers that he has published. He has been a visiting professor or fellow at research institutions throughout the world, including the Centre for Strategic and International Studies, Jakarta; the Institute of Southeast Asia Studies, Singapore; Parahyangan University, Bandung; De La Salle and Ateneo Universities, Manila; the East-West Center, Hawaii; Ohio University; Shorenstein APARC, Stanford University; and Prince of Songkla University, Pattani, Thailand.

Dosch has worked as a consultant for the German Ministry of Economic Cooperation and Development; the European Commission; the United Nations Development Programme (in Vietnam); and the Bertelsmann Foundation.

Donald K. Emmerson is the director of the Southeast Asia Forum (SEAF) at Shorenstein APARC, a senior fellow at the Freeman Spogli Institute for International Studies, and an affiliated scholar with the Abbasi Program in Islamic Studies and the Center on Development, Democracy, and the Rule of Law, all at Stanford University.

Emmerson's recent publications include articles on Southeast Asian regionalism in the *Journal of Democracy* (July 2008), *Contemporary Southeast Asia* (December 2007), the *Japanese Journal of Political Science* (August 2005), and *The Pacific Review* (March 2005), and on US-Indonesian relations in *The Indonesian Quarterly* (March 2006); and chapters in *Southeast Asia in Political Science* (2008), *The Inclusive Regionalist* (2007), *Religion and Religiosity in the Philippines and Indonesia* (2006), and *Indonesia: The Great Transition* (2005).

Emmerson has spoken on Southeast Asian subjects at universities and research institutions in Australia, Hong Kong, Indonesia, Japan, Malaysia, the Philippines, Singapore, Thailand, and Vietnam, among other countries. He has testified before the U.S. Congress on Asian affairs, and has monitored voting in Indonesia and East Timor for the National Democratic Institute and the Carter Center. In 2008–2009 he served on the advisory boards of the International Forum for Democratic Studies, the National Bureau of Asian Research, and several academic journals.

Before moving to Stanford in 1999, Emmerson was a professor of political science at the University of Wisconsin-Madison, where he won a campus-wide award for excellence in teaching. His Ph.D. is from Yale University.

Kyaw Yin Hlaing is an assistant professor in the department of Asian and international studies, City University of Hong Kong. He specializes in mainland Southeast Asia. His research and teaching interests range from political and social movements and democratization to state-society relations and political culture.

Kyaw's current research topics include the perceptions of Muslims by Buddhists in Myanmar and the dynamics of state-society relations and ethnic politics in that country. He coedited *Myanmar: State, Society and Ethnicity* (2007). His other publications on Myanmar include articles in the *Journal of Southeast Asian Studies* (February 2008), *The Fletcher Forum of World Affairs* (Winter 2008), *Contemporary Southeast Asia* (August 2007), *Southeast Asian Affairs* (2006 and 2005), and *Asian Survey* (2005); and chapters in *Myanmar* (2007), *Civil Society and Political Change in Asia* (2004), and *Reconciling Burma/Myanmar* (2004).

Kyaw's M.A. and Ph.D. are from Cornell University.

David Martin Jones is a senior lecturer in political science at the University of Queensland, Australia. He was a lecturer/senior lecturer in the School of Government at the University of Tasmania (1995–2004) and the Department of Political Science in the National University of Singapore (1989–1995). He has also held academic positions at the London School of Economics and the Open University, UK.

Jones' many books include (as coauthor) *ASEAN and East Asian Regional Order* (2006); (as editor) *Globalization and the New Terror* (2nd ed., 2006); and (as author) *The Image of China in Western Social and Political Thought* (2001) and *Political Development in Pacific Asia* (1997). His articles on Australian foreign policy and regional developments in Southeast Asia have appeared in journals such as *Comparative Politics*, *International Security*, and *Orbis*. Periodicals that have published his work on transnational Islamist violence include *International Affairs*, *The National Interest*, and *Studies in Conflict & Terrorism*. Since 1997 he has regularly commented on political violence and political change in the *Australian Financial Review*.

Jones is an international board member of the Centre Universitaire Juridique de Recherches sur les Menaces Criminelles Contemporaines at the University of Paris II, and has served on the board of *Studies in Conflict & Terrorism*. His 1984 Ph.D. in government and political theory is from the London School of Economics.

Erik Martinez Kuhonta is an assistant professor in the department of political science at McGill University, Montreal, where he teaches courses on Southeast Asian politics, developing countries, and the relationships between development and inequality. He coedited *Southeast Asia in Political Science: Theory, Region, and Qualitative Analysis* (2008), which includes his chapter on "Studying States in Southeast Asia." His other publications include articles on democracy and sovereignty in Southeast Asia in *The Pacific Review* (September 2006), on U.S. Asia policy in *Harvard Asia Quarterly* (Fall 2004), and on the political economy of equitable development in Thailand in *American Asian Review* (Winter 2003).

Kuhonta has held fellowships at Shorenstein APARC at Stanford University, and at the Asia Research Institute in the National University of Singapore. His 2003 Ph.D. in politics is from Princeton University. His doctoral dissertation compared the political foundations of equitable development in Malaysia and Thailand.

Michael S. Malley teaches comparative and Southeast Asian politics at the Naval Postgraduate School, Monterey, California. His research interests include the formation, failure, and survival of state, regime change in Southeast Asia, and provincial politics and political economy in Indonesia.

Malley's publications on Indonesia include chapters in *Local Power and Politics in Indonesia* (2003), *Ethnic Conflict* (2002), *Social Cohesion and Conflict Prevention in Asia* (2001), and *Indonesia beyond Suharto* (1999), and articles in *Asian Survey* (January–February 2002), and *Southeast Asian Affairs* (2001).

Before joining the School in 2004, Malley taught in the political science department at Ohio University. He earned his Ph.D. in political science at the University of Wisconsin-Madison, his M.A. in Asian studies at Cornell University, and his B.S. at the School of Foreign Service, Georgetown University. He has also spent time in residence at the National University of Singapore, and at Gadjah Mada University in Yogyakarta, Indonesia, and the Institute of Teacher Training and Education (IKIP) in Malang, Indonesia.

Rizal Sukma is executive director of the Centre for Strategic and International Studies (CSIS), Jakarta. He also chairs the International Relations Bureau of the Central Executive Board of Muhammadiyah, the second largest Islamic organization in Indonesia.

Sukma's record of public service includes advisory positions with the Indonesian Department of Defense and the Syafi'i Ma'arif Institute for Culture and Humanity, and a visiting lectureship at Muhammadiyah University, Malang. He has served on legislative drafting committees of the People's Representative Council dealing with defense issues. In 2007 he was a visiting scholar at Columbia University.

Among his many publications are *Security Operations in Aceh: Goals, Consequences, and Lessons* (2004), *Islam in Indonesian Foreign Policy* (2003), *Indonesia and China: The Politics of a Troubled Relationship* (1999), and a co-edited volume, *Islamic Thought and Movements in Contemporary Indonesia* (2007). He received his Ph.D. degree in international relations from the London School of Economics and Political Science (LSE) in 1997.

Surin Pitsuwan, a native of Nakorn Sri Thammarat in southern Thailand, is the secretary-general of the Association of Southeast Asian Nations, a position he assumed on 1 January 2008 for a term of five years.

Highlights of Surin's lengthy record of public service includes his efforts to resolve conflicts in Southeast Asia as a member of the "Wise Men Group" advising peace negotiations between the Acehnese Independence Movement (GAM) and the Indonesian government, and of the National Reconciliation Commission charged with bringing peace and security back to Thailand's southernmost provinces. He also led efforts in ASEAN to help restore law and order in East Timor.

The International Crisis Group and the United Nations Human Security Trust are among the international bodies on which he currently serves as an advisor. Previous service has included participation in the World Commission on the Social Dimension of Globalization (2002–2004), the United Nations Commission on Human Security (2001–2003), and the International Commission on Intervention and State Sovereignty (1999–2001).

From 1997 to 2001 Surin was Thailand's minister of foreign affairs. His service to ASEAN during that time including chairing the ASEAN Ministerial Meeting and the ASEAN Regional Forum.

In addition to his diplomatic service in ASEAN and the Thai government, Surin has had political, academic, and journalistic careers. He was returned to Thailand's National Legislative Assembly eight times since first running for a seat from Nakorn Sri Thammarat in 1986. He became a deputy leader of the Democrat Party. Previously he taught in the faculty of political science at Thammasat University, Bangkok; and for many years he also wrote columns for Bangkok's leading English-language dailies, *The Nation* and the *Bangkok Post*.

Surin has a 1982 Ph.D. in Middle Eastern studies and a 1974 M.A. in political science, both from Harvard University. He earned a B.A. in 1972 from the Claremont Men's College, California. In the 1970s he studied Arabic and did research in Cairo. His interest in Islam is illustrated by his current service as an academic advisor of the Oxford Centre for Islamic Studies in Oxford, UK.

Simon SC Tay teaches international law at the National University of Singapore. He also heads the Singapore Institute of International Affairs, a nongovernmental think tank that represents Singapore in the ASEAN Institutes of Security and International Studies network, and chairs the National Environment Agency for environmental protection and public health in Singapore.

Tay's current work on international law and public policy is focused on sustainable development and issues of peace and governance, in ASEAN and in Asia generally. His many publications include edited or coedited books such as *Democracy and Elections in Asia* (2006), *Pacific Asia 2022* (2005), *The Enemy Within: Combating Corruption in Asia* (2003), and *Reinventing ASEAN* (2001), and articles in *Contemporary Southeast Asia*, *Georgetown International Environmental Law Review*, and *Southeast Asian Affairs*, among other journals.

In 2003 Tay was a visiting professor at Harvard Law School and Tufts University's Fletcher School of Law and Diplomacy. From 1997 to 2001 he was selected for three terms as a nominated member of Singapore's parliament, where he led public consultations on the National Concept Plan and the Singapore Green Plan 2012, and on Singapore in the twenty-first century. In 1993–1994 he was a Fulbright scholar at Harvard Law School, where he won the Laylin prize for the best thesis in international law.

Tay serves on a number of international and regional advisory panels, including the Asia-Pacific Forum for Environment and Development, and on the advisory boards of the Asia Society, the Open Society Institute, and the Yale University Center for the Environment, among other organizations. He is a founding member of the Worldwide Fund for Nature's regional office in Singapore.

Termsak Chalermpalanupap is the director of research and special assistant to the secretary-general (SG) of ASEAN at its Secretariat, located in Jakarta. Prior to holding these positions he served as assistant director for economic research and external relations at the Secretariat.

Termsak assists the ASEAN SG on matters related to ASEAN and East Asian political and security cooperation, and to the various ASEAN organs and venues, including the Standing Committee, the Senior Officials Meeting, the Ministerial Meeting, and the Summit. He also conducts research on political and security issues of interest to ASEAN.

Termsak's recent publications include chapters in *East Asian Regionalism* (2005) and *Strengthening ASEAN Integration* (2001). From 1972 to 1992, he worked at *The Nation*, an English-language daily in Bangkok, as reporter, chief, reporter, news editor, and finally, as editor of its editorial pages.

Born in Bangkok in 1952, Termsak received a B.A. in international relations from Chulalongkorn University (Bangkok) in 1977, and an M.A. and Ph.D. in political science from the University of New Orleans (Louisiana) in 1982 and 1986, respectively.

Recent and Forthcoming Publications of the Walter H. Shorenstein Asia-Pacific Research Center

Books
(distributed by the Brookings Institution Press)

Karen Eggleston, ed. *Prescribing Cultures and Pharmaceutical Policy in the Asia-Pacific.* Stanford, CA: Walter H. Shorenstein Asia-Pacific Research Center, forthcoming 2009.

Donald Macintyre, Daniel C. Sneider, and Gi-Wook Shin, eds. *First Drafts of Korea: The U.S. Media and Perceptions of the Last Cold War Frontier.* Stanford, CA: Walter H. Shorenstein Asia-Pacific Research Center, forthcoming 2009.

Steven R. Reed, Kenneth Mori McElwain, and Kay Shimizu, eds. *Political Change in Japan: Electoral Behavior, Party Realignment, and the Koizumi Reforms.* Stanford, CA: Walter H. Shorenstein Asia-Pacific Research Center, forthcoming 2009.

Henry S. Rowen, Marguerite Gong Hancock, and William F. Miller, eds. *Greater China's Quest for Innovation.* Stanford, CA: Walter H. Shorenstein Asia-Pacific Research Center, 2008.

Gi-Wook Shin and Daniel C. Sneider, eds. *Cross Currents: Regionalism and Nationalism in Northeast Asia.* Stanford, CA: Walter H. Shorenstein Asia-Pacific Research Center, 2007.

Stella R. Quah, ed. *Crisis Preparedness: Asia and the Global Governance of Epidemics.* Stanford, CA: Walter H. Shorenstein Asia-Pacific Research Center, 2007.

Philip W. Yun and Gi-Wook Shin, eds. *North Korea: 2005 and Beyond.* Stanford, CA:Walter H. Shorenstein Asia-Pacific Research Center, 2006.

Jongryn Mo and Daniel I. Okimoto, eds. *From Crisis to Opportunity: Financial Globalization and East Asian Capitalism.* Stanford, CA: Walter H. Shorenstein Asia-Pacific Research Center, 2006.

Michael H. Armacost and Daniel I. Okimoto, eds. *The Future of America's Alliances in Northeast Asia*. Stanford, CA: Walter H. Shorenstein Asia-Pacific Research Center, 2004.

Henry S. Rowen and Sangmok Suh, eds. *To the Brink of Peace: New Challenges in Inter-Korean Economic Cooperation and Integration*. Stanford, CA: Walter H. Shorenstein Asia-Pacific Research Center, 2001.

Studies of the Walter H. Shorenstein Asia-Pacific Research Center
(published with Stanford University Press)

Jean Oi and Nara Dillon, eds. *At the Crossroads of Empires: Middlemen, Social Networks, and State-building in Republican Shanghai*. Stanford, CA: Stanford University Press, 2007.

Henry S. Rowen, Marguerite Gong Hancock, and William F. Miller, eds. *Making IT: The Rise of Asia in High Tech*. Stanford, CA: Stanford University Press, 2006.

Gi-Wook Shin. *Ethnic Nationalism in Korea: Genealogy, Politics, and Legacy*. Stanford, CA:Stanford University Press, 2006.

Andrew Walder, Joseph Esherick, and Paul Pickowicz, eds. *The Chinese Cultural Revolution as History*. Stanford, CA: Stanford University Press, 2006.

Rafiq Dossani and Henry S. Rowen, eds. *Prospects for Peace in South Asia*. Stanford, CA: Stanford University Press, 2005.

The authorized representative in the EU for product safety and compliance is:
Mare Nostrum Group
B.V Doelen 72
4831 GR Breda
The Netherlands